Best wishes, Peter.
It was good to meet you.

S. Marguerite Mae, CSC

STOLEN DAUGHTERS, VIRGIN MOTHERS

STOLEN DAUGHTERS, VIRGIN MOTHERS

ANGLICAN SISTERHOODS
IN VICTORIAN BRITAIN

Susan Mumm

Leicester University Press
London and New York

LEICESTER UNIVERSITY PRESS
A Cassell imprint
Wellington House, 125 Strand, London WC2R 0BB
370 Lexington Avenue, New York, NY 10017–6550

First published 1999

British Library Cataloguing in Publication Data
A catalogue record for this book is available from the British Library.

ISBN 0-7185-0151-9

Library of Congress Cataloging-in-Publication Data
Mumm, Susan, 1961–
   Stolen daughters, virgin mothers : Anglican sisterhoods in
Victorian Britain / Susan Mumm.
     p. cm.
   Includes bibliographical references and index.
   ISBN 0-7185-0151-9 (hardcover)
   1. Monasticism and religious orders for women—Anglican Communion—
History—19th century. 2. Church of England—History—19th century.
3. England—Church history—19th century. I. Title.
BX5185.A1M86 1998
271'.983'0904209034—dc21   97-34291
                                                    CIP

Typeset by BookEns Ltd, Royston, Herts.
Printed and bound in Great Britain by Cromwell Press Ltd, Trowbridge, Wilts.

CONTENTS

APPENDICES

ACKNOWLEDGEMENTS

I would like to thank the Mothers Superior, Archivists and Sisters of the many communities who allowed me access to their records, and who often lavished hospitality on me as well. Librarians and archivists at many universities, record offices and other repositories were almost invariably accommodating and helpful. Special thanks must go to the staff at Lambeth Palace Archives and the Church of England Record Centre. Funding for this research was provided by the Social Sciences and Humanities Research Council of Canada, the Overseas Research Fellowship, the Association of Vice-Chancellors and Principals of the Universities of the United Kingdom, and Atkinson College, York University, Toronto. Finally, without Valerie Cromwell's advice and guidance this project would have been impossible. My gratitude to her is inexpressible.

LIST OF ABBREVIATIONS

The names of religious communities mentioned in the footnotes are abbreviated as follows:

All Hallows	Community of All Hallows
All Saints	Community of All Saints Sisters of the Poor
Charity	Community of the Sisters of Charity
CRJBS	Community of Reparation to Jesus in the Blessed Sacrament
CSC	Community of the Sisters of the Church
CSCR	Community of the Servants of the Cross
CSJB	Community of St John the Baptist
CSKE	Community of St Katharine of Egypt
CSMC	Community of St Mary at the Cross
CSM&SJ	Community of St Mary & St John
CSM&SS	Community of St Mary & St Scholastica
CSMVB	Community of St Mary the Virgin, Brighton
CSMVW	Community of St Mary the Virgin, Wantage
CSP	Community of St Peter
CSTM	Community of St Thomas the Martyr
CSW	Community of St Wilfred
Epiphany	Community of the Epiphany
Holy Comforter	Community of the Holy Comforter
Holy Cross	Community of the Holy Cross
Holy Family	Community of the Holy Family
Holy Rood	Community of the Holy Rood
MCSD	Missionary Community of St Denys
NSSJD	Nursing Sisters of St John the Divine
Park Village	Society of the Holy Cross; usually known as the Park Village Sisterhood
SHUT	Society of the Holy and Undivided Trinity
SMHT	Society of the Most Holy Trinity
SSB	Society of the Sisters of Bethany
SSM	Society of St Margaret
SSM Scotland	Society of St Margaret, Scotland
SSP	St Saviour's Priory, Haggerston

Other abbreviations

LPL	Lambeth Palace Library and Archives
PH	Pusey House Library and Archives

When quoting from community archives, spelling has been regularized throughout. Abbreviations, which are very common in the convent MSS, have been written out for ease of reading.

INTRODUCTION

This book is a contribution to bridging the distance between historians of religion and of women's history by examining women's religious communities in the Victorian Church of England. Church history tends to neglect the role and importance of women in religion; women's history has not shown much interest in those women who it is assumed conformed to convention by being religious.

Women's religious communities are the one area of women's experience which would seem to fall naturally within the remit of church historians. While a certain amount has been written on the subject, virtually all has focused on the men who were associated with sisterhoods. These few priests have received a disproportionate amount of attention from historians of the Oxford Movement; the thousands of women involved in one important practical consequence of that movement, the sisterhoods, remain shadowy, even peripheral, figures. The emphasis of this material allows us to forget its paradoxical nature, as noted by a former Anglican sister, who later founded a Roman Catholic community, more than a century ago: 'Men wrote the Tracts for the Times ... but it was women who first carried all this theory into practice.'[1] Some readers may object that this book merely reverses this imbalance: my response to this is that there are plenty of histories of the Victorian church that describe the lives and careers of Newman, Pusey and John Mason Neale: one of the central purposes of this book is to re-introduce to history the nameless women of the sisterhood movement.

When one turns from church to women's history, it must then be asked why the sisterhoods, and indeed religion in general, have been of so little interest to historians of women's roles and experience.[2] These scholars tend to be suspicious of the intellectual and feminist credentials of devout women: sisters would be doubly implicated within that subset. When they are mentioned, nuns, and indeed all women whose religion has been central to the way in which they choose to live, are too often portrayed as meek, subservient, otherworldly; lacking the character and drive which makes historical personages memorable and important. This portrayal of the religious woman as inevitably ineffectual and subordinate means that sisters have been seen as mediaeval throw-backs, anachronisms whose historical significance is nil. This ahistorical and unhelpful portrayal ignores the evidence that these sisters, and many other women, saw religion as an empowering and enabling force, not as a restrictive or crippling limitation on their human potential. Religion could be, and sometimes was, an avenue for successful revolt against male authority and conventional morality. Revolutionary potential aside, those who ignore religion cut themselves off from the mental universe of the many women in the past whose religious beliefs, conflicts and activity were central to their self-image.[3]

Thus, for a variety of reasons, the centrality of religion to women's experience in Victorian Britain has been overlooked.[4] Anglican communities generated an enormous amount of controversy in their first decades of existence, with almost all published comment being partially or wholly negative. Viewed by their contemporaries as a threat and a menace, in this century they have been dismissed by a shallow and complacent orthodoxy which pigeonholes them, almost unexamined, as groups of pious women who turned their backs on the world in order to serve God more perfectly. By divorcing them from their social context, this patronizing view has stripped their actions of all importance and has ignored the social significance and social consequences of the rebirth of religious communities within the English church. This misconstruction of the importance and impact of the sisterhoods provides the broad context for their neglect.

More generally, why write a book on Anglican nuns and their work in Victorian England? After all, the very idea of nuns seems to contradict the image of Anglicanism as part of the Protestant tradition. Furthermore, why another book on women's religious work when most British women no longer participate in any form of organized religion? But, as in so many areas of the historical investigation, it is dangerous to limit our pursuit of the past to the preoccupations of the present. An understanding of the phenomenon of the 'sisterhood movement' within Anglicanism illuminates for us one small corner of the Victorian world: one where ideas about the proper role for women, the influence of religion and the power of philanthropic endeavour coincided and, sometimes, collided.

It is occasionally claimed that discussion of Victorian women in feminist terms is so anachronistic as to be meaningless: in other words, if a group or individual would have rejected the 'feminist' label (assuming it had existed), they cannot be termed feminist: this is an example of the 'no name, no thing' fallacy. As well as being one aspect of the nineteenth-century epidemic of philanthropic activity, sisterhoods can legitimately be placed within the story of the advancement of women, as an example of *feminist practice*. Since until very recently the history of feminism has concentrated on the lives of individuals, 'feminist practice', as Rendell terms it, has been comparatively neglected. By feminist practice is meant 'the association of women together for a feminist purpose ... the organisation of a range of activities ... around the claims of women to determine different areas of their lives'.[5] Under this definition, sisterhoods can be seen as firmly rooted in the feminist tradition, both by their fierce commitment to their women-created organizations and by their dedication to improving, or at least ameliorating, the lives of working-class women and their children.

While academic neglect has been widespread, paradoxically there has been, and continues to be, enormous popular interest in nuns. This ranges from romanticized depictions of the 'good sisters', through the idea that all women of religion are psychologically abnormal, to the depths of 'convent' pornography. All popular views suffer from a great deal of superficial stereotyping and from a complete failure to understand the reasons why women joined communities and the reality of how communities were formed. The cultural and social significance of sisterhoods is obscured by these various popularizations as much as by the lack of serious study devoted to the subject; cultural icons as potent as that of the nun resist re-evaluation.

Three explanations are offered for the popularity of Anglican religious communities for women in the nineteenth century. One view, born in the Victorian period and long accepted almost without question, sees sisterhoods as yet another aspect of Victorian England's solution to the problem of 'superfluous' women. Sisterhoods were believed to provide such unfortunates with a church-based replacement for marriage and family life: in other words, those who entered communities merely sought to replace the patriarchal structure of the Victorian family with the equally patriarchal structure of the Victorian Church. The last decade's resurgence of interest in these communities has been accompanied by a rethinking of the social meanings of sisterhoods. This has led to a refutation of the traditional understanding of sisterhoods, instead arguing that the communities were proto-feminist organizations which subverted the limitations placed on the activities of middle-class women by providing them with divine sanction for otherwise unorthodox acts. This perspective assumes that women were attracted to sisterhoods by the opportunity they offered to translate subversive intellectual and vocational drives into the more acceptable language of religion.[6] Thus the Anglican sisters are transformed into incipient feminists, seeking freedom from male control as well as the opportunity to exert authority within the all-female structure of the convent. Most recently a third view has proposed that these communities should more properly be viewed neither as traditional nor proto-feminist institutions, but instead as providing a valuable alternative to both in a time of transition.[7]

These three positions share a common weakness. They are based almost entirely on secondary sources, and indeed almost entirely upon a very few well-known quotations which are dragged out time and again in order to 'prove' something about the nature of Victorian society. Overall, very little is known about the Anglican religious orders for women. There has been little interest in the orders as a way of life. No one has troubled to examine the existing records of these communities to see why women joined them, to discover whether the convent satisfied their aspirations for their lives or, indeed, what life in an Anglican religious order in Victorian England was like. These are the gaps which this book begins to fill.

More specifically, the purpose of this book is threefold: first, to chart the growth of the sisterhood movement to 1900; secondly, to find out what kind of career convent life offered to women, and whether early entrants were motivated primarily by motives of religious devotion or of social service; and finally, to re-examine the public debate on the topic in order to see if anything can be learned from the attacks of contemporary observers as to whether and how sisterhoods threatened Victorian norms. The common thread running throughout the book is its exploration of the ways in which becoming a sister allowed a woman to circumvent the social and cultural restrictions placed on her more conventional counterparts. Community life gave Victorian women the freedom to choose to leave the family home without marriage, to participate in the government of a semi-democratic institution, and to undertake demanding and meaningful work at a time when women were believed to seek employment only in response to dire poverty.

In the course of my research, several themes began to stand out. They seem to me to be central to an accurate understanding of the phenomenon of the Victorian Anglican sisterhoods. First, the sisterhoods actually drew a larger number of women into more communities than had previously been realized. This indicates that the movement was more numerically significant than had been thought, which in turn makes the outpouring of written comment on the subject of sisterhoods seem less grotesquely dispropor-tionate. Second, the first generation of Anglican sisters seem to have been motivated more by a desire to undertake meaningful work which also addressed the inequities in their society than by an overwhelming personal piety and a desire to attain personal holiness. Among the next generation of members, many reversed the two imperatives. From this follows the third finding, that the communities changed over time. In general, a sisterhood in the 1860s tended to be a more radical organization than the same sisterhood in the 1890s: there is evidence for an overall transition from innovation to conservatism. Connected to this, the motivation for joining such a community also shows signs of change over time; as the social welfare impulse weakens, a primarily religious motivation grows. Lastly, the communities show very few signs of conforming to the traditional argument that they attracted women seeking surrogate male authority through the church: on the contrary, they were formed of women often uninterested in, or even antipathetic to, the formalities of the church hierarchy. Their attention was focused instead on improving, as they saw it, the condition of the working class in general, and of working-class women and children in particular. They were important agents in the Victorian outpouring of philanthropy as well as in the first wave of British feminist practice.

A comment on primary sources

Archival materials relating to Anglican sisterhoods are found primarily in convent holdings, and vary greatly in amount and content from community to community. Furthermore, the communities differ enormously in openness to researchers. A few communities refuse or severely limit access to their records, while even the most open of the still-existing communities do not permit full or unrestricted access. (My original intention had been to carry the study through to 1914; the almost universal reluctance of communities to allow the use of twentieth-century records meant that the terminal date had to be revised to 1900.) Some communities refuse access as a result of the insensitivity of earlier researchers. The extreme reluctance of many communities to allow an outsider access to their nineteenth-century records is the single largest problem faced by the researcher in this area.

Many communities possess few records. The vow of poverty and the pressure of active work meant that when paper ceased to be immediately useful, it was discarded. An instance of the low priority given to record-keeping in communities overwhelmed by active work is the case of the Community of Reparation to Jesus in the Blessed Sacrament. It was not until 1897, when Reparation was twenty-eight years old, that it was decided to purchase a book in which to record the names of women who were professed.[8] The communities' disavowal of material accumulation means that personal papers and community records were often systematically destroyed at intervals, if ever kept at all. Within these limitations the scope of the study is as comprehensive as possible; I worked in the records of every community founded before 1900 which would grant me access. I consequently gained at least limited access to the records of twenty-eight communities.

Most of the archives of expired orders have been destroyed or have disappeared, but a few have found their way to the Pusey House archival collection. As a general rule, the larger and earlier-established communities have survived; many smaller and later ones have not, and with them died their records. While this certainly marred the representativeness of the study, every attempt was made to avoid distortion when depicting the movement as a whole. In such circumstances there is always the problem of skew: it is difficult for the researcher to avoid being seduced by complete archives, and so neglect equally important organizations whose records are meagre. I have worked on the principle that records that have managed to survive should be employed, even if they lack typicality. Since large and middling communities have survived with greater frequency than very small ones, the archival materials of the first type are much more likely to still be in existence and to be at least partially available to the researcher. Thus the activities and experiences of the smaller (and often later-formed) sisterhoods are under-represented in this book. The papers of several bishops involved with sisterhoods were used at Lambeth Palace Library, and some information on deaconesses was available at the Church of England Record Centre.

Community records were supplemented by the pamphlet collections at Pusey House, Oxford, and St Deiniol's Library, Hawarden. No student of Victorian pamphlet literature can fail to notice the importance of the medium as a cheap and quick way of spreading ideas and opinions; because it was so speedy and inexpensive, it can, to a certain extent, serve as a gauge to the concerns of the time. It is important to note that one of the greatest of the pamphlet debates was devoted to the question of the legitimacy of the establishment of religious orders for women within the Anglican Church. Because the establishment of women's communities provoked 'such impassioned discussion, it provides the modern scholar with a valuable prism within which to analyse gender and class issues' in Victorian society.[9] This material has been used extensively.

Prescriptive literature, with its great emphasis on the imperative and religiously motivated necessity for women to remain within the home, is useful and important. But the successful rejection of home and family by thousands of women who experimented with community life reminds us that we must look also at the material and social culture of the sisterhoods themselves, which often portray a world-view at odds with the prescriptive literature which purports to describe and explain them. This work attempts to do both: to examine the mass of controversial literature enveloping (almost crushing) the communities, and to study the women who joined, and the nature of the organizations they created.[10]

Terms of reference and terminology

When one sets out to write a social history of a religious movement, one crucial question is that of scope. Will the historian foreground and evaluate the religious beliefs of the group, or focus upon describing the life and activities that emerged from those beliefs? It was a question I struggled with in the writing of this book: and reluctantly I concluded that the story of the theological revolution behind the Victorian sisterhood movement is a task that would swell this book to unacceptable proportions. The book you are holding is a social history and makes no claim to be a comprehensive guide to the religious beliefs and practices (which varied considerably) of the ninety-odd Anglican sisterhoods established in nineteenth-century Britain. That story remains to be written by someone else. Of course religion cannot be separated out from the motivations and the activities of sisterhoods. It is important, and the whole history of the sisterhoods is saturated with it. But it is not the main theme of this book.

I cannot leave the question of religious belief, however, without saying something about religious terminology. It may disturb those who are well-versed in church history that the terms 'sister' and 'nun' are used indiscriminately in the text. This is done deliberately, for the reason (which I believe to be a good one) that the women I am writing about made no meaningful distinction between the terms. They referred to themselves as both sister and nun without any indication of being aware of the difference in canon law or in Roman Catholic usage between the words. To these Victorian Anglicans, sisters and nuns were women who banded together in a community structure, wore a common dress, and made (usually) more or less binding promises to live a life of poverty, chastity and obedience.

... never since the Reformation has conventual life been so interesting to the body of English women, and to the whole nation through them: at a time when – partly through religious enthusiasm, stimulated by self-chosen teachers and counsellors, partly from the failure of family life, hitherto the English ideal, to satisfy woman's growing aspirations – the cloister has assumed a reality as a possible sphere and refuge ...*

* [Anne Mozley], 'Convent life', *Blackwood's Edinburgh Magazine*, **105** (1869), p. 607.

PART I OVERVIEW

CHAPTER ONE

'THOSE WICKED NUNS': THE FORGOTTEN STORY OF THE SISTERHOOD MOVEMENT

Anglican sisterhoods take their place in a long tradition; Christian women were among the first to form women-only groups, with the earliest established in the second or third century AD. The importance of the nineteenth-century Church of England movement lies in their being the first successful communities for women in the post-Reformation Established Church in Britain, although several attempts had been made in the seventeenth and eighteenth centuries. When the poet laureate Robert Southey resurrected the idea in the early nineteenth century, he imagined that they would operate as both refuge and resource: places of refuge for unmarried women and as sources of charitable relief and trained nurses to ameliorate the suffering of the poor. Indeed, it was as a tribute to Southey that the first sisterhood, the committee-established Park Village community, was founded in 1845.

The sisterhood movement grew rapidly in a glare of publicity. By the century's end, Anglican sisters were the largest group of full-time, organized women church workers within the established church. Most estimates calculate that there were between 3000 and 4000 members in 1900, living in around sixty communities.[1] This is almost certainly a conservative estimate, as my own research has unearthed more than a dozen Victorian communities whose existence has been forgotten; although some of these forgotten communities were undoubtedly short-lived, there is no doubt that more than ninety sisterhoods were formed in the first fifty-five years of their revival. Archival research suggests that approximately 10,000 women in all had passed through ninety-odd communities between 1845 and 1900, staying for anywhere from a few months to a lifetime.[2]

The urge to create or join women-only groups which were dedicated to social service and devotion was not confined to Roman Catholics and Anglicans in nineteenth-century Britain. Quakers made attempts at the same ideal, and the Wesleyan Methodists established the Sisters of the Poor in 1887 in direct imitation of Anglican orders. Deaconess orders also enjoyed a resurgence among a number of denominations, both in Britain and on the continent. The popularity of such organizations created much alarm among those dedicated to keeping women in the home. A number of contemporary observers saw in sisterhoods a viable and ever-more popular alternative to the ordinary life of a Victorian woman, and thus an implicit criticism of marriage and family life. As Penelope Holland warned in 1869, women's religious communities were increasingly perceived as an attractive escape from a lifetime of female domesticity or trivial social activity: 'in the present day there is scarcely any alternative for a girl in fashionable society, between reckless dissipation and a convent life. The latter is being chosen oftener year by year'.[3] One of the more dispassionate critics of community life agreed that the interest in the movement was growing: she saw the attractions as being a combination of religious enthusiasm and the sisterhoods' ability to offer a sphere to women aware of '*the failure of family life* ... to satisfy woman's growing aspirations'.[4] 'A sort of agitated interest in them is constantly increasing', wrote Sarah Wister in 1873, one of many testimonies to the enormous attention bestowed on these groups.[5] The 1901 census would seem to confirm the attractiveness of the religious life: of professional women over the age of 45, sisters comprised the third largest group.[6]

The first Church of England community commenced in the year of John Henry Newman's secession to Rome, and this naturally draws us to place the sisterhoods within the framework of the Oxford Movement. Newman's writings (in particular *Lives of English Saints*, published in 1844) were an important influence on the pioneering generation of sisters. A number of women who joined communities, including the first woman to be professed in the Anglican Communion, traced their decision to their reading of Newman's books. This is not the place to offer a pocket history of the Tractarian movement, nor of its successor movements: Ritualism, Puseyism and Anglo-Catholicism.[7] Suffice it to say that all these varied expressions of the Oxford Movement agreed on the primacy of the sacraments as a means to salvation, rejecting the dominant conversion model insisted upon by Victorian evangelicalism. Beyond that, they varied widely in their attitudes toward ritual and authority; but they again came close to unanimity in their insistence on active work and charity: both as a form of spiritual discipline and to obey the commands of Christ.

Anglo-Catholicism offered, even for those women who did not enter communities, a busy and demanding life: daily services, the duty of regular self-examination, an obligation to work among the poor, and an almost Methodist attention to regularity of life. It was 'virtually a full-time occupation, with a variety of activities useful and (in their own terms) important'.[8] Women who were active in Anglo-Catholicism were almost certain to be exposed to sisterhoods through circles of like-minded women, which often included associates or members of communities. Communities must be seen as part of a larger Anglo-Catholic system; what was sometimes known as the 'London–Brighton–South Coast religion' is reflected in the geographic distribution of the convents established.

Most communities, with the general exception of those founded in the province of York, tended to cluster at the extreme ritualistic end of the Anglican spectrum, although not all of the women who joined them were attracted to this element. This is consistent with the influence of the Oxford Movement on the sisterhoods, except for those directed by E. B. Pusey, who assumed public leadership of the Movement after Newman's secession, as being that of the second generation of Tractarians. One durable contribution of the Oxford Movement is the sisterhoods which flourished long after the original leaders of the Movement were all dead; in their two-fold emphasis on doctrine and practice, they were central to perpetuating its spirit, if not its name. Certainly the delayed social effect of the Oxford Movement shone forth most brightly in the communities, aligned as they often were with the socialist slum clergy. Some contemporary observers went so far as to claim that the High Church movement would never have become a force in British society if it had not been for 'the active and personal contribution of women', particularly sisters.[9]

Much to its dismay, the Victorian Church of England discovered that even a remarkably conservative institution can harbour radicalism. By the 1830s the late eighteenth-century evangelical impulse had lost much of its original spiritual vitality to become a stultifying and rigid social captivity, often seeming to be more concerned with Sunday travelling than with serving God in this world. However, this same impulse took on a new shape in the Oxford Movement, which was as radical in its desire for holiness as the Clapham sect had been. Women found that a shared religious faith could transform their lives, as religion provided the motivating force behind their attempts to organize themselves and create philanthropic institutions aimed especially at their own sex. Of all the women-generated groups in Victorian society, it is sisterhoods which brought this tendency to its furthest and most developed form. After the first phase of the Oxford Movement ended, the sisterhoods showed the Church that the combination of High Church theology and women-oriented institutions could be an extremely trouble-some thorn in the flesh. Allchin reminds us of the paradox implicit in 'the fact that a theological movement so traditional and conservative [as the Oxford Movement] should have found itself coming into alliance with the most radical political and social points of view'.[10] One contemporary witness says that in her circle, evangelicals were derided for their 'lax and easy-going religion', and 'again and again' she heard the 'High Church party held up as the only one which understood a really active, working life'.[11]

In the spring of 1845 the first Anglican religious community for women, the Park Village sisterhood (officially styled the Sisterhood of the Holy Cross), commenced work in the slums of Somers Town and Camden. The backgrounds of the first three women to join were to be typical of later members of many sisterhoods; one was the daughter of a country clergyman, another the daughter of a Scottish Episcopalian bishop. It is also typical that nothing can be discovered of the background of the third. Indeed, most of what is known of this small and short-lived community comes from only one source: the unabashedly hostile autobiographies of two former members.[12]

However, Park Village was to be anomalous in many ways. Uniquely among all Victorian sisterhoods, it was not founded by a woman, but was established and financed by a committee of prominent men (including Gladstone, Lord John Manners, and Lords Clive, Lyttleton and Camden) as a memorial to Robert Southey. Park Village's mandate, first described by Gladstone in a privately issued circular, was fourfold: '1. Visiting the poor in their own homes. 2. Visiting hospitals, workhouses, or prisons. 3. Feeding, clothing, and instructing destitute children. 4. Assisting in burying the dead.' The community contained the seeds of failure from the outset. It was fatally weakened by its lack of a natural leader, created as it was by a committee rather than, as all the other sisterhoods were, by a woman of strong character who could draw others to join her. It seemed directionless. Extreme experiments in asceticism were another factor in its failure, and the early members could not agree whether their goal was the performance of good works among the poor or a less active life of devotion and contemplation. Most of its members joined the second community to be formed, the Society of the Most Holy Trinity (Ascot Priory), when it absorbed Park Village in 1856.

Within five years of the foundation of Park Village six sisterhoods had been established. The best known of these was Ascot Priory, located in Plymouth. It was this community, founded by Priscilla Lydia Sellon, which largely attracted the great swells of public hostility in the 1850s, and the sisterhood suffered permanent damage as a result.[13] Public inquiries and pulpit denunciations of Ascot Priory centred around the ritualistic practices of the group, as well as the autocratic figure of the founder. The founder of Ascot Priory, however, was certainly one of the most influential figures of the sisterhood movement, and her character and achievements had a profound impact upon Victorian beliefs about women's communities.[14] Lydia (she did not use her first name) Sellon, the daughter of an affluent naval commander, was probably born in 1821, and was reared by a Scottish Presbyterian governess after the early death of her mother. She came under the influence of the Oxford Movement around 1830, but although she visited Park Village, she was repelled by the group's extreme asceticism, and eventually decided to form her own community. Ascot Priory was founded in response to the Bishop of Exeter's public appeal for workers willing to come to the appalling slums of the Devon seaports. By 1851 Sellon's community, as well as having supplied a number of nurses for Florence Nightingale's hospital in the Crimea, was running an orphanage, a training school for sailor boys, a refuge for girls, a home for elderly seamen, a large industrial school, six model lodging-houses, a soup kitchen, five ragged schools, a convalescent home and a hospital, with sisters working in Devonport, Bristol and Alverstoke in Hampshire. Soon the community was working in Bethnal Green and Bradford-on-Avon as well. (Ascot Priory established a London presence by absorbing a small sisterhood in Pimlico in 1854.) However, because the sisterhood suffered from so much negative publicity in its early years, it found it more difficult to attract members or financial contributions than did other sisterhoods.[15] It is said that when women declared their intention of entering a sisterhood, they were commonly advised 'anywhere but Devonport' (Devonport is yet another name for the community, which was officially styled, but seldom called, the Society of the Most Holy Trinity). The sisters of this community gradually retreated to Plymouth, developing a tendency toward the contemplative life (Florence Nightingale noted with some contempt that Sellon 'retreated from the world') and the group became increasingly divorced from the philanthropic impulse which had given it birth.

It is an odd twist of history that the first two communities for Anglican women were both untypical of the movement as a whole. A contemporary description claims to be representative of the way communities were generated, and indeed it does closely follow the experience of many foundations in the 1850s:

in a neglected corner of a slumbering diocese, where ... people were most solidly established in their satisfaction with things as they were, and in contempt of every new idea, two ladies were brought together by a common desire to rescue the sinful. They took a house in the country and began to receive penitent women. Other ladies joined them, fired with the same spirit . . . Their plan of a common life gradually developed in a rule accepted by all. They left pleasant homes, useful and easy lives, for repulsive work, poverty, and the ridicule of their neighbours.[16]

One sisterhood whose development followed this general pattern was the Community of Saint John Baptist (usually known as 'the Clewer Sisters'). This community was formed in 1851 at Clewer, near the Windsor military camp, as a refuge for prostitutes who wanted to leave the streets. The Clewer sisters ran a penitentiary for such women, which provided a two-year course of 'penitence'. Its founder, Harriet Monsell, was the daughter of an Irish MP and baronet. The childless widow of a clergyman, she dedicated herself to God beside her husband's deathbed.

Long considered one of the most fashionable of the sisterhoods, Clewer attracted many members from the aristocracy and upper gentry. Monsell skilfully cultivated her family ties with persons of influence, such as Archbishop Tait and the Royal Chaplain, in order to maximize the desirability of the community to potential members. Her success in this was evidenced by the private visit of Queen Victoria and one of her daughters to the community in 1864. By 1900 Clewer had enrolled more than 300 sisters stationed in over fifty sites scattered around the United Kingdom, and worked largely in the USA and India as well. One contemporaneous group with a similar development was the Community of All Saints — in early days often called the Sisters of the Poor. It was founded in the slums of Marylebone by the 'immensely rich' Harriet Brownlow Byron, daughter of a former MP and Deputy Lieutenant of Hertfordshire.[17] Specializing in nursing, this community also counted over 300 members by 1900, and was spread even more widely than Clewer.

Two more communities deserve brief mention. The Community of Saint Mary the Virgin, Wantage, was one of the very few communities which did not discriminate between sisters on the basis of their social status. Instead it placed all members in a single order. This was exceptional at the time, as almost all other sisterhoods divided their members into choir and lay sisters, based on social status and financial contribution. Its leader from 1850 to 1887 was the daughter of a Sussex farmer; Harriet Day's humble background, in addition to the lack of social barriers within the community, attracted many intelligent, ambitious women who had been financially self-supporting before entering the community. This community also concentrated on working with prostitutes, although it gradually expanded into schools and teacher training.

The Community of the Sisters of the Church is the only sisterhood founded relatively late in the century (1870) to grow at the rapid pace of the communities of the 1840s and 1850s.[18] The Sisters of the Church's founder, Emily Ayckbowm, was a woman with an acutely sensitive social conscience and extraordinary charisma. Her remarkable vision gave rise to a fast-growing community which ran orphanages and schools, as well as a myriad of other projects. After only twenty-five years of existence, the community, despite a barrage of negative publicity in the 1890s, had established twenty-eight schools, five large orphanages, three convalescent homes, nursed children in a 500-bed seaside convalescent hospital, and was feeding hundreds of unemployed East Londoners every winter.[19] Charles Booth encountered Ayckbowm's sisters, whose methods did not meet with his approval, repeatedly in his explorations of late-Victorian poverty. Even Booth, who disliked their refusal to submit themselves to the authority of the bishops, had to admit that their 'enthusiasm and zeal' had allowed them to 'spread all over the world, showing astonishing force and vigour'.[20]

By 1900 more than ninety sisterhoods had been formed for women wishing to live the monastic life within the Church of England. Aside from the two early amalgamations, only a handful failed, and none 'went over to Rome' during Victoria's reign.[21] Most of these nineteenth-century foundations were still functioning in the 1960s, in great contrast to Anglican communities for men. Of the eighteen men's communities formed in the nineteenth century, eleven had become extinct before 1900, usually after only a year or two of life. Typical were the Brotherhood of St James, which survived for six months in 1855, and the Order of St Joseph, in existence for the greater part of 1866. Two of the remaining seven had already become Roman Catholic before 1900, and a third was to join them shortly after the end of the century. Others were wracked by scandal.[22] None were to attain anything approaching the size, importance, or public face which many of the women's communities enjoyed.

As later chapters will make clear, Anglican sisterhoods as they evolved bore little resemblance to Southey's description. They were not to be, as Southey had imagined, a home for superfluous women or an employment agency for reliable nurses, although to a certain extent they fulfilled these functions. The following chapters will demonstrate that Anglican sisterhoods became much more than their initial projector had ever envisioned. Their inventive and evolving community structures gave women independence, autonomy and control over their own lives; they provided a nurturing woman-affirming environment while also providing creative, fulfilling work. The work they did became a significant element in the history of Victorian philanthrophy, as well as giving the lives of the sisters profound meaning. Both in their convents and in their work, religious communities empowered women. They validated the worth of women, their abilities and their labour, 'in a world that seemed materialistic, godless, and male'.[23]

The following chapters will examine how and why women entered sisterhoods and the lives they lived there, the government and administration of communities, and sisterhood projects among the poor. The final section of the book discusses popular responses to the sisterhood movement, from the clerical establishment, Victorian feminists and the general public.

PART II   THE REALITY OF SISTERHOODS

CHAPTER TWO

'THE EAGER LIFE HERE JUST SUITS ME': THE ATTRACTIONS OF CONVENT LIFE FOR VICTORIAN WOMEN

Why did women join these new institutions? The motivation of those who joined Anglican communities in the nineteenth century is crucial to our understanding of how and why the communities fared as they did. Almost always motivations for such a momentous decision were mixed. Religious impulses, a desire to help the poor, a wish for a 'career', disinclination for marriage, an interest in living with other women, and many other factors merged in these decisions. Much of the rest of this book tries, in different ways, to answer that all-important question, why – why women joined and stayed in communities.

However, our cultural presuppositions about religious communities as they exist today may lead us to make unwarranted assumptions about these Victorian sisterhoods. Women today who join such groups are invariably seen as being deeply devout: after all, the caring professions and communal living arrangements mean that women who wish to live with other women and work among the disadvantaged do not need to join sisterhoods to carry out these desires. But for much of the nineteenth century, this was not the case in Britain. This meant that women joined sisterhoods who today would not dream of making such a choice, and we would be wrong in assuming that all Victorian sisters were profoundly religious. While in one sense it is probably impossible for a historian to study the nature and depth of the religious commitment of Anglican sisters, it is possible to chart some general trends in an area which was normally treated with strict reticence by the sisters themselves.

It is difficult to gauge the religiosity of sisters; the life of prayer is usually a silent one. The conventional rhetoric of spiritual testimony must always be taken into account, with its tendency to darken the pre-conversion picture in order to heighten the contrast with the sanctity of the present. However, I have made the decision to take the record more or less as it stands, although some may consider this naive: if a sister or an ex-sister records that she was uninterested in religion when she entered a sisterhood, I pay her the compliment of taking her at her word.

First, it is clear that a religious motivation of some sort was almost always present in the decision to join a community, although the extent of the part it played varied a great deal. The picture is complex: first, sisters believed that they were called directly by God, and that their vocation set them apart from the ordinary life of women, making marriage or independent spinsterhood impossible. Unlike the clergy, whose sense of vocation may often have been mixed with social, economic or professional reasons for the taking of orders, sisters cut themselves off from all recognized roles for Victorian women. This made the concept of vocation a central issue. Second, a great number of women joined communities, especially in the early years, because they were widely perceived to be the only outlet for women who felt called to a life of social service. For some of these women, the religious impulse was secondary, or even absent. Perhaps, for most who joined, the two motivations were inextricably interwoven. It is clear that in general Victorian sisters saw life as a vocation of service, not to a husband or to a priest, but to Christ in His poor. Their work, central as it often was, was imbued with religious belief and feeling, even if it was seldom expressed. As one opponent of the movement admitted,

> The reasonable attractions of sisterhoods seem to consist in their offer of training, protection, and authoritative direction in work which provides food for the affections while promoting the salvation of souls and the glory of God.[1]

The great majority of women who entered Anglican communities were conventionally religious; many were extremely devout. However, it would be a mistake to assume that all Anglican sisters shared a homogeneous and utterly conventional religious background. In this area there seems to be strong evidence of change over time, a change which is most clearly expressed in the different attitudes toward religion among first- and second-generation sisters. First-generation sisters 'came for the work, not the life', according to contemporary observers. One second-generation sister, herself a historian, depicted the attitude of one of her colleagues as typical of first-generation members. When visited by the chaplain, Sister Mary Pascal reported,

> he asked me if I was progressing in my spiritual life. I said, I really don't know. I am interested in my work; I am always at Office; I have my time of devotion. What more does he want me to do?

Sister Elspeth went on to say that 'it was all that those earliest Sisters had as an ideal, and they lived up to it faithfully. Only a few in those days wished for more time for devotion ...'[2] She claimed that her contemporaries had reversed these priorities and placed the date of the change at around 1900, when social work and teaching were becoming very widely accepted as female professions. There is evidence that for many first-generation sisters, the impetus to join was an urgent desire to cease being collaborators with social and economic injustice; they were no longer 'content smilingly to lie on a bed of roses while they know that thousands around them sleep on thorns'. The single-minded search for personal sanctity sometimes imagined by outsiders was a rarity in the early days of sisterhoods.[3] In all the successful early Anglican communities, the desire to do good weighed more heavily than any devotional impulse. When Benedicta Bostock joined the Benedictine community of St Mary's Abbey, she was asked the reason why she wished to become a nun. Her answer was simple: 'The Poor Law'.[4]

Part of this tendency towards a vocation of social service in a community's first generation may also have been inherent in the selection process. The founder of Clewer, when interviewing potential members, placed more emphasis on general mental ability than on religious faith. She believed that women possessing common sense could be instilled with religion, but that piety unaccompanied by common sense was of no value to a community. The founder of All Saints shared this attitude. One sister remembered 'we old (first) sisters were trained for *work* and not for the religious life ... [Mother Harriet] was always saying *Work* and Pray – or, that work must come first, and Meditations, Devotions, etc. must make way if the work came.'[5] Significantly, even secular philanthropists saw the sisterhood movement as the beginning of organized and trained social work.[6]

As the example of Clewer makes plain, communities did not always require a high standard of belief from incoming members: in the days of few workers and many pleas for assistance, Mothers Superior had a natural inclination toward the recruitment of practical, sensible women who were not afraid of work; increased religiosity, it was assumed, would come as the sister became more immersed in community life. One sister, according to her biographer, was not even a Christian at the time she joined what was to become the Community of the Holy Rood. Dora Pattison (sister of the sceptic Mark Pattison) was tormented by her disbelief in the authenticity of the Bible, and it is possible that she may have joined Holy Rood in the hope that sisterhood life would strengthen her faith. In fact, it seems that sisterhoods actively encouraged women with 'doubts' to enter. Community life, it was claimed, would provide scope for those 'oftimes tormented with infidel doubts': presumably work for God would assuage doubts of His existence.[7]

Some did not doubt, but were profoundly ignorant of Christianity. A lay novice in another community is said to have 'known nothing of any kind of religion whatever'. In the All Saints novitiate the novices were reported as having a distaste for religious discussions, and the level of religious sophistication is indicated by one admitting that she found the training interesting because she 'knew next to nothing of the Bible'.[8] Others held beliefs that were not orthodox. The founder of Wantage was a convert from Socinianism, an ancient heresy which disbelieves in the divinity of Christ, seeing him as only a good man. An ex-sister described herself as 'more of a Deist than a believer in Christ' during her years in a community.[9]

Others simply seem to have had little interest in religion at all. One sister, who later became the Mother Superior of Saint Saviour's Priory, described her life at the time she decided to enter a community as being completely devoid of religious concern or sentiment. Some actively disliked devout practices. The same All Saints sister who claimed to know nothing of the Bible described her religious background as eclectic and religiously tolerant:

> I was not brought up in any definite school of thought: mine was a family of mixed religions, Quaker, Anglican, and Papist, and I was left to think as I chose. I probably would have answered, if questioned, that one religion was as good as another ...

While this individual wrote this from the perspective of her later conversion to Roman Catholicism, the fact that her latitudinarianism was not seen as problematic while she was an Anglican sister is important to our understanding of the formative years of these organizations.

At the other extreme, deaconess orders (where Evangelical ministers organized women to work as 'the handmaidens of the clergy' under close supervision) refused to allow women with suspect spiritual credentials to join them. Louisa Twining tells with approval the story of a woman who volunteered to be a deaconess. When the pastor-founder of the deaconess order queried her motivation he found that 'it was her love and pity for suffering humanity that induced her to help her fellow-creatures; but this answer did not satisfy him ...', and her application was rejected.[10] This insistence on religious uniformity, and the rejection of candidates whose motivation would certainly have been acceptable to a sisterhood, may have accounted in part for the steady haemorrhage of members experienced by some deaconess orders; loss of deaconesses to the more tolerant sisterhoods was a constant problem for several of the deaconess communities.

The claim that there was a predisposition toward usefulness over devotion within communities until late in the century is reinforced by accounts of the lives of pioneering sisters. Some were no more inclined towards devotion even after years of community life. Sister Sarah, the daughter of a Scottish Episcopalian bishop, worked for eleven years at Ascot Priory. 'Devoted to the poor, who "loved her as a mother", "capable and trustworthy", she did not like the religious aspects of sisterhood life, to the degree that she would have preferred to "take service as a housemaid." '[11] Some who loved the work were reluctant to take the vows with their implication of lifetime commitment. Sister Eliza of Wantage voluntarily remained a novice for eight years and was told finally that if she would not be professed, she would have to leave. 'This was a great sorrow for she loved her liberty and had no wish to be tied down to Rule.'[12] One former sister lost her belief in the existence of God nine years before she left her community, and another concluded that 'I suppose I was naturally more of a "social worker" than a sister of charity ...'[13] Others were unable to overcome their distaste for the performance of their religious duties. One All Saints sister, described as 'a good Christian of the ordinary type', felt 'oppressed' by the religious activities of the sisterhood. To assuage her discontent, the community proposed to relax her religious obligations and find her congenial employment within the sisterhood.

Women who joined communities were seldom looking for paternal clerical authority to shape their lives. A number of sisters disliked and avoided priests: indeed, lack of contact with priests was at least occasionally mentioned as one of the advantages of a devotional life structured by a sisterhood. Other sisters simply defied their confessors when their advice seemed inappropriate.[14] The co-founder of Clewer explained that the motivation for community life was social, not spiritual.

> The necessities of our helpless poor, and a consciousness of the increased power obtained from combination ... have led to the idea of working together in a body. Hence societies are formed ... *The need of doing the work has led to developing the life; not the life looking abroad for a work to which to attach itself.*[15]

While this could be seen in part as defensive posturing in a society that was initially hostile to the sisterhoods, it is certainly true of the early years of Clewer, and of a number of other sisterhoods as well.

It was not uncommon for early members to have been valued much more for their secular abilities than for their spirituality. For example, the assistant superior of All Saints was described by the disapproving male warden as 'a woman of great power, very strong will, very fair abilities, but she never comes to her duties as a Sister, never to Chapter of Faults, seldom to Offices in Chapel'.[16] This particular sister spent the whole of her adult life in a large community, holding a variety of prestigious posts, and her disregard for her religious obligations seems to have concerned no one other than the warden. All Saints' Sister Mary Pauline, a good organizer and fundraiser, was often sent as troubleshooter to works which were floundering. She was remembered by her community as an excellent administrator whose good judgement meant that she was consulted by priests and members of the nobility, but as never keenly interested in religion.[17]

This priority of work over piety was sometimes made explicit: the Rule of the Sisters of Charity stated that service to the poor took precedence over religious duties.[18] The original Rule of All Saints specified that offices would be said as work permitted, and the founder of the Sisters of the Church refused to consider saying more offices, pointing out that such demands were 'totally unsuited to such a Society as ours'. The community's novices were advised to omit part of the prescribed devotions if they seemed 'burdensome and a strain, especially if they are much employed in studying, teaching, or writing'. The Rule of Holy Rood went further: 'the sisters appointed to the schools, or care of patients or Mission Work will not attend Offices, which would interfere with their duties'. One Mother Founder, when contemplating the near-approaching death of a sister, admitted 'I try to think mostly of the joys that are in store for her – but she would be a great loss in our works.'[19]

As time passed, however, a growing number of communities experienced increased tension between the goals of women who entered for an opportunity of social service and those whose primary object was devotional or even ascetic. The speed with which the change took place varied greatly from community to community. This issue was discussed at Chapter in the Community of All Saints in 1895, when the following bit of gossip was relayed by the Mother Superior:

> The Clewer Mother said to one of our Professed Sisters a little while ago 'we were formed more for work, you for the Religious Life' ... Clewer at the time is divided I know: between those who wish for a more Religious Life and those who do not ...[20]

In 1883 one observer was able to say that in most sisterhoods 'their primary end is the life, not the work', although some disagreed vehemently; the Mother Foundress of one community simply dismissed this book as the product of a profound ignorance of community life.[21] However, a community founded near the close of the century (1898) proclaimed the primacy of the religious life very distinctly in their Rule: 'What Sisters are is far more important than what they do: their life comes first and their work second ...'[22] By this time, as the embryonic welfare state was being discussed with increasing seriousness, and as opportunities for women's employment grew, it is possible to notice a change of emphasis in the new entrants in even the older sisterhoods. They were now much more concerned with the development of the 'inner life' than had been earlier recruits. The tensions that arose from this gradual change, from communities as groups whose members were oriented toward social work to groups oriented largely toward personal holiness, was made clear by the Sisters of the Church's experience in the 1890s. When the community curtailed its religious observances due to the demands of their work (an indication in itself that the leading members still valued their social services above all else), some sisters left the community. They claimed to have done so because of their dissatisfaction with the continuing priority given to active work over religious devotion.[23] The strongest reformulation of the purposes of a sister was to come in 1908 at the Pan-Anglican Congress: 'in the mind of a good Sister the idea of her life in God always comes before the thought of her work for God'.[24] Love of work, and love of God: these two things were the prime motivation of those who joined pioneering sisterhoods, although the mix varied from sister to sister, community to community, and over the passage of time.

Regardless of the initial spiritual or social motivation which prompted these Victorian women to join Anglican communities, it is clear that many of them found happiness in the sisterhoods. What the student of their archives remembers most clearly is the sense of fulfilment and of happiness expressed movingly in their memoirs, diaries and letters. St Saviour's Priory's Mother Kate perhaps put it best: describing her call and its result she wrote

Something suddenly seemed to come into my heart that put everything in a different light before me ... And I was not disappointed with the reality of my daydreams ... I have my heart's desire granted, though in a far different way to what I had ever expected.[25]

Becoming a sister

For any sisterhood to endure and thrive, a steady supply of new members was necessary. There were three reasons for this. First, it was imperative that active workers who died, left or grew too old to continue their labours be replaced. A community which could not attract a second generation died out with dismaying speed, as a few of the smaller sisterhoods were to discover. Second, large numbers of candidates were needed in order to ensure that obviously unsuitable women were not taken simply through shortage of numbers or out of lack of choice. Third, a large novitiate was a sign of status among the sisterhoods, and communities which grew rapidly attracted yet more aspirants: as a priest associated with a smaller community wrote in frustration: 'I am afraid the tendency of the day is for would-be sisters to crowd into the big Communities.'[26]

Therefore, the attraction of prospective candidates, the selection of suitable women and the training of new members were of the highest importance in ensuring the survival and prosperity of the community. This task of regeneration was the joint responsibility of the entire community, although certain aspects of it were shared out to community office-holders. Normally the Mother Superior was the person first approached by an aspirant, and all sisters were given the opportunity to vote on the candidate's suitability after a period of testing. However, the Novice Mistress, who undertook the supervision of a two- to four-year period of specialist training of the newcomers, bore the brunt of responsibility in the intervening period.

The first step in the actual process of becoming a sister was application: this was a relatively informal process, where the applicant contacted the Mother Superior by letter, explaining her background, her reasons for wishing to enter, and supplying a reference, normally to her clergyman or spiritual director.[27] The Mother Superior would then appoint a time to interview the candidate, and to show her the community if she were unfamiliar with their work. The practical emphasis of the interview must have dispelled any remaining traces of romantic illusion. An early Clewer sister described her first meeting with the community's founder as a demanding exploration of what she could contribute to the corporate life:

> She ... said, 'I hear you want to be a Sister.' I assented. 'What can you do?' was her next question. I hesitated, and she began to cross-question me as to my capabilities ... I was impressed with her strong practical sense, and great devotion to her Community, and that the question in her mind was whether I should be of any use in it. It was a very business-like visit ...[28]

This sort of introductory visit was often unnecessary, as sisterhoods always attracted members from among the associates (lady helpers) of their own or other communities, as well as from the networks of charitable ladies with whom they came in touch.[29] Family and social ties also played a part. A significant number of enquiries came from women who had sisters or other relatives living in Anglican communities. A few women followed their governesses into communities, and it was not uncommon for mistress and maid to enter together, the maid of course becoming a lay sister. Lay sisterhood was the role offered to working-class women in sisterhoods, and candidates for lay sister status had frequently been brought up by, or had strong ties to, the community, through being raised in a sisterhood orphanage or industrial training school or by having worked for a community as a paid servant. The late Brian Heeney, who believed that the Church Army, with its 192 working-class women members in 1900, was the biggest source of 'female proletarian Church workers', must have been unaware of the number of communities with lay orders.[30] The number of lay sisters in Anglican communities, although impossible to determine accurately from surviving records, was at least double that.

If the aspiring sister's interview was successful, she was invited to spend some weeks with the community as a visitor, living in the house and observing their work. This visit could be a shock to women who envisioned sisterhoods as romantically cloistered affairs, or who had not considered what they had to offer to what the founder of Clewer called 'the most practical of things, the life of a Sister'. It was not unusual for women to leave the next morning, dismayed by the unromantic simplicity of life and the hard work expected of members.[31] During this visit both the community and the applicant would be forming opinions about the possibility of a permanent relationship: the community scrutinizing the woman, the woman asking herself if this sisterhood (or indeed any sisterhood) was right for her. If, after a few weeks, the woman seeking admission wished to persevere, she became a postulant. Postulancy, which lasted around six months in most cases, involved helping with the work, sharing the community's devotions and meals, and becoming generally acquainted with the sisterhood's philosophy, rules and personnel. Those women who did enrol as postulants found that their lives were instantly filled with a regular routine of activities which were intellectually, emotionally and physically demanding. Postulancy could be a time of great stress for candidates, as they endeavoured to test their vocation for community life, struggled to learn new and taxing skills, while at the same time often bearing the brunt of their families' anger or dislike of their choice.[32] One sister wrote of her family's dismay at her decision to enter a community as being of a piece with the wider culture's enmity:

> It was not an easy thing to enter a Religious Community in those days. Much suspicion and ill was thought of them and the dress of a Sister disliked and scoffed at. When at length I received the Habit, I remember as we walked in the street, passers by often scoffed or showed positive hatred of our outward dress – 'made faces' at us and called us 'sisters of Misery', etc! And one's own relations even pitied us.[33]

At the end of the six months of postulancy the community voted on the question of whether the postulant would be admitted to Clothing, thus becoming a novice. Most communities required a two-thirds positive vote before a woman was allowed to remain. Sisterhoods were acutely aware of the potential for disruption if unsuitable candidates were permitted to enter the novitiate, and it was usual for the sisters to reject one-third to one-half of the postulants. Generally almost another one-third left of their own volition. This selectivity must have left the successful candidates feeling especially privileged. One sister wrote of her pleasure at being clothed in terms which are more resonant of a career than of a religious ceremony, saying 'there was the feeling of being promoted'.[34] A woman who failed her election to the novitiate might be allowed to try again later, be urged to try a community more suited to her personality, or simply sent away as unsuitable. Of course, many women, after six months' experience of the life, chose to go away voluntarily, finding community life other than what they had envisioned.

The novitiate

In the relatively experimental communities of Victorian Anglicanism, clothing was seen as the real entrance into the inner life of the sisterhoods. At clothing, women received the habit of the community with some small modifications, intended to mark her probationary status as a novice. It was at clothing that the new sister was given her name 'in religion': in most communities this was selected by the Mother Superior, but in some groups the novice herself was asked for a suggestion. This was often her own Christian name or a variant of it, but in some communities the new name was entirely different.[35] This was now prefixed with 'Sister'. The novitiate lasted anywhere from two to four years for choir sisters; in the early days it was occasionally shortened for exceptionally gifted women or those whose special talents were in demand. Lay sisters almost always had a longer novitiate: four years was typical. Occasionally, gifted novices were given great responsibility astonishingly early. All Saints' Sister Elizabeth, who organized the nursing at University College Hospital, was still a novice when she undertook the task. Several professed sisters worked under her direction there, indicating that the sisterhoods could give precedence to talent over rank when the work demanded it.[36] In order to ensure that each novice received individual attention, fast-growing communities often had to subdivide the novitiate. For example, the Sisters of the Church's novitiate was so large that in 1888 it was divided into Junior and Senior branches, each with its own Novice Mistress: the Junior novitiate, which comprised those who had been clothed for less than eighteen months, contained forty choir and twenty lay members. Novice Mistresses took great pride in turning out future leaders of the community, for in this way they shaped the sisterhood's future. One Novice Mistress's brief summing-up of her term in office makes her gratification plain: ' ... I had a large and important Novitiate – so many Novices who were trained during the 6 years I was Mistress became afterward, Sister Superiors or heads of work ...'[37]

Communities utilized women's services in education, in ministering to the sick, in charitable labour, and in the maintenance of their own communal life. One aspect of the seriousness with which they took their work was their emphasis on training. These organizations viewed the novitiate as a period of intensive training for practical work as well as for spiritual duties, at a time when most secular commentators assumed that womanly instincts would suffice for caring work, and that training was unnecessary. That sisterhoods insisted on training their personnel was seen as additional evidence of their unnaturalness. More liberal observers praised communities for their 'just sense of the necessity of a fitting preparation before [they] can efficiently undertake duties so difficult and important'.[38]

The training in the novitiate was not a mere nominal acquaintance with the community's projects. One former All Saints sister remembered 'And how we worked! The training of the novitiate was practical in the extreme.'[39] During the novitiate the novices attended classes, studied and wrote examinations, and did practical work within and outside the convent under the supervision of sisters who were specialists in their areas. Some women found the adjustment a trial: Sister Emily Gertrude, who had enjoyed 'a gay youth', escaped from the pressure by dancing, with a chair as her partner, during her novitiate at Wantage.[40] Women from sheltered backgrounds often found their first experience of work exhilarating, and one former sister described her first day of manual labour (in the third person) as a transformative experience.

> For the first time Maude realised herself as really a Sister of Mercy, and a strange feeling of exultation filled her heart. She felt that she could walk miles in her thick shoes, and carry no end of things in her gloveless hands, and with a glowing love to all whom she met, help to mitigate the sorrow and suffering around her ...[41]

The first three pages of the memoirs of Sister Caroline Mary, the second Mother Superior of All Saints, chronicle her delight at the active life of the sisterhood; the long account of all the things she was able to *do* after becoming a sister is telling, as is her obvious pleasure in being given work and responsibility. The founder of the Sisters of the Church agreed, writing 'Talk of the pleasures of Society, they are dull and vapid compared to such excitements as these!'[42]

Novices, especially those from the middle and upper classes, spent a considerable portion of their novitiate familiarizing themselves with domestic work, jobs that in their own homes had always been performed by servants. It was found that these women, mostly from comfortable backgrounds, needed instruction in basic skills such as knowing when water was boiling, and in how to clean a saucepan. That they had always been looked after by servants is underlined by the necessity for instructions such as the following: 'be careful that water spilt is dried up at once, to avoid ruining the ceiling underneath ... close bed-room and passage windows in wet weather, as the rain injures blinds, wall-papers, and wood work ...'[43]

Nor was it possible to assume that these lady novices compensated for their lack of practical skills by a superior academic education. Just how much training was sometimes necessary is clear from a passage in the All Hallows constitution, which states that the Novice Mistress is responsible for the secular culture of choir novices who had received 'a deficient education': the regulation goes on to state that no choir sister should be professed until she can 'read aloud intelligently, express herself sensibly in a legibly written letter, and work mentally such arithmetical questions as are necessary in housekeeping or ordinary business'.[44] This regulation, designed for the training of middle- and upper-class women, is a striking indictment of the substandard education many Victorian women of the middle and upper classes received. Equally striking is the practical helplessness of some Victorian ladies. Another early sister admitted that when she first shopped for the community she had no idea of the value of goods: she did not know whether a farthing or a sovereign should be offered in payment for a loaf of bread, and had difficulty in making change. In her home, such knowledge had been the province of servants.

Training of the novices varied according to the sisterhood's resources, size and mission. The Community of All Saints, struggling to deal with a novitiate of forty or fifty women at a time, opened a branch house in Finsbury in the 1890s for the sole purpose of providing more work for their novices.[45] Most of the nursing sisterhoods (nine of the first ten communities nursed) preferred to recruit women who had some hospital training, but were willing to provide nursing education for sisters, both choir and lay, who demonstrated ability.[46] Some sought training abroad. A few of the early sisterhoods sent women to Kaiserwerth, where Florence Nightingale had trained, but this German deaconess institution soon demonstrated its lack of tolerance for High Church Anglicanism by sending away a woman who proved to be guilty of membership in a sisterhood.[47] The Nursing Sisters of St John the Divine advertised that 'to those of a lower station they give full training, and a position for life'.[48]

In the 1840s and 1850s the provision of training in England for nursing sisters was difficult, as few hospitals were willing to train 'ladies', or indeed to believe that nursing required any training whatsoever. After prolonged negotiations, sisters were allowed to attend teaching hospitals like Westminster, although the hospital demanded that they lay aside their title, habit and cross during the training. Typically, the hospital training undertaken by a sister lasted about nine months, and by the standards of the time was considered extremely thorough.[49] Before long, some sisterhoods built up a core of experienced nurses, who were then able themselves to train their new recruits in their own wards. Women such as Holy Rood's Sister Lucy, who held an Honours Nursing Certificate from London Hospital, were quickly employed in training their fellows.[50] Some opened their training facilities to women who wished to be nurses without being sisters. Ascot Priory opened a training school for military nurses in 1854, and from 1857 the Nursing Sisters of St John the Divine routinely trained secular nurses in their wards at King's College Hospital. This was an earlier training school than Nightingale's. By 1861 Nightingale was actively involved in the Nursing Sisters of St John the Divine's training schemes for midwives.[51] Even when well-established, sisterhoods continued to send members abroad for training unavailable at home. The Sisters of the Church sisters travelled to the continent to study nursing in French and German children's hospitals before opening their own convalescent home for children.[52]

Sometimes communities attracted trained professionals who had come into contact with the sisterhood in the course of their work in the same locale. An Edmonton social worker entered the Community of the Holy Comforter, also in Edmonton, in 1895; it is probable that the future Mother Monica first encountered the community in the course of her duties: it is certain that she continued her social work after her profession.[53] Communities which ran schools often attracted their hired teachers into their ranks. Teaching sisterhoods such as the Sisters of the Church actively recruited trained teachers into the novitiate, and sent virtually all their choir novices to teacher training classes, often at Bedford College. (The Sisters of the Church's training is discussed at greater length in Chapter Four.)

Sisters, uniquely, were trained both for skills and for a certain kind of life. During the novitiate they were expected to demonstrate their aptitude for both. Throughout the novitiate the candidates were under the close scrutiny of the Novice Mistress, and more generally under that of the entire community. All knew that at the expiration of the novitiate, they would be expected to vote on whether the novice would be received as one of themselves or sent away. This decision was taken very seriously. Bennett tells us: 'The training of the novitiate was searching, and the sisters were not afraid to vote against a novice if she was not considered satisfactory.' At the same time the novices were studying the Rule, in order that they might make an informed decision about whether the community's philosophy and regulations were acceptable to them.[54]

One early member described her experience of the novitiate as very much influenced by the personality of the Novice Mistress. It is noteworthy that sentiment seems to have played little part in their training.

> She [the Novice Mistress] had all the qualities necessary for her post. What struck me ... was her power to get the most, spiritually, intellectually, and physically, out of those in her charge ... she made us feel that she expected the very best from each individual novice, and she received a loyal response to her expectations ...
>
> There was a tremendous esprit de corps in the novitiate; perhaps as a result of her particular temperament, it was more the spirit of a regiment, or a school, than that of a home ...[55]

The novitiate was no sinecure. Communities sent away between one-third and one-half of their novices, with some rejecting well over half as (in the phrase universally used) 'unfit for the life and work'. This was in addition to the 30 to 50 per cent weeded out at the stage of postulancy. Of thirty novices who did not achieve profession at All Saints between 1900 and 1910, the reasons recorded by the community were varied. Eight left for reasons of health, seven were described as having 'no vocation', and an equal number were cryptically described as 'unsatisfactory'. Five failed their elections to profession (meaning that at least one-third of the community felt doubts as to their suitability), and two were described as 'not ready'.[56] The large number of women turned away for health reasons is a powerful reminder of how demanding sisterhood life was; women without excellent physical stamina often found the work simply too hard. Mental health was also considered: the 'morbid' were forced to leave. Expulsion for any reason could occur at any time during the novitiate; 'no desire on her part to stay would have the slightest effect – she would be told firmly and kindly that she must leave, and the sooner the better. Neither would the size of her income make any difference ...'[57] A novice could be considered unsuitable for many reasons, including weak health, stupidity, laziness, or the belief that her temperament made her better suited to a different community, one with a different emphasis or type of work. Some were simply not ready, and were advised to try again after a few years' experience of life.

Self-selection was also at work throughout the novitiate, with many women realizing that they did not wish to make a life commitment to a sisterhood. Novices were free to leave at any time, and those who doubted their vocation were generally encouraged to do so. Some expressed ambivalence about the commitment involved in becoming a full sister. Bennett again: 'though I did not want to leave the Community, I dreaded the thought of profession'.[58] Novices who failed their election to profession by a narrow margin, or who it was felt needed more time to consider their future, were sometimes allowed to spend an extra year in the novitiate. If the second election was failed, the novice was compelled to leave. As one sister warned prospective candidates, communities elected or rejected candidates fully aware that a mistaken election could cause the entire body of sisters years of anxiety, discomfort or misery:

> It is no easy matter to obtain entrance into a sisterhood. A woman may have a sincere desire for the life, be well adapted for it, and perhaps have a good fortune to bring with her, and yet may be rejected, on offering herself for the Novitiate. If received then, she may be rejected, when proposed for Profession; and, though she pass through that ordeal, she may, in some Houses, at any future time be requested to leave the Sisterhood, should it appear desirable to a majority of three-fourths of the Sisters.[59]

In the early years of the Anglican sisterhoods the communities had to deal with women influenced by fashion, as well as with all the ordinary types of unsuitable candidates. As a result of the Victorian craze for all things mediaeval and the pseudo-Gothic, the idea of the 'romance of life in a cloister' took hold of the imaginations of many, some of whom wished to carry it out within the Anglican Church. Marion Hughes's Oxford-based community, the Society of the Holy and Undivided Trinity, attracted a disproportionate number of this type of candidate. This was unsurprising, given that the founder confessed to sharing this weakness for the picturesque aspects of conventual life. The community's stability and growth suffered as a result.[60] Other sisterhoods, perhaps observing the turbulence of the Society of the Holy and Undivided Trinity, emphasized that such impulsive romantics could do grievous harm to a community, in that 'they enter upon duties, and assume a position, falling from which they may, in no small degree, disorder and shake the whole'. The remedy for this attitude, it was believed, was in a minimizing of the 'mediaeval' aspects of community life, as well as making the selection process as testing and as democratic as possible; 'it is very wholesome then for us to live in this our simple, unadorned, and formless household'.[61]

Because communities expected only a portion of their postulants to endure until clothing, very few troubled to record the number of postulants who tried the life. However, it is possible to study the novitiate of All Saints between 1891 and 1910, when the Novice Mistress kept a tally (not necessarily complete) of the names of those who came to try their vocations. During that period she recorded the reception of 103 postulants: 79 (77 per cent) were clothed and entered the novitiate, and 53 were professed. These represent 51 per cent of all the postulants and 68 per cent of those who persevered to clothing. Of these 53, 45 women, or 85 per cent (32 choir sisters and 13 lay sisters), remained for life. So, from this cohort overall, only 51 per cent reached profession and 43.6 per cent made a lifetime commitment to the sisterhood.

A second list of All Saints novices covering the first decade of the twentieth century makes the important distinction between lay and choir aspirants: it indicates that 43 lay novices and 40 choir novices were clothed. Sixteen (37 per cent) of the lay novices were professed, as were 22 (55 per cent) of the choir novices.[62] Overall, All Saints seems to have retained about 50 per cent of its aspirants, but lay aspirants were less likely to remain than those of a higher social status. This would indicate that although many working-class women considered the life, lay sister status was less attractive to

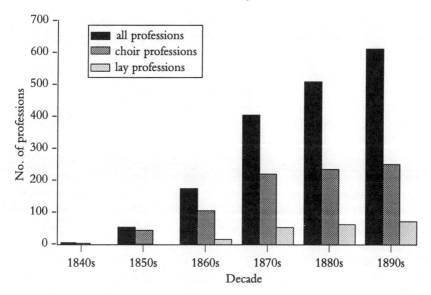

Figure 2.1 Professions by decade and order

them once they had actually had a taste of community living; it may be that there were fewer rewards for working-class women within the sisterhoods. Be that as it may, of those who did attain profession, the vast majority remained within the community permanently, indicating the success of the earlier weeding-out processes, the postulancy and the novitiate.

Profession and the vows

Profession ceremonies were the high festival of sisterhood life, along with the annual commemoration of the community's patronal dedication. These ceremonies were closely modelled on their Roman Catholic equivalents. At profession, the novices would wear wedding dresses at the beginning of the ceremony, which would be changed for the dress of a professed sister after the taking of the vows. During the ritual a black veil was placed over the white veil of the novitiate, and some communities also exchanged the cross worn by novices for one of a different type. The bestowing of a 'wedding' ring at profession was not normal practice in most Anglican communities until relatively late in the century.

The purpose of the profession ceremony was to initiate the novice into full membership in the community. This was done through the taking of the profession vows. Anglican sisters took the three vows of chastity, poverty and obedience. These vows were seen as correctives to the 'three elements of evil': sensuality contrasted with chastity; covetousness with poverty; and pride (in the sense of self-sufficiency) with the promise of obedience. At least one community added a fourth vow, that of charity.[63] Normally the vows were made in the presence of a dignitary of some sort: a bishop (if a sympathetic one was available), or the clergyman most closely associated with the community, or the Mother Superior. It is important to make a distinction here – the vows were not made *to* the presiding authority, but were simply *received* by him/her. The vows of poverty, obedience and chastity were made *to* the community as a whole, or sometimes to God.[64]

Poverty

In striking contrast to the gross materialism of the Victorian homes they had left, women who took the vow of poverty renounced the whole concept of individual ownership. Private possessions were forbidden in the rules of all communities, and sisters were encouraged to consider nothing as belonging to themselves personally; the community would supply them with what they needed.[65] The accumulation of objects was in direct contradiction to both the letter and the spirit of the sisterhoods, and it was accepted that the love of such things could interfere with one's vocation. The Mother Foundress of the Society of the Holy and Undivided Trinity wrote of one woman who left the community:

> Mr Harmon came and packed up the remainder of Maud Grindle's clothes and books and pictures – such a large collection of what she called *her own* that no wonder she has lost her Vocation – she by those trifles so completely broke her vow of Poverty.[66]

Sisters in this community were allotted the following, which is a relatively lavish provision compared to some other sisterhoods:

> A new habit once a year, the old one being kept in case of need;
> Two pairs of shoes and stockings;

One cloak;
Five shifts, drawers, night shifts and caps;
Five boddices [sic]; five hoods and caps;
Seven tippets and straps;
Two petticoats;
Three flannel petticoats;
Twelve pocket-handkerchiefs and [sanitary?] towels;
Two pairs of stays;
Five pairs of stockings;
A workcase; thimble; scissors, needles, cotton, knife; notebook; Bible;
The Paradise of the Christian Soul; office book; rosary.[67]

Poverty meant a genuine reduction in the standard of living for these upper-
and middle-class women. The sisters of Saint Saviour's Priory lived a life
modelled, as closely as possible, on the material status of working-class
artisans in East London, where the community was based. When dentists
were required, they visited the students at Guy's Hospital, and 'clothes had to
last forever – shoes came from jumble sales'. Food was adequate in quantity
but of 'rough' quality; 'the food and clothes of the sisters shall be only such as
become the poor'.

Their individual cells were simply furnished. Each contained a wooden
chair, an iron bed with cheap red blankets, a wash stand constructed from a
soap box, jug, basin, carbolic soap, toothpowder, a hot water can (hot water
was rarely provided) and a mug. The room also contained a gas light, one
tiny table, and a mat. The other furniture was a clothes cupboard and one
bookshelf. Invalid sisters lived a life of comparative luxury: they enjoyed, in
addition to the above, 'fireplaces and bigger windows, with a table big
enough to write on and a chair with arms'. Although the sisters had
everything necessary for living, the extreme bareness of their cells and
convents compared with the opulence of mid- and late-Victorian homes
shocked many who visited them. The goal was to avoid exceeding the
standard of comfort 'we should desire to secure for all the poor: roughly
speaking, such conditions as suffice for health and efficiency'.[68] Some critics
of communities felt that such plain living was an outrage to the sensibilities
of ladies; the level of anger expressed suggests that the sisters' (very
orthodox) rejection of materialism was an affront to the sensibilities of their
society as well.

Chastity

Of the three vows taken in Anglican sisterhoods, the promise of chastity attracted the least attention. In Victorian Britain, it was assumed that any respectable unmarried woman would inevitably remain chaste. In light of this, the vow of chastity was usually explained as being a promise that the sister would not contemplate marriage. It also served to emphasize the distance between the sister and the biological family. As the Community of St Peter's spiritual counsels described it, 'chastity constitutes the most intimate ground of separation from earthly ties'.[69] Most community rules also included exhortations to modest and decorous behaviour in the section on chastity.

Virginity was not a prerequisite for entrance into a community, as witness the steady trickle of widows into the orders: both Clewer and Holy Rood were founded by widows. Unlike some Catholic orders, Anglican sisterhoods also admitted illegitimately born women into their sisterhoods. More problematic were the cases (which must have been extremely rare) of the admission of women with prior sexual experience outside marriage. The Mother Superior of the Community of the Holy Family felt compelled to consult the Archbishop of Canterbury before admitting a woman who had indulged in sex play, and perhaps intercourse (the woman herself seems to have been unsure), while in her teens. The incident was described to the Archbishop in veiled terms. 'At the age of 15 [she] committed or attempted to commit an offence against chastity with a boy of $14\frac{1}{2}$.' Mother Agnes based her opinion that the woman involved was probably still a virgin on the grounds of the youth of the boy involved, and the Archbishop discreetly concurred.[70]

Obedience

The vow of obedience was almost universally misunderstood by Victorian observers of sisterhoods. They saw it as a promise of obedience to the Mother Superior. In actual practice, the promise to obey applied first of all to the rules and constitutions of the community, and secondarily to figures of authority. Even then, it held fast only as far as they made requests consonant with the community's constitution and ethos. 'Obedience implies a steadfast and habitual regard for the spirit and rule of the Community and its established customs; and a generous and immediate submission to all lawful authority.'[71]

The Rule of the Community of the Holy Family, a teaching order whose founder and first four members were all Newnham graduates, stressed the idea that obedience must be intelligent.

Sisters' obedience cannot be too perfect; but it is quite possible that too little liberty may be left them. In our Community it is intended that all Professed Sisters shall have a real though limited initiative and responsibility. They are to think for themselves and must be encouraged to do so. Head Mistresses and Sisters in Charge must be allowed, as far as is possible, to work in their own natural way, making their own experiments, and, if need be, learning by their own mistakes.[72]

The vow of obedience was seen by outsiders as unnatural, given as it was to a corporate group headed by a woman: of course the vow of obedience to a man in a marriage ceremony was seen as eminently fitting for women. Much of the opposition to this vow was expressed as part of a wider critique of sisterhoods, which will be discussed in Chapter Six.

The vows were full of meaning for the sisters who took them. They saw them as setting them aside from the ordinary lives of Victorian women, as a symbol of their commitment, and as a help in the inevitable moments of discontent or doubt that were to come. One sister wrote: 'The Vows ... so freely stigmatised, because so thoroughly misunderstood, are in their reality, a stay, a bulwark, and a comfort, for the want of which nothing else can make up.'[73] E. B. Pusey warned that if Anglicanism persisted in its rejection of women willing to dedicate themselves for life, such women would turn to Roman Catholicism, which would at least allow them to commit themselves to their call.[74]

Because the vows were not recognized by the civil or religious authorities, women could not be constrained by them. At the same time, sisters certainly saw the vows as highly significant, and very different from an ordinary promise. The special meaning of their vows is made clear by the reaction of one of the minority of women who later regretted taking them. Although she had enjoyed her novitiate, she wrote 'I would have given anything to have undone the morning's work in the evening of my Profession day.'[75] Sister Margaret Emily was in the minority. Generally, women attracted to sisterhoods wanted to make the commitment entailed in the three vows. Part of the Victorian history of the communities was their struggle to take the vows of obedience, poverty and chastity openly. They were motivated primarily by the conviction that they and their companions had been called by God to the life of a sisterhood. It follows that the primacy of the vows increased as communities became more inner-oriented, as the century drew to a close. The advantage of the vows was that as well as providing stability, they assisted in the simplification of the sister's life. As the Convocation Report on Sisterhoods put it: 'they feel that this call requires them to give up their personal freedom of action, and to obey a settled rule: they have no mind to marry, or even to be free to marry; they will have nothing more to do with the distractions and cares which attend on the possession of this world's goods'.[76] Among the defences of the vows, the idea that the vows simplified life was important; it was argued that they allowed sisters to work more efficiently and freely, since so many of the ordinary questions of life were taken care of by the Rule.

Although early historians of the Oxford Movement, such as Sparrow Simpson, often state that 'no vows were taken in the early years of the movement', this was not the case.[77] Generally, Anglican sisters at first made their vows privately, as promises of chastity, poverty and obedience were forbidden by the church authorities, although it was admitted that women could not be prohibited from considering their promises as constituting a commitment for life.[78] In some communities, the discrepancy between episcopal prohibition of vows and the practice of taking them was explained away with considerable ingenuity: at All Saints, several sisters wrote letters describing their understanding of the practice in the 1850s:

> When I told our Mother Foundress that 'I wished to be a Sister' she said *most* strongly that I must remember I should be bound 'for the rest of my life in this world'. [She also said] 'Although there was a Statute which *verbally* released Sisters, it had been put in by the Bishop, and really was never intended in the founding of the Comty, but our Vows were *binding for Life*.' [The Novice Mistress taught that] ... this is a free country & if any one chose to break their vows, they were at liberty to do so, but we were taught it was a deadly sin, at least that was always the impression conveyed to me, as a Priest or a married woman may break their vows. At any rate we were always taught that the vows were life-long, & she said that clause [prohibiting vows] was put in by our first visitor, the Bishop of London. We have never liked it & always wished to get rid of it ... It seems to me that in a free country no one can compel vows to be kept, or forbid them to be made if we like to do so. Surely the freedom must be allowed to both cases.[79]

Because the vows could not be made openly, in some communities there was confusion over whether the promises were binding for life or for only as long as a woman remained within the sisterhood. Some sisters argued that a woman who left need take no other action to sever the connection, while others believed that living outside the sisterhood did not mean that a woman ceased to be a sister. A former All Saints sister explained to the Archbishop of Canterbury that her vows were binding for life, and that she wished them to remain so.

> I firmly believe and hold that once a Sister *always* a Sister, and that the Bishop can only and is only asked to release me from outward membership of my Community, but this does *not* touch my vows at all ... *I will still be a Sister.*[80]

Others felt that the lack of dispensation meant that a woman who left committed a serious sin.[81] If the vows were binding for life, a power of dispensation was necessary; this raised the question of who in the Anglican Church had the power to dispense vows? This question was not satisfactorily settled in the nineteenth century; most women who left seem to have concluded that they themselves held the power to make void their vows without clerical assistance. But for the majority of Anglican sisters, who remained active members of their communities from the time of making their vows until death, the question of dispensation never arose. They valued the taking of their vows as a defining event in their lives, equivalent in significant ways to ordination to the priesthood. Even more importantly, the taking of vows embodied key values for these new organizations: they provided a symbol of commitment, a sense of stability for both the membership and the institution, and the key ultimate ritual of initiation into a new way of life.

Lay status and social class in the convent

Most communities, imitating traditional Roman Catholic practice, divided their sisters at clothing into two classes, choir and lay. The special status of lay sisters and novices is of considerable interest. However, not all communities made provision for lay sisters. Those that did not wished to submerge all class distinctions in a common vocation and shared work. Wantage was the biggest single-order sisterhood, but even there social class could be productive of tensions. Their Rule warned members against preoccupation with social background, arguing that the danger of pride was common to all, although taking different forms in different social strata.

> Take heed that there be not in any of you a feeling of vanity because you are admitted to the society of those with whom you would not elsewhere be on equal

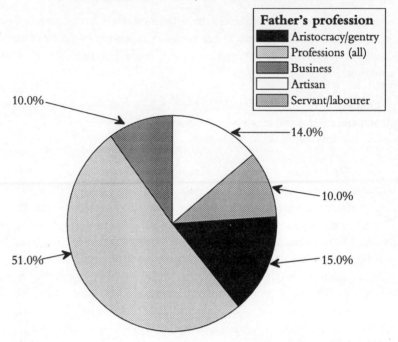

Figure 2.2 Social class of sisters professed 1845–1900 (all orders)

terms ... Else would such communities become useful to the rich, and not to the poor, if the poor be inflated with vanity, and only the rich be humbled. On the other hand, let not any of you despise those, who, in the world would be beneath you in rank and fortune. Rather rejoice ... in the society of your poorer sisters. What advantage is there in 'dispersing abroad and giving to the poor' if the heart become prouder in despising riches than it was before in possessing them?[82]

The Sisters of the Poor (the Community of St Mary at the Cross), based in Shoreditch, was composed of a single order, and accepted postulants from any rank of life, whether wealthy or penniless. These women did all their own housework, seeing it as 'an occupation full of dignity that no woman need be ashamed of'.[83] In order to maintain an equal footing within the convent, members were discouraged from talking about their families and background, and their differing financial contributions were normally kept secret. However, differences in accent and education must have made social origin fairly obvious in the case of most sisters.

It was at clothing that the difference between the lay and choir aspirants became obvious (see Table 2.1). While there is no question but that sisters

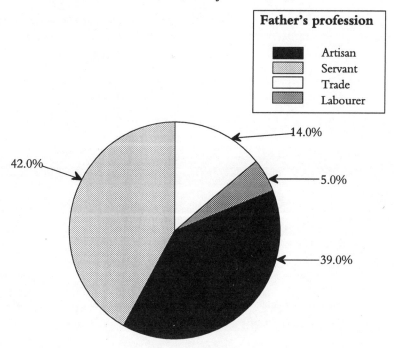

Figure 2.3 Social background of lay sisters professed 1845–1900

transgressed social as well as geographic boundaries in their work with the poor, the lay/choir division within the sisterhoods forces us to ask whether and how sisters maintained social boundaries within their own communities. As with all aspects of the Anglican religious experience in the nineteenth century, the record is one of experimentation and diversity rather than regulation and conformity. The lives of lay and choir sisters in some communities were virtually identical, while in others there was considerable divergence. E. B. Pusey had been the first to suggest the incorporation of lay sisters into Anglican sisterhoods, and he assumed that, if women from working-class backgrounds were not admitted as a separate order, it would not be possible for them to participate in the religious life at all. He does not seem to have envisaged the possibility of a classless community, although, as has been mentioned, a very few nineteenth-century orders did away with the distinction; the most important of these was Wantage.

Lay sisters were drawn largely from the respectable upper levels of the working class; their fathers were described in community records as farmers, artisans, small tradesmen or shopkeepers. Unskilled occupations, such as farm

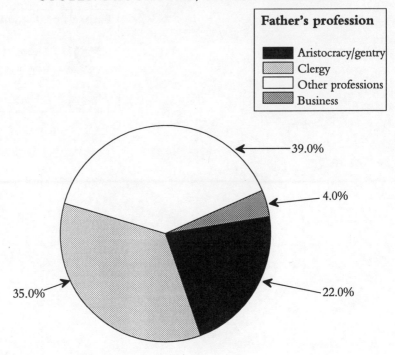

Figure 2.4 Social background of choir sisters professed 1845–1900

labourer, were rare.[84] Those working-class women who entered the communities with an employment history of their own tended to have been domestic servants, although a substantial minority had been infant school-mistresses, matrons or ward nurses in hospitals. Between communities there could be considerable social difference; the daughter of a minor official could count on lay sister status at All Saints; an identical background would entitle her to choir sister status at the Society of the Holy and Undivided Trinity. It seems likely that prospective members of equivocal status took such subtleties into consideration when choosing where to try their vocation.

Choir sisters typically came from an upper- or middle-class background, with a very strong representation from clergy families: almost 35 per cent of all Victorian choir sisters were the daughters of clerics. Aside from clergy daughters, it is striking how many of these women were related to men who exercised some power in Victorian society, and who either formed the elite of wealth and birth or assisted in governing the country and its empire. Whether members of the aristocracy, the landed gentry or the political world or highly placed in the military or the law, these men exerted influence on the

Table 2.1 Class backgrounds, based on father's occupation, of sisters professed 1845–1900 (percentages)

Class background	All sisters[a]	Choir sisters[b]	Lay sisters[c]
Aristocracy/gentry	15.0	21.9	
Clergy	24.0	34.9	
Other professions	27.0	39.0	
Business	9.9		
Merchant		4.8	
Trade			13.8
Artisan	14.2		38.8
Labourer			5.5
Servant/manual worker	9.9		41.6

[a] N = 211 sisters for whom this information is given. This figure includes 29 sisters who joined single-order communities.
[b] N = 36
[c] N = 146

world around them. The daughters or sisters of this elite, suited to such work by their class and background, were barred from such activities by their gender; some of them saw in sisterhoods the possibility of exercising authority and fulfilling their ambitions in an alternative sphere.

Several of the sisterhoods, especially All Saints and Clewer, had the reputation of being 'fashionable' communities. This reputation is interesting in light of the frequently expressed concern that some women became sisters from a desire to improve their social standing. Opponents of sisterhoods went so far as to claim that women stayed in communities because of the 'earthly distinction' they derived from their status as sisters. Typical was the claim that parochial mission women, Bible women and parish nurses came from a lower social class than did sisters, and 'occupied about the same relationship to a Sister as a Scripture-reader did to a parish priest'.[85] Of course, the absurdity of the claim lay in that a sister, as long as she remained one, would benefit very little from her status, as all within the community were (in theory at least) equal. However, the belief that becoming a sister raised one's social status was widespread among both supporters and opponents of the movement. The rise in social position entailed by sisterhood status must have sometimes proved difficult to handle gracefully, given the number of warnings against pride directed to lay sisters. Characteristic of these warnings was this by an anonymous writer (internal evidence indicates that she may have been a sister at East Grinstead) who protested:

> I would have it understood – and that thoroughly – that we drop our worldly rank on entering ... and do not take up a rank we never had before. We are all equal. But it is because the titled lady descends to the level of her humble Sister, *not* because the humble Sister rises to the rank of the titled lady.[86]

That this lesson did not sink in easily is obvious from the number of times it seemed necessary to repeat it: after all, it must have been a heady experience for a former cook to see 'ladies' rise when she entered a room and to be invited to dine with members of the aristocracy.[87]

Whether communities were composed of one order or two, their rules and constitutions assumed that gentlewomen were the natural leaders of these institutions. In their fullest development, most communities envisioned themselves as an idealized microcosm of the social order of Victorian England. Ladies would be 'most helpful in directing the work of others of a lower social condition'. Under upper-class guidance middle-class women would become tolerable leaders themselves. Lower-middle-class and working-class sisters would do the work: these groups would 'provide us with admirable teachers for our schools, nurses for our Hospitals, ... and helps in training the elder children in domestic service'.[88] Exceptions to the assumption that upper-middle or upper-class women would take the positions of leadership within the sisterhoods were rare. Wantage was the most important anomaly, and here it happened as an *ad hoc* response to circumstances (the original Mother followed Manning into the Roman Catholic Church), rather than as deliberate policy. This community chose its first permanent Mother Superior from an upper-working-class background: Mother Harriet, the daughter of a working farmer, was elected by the community in 1853. Despite her lack of social standing, for 37 years her attractive personality and great ability enabled her to govern a community drawn from all ranks of life, at a time when the upper classes required the lower to remain subservient and respectful.

Some sisterhoods, while comprising two orders, clearly did not see the lay/choir division as being etched in stone. The Communities of the Holy Name, Holy Family and St Thomas Martyr allowed sisters of outstanding talent but inferior background upward mobility within the communities. In these orders women clothed as lay sisters could be professed as choir sisters, if their abilities warranted such promotion. Two such lay sisters, after promotion to choir status, became Mother Superior of their respective communities. Sister Emma, born in Highgate in 1839, entered the Community of the Holy Name as a lay postulant in 1867. She was clothed as a lay novice in 1868, but was professed as a choir sister in 1870, and was appointed Sister in Charge of the Wolverhampton branch house in 1876. Her promotion thereafter was rapid. She became Novice Mistress in 1877, Novice Mistress of the Choir Novitiate in 1887, and was elected Mother Superior in 1888. She was re-elected in 1891 and 1894, but lost her bid for a further re-election in 1897; sometime after 1897 she left the community. We cannot know if her decision to leave was connected to the loss of her position as Mother. Sister Jane of St Thomas Martyr entered the community as a lay novice in 1866, was professed as a choir sister in 1870, and six years later was elected Mother Superior, a post she retained for 24 years.[89] There are other cases of lay to choir elevations and (rarely) the reverse as well; this final demarcation of status normally occurred after clothing but before profession. However, the late-Victorian Community of the Holy Name made provision in its Constitution for elected elevation after three years, evidently envisioning frequent transfers from lay to choir status.[90] Unusually, All Hallows allowed the elevation of lay sisters to choir status only after lay profession.

The limits to lay sister status were in general clearly defined. Some sisters who entered dual-class communities were obviously borderline cases: these were women whose family standing and own education were indeterminate. A good education generally made women from humble backgrounds eligible for choir status. A woman from a wealthy background may have posed a dilemma for a community if she was eager to become a sister and seemed to possess a genuine vocation, but was unfit to hold a position of any responsibility. One example of what was a rare situation is that of Sister Margaret Monica, professed as an All Saints sister in 1893. The daughter of a wealthy banker, she entered as a choir sister, but community records describe her as 'mentally deficient'. Her Novice Mistress argued the case for her profession in supremely pragmatic terms: 'she is giving all she has: this is her one desire; she is well-dowered and will never be a charge upon the Community. She is sweet-tempered and very obedient, and can do a lot of hard manual work gladly.' In practical matters Sister Margaret Monica took on the role of a lay sister (albeit a very well-dowered one): she was not allowed to vote on important questions, and was employed entirely in manual labour.[91] A lay sister in all but name, her case demonstrates that communities displayed a considerable degree of flexibility in weighing the relative importance of background, wealth, education and intellect.

Lay sisters were treated differently from their choir companions in a number of respects, and this differentiation began as soon as the prospective sister entered the convent. Lay sisters tended to enter at a younger age than choir sisters: the average age of lay profession was 30, meaning that most had entered the novitiate at about the age of 26. (Lay sisters generally had a four-year novitiate, as opposed to the choir sisters' two years.) Choir sisters were usually slightly older when they entered: with profession averaging 33½ years, clothing would have been at around the age of 30 or 31. The average age of all sisters at profession (including those in single-order communities and those whose status is unknown) was 34 years 3 months. This would indicate that women entered communities at a slightly older age than the average age of marriage for their class, with the difference for the choir sisters being considerably greater.[92]

As mentioned above, lay aspirants generally underwent a significantly longer novitiate than did their choir equivalents. In some communities, they did not attend the instructions given to the choir novices. This both suggested that it was not seen as important (or desirable) for lay sisters to have a sound theological education and signalled the importance of lay novices devoting themselves to domestic duties rather than to study. In at least one community, lay sisters had a different chaplain, suggesting, rather bizarrely, that their spiritual needs may have been seen as different as well.[93] Lay sisters in the Sisterhood of All Saints were urged in their *Rule* to 'strive against their own carnal wills': I can find no equivalent admonition for choir sisters; however, All Saints did not require a longer novitiate for lay sisters. In most communities, they had a limited number of services to attend in chapel, but generally the entire community took recreation together. After profession, lay sisters were restricted from holding certain high offices within the communities, although a number of lesser official roles were open to them. Most importantly, in the semi-democratic structure of the communities, lay sisters were prohibited from voting in chapter. (There were exceptions to this: one of the largest communities, All Saints, elected superiors by the vote of *all* sisters.)[94] Despite their lack of a formal voice, they were still allowed some input into lay elections. The practice of the Society of the Holy and Undivided Trinity was typical: when a lay novice was up for profession, the lay sisters, although technically voteless, were consulted by Chapter before a decision was taken. (Chapter – discussed in more detail on pp. 65–6 – was the governing body of the sisterhood and was made up of senior members of the community.) However, lay sisters managed to make their voices heard in other ways as well: one Holy and Undivided Trinity choir sister was dismissed by Chapter at the request of the lay sisters, after complaints of her bad temper. The same sisterhood's lay sisters also managed to protect their position by the use of less commendable devices, in one instance forcing out by unkind treatment a lay novice who they believed would not be strong enough to take her share of the work.[95]

Lay sisters could be distinguished, both before and after profession, by their dress. The lay habit was often an easily washed dark-blue cotton rather than black serge. In some communities lay sisters received silver rather than gold rings at profession. These visible signs of social and functional inferiority provoked resistance in some lay sisters: the Society of the Holy and Undivided Trinity experienced an 'apron rebellion' in the early twentieth century, when the lay sisters revolted against having to wear an apron over their habits. This dissatisfaction was based only superficially on the lay sisters' dislike of being differentiated in dress from the choir sisters. Not satisfied with being permitted to doff their aprons, two years later the lay sisters were 'clamouring' for admission to the choir novices' sitting room.[96] Some communities practised rituals which symbolized the essential equality of the two orders; the lay members of the Society of the Sisters of Bethany waited on the choir sisters at table, but they in turn were waited on by the choir sisters.[97] While this inversion of status was important for symbolic reasons, its primary purpose was the instilling of humility in choir sisters rather than representing an improvement in status for lay members of the community.

Some women came to regret that they had entered communities as lay sisters despite a background which might have been suitable for choir status in a different sisterhood. This may account in part for the higher rate of attrition among lay sisters. (Some lay sisters seem not to have been particularly working-class in upbringing, and most were reasonably well-educated: one fictionalized representation of East Grinstead shows the lay sisters having scrubbing lessons before they could teach this skill to the orphans they trained for domestic service.) In particular, the better-educated lay sisters seem to have found their status problematic, which indicates something about the level of perceived inequality between the two orders.[98] One All Saints lay sister, the daughter of a London builder and sister of a prosperous businessman, left the community with her brother's support because of dissatisfaction over her lay status. However, a year later she returned at her own request and submitted to the discipline of losing her seniority within the community. Her conflict must have been resolved to some extent as she remained within the community until her death 47 years after readmission.[99]

In many ways, the convent provided an attractive home for working-class women, at any rate for those whose alternative career opportunities were limited to domestic service. The domestic work they performed was not very different from that which they would have done in private employment, although it was necessary for the women to become expert at the arts of cooking, cleaning and shopping for very large numbers. While they did not receive wages, they were given generous leisure time and holidays.

Because they had deprived their families of daughters who might have contributed to the family economy, communities sometimes went to great lengths to assist the families of lay sisters. This assistance could include the payment of a regular allowance as compensation for the wages the sister would have sent home from service. Sometimes assistance reached far beyond the lay sister's parents. The story of how Sister Amy entered the Community of All Saints is an interesting one, combining as it does incest, alcoholism and gentle religious blackmail. Sister Elspeth tells the story:

> She [Sister Amy] was a maid in one of our branch houses and confided to the Sister in Charge a very real trouble. Her elder sister was living in sin, with a man who was really the husband of another sister. There were five children; and the man was drinking heavily and becoming brutal. The Sister [Sister Maude] told her that if she would offer her own life to God in religion, He would find some way out for them all. And He did. Sister Amy came in, and found herself quite happy in the religious life. Our [Novice] Mistress managed to get in touch with Harriet [the elder sister], who was by no means unwilling to leave the man, if a way could be found. To cut a long story short, Harriet and the children ran away secretly. Harriet went to Clewer and served her time in the House of Mercy there for two years. The children were disposed of in our Homes. The man never traced them. At the end of two years, we sent the whole family to the Cape: Harriet had had a nurse's training at Clewer and finally went to nurse on Robben Island at the Lepers' Government Hospital (not out of devotion but because the pay was good, and the danger, with modern precautions, negligible). The children went to our Schools; two trained as teachers. [Added note] Wonderful things happened to all that family, which would take too long to add here . . . Sister Amy led a quiet and uneventful life in religion, and never regretted her offering.[100]

The convent may have seemed a haven to this woman, whose family experiences probably led her to regard marriage as an unjustifiable risk. Women who chose lay sister status over conventional domestic employment may also have welcomed their freedom from the possibility of seduction or sexual harassment by employers, which was a notoriously common occupational hazard of service.

Most importantly, lay sisters were assured of a home for life. This was in marked contrast to the often pitiable situation of the overworked general servant who, if she suffered a long bout of illness or became permanently incapacitated for work, would almost certainly lose her post, and with it her home. Within a community, lay sisters were free from the fear of unemployment and of finding themselves out of place without a recommendation. The lay sister who fell ill could be sure that she would benefit from the best nursing the sisterhood could provide, regular medical attendance, a proper diet and the prayers of her fellow sisters. Those who became permanent invalids were encouraged to take up alternative forms of work which could be performed from their beds, and a number of them used this opportunity to develop latent artistic abilities. For example, Sister Barbara, the daughter of a Bradford locksmith, although confined to her bed for many years, taught herself to carve wooden figures which found a ready sale. The community records mention the great pride and satisfaction she derived from her ability to contribute the money she earned to the sisterhood's funds.[101]

The daily lives of most lay sisters probably presented a long round of domestic chores, very similar to what they would have been in a large household, but immeasurably better than the life of the maid-of-all-work, in that they became specialists in one area of domestic management and had regular blocks of time set aside for rest and recreation. That community life was often attractive to working-class women who had the opportunity to observe it at close quarters is indicated by the steady trickle of industrial girls, orphans and former paid employees of the communities who entered as lay sisters.[102]

Lay sisters of ability could look forward to some advancement within the community because the orders were eager to capitalize on the skills of their pioneer members. Working-class sisters who demonstrated talent were highly valued and regularly promoted. A good example of a working-class woman who enjoyed a satisfying and responsible career within an Anglican religious community was Sister Agatha of All Saints. The daughter of a captain in the Merchant Service (a background that would have qualified her for choir status in some less fashionable sisterhoods), her first position after profession in 1864 was in the convent workroom. As the result of her obvious ability and intelligence she was soon selected to train as a nurse. She then nursed at University College Hospital for a decade, and worked for two years in South Africa, helping to establish the community's hospitals there. The culmination of her career was her thirty years' service as the Sister-in-Charge of the men's ward of the All Saints' Convalescent Hospital, Eastbourne, where she had eleven other lay sisters, as well as choir novices, working under her supervision. (The hospital at Eastbourne is interesting as it seems to have been administered and run almost entirely by lay sisters, often former ward nurses. The sister in charge of patient admissions and the head of the dispensing department were both the daughters of London tradesmen. Sister Elspeth recorded: 'All the Lay Sisters liked Eastbourne, where there were usually twelve of them; they had good quarters and responsible work.'[103])

The rules of most communities contained a provision insisting that lay sisters should be treated with consideration and courtesy. The very commonness of this regulation probably indicates that some choir sisters had difficulty treating as equals these women, who were usually the social equivalent of the servants they had employed before entering the convent. A certain level of formality was insisted upon; unlike the practice in Irish Roman Catholic convents, choir sisters were not permitted to address the lay sisters by their first names alone, without the prefix of 'sister'. In general the form of address used for both orders was the same, although one community did insist that its members refer to choir sisters as 'the Sister —', while lay sisters were denied the definite article, and simply called 'Sister —'.[104]

One area where the lay sisters were not restricted was in the pursuit of personal holiness. The necrologies of lay sisters laid much more stress on their spiritual excellence than did the equivalent accounts of choir sisters. Typical in its assessment was this summary of the character of Sister Mary Julia, both in its stress upon holiness and in its faintly patronizing tone. She was described as a 'sweet, sweet soul, most holy child', and her contemporary, Sister Mary Matilda, the daughter of a draper's assistant, was assessed as a 'dear holy simple faithful religious soul'.[105] Perhaps the choir sisters who were the chroniclers of the orders believed that domestic labour improved the character, but it is also possible that, not knowing them well, the choir sisters simply did not know what to say about their lay colleagues. In my reading of the records this seems unlikely; in Anglican orders the personalities and abilities of lay sisters seem to have been strongly marked and well-known within the community. This may be in part due to their being a small minority within most communities; lay sisters generally comprised less than 10 per cent of the membership. Choir sisters were much more likely to be lauded for their business acumen or intellectual distinction, although there are exceptions in both directions: choir sisters praised for their humility and love of poverty, and lay sisters memorialized for their administrative capabilities. One lay sister who fell into this category was Sister Mary

Winifred, who entered the All Saints sisterhood when the woman whom she had served as maid also entered. The record's comment is revealing, both in its appreciation of her unusual ability, and in its suggestion that her talents were underutilized in the community: 'She was a person of intellect and had read a great deal in deep ... books, but she also did all her household duties carefully and well.'[106]

For some working-class women, the convent may have provided a protected transition from rural to urban life. Entering the community as lay sisters allowed women from working-class, usually provincial, backgrounds to become accustomed to the metropolis without running any of the hazards traditionally encountered by young women on their first introduction to London. From within the security of the sisterhood they gained experience in the management of an extremely large and complex household, training which served them well if they chose to leave the community.[107] A lay sister who decided to leave would be provided with an extremely complete outfit, money and highly respectable references. Most importantly, she left with skills which were increasingly in demand in an age which depended upon institutions to manage the problem of the unemployed or unemployable. It seems likely that their employment prospects were also enhanced by the social skills learned through sharing recreation, work assignments, worship and daily life on an intimate basis with women of a much higher social class. Many of them went on to become the matrons of large institutions, such as workhouses, asylums, almshouses and hospitals.[108]

Associates

As well as a Superior, professed sisters, novices and postulants, there was one other important, although less visible, group of women in any community's make-up. Sister associates were women who could not, or did not wish to, formally enter the community but who were interested in its work. Because communities often undertook more varieties of social work than their own sisters could staff, it was imperative to have large numbers of essentially leisured associates in order to carry out their manifold projects. Being an associate involved a significant level of commitment. In the early years of many sisterhoods all sister associates were expected to devote six months of every year to the community, living and working with them and wearing a habit. While at home they followed a simple rule of life.[109] By the end of the century the rule with regard to residence and active assistance had relaxed to the point where most associates simply contributed financially to the work and followed their rule, although a sizeable number continued to offer direct assistance. Martha Vicinus puts the ratio of associates to sisters at ten to one. While this is roughly accurate for the largest and best-known communities, smaller groups had far fewer associates, and this hindered them in fund-raising and in publicizing the community within the charitable classes. St Thomas Martyr, for example, enrolled only eight associates before 1900, in almost the first half-century after its foundation.[110]

In the early years of the communities' development, many women served as associates while waiting to overcome family objections to their vocation. Some women managed to acquire substantial training during this period of anticipation. Harriet Bouverie spent part of every day working at the All Saints convent during the lifetime of her sister, whom she could not leave, and Sister Mary Gertrude worked as a volunteer at All Saints' Eastbourne Hospital for a number of years before her mother would consent to her entering the novitiate. Sister Caroline Mary, All Saints' second Mother Superior, helped at a home for incurables in Soho, assisted at a charity school in Bognor and finally trained as a nurse at University College Hospital while waiting for her mother to consent to her joining the community. Her profession took place seven years after Caroline Mary had become an outer sister (the term used by All Saints for associates), and nine years after she had first requested permission to join, at the age of 25.[111] Those nine years had been spent trying to live a compromise life demanded by her mother and ultimately repudiated by the daughter, who explained it thus:

> she wished me to lead a life 'out of the world and devoted to the poor', in her home – our Lord had called me, as a child of 12, to give up father – mother ... to take up the Cross and follow Him. This *could not* have been in any other way, but by becoming a Religious, and entering a Religious Community.[112]

In their efforts to fulfil both their family duties and their desire for community life, some women undertook a hectic juggling of responsibilities that seems more typical of the late twentieth century than of the mid-nineteenth. Anne Wigram, later Sister Anne, the only child of a wealthy widower, attended 7 a.m. mass daily at the convent, and afterwards returned home to preside at her father's breakfast and see to the housekeeping. She would then return to All Saints to work until 7 in the evening, when she went home, dressed for dinner, and spent the evening with her father. She continued this routine for four years before entering the sisterhood in 1862.

The All Saints archives record that many were forced to undergo an 'outside novitiate' in this fashion.[113] (This does not mean that their term of probation in the community was shortened, however: Wigram for one underwent the normal two-year novitiate.) Some were denied even this nominal tie by parents who demanded complete mental as well as physical devotion to the duties of the domestic sphere. The woman who eventually became Sister Catherine of All Saints was unable to fulfil her wish to become an associate in 1855: her father refused his permission out of fear that it might take her interests away from home. She finally became a postulant eleven years later. In her recollections, Sister Frances Emily wrote that she was ultimately allowed to enter All Saints not long after a holiday abroad with some of the sisters. 'I came into the Novitiate the following February. I had been waiting eighteen years.'[114]

Of course, long delays of this kind doubtless encouraged many women to give up the idea of becoming a full-fledged member of a community, especially if there seemed little chance of family responsibilities ending. These women contributed in other ways to the community life they could not share, through voluntary work in the community's projects or by financial contributions. A large and beautiful chapel at All Saints' Eastbourne Hospital was the gift of a woman who had given up her ambition to join the community because she felt it was her duty to be a mother to her brother's children. Others made more eccentric accommodations. A Mrs Palmer founded a sisterhood in London called St Saviours; she presided over the community by day in the habit of a sister, but returned home at night to her banker husband.[115] The founder of the Community of the Holy Rood, although a widow at the time she established the sisterhood, had children who were still at school when their mother became a nun.

Overall, and especially in the early years, associates occupied an equivocal position. Some were women who were awaiting an opportunity to become a fully-fledged member of the community, others were married women who may have regretted that no such alternative was open to them when they were young; yet others were women who wanted to assist the community's charitable projects but who had no desire for a further commitment. The most important function of associates, at least initially, was the practical assistance they offered, both at the mother house and at the various branch houses, where they worked under the supervision of the sister in charge of the enterprise. There is evidence that the commitment was not wholly one-sided. Associates of East Grinstead, after nine years' service, became 'sisters Associate for life; and the Society is bound to take care of them, as of Choir and Lay Sisters, in sickness and old age'.[116] As time passed, associates became less frequently potential members of the community and took on more the function of serving as the community's secular friends, and as such were more likely to assist in fund-raising than in actual community work. At all times, associates were almost invariably 'ladies': lay associates seem to have been rare or non-existent.

The end of community life

For any individual, life in a sisterhood could come to an end in one of two ways. For the great majority of professed sisters, the association came to an end only with death; for some, however, the tie was broken earlier by departure, whether voluntary or enforced. Overall, about 20 per cent of Anglican sisters seem to have left their communities before death.[117] This figure, based on community profession rolls, is probably slightly low, since a number of communities edited their rolls to remove the names of sisters who lost their vocations, because such departures were sometimes regarded as a 'betrayal' of the community. However, it is often possible to reinstate these women from information found in other community sources, and I have done this wherever possible. Many of these who left converted to Roman Catholicism or entered other Anglican orders. Once women had settled into the life of the sisterhood, decisions to leave were relatively rare: most of the 20 per cent who did not persevere left fairly soon after profession.[118]

It was more common for lay sisters to leave, perhaps out of discontent over their subordinate status or from a desire to better themselves. Of those who are known to have been professed as lay sisters, 28.8 per cent, or more than one-quarter, later left. It is noteworthy that in the one single-order community for which this information is available, only a very low 13.6 per cent left; this may indicate a high level of satisfaction with their position within a relatively egalitarian community.[119] Communities did not feel that their obligations to former sisters ended with the end of the formal tie: some kept in contact for years, and communities provided continuing financial support for members without private means. Sister Winifred of All Saints was only one instance of a very common practice. She had worked at the community's branch house in Edinburgh, and left due to poor health. The community had allowed her £100 a year for the last three years before her final departure, while she had been living with a 'mental attendant'. (This is the only clue given as to the nature of her health problem.) When she

Table 2.2 Reasons for leaving after profession

	%
Roman Catholic conversion	36.4
Transfer to another C of E order	22.8
Dismissed	14.1
Requested release	6.7
To found new order	3.0
Insanity	2.4
Illness	2.4
To marry	1.9
To work alone	1.9
Parental demand	1.2
After discipline	1.2
Other	6.0

decided at the end of that period to make a complete break with the sisterhood because of her continuing 'bad health', she was offered an annuity of £125 a year for life.[120] Holy Name lay sisters had money invested for them annually, to provide them with an income if they should ever decide to leave.

At All Saints, the inability to work with others was defined as the most serious personnel problem encountered by the community. Most women, of course, joined sisterhoods with little experience behind them of joint co-operative work, given their home educations and exclusion from the workplace. Other types of sisters could also prove thorns in the flesh. Communities pointed to three types of improper motivation which were difficult to weed out before profession. There were women who joined in order to get a secure home, those who did so in the hope of improving their social position, and those who entered because they had 'an affection to live with some particular Sister'.[121] The third type of difficulty raises the question of sexuality within religious communities. While there are a small number of cases in the archives of sisters who left to live with another sister who had been expelled, it would be wrong to assume that overt homosexuality was necessarily always the underlying cause of this. I have only encountered one less-than-veiled reference to a sister/sister relationship which could be labelled lesbian. These were two sisters, raised in an orphanage, who both became lay sisters. Each became attached to a choir sister. The community's chronicler wrote, 'It was not a good relationship, but [lay Sister] Josephine stayed with Sister M. R. after she left the community and in fact until she died. [Lay] Sister Virginia [Josephine's biological sister] came in out of her affection for Sister Mary Isabella. Best to say no more.'

Very occasionally women left communities to marry men with whom they had come in contact in the course of their professional duties. For those that remained, the very hazards of married life may have been another incentive for choosing and re-choosing the community. One sisterhood lost a member when she decided to marry the doctor with whom she had nursed. Less than a year later, she was dead, after giving birth to a still-born infant. Another woman, leaving a sisterhood to marry, returned eight years later, widowed and bereaved of her children.[122] Such incidents (although leaving a sisterhood to marry was rare) must have underlined for the remaining sisters the unavoidable dangers of even happy marriages. Such episodes were carefully recorded in community archives, perhaps reflecting the communities' wish to emphasize that those women who entered joined through choice. A great many memoirs of Victorian sisters mention their physical beauty, or stress that they refused offers of marriage before determining to become a sister.

Sometimes sisters left en masse to form a new community, such as the eighteen who left the Sisters of the Church in 1894, most of whom combined to form the Communities of the Ascension and of St Michael and All Angels. Neither community was to have the dynamism or the longevity of the Sisters of the Church. Earlier the Sisters of the Church's founder had written in her diary that the loss of members was probably healthy: 'I never could regret the departure of half-hearted people, but looked upon it as God's good providence towards the Community, relieving us of those who might become a terrible trouble as they grew older.' The 1894 exodus was led by the Novice Mistress; it seems likely that she had grown frustrated with her position, and felt that her only chance of becoming Mother Superior was in her own community.[123]

There are instances of sisters in other communities with well-established founders leaving for reasons that appear to be connected with unsatisfied ambition. One example was Sister Ellen, who was Novice Mistress when she left her community in 1857. Her reason for leaving was her belief that the Mother Superior should be elected every three years, thus giving other women an opportunity to lead the sisterhood. She took one sister with her, who later returned.[124] With founders usually governing their communities for life, first-generation sisters who aspired to the role of Mother Superior must have seen their chances of ruling as slim. This undoubtedly motivated some talented women to leave established orders and attempt to found communities of their own. Sister Clementia decided to leave All Saints when her plan to make the South African branch independent of the mother community was rejected; she later became the Mother Superior of another community. Of another sister who left it was written: 'If Sister Gertrude had been advanced ... to the office of Sister Superior or been chosen on the Council it would have no doubt taken away [her] determination to leave the Community.'[125]

Old age and death

Sisters did not retire in the conventional sense of the word. Many continued their specialist work, such as teaching in schools, until they were well into their eighties, and it was common for sisters displaced from their primary work to take up another. For example, one of the Sisters of the Church took up basket weaving after losing her sight. She was also recorded as being 'astonishingly fleet of foot' at the age of 97: it is perhaps equally astonishing that at 97 her capacity for speed had been called out.[126] Sister Bessie of Wantage took up what her community called 'her second great work' after retiring from the classroom in her sixties, when she undertook the organization of a national guild for women teachers. Sister Lilian, who died 64 years after her profession, retired after running a Sisters of the Church orphanage for many years. She then became the community's secretary and accountant, and was noted as a keen gardener and skilled maker of dolls' beds (sold at fund-raising bazaars) until her death in her nineties.[127] Although such second careers were usually less physically demanding than the first, this was not always the case: the Sisters of the Church's Sister Jane volunteered at the age of 60 to emigrate to Australia in order to run an orphanage housing 160 children.[128]

Sisters who became infirm were cared for within the convent; those who required more intensive nursing were normally sent to stay with one of the specialist nursing sisterhoods (often the Community of St Peter) in preference to hospitalization. This nursing was probably of a high standard: Susan O'Brien, discussing Catholic sisters, points out that it 'was of a level only possible in an all-woman community where the care of children, husband, and relatives could not take priority over their own health'.[129] A few sisters chose to live with members of their own family, normally a sibling, as their infirmities increased, although these women generally retained the habit as a signifier that they did not wish to renounce their allegiance to their community.

The average age of death for all sisters in my study was 73 years and 6 months. Lay sisters died about three years earlier than choir sisters, on average. This three-year gap in age between choir and lay sisters is interesting. It almost certainly can be attributed to living conditions in childhood, as all sisters shared the same food, clothing and shelter after joining communities. Age at death for Anglican sisters compares favourably with the average life expectancy of female members of British ducal families: the cohort born between 1830 and 1879, if they survived to the age of twenty, could expect to live to celebrate their sixty-sixth birthdays, over six years less than these Victorian nuns.[130]

The death of a community member was a solemn event, and all communities surrounded it with rituals which were rich in meaning. Accounts of deathbeds make it plain that the dying sister was usually surrounded by her companions throughout. The sisters shared fully in the Victorian preoccupation with edifying deathbeds, and community necrologies often emphasize the death of the sister as opposed to her life. Wantage's archives have some interesting deathbeds, and the Sisters of the Church's records typify the interest in a 'good death'. Overall, suicide was rare. There is evidence of two suicides (one certain and one probable) in the biographies of approximately 2200 sisters; the undoubted suicide was of a novice considered mentally unstable by her family, who killed herself while on a visit to her parents. The woman's family exonerated the community concerned, but the coroner suggested the sisterhood had been 'over-working' her.

At the passing of the sister, the chapel bell was tolled for ten minutes, during which all members would assemble in the chapel, where the Litany for the Dead was then said. The body was laid out by other sisters, and was clothed in the habit, veil and crucifix worn by the sister in life.[131]

The coffin remained in the chapel or mortuary chapel until the funeral. During this period it was continually watched over by other sisters.[132] Even the task of watching over a coffin could be perceived as a rewarding experience: Caroline Mary, who was at this time the Novice Mistress of All Saints, recorded her feelings after performing this office for the late Sister Mary Christina, who died in 1873. Her account makes it clear that spiritual lessons could be found even in the task of watching over a dead companion.

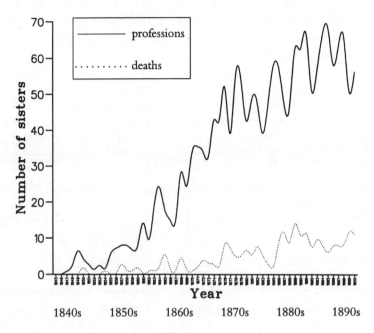

Figure 2.5 Professions and deaths by decade

I and my novices, took watch there [in the mortuary chapel], day and night till she was buried, and never in my life have I seen such a *lovely* corpse. She was not at all what is called 'pretty' in feature ... but as she lay dead in her coffin, a wonderful beauty came on her perfectly reposeful face, and day to day seemed to increase, so that we could not but be sorry, when after four days and nights, the time came for her to be carried to her grave ...[133]

Special music such as the Requiem, the Placebo and the Litany for the Dead would usually be sung during the period of watching. Community funerals were conducted with state. The Mother Superior read the first part of the burial service before the coffin was removed from the chapel, and the Nunc Dimittis was sung as the coffin left the convent, with the chapel bell again tolling throughout. Public processions through the streets to the cemetery were conducted in some communities. Typical is this account of a Holy Rood funeral: 'shops, works, and business premises closed on the day of Mother Elizabeth's funeral. Dense silent crowds lined the streets along which her coffin was carried.'[134]

In their 'Spiritual Counsels', members of the Community of St Peter were advised to keep their sorrow at the death of sisters within bounds. They were admonished to consider the sister's existence as continuing on another plane, a belief which probably helped to alleviate the sense of loss and separation which accompanies death.

> Do not grieve unduly when the Master's Call comes for one of your Community; rather rejoice ... Feel, not that death has separated you from your Sister, but that the same Life ... is being lived beyond the Veil in greater fullness and perfection ... Never cease to love and pray for her; rejoice in the thought of her prayers for you ... [135]

On the anniversary of profession, All Saints sisters were prayed for at Mass for 25 years after their death.

Overall, the typical Anglican community at any point in its nineteenth-century development would have held the following categories of women: professed sisters, probably both choir and lay, novices of both types, and postulants, as well as visitors and enquirers. Very probably associates would also be present, as would industrial girls, orphans or incurable patients, depending on the mission of that particular sisterhood. Most typically a servant or two was employed, but far fewer than such a large household would normally require. Given such large numbers of individuals living communally, it follows that the management and daily regulation of community life was of paramount importance. This is the theme pursued in the following chapter.

CHAPTER THREE

'A FREE PERSON IN A COMMUNITY OF EQUALS': THE GOVERNMENT AND DAILY LIFE OF SISTERHOODS

A religious community was a highly authoritarian organization, with a clearly delineated structure of command. At the same time there was limited membership representation, based largely upon seniority, age and class. In yet another sense, all sisters were equal participants in a democratic system. The emphasis varied from community to community and over time. Very generally, in most sisterhoods the founding member (the Mother Foundress) governed, and had fewer checks on her authority than subsequent Mothers Superior would have. But even in the case of the founder, the Mother's authority was kept in check by the community's Rule. In others, such as East Grinstead, the government was essentially constitutional in nature, with authority vested in the body of professed sisters.

The founder

The woman who founded the community, known to her followers as the Mother Foundress, earned her office by right of her ability to draw others to join her and normally held office for life. Most successful Mother Founders were women of strong character and of high educational attainment. Their childhoods commonly demonstrated 'unfeminine' behaviour: typical was this memoir of Mother Lavinia, founder of All Hallows. 'She was very amusing in the nursery and schoolroom, though at times rather a disturbing element. Gifted with a natural power and inclination to command, it was not easy for her to yield her will to another.' Most were described in community memoirs (childhood friends of the founder often joined the sisterhood) as strong-willed, active and intelligent girls; many were given a 'boy's education' by proud fathers.[1]

The founder of the Sisters of the Church, Emily Ayckbowm (whose decision to form a sisterhood was inspired in part by reading Kingsley's *Yeast*), planned the community long before it came into existence. She and two friends (both of whom joined the fledgling organization) enthusiastically planned and discussed the proposed foundation. They met

> to make plans together, which their governesses were apt to consider wild and impossible, nay, revolutionary, and – unladylike. To live with the poor, and like them; to care nothing for fashion or luxury; little even for comforts and the thousand things which people are apt to call necessaries – and all this for the Quixotic purpose of doing good.[2]

Ayckbowm clearly saw the founding of her community as a call from God, and as a greater destiny than the ordinary portion of middle-class women. Her energy and desire to help others could not be satisfied by the life the world offered her. She wrote, 'It seemed to me that I must be put into the world for some good purpose, something a little beyond sitting still with smooth hair, and a bit of woolwork in my hand.' On the first day of the Sisters of the Church's existence, when she was its sole member, Mother Emily demonstrated her conviction that she had been called to help create something destined to be both important and lasting. 'I ... earnestly thanked God for bringing me one step nearer that great work which I felt sure awaited the new Community.'[3]

Some founders were less immediately sure of their calling. Etheldreda Benett, who founded the Sisters of Bethany after training at All Saints, received a letter encouraging her to persevere in her ambition to found her own community rather than to join an existing sisterhood. The letter sheds some light on what qualities were considered essential for founders of Victorian sisterhoods.

> He [God] has given you a capability of forming a plan beyond many others. Then you have fortune and position in Society as would give you access into the highest ranks, indeed ... You have besides ... a capability of entering into other people's mental distresses, which could be all turned to account as the Head of such a Society ...[4]

Bethany was founded to provide retreats for women, and as such was devoted to the 'mixed' rather than to the 'active' life from its inception. Its 1862 retreat for women was the first in the Church of England's history.

Mother Ethel was not alone in having had considerable experience of life in another community. Founders were sometimes acutely aware of their own need for training; after the establishment of the first few communities, several women who fully intended to create, rather than join, a group trained in the established novitiates of All Saints, Clewer and East Grinstead. The archives of All Saints proudly notes that the founders of four other Victorian communities were trained in their novitiate. Many women who dreamt of forming sisterhoods travelled abroad to study Catholic communities and, if possible, to pick up some rudimentary training from them.[5] During such visits the Anglicans had little opportunity to scrutinize the inner life of Roman sisterhoods. As 'heretics', the Anglicans were seen as foolishly presumptuous in their desire to initiate communities. They were assured by their hosts that their attempts were doomed to failure, as only Roman Catholics had access to the true sacraments, which were perceived to be crucial to a society's success. But these visits gave the Anglicans their only chance to observe the externals of community life, and this is indeed where the Roman Catholic influence was most prominent in the communities they founded. Of course, reading Catholic manuals on the religious life was another way that Anglican founders gained information on the traditions, theory and customs of communities.

Trained or not, charisma in the founder was a necessity for the successful formation of a society. Not all Mother Founders had immediately likeable personalities: several were formidable and dignified women who (to novices at least) could appear frightening. In a society which accepted female amateurism and emotionalism, these founders' demands for competence, reliability and self-control could make them seem distant and unsympathetic until they were better known. Perhaps the alarming professionalism of the first encounters with the Mother heightened the contrast with their later feelings about her: there are countless comments in community archives about how warm and loving the Mother was, 'once I came to know her'.

The fastest-growing groups, among other advantages, tended to have founders who welcomed the opportunity to delegate responsibility and who attempted to draw out the best abilities of all their members. They respected the strengths of their recruits. As the Sisters of the Church's founder wrote: 'we are particularly fortunate in having such a band of *capable* Sisters who can do anything'.[6] The style of governance of the Mother Foundress of Clewer, Harriet Monsell, assisted in the attraction of large numbers of women to its novitiate, quickly making Clewer one of the largest sisterhoods.

Her feeling was that those who ruled should share ... with others, making all feel it to be a common work ... Strong and self-reliant herself, she was most generous to others ... giving scope for their special gifts and energies. Strong individualities of character were a positive pleasure to her; they called out her intelligence and her sympathies, for there was in her a very real love of liberty, and she would encourage a true freedom in others ...[7]

Clewer's founder was also extremely well connected in high society as well as in ecclesiastical circles, as were a number of other Mother Foundresses. This social strength can only have benefited the fledgling movement.

As in so many things, the founder of Ascot Priory was an exception to all of this. Given the small size and slow growth of this community, her practice would not be important, except that this first permanent foundation generated an enormous amount of public scrutiny. Sellon's style of governance formed the stereotypes about Anglican sisterhoods for a generation. She has been described as a woman of 'strong mind, deep feeling, and of extraordinary ... ambition'; and she became notorious for demanding unwise extremes of obedience from the sisters in her community. The daughter of a naval commander, and an extremely autocratic personality, her model was one of military discipline and unquestioning obedience, taken to an absurd degree. Her community was described by one observer as 'a monarchy without a parliament'.[8] It violated the norms very quickly established in almost every other Anglican community.

> There were no chapters, no elections of Novices, *everything* depended on the superior's *dictum* ... I could not help knowing that English girls would not join it unless there were some change in the Constitution.[9]

However, the community did survive, and presumably those who stayed were able to tolerate Sellon's autocracy. Her brilliant mind and forceful personality made the community a very pleasant place for those who could tolerate her rule, as witnessed by one former member:

> I know that the mother and sisters were honourable, hard working, kind, generous, trusting, united, happy in their work, and in their devotion to God, and to their fellow-creatures. They were but human, and made mistakes like others, but there was nothing base or false among them, nothing mean or selfish, but much to admire and much to love; and I never spent so happy a time as my first months at Devonport; never met, and had intercourse with so many gifted devoted people ... who seemed carrying music in their hearts – the music of intense love to God and man.[10]

While founders normally ruled the communities they had established for life, several Mother Foundresses retired from the post of Superior as the result of pressure for change from within the community.[11] It must have been a painful experience to abandon control of a community which one had created from nothing and then directed for decades. The founder of Clewer wrote, with some restraint: 'it was very difficult to open my hand and let drop all the threads of Superiorship . . .' She found it so frustrating to watch another do the work which had been hers for 23 years that she retired to a branch house at Folkestone in 1875, safely away from the seat of community power at Windsor. There she gave herself up to contemplation and prayer until her death in 1883.[12]

Whether autocratic or democratic in her style of governance, the founder was usually concerned that the community might change direction or even dissolve after her death. Some attempted to avoid this by influencing the choice of their immediate successor, who would be known as the Mother Superior, never as Mother Foundress. This attempt was often unsuccessful, with the community ignoring the advice or arrangements of their first Mother.[13] This rejection of the Mother's wishes for the succession may indicate conflicts about the direction the community was taking, or doubts about the strength of the successor. In any case, power struggles over the leadership were not uncommon at the death of the founder, and it was not unheard of for an unsuccessful contender to leave her community, often to attempt to found another.

The Mother Superior

After the death or retirement of the Mother Foundress, a Mother Superior was elected by secret ballot of all professed choir sisters; normally a two-thirds majority was required for election. Nominated by her peers to a term usually no longer than three years, and eligible for re-election for a limited number of terms, subsequent Mother Superiors were to be 'respected and honoured as a Mother'.[14] The role of Mother Superior was dual: she was expected to provide maternal support for the community and to serve as chief administrator in a complex and controversial organization. Not all women combined maternalism and business ability in equal measure, and often the Assistant Superior was selected as a counterpoise to the strengths of the Superior. Mothers Superior were expected to have the qualities of leadership and personality required for both growth and stability: when Sister Ella Mary was elected Mother Superior of the Society of the Holy and Undivided Trinity one sister recorded in her journal:

[she was] unanimously voted for, much to the general satisfaction, for all felt that that [sic] her 7 years as Assistant Superior well qualified her for the office and she is much loved for her humility, gentleness and loving disposition.[15]

Mothers Superior were treated with reverence equivalent to that accorded to dignitaries of the church. It was normal for all sisters to curtsey or bow when passing the Mother, and it seems that this practice created an awkward moment when Queen Victoria was making a private visit to Clewer in 1864. She observed, with some displeasure, that sisters were curtseying as they passed her and the Mother Superior on their tour of the convent. When she complained of this recognition on a visit which was intended to be strictly private, Mother Harriet was forced to explain that the sisters were curtseying to their Superior rather than to their Queen.[16]

Most rules restricted the Mother to three consecutive terms of office.[17] Just as a few foundresses struggled with the loss of their position, it was difficult for former Superiors to accept the relinquishment of their power at the end of their term of office. The pain of this transition must have been exacerbated by the tendency, in some communities, for the new Superior to exclude the former Superior from office-holding while consolidating her authority. Mother Mary Augustine of All Saints, who kept a detailed diary throughout her twelve years as Mother Superior, has a single poignant entry for the year following her failure to be re-elected: 'Did nothing this whole year.' Another potential rival to the new superior was sent to a branch house with unlimited wool and instructed to knit sweaters.[18] Such underuse of talented sisters was usually temporary: once the new Mother had confidence in the loyalty of the community, former Mothers often took high positions within the sisterhood, but usually at a distance from the mother house.

Other office-holders

The Mother Superior had the right to appoint her subordinate office-holders; chief among these were the Assistant Superior, Bursar and Novice Mistress. When a new Mother Superior was elected, she made new appointments to the community's other positions of authority, in order to ensure her co-workers were in sympathy with her ideas and to break the power of those who had governed under the former Superior. Only office-holders of really exceptional ability would be retained after a transition at the top.

Assistant Superiors filled a largely administrative position; the Bursar's mandate was the control of the community's often extensive investments, income and other financial resources; and the Novice Mistress had the responsibility for nurturing and shaping the next generation of the community. While large communities had a great number of minor office-holders as well, the roles mentioned above were always considered to be the most important, responsible and prestigious positions. Women who held the posts of Assistant Superior and Novice Mistress were especially likely to become Mothers Superior in time. That these posts were considered to demand considerable maturity is indicated by the Sisters of the Church's policy of not promoting to Assistant Superior before the age of 40.[19]

Authority within the community structure

All of these posts, as well as that of the Sisters Superior (sometimes called the Sisters-in-Charge) who were assigned to run one of the many branch houses, provided women with an outlet for ambition and energy. It gave them the constant opportunity to develop and improve administrative skills, a chance to exercise authority and a 'public' role. A Mother Superior, especially, held a position which had no secular equivalent in Victorian society. Frances Power Cobbe, always hostile to sisterhoods, admitted the paradoxical truth that a woman of ability could expect to find far greater scope for her abilities within a convent than outside one.

> it is quite possible that a convent may prove to her a theatre whereon she may develop wonderful abilities for the government of the community and the direction of noble enterprises. In whatever line may be the bent of her disposition, she may find a field wider than the private life of a woman can often supply, and female saints ... beckon her to follow their example, and rise to their glory. We have all heard somewhat of these powerful lady-abbesses, Anglican no less than Roman.[20]

All members of the community were expected to show obedience to the Mother Superior. The Superior decided who would undertake what work, where, and for how long, although sisters did have a limited right to refuse to undertake projects. This power of refusal applied when a community decided to undertake a new line of work, for example, when a nursing order decided that they would also work with the mentally handicapped. In such cases of 'a vocation within a vocation' volunteers were always asked for.[21] Additionally, communities could show flexibility when obedience clashed with a sister's strong desires. When Sister Helen of All Saints was asked by the authorities to develop a system of training nurses for insane asylums in New York State, her community refused to let her go. She went anyway, and spent three years at Bellevue. By 1876 the nursing school was well-established and she returned to England, still in her habit, 'and made her peace with the community'. She spent the rest of her life filling a responsible position in the sisterhood, so whatever discipline imposed on her for her disobedience clearly did not involve the loss of rank or of seniority.[22]

Sometimes the authority of the Superior was quite explicitly restricted by the Rule. The first Rule of Wantage stated that the sisters

> shall be presided over by one of themselves, who shall be chosen by themselves ... and shall be called the 'Superior', whose position shall be that of the Head of the Family ... exercising no further control over ... her fellow-workers ... than is necessary for the orderly regulation of a family, and the well-doing of the chief work.[23]

This harmonized with Wantage's non-hierarchic internal structure, most marked in its abolition of lay sister status. The potential abuse of authority by Mothers Superior was very worrying to their secular contemporaries, especially since it was a Victorian axiom that no woman could hold power without abusing it. Reasonably enough, defenders of the movement maintained that a Mother Superior who misapplied the vow of obedience 'would soon cease to have any [sisters] ... to abuse'.[24] Sisters chose their communities, a luxury denied to them in their families of birth. Presumably those who entered the more autocratically governed communities had a greater tolerance for this form of government; others consciously sought out the more democratically organized, sometimes even single-order, sister-hoods. In either type of community, an all-important difference from the family was the existence of a normative document: the Community Rule. As Charles Grafton, an American bishop with a wide experience of English sisterhoods, pointed out, women who entered sisterhoods had more protection against the uncontrolled exercise of authority than did women who remained within the family.

> In the government of the family, there is a combination of authority and freedom ... The same is found in the Sisterhood, but there is this difference. Family life is exposed to the despotism of selfishness or to the caprices of an unsanctified will. Its

harmony and peace are often painfully disturbed by miserable dissensions. In the family of the Sisterhood there is this protection. Those only can rule who have been trained to obey, and the abuse of power is controlled in two ways. It is checked by the triennial election of superiors, and its use is limited by the Rule.[25]

Protection afforded by the Rule only applied, of course, when the Rule limited the authority of the Superior, which was normally the case: again Ascot Priory was the only real exception to this. In other sisterhoods, Mothers ruled only as long as they observed the spirit of the Rule. One striking example of community sanction against a Mother Superior took place at the Community of St Thomas Martyr in 1876, when Mother Amy, who had been elected four years earlier, felt the strength of a Chapter determined on discipline. The Community's profession roll records that 'in consequence of [Mother Amy's] unsatisfactory conduct all the Sisters were assembled in Chapter, and after a statement of the charges brought against her she was expelled ... from the Community'.[26] Sadly, the discreet recorder of this momentous event gave no hint of the nature of Mother Amy's offence.

The final repository of decision-making power within any sisterhood was the organization called Chapter. Chapter typically consisted of all professed sisters, both choir and lay. It met at regular intervals, and an extraordinary meeting could be called if a certain percentage of the community demanded it. Any member could place an issue before Chapter, after giving due notice.[27] Here any sister, regardless of status, could speak out in the discussion of any question on which she had an opinion. However, if matters went to a vote, the lay sisters were effectively silenced, as they were almost always voteless. Sometimes the Warden (usually a priest who served as Chaplain) was allowed to attend Chapter meetings; but with very few exceptions, he was allowed to speak only when invited to do so, and possessed no vote. Chapter decided which postulants would be admitted to clothing, and whether novices would or would not be professed. Normally Chapter also voted on the dismissal of members. A two-thirds or three-quarters majority in Chapter was required to add, alter or remove any of the community's rules or constitutions. (Normally all business involving mortgages, the letting of property or the use of capital required a three-quarters majority vote in Chapter.) As mentioned earlier, Chapter also enjoyed the power to check the actions of the Mother Superior.[28]

All decisions of importance to the community were debated by a senior group of sisters, the Council, previous to taking them to Chapter. Financial decisions and whether to undertake or give up projects were Council matters.

In small communities, the Council consisted of all professed sisters and was effectively synonymous with Chapter: in larger sisterhoods, chapter sisters elected a number of senior sisters to represent them in council.[29] Mothers, even Mother Foundresses, respected the democratic nature of the process. As Mother Emily explained to the Archbishop of Canterbury when he requested a change in the Sisters of the Church's practice, the granting of his petition was by no means automatic:

> it is impossible for me to decide alone any question of importance; such matters must be referred to the Governing Body of the Community. I will therefore at once call a meeting of the Senior Sisters, and will communicate to you the result.[30]

It should be clear by now that sisterhoods developed on an *ad hoc* basis. Often the Mother Foundress was not joined by other women for a considerable period after 'forming' a community; organizations like Chapter and Council could only emerge as numbers and the demands of business grew. All Saints held its first Chapter more than a decade after the community's foundation, and this was not unusual. The special role of the founder of the community could tend to delay the inevitable development of the central role of Chapter and the Council in governing the community. The following is a detailed summary of the decision-making process in Clewer during the lifetime of the founder:

> [the Mother Foundress] ... would personally examine on the spot into all the circumstances of the case, controlling her own sympathies and love of expansion, till fully satisfied that the proposed work was fitted to the Community's objects and rule, and within its power. *If her own mind was satisfied ... and if the Chapter accepted the proposal*, then her promptness and decision came into full play. She would go into all the details, choose her instruments, press outsiders into co-operation, form links far and wide, and map out the ... future of the work with a quickness and breadth that almost bewildered those who did not know her well, or who were of a less venturesome or less sanguine disposition.[31]

Chapter at Clewer seems to have played a subordinate part in planning compared to its role in most other communities, but was clearly important in authorizing and legitimating plans generated by the founder. However, in at least one community, the decision of Chapter could overrule the founder's wishes, and in virtually all sisterhoods, Mothers Superior succeeding the founder were subordinate to its ultimate authority.[32]

Daily life in the community

Household work

While few members of a community would ever become Mother Superior, all participated in the daily life of the sisterhood. Chief among their everyday concerns was the maintenance of these anomalous households. Sisters worked outside the convent at a multitude of tasks, yet the everyday domestic details of managing a household of up to 130 women had to be seen to. In many communities, no member was exempt from household work. Of the Sisters of the Poor in Shoreditch it was written that 'whatever your servants do for you, that the Sisters do for themselves and for one another. They have no domestic servants, but cook, wash, and scrub for themselves.' Ascot Priory's statutes made it clear that any sister could be asked to do any work within the community, regardless of social position, 'as it is not considered that any work whatever is degrading'. To Anglican sisters the Victorian horror at ladies doing servants' work was an 'irrational and irreligious' idea.[33]

When communities were small and lay sisters few or non-existent, sharing the housework was a matter of practical necessity. Even when lay sisters were available, all members of orders like the Sisters of the Church took turns doing the cooking, including Superiors and Headmistresses. In June 1875, five years after the community was founded, the Mother Superior and another sister were taking cooking lessons. The depth of their ignorance of domestic chores is indicated by the nature of their first lesson: it was devoted to instruction in the cleaning of saucepans. Shirkers or delicate flowers were not welcome in any active order. The Rule of Holy Rood reminded them that 'all must work at least as hard as women who work for their daily bread'.[34]

For some women this sort of work was unexpectedly congenial, as well as having the added savour of novelty. Mother Kate described her novitiate at East Grinstead in the 1850s as a complete change from her sheltered and idle life in an extremely well-heeled Cheshire rectory, and depicts the manual labour as one of the positive pleasures of her new life: 'I enjoyed the scrubbing most heartily, though it was some time before I accomplished laying a fire with satisfaction.'[35] One former sister described their daily life in terms which can be seen as one long violation of the accepted norms of behaviour for upper-class women. Most deviant of all was their enjoyment of it.

[We] went daily in and out among the poor ... set [our] house in order, pumped water, dusted, scrubbed; prepared soup for the poor; swept the black beetles from under the mattresses; picked them out of the sugar basin; recited services in the oratory; on Sundays carried [our] dinner to the bakehouse; beer ... had to be procured at the public-house near; meat was purchased and brought home by [our]selves. [We] lived, in fact, the life of quite poor people, and were very happy in the busy work of [our] 'religious life'.[36]

Some of the work must have been great fun. One former novice in a Roman Catholic community observed 'nuns have a great objection to help from without; they stain, varnish, whitewash, ... make candles, bind books, frame pictures, &c., *themselves* – often very nicely'.[37] In most communities the routine domestic tasks became the sole responsibility of the novices and the lay sisters, when the order grew large enough for this to be possible. Hired assistance was unusual and, when employed, usually provided a technical skill otherwise unavailable: the Sisters of Bethany were typical in doing all their own work, with the exception of the head laundress, who was a hired employee.[38]

Food

In accordance with the ambition of sisterhoods to live a life similar to that of the poor, the food and drink in communities was of the simplest: bread, cheese and beer formed the original menu at All Saints. Sometimes even this simple diet was restricted: when money ran short (as it often did in the early days of most sisterhoods) the milk and bread and butter had to be measured out in portions for each sister; no one could have as much as she wanted. Indeed, when illness struck, some communities felt it would be wrong to introduce high-priced luxuries and extra care, for as the Rule of the Sisters of Charity put it, 'the servants [the sisters] ought not to fare better than their masters [the poor]'.[39] The deliberate restriction of luxury in purchasing food was unintentionally compounded by the domestic ignorance of many of these upper-class women. As an early All Saints sister remembered,

> our poverty was very real, the allowance for housekeeping being just sufficient if managed by an excellent housekeeper with a knowledge of food values, but our good-looking, cheerful sister in charge had had no experience in such marketing and household management. However we laughed over it ...[40]

Despite these initial difficulties, the food in almost all sisterhoods remained unlike a typical working-class diet in being regularly supplied, of adequate amount and of acceptable, when not excellent, quality. Later communities learned from the experience of the first sisterhood (Park Village), which enfeebled its work by allowing members to fast to an extreme which was detrimental to their health. By the end of the first year of the Park Village sisterhood's existence, three of the seven sisters had disabled themselves for work by overzealous mortification of the flesh. Most later communities wrote into the Rule an admonition that fasting must be moderate and of a sort which would not disable members for active work.[41] Not only was this a sensible restriction on health grounds, it provides one more indication of the priority work initially took over spiritual practice. Sisters who were unable to do hard physical or mental labour due to fasting or other penitential practices were seen as disabling themselves to the detriment of all.

Leisure

Work could not be unremitting. Sisters in virtually all communities had one month's 'rest' in the year, when they could visit their families or travel. In some sisterhoods, such as the Sisters of the Church, all members except a core group of five took their holidays at the same time, when associates would effectively take over the running of the community's projects for a month.[42] The visiting of families seems to have been somewhat problematic, seeing how often instructions are given as to appropriate behaviour while visiting often ambivalent (and sometimes broken-hearted, or furious) relatives. It was charged that members of some communities display a constrained manner in public. The strict regulations on behaviour while visiting their homes must have emphasized their estrangement from their families.[43] Rather than spend their vacations in an atmosphere of domestic unhappiness, many choir sisters chose to travel. In this way the choir sisters continued the pattern of their pre-community lives, with leisured holidays abroad: for example, Mother Harriet of All Saints spent two months on the Continent every year. European tours were very popular, and were often undertaken by small groups of sisters from one or more communities travelling together. One notable trip was the continental sketching tour undertaken by the Mothers Superior of Clewer and East Grinstead and several sisters and associates of the communities.[44] Those sisters who did not travel abroad, but could not return home because of familial disapproval of their vocation, went to branch houses of the community, or to seaside rest homes run by their own or another sisterhood. Bethany paid for their lay sisters' month-long holidays, while choir sisters were responsible for their own expenses.[45]

Each sister was assigned an individual timetable of daily duties, which normally remained unaltered throughout the year. Recreation was timetabled as strictly as hours of work. As well as the month-long annual holiday, and a monthly day of retreat, sisters of all grades had recreation once or twice a day. Lay sisters, unfair as it seems, often had shorter or fewer periods of leisure, although most were allotted a minimum of an hour a day for reading and meditation.[46] Recreation was a communal affair. Smaller communities had recreation as a group, but larger sisterhoods tended to have separate recreation rooms for lay sisters, novices, junior professed and senior professed choir sisters. Letters were written, needlework was done, chess was played. Music and exercise also had a part in recreation: Clewer's community room was supplied with a harp and piano, while All Hallows sisters were encouraged to walk in the gardens as much as possible. Popular authors such as Dickens and Tennyson were read aloud, and conversation was general. Sisters were expected to do their best to be entertaining talkers: one community's rule admonished them to 'each read sufficiently to contribute to the conversation'. All Saints sisters seem to have discussed Italian politics with great enthusiasm; discussion of work was forbidden during recreation.[47] Mental culture was important in virtually all communities, given the stresses inherent in women from many different backgrounds attempting to create a new way of living. An early Ascot Priory sister felt that they succeeded: 'hard work, love, and obedience were all in all. The household was the happiest, busiest, merriest, least constrained, and most united of any I ever was in ...'[48] One contemporary described the conversation of the Wantage sisters in terms which would have made them welcome in any circle: '[its] charm lay in an intense reality, deep piety, simplicity, humility, and a ready wit ... they were very racy though never flippant ...'[49]

Added to the communal leisure was between one and three hours of private devotion and meditation every day. Additionally, in many communities sisters spent one day a week in retreat, and had an additional solitary day once a month.[50] This privacy was a precious commodity in a society predisposed to believe that women's time was always at the disposal of others. It was not uncommon for daughters of the wealthiest homes to be forced to spend the entire day in the company of the entire family in the drawing room, under the pretence of saving fires. Sisterhood life gave women time and space to be alone, allowing them to develop and expand their sense of their own selves. An example of this was Sister Bessie of Wantage, who felt deep gratitude to her community for providing her with 'the luxury of solitude'.[51] In *Cassandra* Florence Nightingale wrote enviously of Roman Catholic sisterhoods, calling them these wise institutions which ... are better adapted to the union of the life of action and that of thought than any other mode of life with which we are acquainted; in many such, four and a half hours, at least, are daily set aside for thought, rules are given for thought, training and opportunity afforded. Among us, there is *no* time afforded for this purpose ...[52]

While at first glance this may seem to contradict my argument that work was the primary focus of almost all communities in their early years, sisterhoods recognized that effective work had to be balanced by both rest and reflection.

In some communities, time for thought and reflection were ample. Bethany sisters had two 45-minute periods of private meditation, one hour assigned to reading, and two hours of recreation each day, as well as one day's solitary retreat every month.[53] This is more than in any other Victorian community, and reflects Bethany's almost unique position as following the 'mixed' life (a combination of work and devotion); virtually all other Victorian communities were 'active'. No wholly contemplative foundation was successfully made during the nineteenth century. Although it seems paradoxical, women who entered communities found an environment both more individualistic and more communitarian than 'normal' domestic life, combining a group-centred existence with large amounts of time spent privately and alone.

Scholarship

Despite this, no Anglican community developed a reputation for scholarship during the nineteenth century. This is only to be expected, given the commitment of these newly founded ventures to active work. However, individual members found time to indulge in many kinds of study. Communities had large libraries, and it was not unusual for the sisters to have two or more hours a day set aside for reading. Neither was the literature available solely devotional: history, newspapers, 'modern books' and biographies were read, as well as popular novels from Mudie including the rather risqué Ouida and unspecified 'American novels'.[54] The neglect of secular scholarship was considered unwise. The co-founder of one community thought it essential to balance the devotional matter with other types of reading to avoid 'minds [which] grow like excrescences – all on one side'.[55]

One teaching order, whose first members were all Newnham graduates, saw continuing academic study as essential to their vocation. This sisterhood enshrined the obligation to continue secular study in the community's rule, calling for 'the largest liberty possible in all necessary studies'. Community life, as envisaged by the Holy Name sisterhood, must 'foster the spirit of a liberal education by giving time and opportunity and means for enlarging our discourse'. More pragmatically,

> Every Sister ought to be so systematically studying at least one subject that she makes real progress from month to month; and the Community must aim at securing this. Generally speaking, each Sister ought to go on studying the subjects in which she has specialized.

A necessary corollary was their determination to refuse to accept novices of 'narrow education and understanding'.[56]

Women entering sisterhoods were advised that the religious life did not require a sacrifice of their intellectual lives. They were reminded that before them lay 'a wide expanse of wisdom and learning, couched in different tongues, compiled in various ages, all relating to their own duties, their own lives, their own hopes ... [In consequence] it becomes almost unpardonable for any ... to abstain from acquiring knowledge ...'[57] Novices at East Grinstead were set to a demanding course of study, including St Augustine in English and ecclesiastical history in French. They were given monthly examinations on their reading. Some of the time devoted to study at the Sisters of the Church was spent writing papers, which were then delivered to the community as a whole, or published in the sisterhood's journals. Sisters with special responsibility for training spent time preparing lectures on theological and practical subjects, as widely divergent as Sister Elizabeth's lectures on the Apostles' Creed and Sister Theodora's class on 'Accounts and Their Importance'.[58]

As a result of their regular leisure time and easy access to books, many sisters were authors. Their productions ranged from contributions to the *Victoria County History* series through hymns to thinly-fictionalized portrayals of sisterhood life. Some of this work was genuine scholarship. Sister Elspeth of All Saints, who had studied in the Oxford School of Modern History, contributed lengthy articles on 'Ecclesiastical History' and 'Religious Houses' to six volumes of the *Victoria County History*.[59] Not only do the sections demonstrate Sister Elspeth's skills in using mediaeval documents and her ease with Latin palaeography, but they are also marked by her distinctive dry wit. Sister Edith Teresa, who ran Wantage's home for female alcoholics, was a classical and Hebrew scholar. She 'had her Hebrew lexicon constantly ... on her knee, even at the age of 90'; mediaeval ecclesiastical history was 'her perpetual delight'.[60] For Ascot Priory, All Saints and East Grinstead, translation from Latin was an important and valued skill, as early communities needed information on the religious life that was often available only in this form.[61] Christina Rossetti's sister, Maria, a choir sister at All Saints, devoted herself to translating the Day Hours of the Church from Latin into English. The community used her translation into the twentieth century. Other sisters employed their classical learning for recreation: Sister Georgiana of Ascot Priory (formerly the Hon. Georgiana Louisa Napier, of Merchiston Castle, Edinburgh) corresponded with her brother in elegant Latin.

Taking the Sisters of the Church as an example, it is clear that for some sisters literary output was an ordinary part of their religious life. Sister Elizabeth wrote two books on the Old and New Testaments, and Sister Jane collaborated on three books on educational theory with Mother Emily. Mother Emily herself wrote a series of popular catechisms for children, which had sold over 300,000 copies by 1904. Books on educational technique were something of a speciality of this community, whose founder spent much of one winter doing research at the British Museum Library. She also wrote regularly for *Our Work* (the sisterhood's main journal), as did many other sisters, and contributed a series of articles on baby farming for the *Church Weekly*, which itself was staffed by members of the community. Also, the regular production of the often highly attractive fundraising magazines required considerable literary and editorial ability. The Sisters of the Church ran competitions among the sisters for stories, articles and drawings for *Our Work*: the winners were recognized by having their productions published.[62]

Another area where research and painstaking skill was required was in the revival of church embroidery techniques, many of which had been lost at the time of the Reformation. John Shelton Reed argues convincingly that the valuing of women's work, such as needlework, which could be used for the decoration of the altar was an important factor in attracting women to the 'subversive' Anglo-Catholic wing of the Church of England.[63] Wantage developed a special expertise in this area; several members had travelled throughout Europe studying examples of mediaeval work and painstakingly relearning techniques which had been lost for centuries. Their school of embroidery had an international reputation, which resulted in commissions from all over the world as well as Coronation work. The surviving examples of their embroidery show strong, brilliant colours and bold design, very unlike the typical 'drooping lilies and tendrilled vines' so popular at the time.[64]

Since most leisured Victorian women had been taught to draw and play to some extent, they had a basis upon which to develop these artistic skills within the community. Sisterhoods attracted talented musicians and artists, whose training and creative abilities could be utilized within the community to enhance the worship of God. They concentrated their talents on the beautifying of the chapel's appearance and the perfecting of its music. For example, Sister Caroline painted the twelve Stations of the Cross in the Sisters of the Church community chapel, and an All Saints sister decorated their first convent. Artists also sold work outside the community as a means of raising funds. Wantage's musicians, skilled in Gregorian plainsong, visited other communities in order to instruct their fellow sisters in the techniques of plainchant, another Victorian revival of an earlier mode of expression.

Relationships within the community

Communities were also concerned with the art of living harmoniously in a large group of unrelated individuals. Social relationships within the sisterhood were always a paramount concern. Women's communities supplied their members with emotional support and sympathy, as well as with maintenance and work. One Anglican deaconess–sister described the comfort provided by her fellow workers in a rare depiction of the inner life of a community.

> I have found out what a blessing a large circle may be. For instance, as evening draws on, you will see some of the sisters coming in, with tired and not over-clean faces, looking, almost asking, for a word of sympathy and love; and then it is such a comfort to feel that we are not working alone, with no one to take an interest in what we do, but that we are mutually linked together, and must do all we can to help and comfort, uphold and strengthen, one another. We all have our share in hearing about the scenes of woe and suffering which have been witnessed during the day; and I think many of us would be soon quite worn out, if we had not this way of relieving our minds.[65]

The necrologies of deceased sisters made clear the importance of congenial and creative personalities in the intimacy of community life. Typical is the tribute to Sister Caroline of the Sisters of the Church: 'Besides being so devout a Religious, she was such an extremely interesting personality – so loving and large-minded in sympathy. All this [was] combined with her really extraordinary artistic powers ...'[66] Sisters did not need to be flawless to be loved and valued. One sister struggled with a lifelong drinking problem. Despite her addiction, the archives of her community record the respect and affection allotted her during her long and useful life as a sister.

Charlotte Mary Yonge, who was associated with Wantage for much of her adult life, was powerfully attracted to the busy, useful life she saw there. 'I think the eager life here just suits me, from the wonderful unflagging feeling about it. It is so much the sparkling, hurrying, stream,' she wrote.[67] As well as pride in the institution they had formed, these women, many of whom had joined communities after leaving unsympathetic or actively hostile families, enjoyed the relief of living among others who understood and shared their interests. Sister Bessie of Wantage wrote to a former pupil: 'we have found our niche ... [and experience] the love and the sympathy and respect which come from long association in work and interest'.[68]

Most sisterhoods did warn against the development of 'particular friendships', a term used in both the Anglican and Roman monastic tradition to describe friendships that took on an intensity that was believed to impair bonding to the group as a whole. The Rule of the Society of the Holy and Undivided Trinity admonishes the Mother Superior to forbid 'undue familiarity between the Sisters', and 'extreme demonstrations of regard', mentioning especially the inadvisability of 'long private communications between the Sisters'. In this community sisters were not permitted to enter one another's rooms without permission or pressing necessity.[69] The concern seems to have been to prevent the possibility of falling in love, or at least to restrict the opportunities for overt displays of intimate affection.

Having said that, it must be remembered that some communities put no restrictions on emotional friendships between members. Clewer was an example of a community whose founder believed that they could be a positive force.

> She would not have love crushed out but wisely directed. To one who was very much attached to herself she wrote: 'I do not think you need trouble yourself because you love me. As a fact you do. All efforts to think or feel otherwise will only be unreal and lead to no good. All you need strive for is to love God more ... Love is of God; it is a Divine gift; do not seek to crush it ...'[70]

The founder of Holy Family, Mother Agnes, put this even more strongly, writing in the Rule: 'Particular friendships between Sisters in the Community are to be cherished ...'[71] As interesting as this advocacy of particular friendships is, it stands almost alone. Few Victorian sisterhoods encouraged such relationships.

The lack of a label such as 'lesbian' probably allowed sisters to display warmth and affection for one another in ways that would have been almost impossible in a more sexually conscious environment. Take for example the habit of one of the first Wantage sisters, as remembered by one of the junior sisters who worked at the printing press with her. 'After a while she would suddenly say "Mia Carissima, you look white, let us have a rest," and ... she would stretch herself upon her bed and take me close to her (the bed was very narrow) and tell stories.'[72] This allowed sisters to manifest tenderness and nurturing love for one another quite unselfconsciously, free from fear of being stigmatized as 'inverts', and their behaviour is squarely within the ordinary range of 'loving female friendship' described by Smith Rosenberg.[73]

The habit

A happy community quickly developed a sense of corporateness, of belonging to something important and distinctive. Of course, the immediate visual marker of a sister was her distinctive uniform. Unlike conventional Victorian ladies' dress, the habits adopted by all sisterhoods were inexpensive, long-lasting and comfortable, and did not require constricting laced stays. The habit of each community typically varied enough to prevent mistakes of identification, and sisters developed deep attachment to their unique garb. To avoid imagining that Victorian Anglican sisters were swathed in sombre black from head to foot, it is worth remembering that the nineteenth-century love of bright colours did not pass these women by entirely. Pale blue facings and cuffs enlivened the Society of the Holy and Undivided Trinity's uniform, the Community of Reparation had a red, white and black habit, Ascot Priory sisters wore purple, and Holy Family members dressed in blue and white. The Park Village sisters wore a blue and red habit with a bell-shaped skirt. One short-lived community, the Order of the Visitation, wore turquoise and white with decorations similar to those which characterized the robes of an archbishop.[74] East Grinstead sisters wore grey in the belief that it was better suited to cottage nursing than black, and was also more pleasing to children. The Sisters of the Church used colour to differentiate between the different functions of their members: choir sisters wore black with grey girdles, while teaching sisters were distinguished by their purple or violet girdles. When the communities began work in Africa and India, they did modify their garments in response to the demands of the climate; white habits of light material were ordinarily worn, although often replaced by the 'English' habit for photographs. Lay sisters normally had a distinctive habit, as did novices, involving a close-fitting frill under the veil and a lighter-coloured fabric, often blue. The sweep of the habit must have been a nuisance at times. Lay sisters' habits had smaller sleeves than those of choir sisters, whose angel sleeves trailed almost to the ground in a number of communities. Fortunately, these could be pulled up and secured with a button at the shoulder for manual labour. Victorian sisters occasionally sported slightly briefer garments: Bethany gave careful directions for the appropriate bathing dress to be worn by sisters at the seaside.[75]

Sometimes the adoption of a habit was subject to experimentation by the early sisters. When the Community of Reparation was in its infancy its first members were burdened with an ungainly and cumbersome habit. The advent of a forcible postulant, Sister Teresa, changed all that.

> The first night Sister Teresa ... said 'When I am a Novice I don't mean to look such a fright as you both do. You would frighten anybody ... You have used far too much stuff and your things are all wrong.' The next day she was as good as her word and quite proud of the result of her labours. She practically ruled the house for the time being.[76]

The habit of Sister Isobel (of the Community of St Cyprian) was also odd-looking; it was of so peculiar a nature that she was ostracized in the French Roman Catholic sisterhoods she visited in 1869.[77] Regrettably, no photograph has survived.

The habit had several advantages. It was cheap, and thus especially appropriate for women who had made a promise of personal poverty. A habit could last for several years, was made within the community and was not subject to the vagaries of fashion. Because it was without a waist and did away with the need for restrictive laced stays and other confining undergarments, a sister's dress was 'as comfortable as any woman can wear.' Underclothing was minimal. A simple cotton shift was all – in the era of voluminous skirts, it was necessary to inform prospective sisters that crinolines were not worn.[78] Additionally, the habit was an instant identifier, came to command respect, and probably assisted in the sense of corporate identification. As an American sister wrote, its importance was even more symbolic than practical to these fledgling organizations: 'It is the badge of sisterly union, and as such is of value to the community in much the same way as a soldier's uniform is to the regiment, or a scholar's gown and cap to the university.'[79] Distinctions of wealth, age and personal taste were blurred by the uniform dress. It also served, for lay sisters at least, the important purpose of cloaking social status. 'The dress of a religious order, like that of a clergyman ... may raise, but cannot lower, the social standing of those who adopt it.'[80] Its uniformity was commended as 'promoting sisterly equality', and being similar in that respect to a clergyman's surplice.[81]

Of course the habit had its disadvantages. Little boys in Southwark were fond of running up behind Community of Reparation sisters and poking their veils over their faces with a stick. Sisters in most Victorian communities soon accustomed themselves to children trailing after them, sometimes tossing stones and chanting 'Old Roman Carfolic'. As the sisters continued to come and go on foot, undeterred, such attentions faded away as they lost their novelty. Adults could also react negatively to the sisters' uniform dress. In 1863 Sister Kate wrote her cousin that it took some time to learn to ignore the attention the habit could attract, saying 'much as I like it I can assure you it is no pleasant thing to walk about – almost every creature one meets stares at one as if one was a wild beast. I am used to it now, but at first I felt most horribly uncomfortable.'[82] The Mother Superior of the Community of Reparation, in Blackfriars, proudly reported that over the course of her career she had 'only' had some stale haddock, a quart of beer, and one bag of flour thrown at her.[83] Truly a victory for Protestant tolerance of the 'unEnglish' habit.

While the sisters themselves looked on the habit as their chaperone-substitute in public places, nothing, however, created so much opposition in early years as this garment, which was seen as symptomatic of all the worst abuses of the Roman church. Part of the public excitement over the habit may have resulted from the relative novelty of the attire: members of Roman Catholic orders in England wore ordinary dress until 1870 or later, whereas Anglicans wore a distinctive habit from the first foundation in 1845.[84] While detractors of sisterhoods accused wearers of the habit of everything from sexual immorality to vanity, sisters defended the use of a uniform costume as practical and indeed necessary. The habit was described as providing a passport into the worst and most lawless slums, allowing the wearer to go with impunity anywhere, alone, at any hour of the day or night. It was perceived as providing 'all the introduction they need in addressing the degraded and desperate'.[85] (On at least one occasion, the Anglican habit also served a political purpose: William Smith O'Brien, instigator of the outlawed Irish Confederation and leader of the Young Ireland Rebellion of 1848, is reported to have escaped from the police in the habit of an Anglican nun: Harriet Monsell, founder of Clewer, was his sister.[86])

Community identity

The sense of corporateness extended far beyond the uniform dress. Anglican religious communities varied from tiny groups in a single location to large organizations working in up to sixty centres scattered across the world. Most community mother houses contained the following types of personnel: professed choir and lay sisters; choir and lay novices; postulants; sister associates; visitors; and inmates from 'outside', such as incurable patients, penitents, students, or orphans. To avoid conflict, it was essential to develop an attitude that the community provided a sense of belonging, of identification with its cause. One of the more intangible and yet important aspects of living in community for Victorian women would have been the sense of corporate identity. Women were not used to belonging to voluntary organizations in the same measure as men: clubs, the military, public schools, all created a sense of belonging for men which became an important part of their sense of self. Sisterhoods were one of the few such organizations for women only, and as such fulfilled a similar function for their members. If, in Victorian eyes, a woman alone appeared incomplete, communities provided opportunities for corporate completeness, without the utter deprivation of legal existence and ownership of property required by marriage.

As communities grew, so did their members' pride and confidence in the alternative life they had chosen and helped to create. While individual women had given up all of their personal wealth to join a sisterhood, they exulted in the corporate wealth, reputation and size of their community. Vicinus puts it well: 'the most obvious manifestation of the "New Woman" life-style was the particular pride felt among Anglican sisters [and others] ... in plain living, plain clothes, and plain food ... The wealth of the community expressed itself in its size, numbers, and influence ...'[87] Communities' archival material expresses with great intensity the sisters' sense of complete identification with the group's achievements, and of their feeling of excitement in building an alternative culture, with the community at its heart and their commitment expressed in service to others. It could be experienced as a life which allowed for an unanticipated level of self-fulfilment, as Sister Leonora describes:

It was the sense of a happy religious strictness, with a delightful margin for originality of life, expression and freedom, and the drawing out of talents perhaps undreamt of before, that made life under Mother [Emily]'s auspices so charming ...[88]

Women within the communities were valued for what they could contribute to the corporate life. A woman who founded a deaconess community wrote of one advantage that sisterhoods had over her own organization, where deaconesses worked as isolated units, one to a parish: 'one may have a talent for teaching, another may be specially good at visitation, a third may have musical tastes, and yet another may excel in Church embroidery: in the Community scope is found for all, each offering her share to the corporate life of the whole'. Sisterhoods provided women with a tremendously affirming environment, where 'the worthwhileness of what they were doing with their lives and their time was continually re-affirmed – a degree of support enjoyed by few outsiders'.[89]

Community finance

This chapter has so far considered the internal supports of the communities, but a crucial external prop – money – cannot be neglected in a balanced portrait of the administration and operation of sisterhoods. Despite the importance of the material basis of communities, little is known of the financial affairs of the sisterhoods. They themselves tended to emphasize their spiritual and social service achievements, mentioning money only when it was in short supply. Money arrangements were often excessively impromptu. The Sister Bursar of East Grinstead in the early days of the community simply kept the funds for day-to-day needs in the pocket of her habit. The Community of St Mary and St Scholastica had no bank account; all of the sisterhood's finances were distributed by Mother Hilda. As late as 1909 the Community of Reparation went through a financial crisis, largely as a result of fiscal ineptitude. When asked to forward their books to an official auditor, they were unable to comply, as no books were kept.[90] Even a considerably better organized community, such as the Nursing Sisters of St John the Divine, kept no permanent accounts of the Sisters' Fund, with the sister in charge of it administering it on an *ad hoc* basis, and keeping no record. This had unfortunate consequences. When the St John the Divine sisters left King's College Hospital in 1883, the hospital's Committee kept possession of the

Sisters' Fund, due to carelessness in the drawing up of the institution's constitution. The sisters had over £15,000 in the fund at this time, mostly derived from their own personal contributions since 1868. This money was never recovered.

The minimal record-keeping within the communities has meant that no usable internal budgets for our period have survived. What follows is therefore necessarily an incomplete and imperfect picture, based upon casual mentions of financial affairs in various publications.[91] In the absence of financial records, it is difficult to estimate how much money was required for the support of the communities. Although Bishop Grafton, in the only discussion of the question that I have found, estimated that twenty-five shillings a week would more than cover the expenses of a sister, this was probably based on his knowledge of the sum paid by choir sisters for their maintenance in many communities, rather than on any practical under-standing of their housekeeping expenses.[92] The 1870 parliamentary inquiry into convents and monasteries heard testimony to the effect that it cost Roman Catholic convents £12 a year, on average, to supply one nun with food, clothing, shelter and the other necessaries of life.[93] It is probable that the figure for Anglican sisterhoods would have been very similar. Overall, £12 to £15 per woman per year was close to the real cost of maintaining a sister.

All of the Anglican communities took the vow of poverty very seriously and attempted to make the life of their individual members very much like those of the poor with whom they worked, in terms of material goods. One woman from a wealthy military background expressed the difficulty she faced in replacing romantic ideals of 'Holy Poverty' with real simplicity of life when she joined in the late 1850s a sisterhood with a reputation for being very 'aristocratic'.

> I had not minded the plain food at supper, but the coarse tablecloth, the mugs and steel forks instead of shining silver and glass, had been difficult to ignore ... it was not pleasant to face spending the rest of one's life amid such bare surroundings without carpets, curtains, or any of the things that make a house attractive.[94]

Despite their plain living, sisterhoods did offer long-term economic security to their members: when Sister Margaret Emily decided that she had been mistaken in becoming a sister, she added that 'if I remain in the Community it will be from the motive that I am provided for the rest of my life ...'[95] For women from the struggling sections of the middle class, the security offered by a convent (greater in some senses than that offered by marriage, in that the

death of an individual did not threaten the community's financial position)
must have been a genuine attraction.

Early sisterhoods derived their funds from varied sources. One of the most
common was the income of the sisters themselves, many of whom were of
high social standing, and had correspondingly large sums of money at their
disposal. Generally, the minimum yearly contribution requested of a choir
sister was fifty guineas, or a lump sum of £500, but care was taken that the less
affluent not be stripped of their money. The constitutions of All Hallows
specified that 'No one will be required to give all that she has, even of
income.'[96] Many did so voluntarily, however. Lay sisters brought no money:
domestic labour was their contribution. Although there was no upper limit
on the annual contribution, women were told that only their income was
welcome; the rules of most communities forbade the donation of capital,
except in the form of legacies. While many women did choose to give their
entire incomes to their communities, they were also urged to make decent
provision for any family members who required assistance.[97]

The large amounts of money (and sometimes jewels) brought in by sisters
suggests that many women had control of their own money, and thus could
join despite parental opposition. Since so many women joined against the
wishes of the family, it is reasonable to suppose that the money they
contributed was theirs in their own right. One of the most striking outcomes
of my research was the sheer amount of evidence as to the number of middle-
class Victorian women who enjoyed financial autonomy, even if their capital
was modest. Many women benefited from bequests from other relatives such
as grandparents and aunts and uncles; this money was presumably intended to
support them if they did not marry well. Furthermore, the large number of
sisters who brought significant sums of money into the convent with them
indicates that the widespread assumption that Victorian women had no
control over their money is inaccurate, or at least incomplete. At the same
time, there are cases of parents using financial coercion to keep daughters out
of communities.[98]

Near the time of final profession, the new sister made a will in which she
was free to leave her property as she wished. Bethany was typical in giving
sisters six months after profession in which to arrange their financial affairs;
this meant that a choir sister would have about four years between entering
and the time when she was forced to decide what to do with her money.
Most seem to have divided their capital between their communities and their
families. Any property acquired after profession was assigned to the
community if the sister had not disposed of it otherwise within six months

of acquisition.[99] However, sisters were free to change their wills at any time. Sister Isabella Mary of the Divine Love, a member of the Society of the Holy and Undivided Trinity, changed her will after the death of another sister to whom she was attached, leaving her substantial fortune to her family. A woman who left a sisterhood would not receive back her annual contributions, but most constitutions stated that the community had no other claim on her, nor she upon it.[100] Epic struggles sometimes took place nonetheless, as departing sisters demanded back less easily transferable valuables, such as an inheritance of diamonds that had been incorporated into the community's chalice. For those who were less well off, in spite of their formal declarations of non-responsibility, communities seem in actual practice to have supported until death individuals who left the order but were without an independent income. At least one community invested money on behalf of lay sisters: Holy Family lay sisters had £8 a year of the community's money invested for them from the time of clothing to the age of sixty-five, to be turned over to them if they left or were sent away.[101]

The actual amounts brought into the communities by individual members cannot normally be ascertained, as the amount agreed upon varied from case to case and was kept secret between the entrant and the Mother Superior. Indirect evidence would seem to indicate that these amounts were often substantial: when one sister in the community of the Sisters of St Mary became a Roman Catholic, she took with her half the community's property.[102] She later unsuccessfully sued the community for the return of her money, wishing to bestow it upon a Roman Catholic order. The legal case is interesting because it shows that the sums involved could be large. Out of capital of 8000 guineas and the income derived from another 13,000 guineas, 7000 guineas had been given to the Sisters of St Mary at the Cross to build their hospital and convent, and the income from about 1800 guineas worth of railway stock was used to finance the community's work with the poor: this was the financial contribution of just one member. Similarly, when several members of Saint Saviour's Priory left the Church of England in order to establish a Roman Catholic order, they took with them all the community's income and the convent property, as well as the bulk of its furnishings and fittings.[103]

The founder of the Sisters of the Church brought in £9000 capital, as did several other sisters: Ayckbowm also contributed her income of £300 to £400 per year. The sisters in this community were expected to contribute £50 a year; the amounts actually given by those with private incomes varied from £70 to £450. Because the community did not refuse women without money, many seem to have been relatively poor. More than half of the sisters contributed little or nothing, although the contributions of members like Sister Theodora must have gone some way toward making good such losses. Long an associate of the Sisters of the Church, she was unable to join the community until after the death of her father and siblings, when she was 50. Not only did she give large amounts of money to the community (her contributions built the school at York, among a number of other projects), but she controlled the community finances from the late 1890s on. The records say that 'her splendid talent for business and finance' was discovered at the time when the sisterhood was under attack over its financial record-keeping.[104] Whether independently wealthy or not, all Sisters of the Church sisters were permitted 'to keep one shilling in [their] pocket for use in case of need'.[105]

Most communities divided their accounts into two types. That which supported the sisters and built the convents, usually known as the Sisters' Fund, came entirely from the private means of community members. This fund could be substantial. Ascot Priory, a relatively small sisterhood, used the income of its members to purchase two sites and build two magnificent convents. The Sisters' Fund of the Nursing Sisters of St John the Divine, another small community, contained over £15,000 in 1883.[106] Earnings from private nursing and other employment went into the Sisters' Fund. Most of the teaching sisterhoods had members employed in board schools by the 1890s, whose government-paid salaries were paid to the community.[107] Even in the one sisterhood where an elected council of men managed the funding for community projects, the sisters managed the Community Fund – this was, after all, their own money.[108] The Rule of the Community of the Holy Family provides a salutary check to those who assume that the concept of 'ethical investment' was unknown to the Victorians. It states that the community must

> fulfil its social obligations. In investments and spending of money, it shall have regard to the moral character of the investment and to the social conditions of the work for which it pays.[109]

Several of the communities were accused of misappropriation of donated funds, although none of the accusations seem to have had a basis in any sort of dishonesty. The irregularities that certainly existed seem to have been the result of the sisters' lack of business experience or simple auditing errors. The problem was compounded by the casual attitude evinced toward record-keeping in many communities. In part this was because some sisters viewed money as a potential evil, such as Mother Kate, who came from an old and wealthy Cheshire family.

> Her choice of a life of poverty, and her love of that state, had filled her with a horror of anything like hoarding. Money, she felt, must pass quickly through one's hands lest they be soiled by holding it, and must be diverted unstintingly to the service of others.[110]

The Sisters of the Church Sisters' Fund 'if left intact, could pay off interest and quite £2,000 a year' of the large debts accumulated from their ambitious school-building projects. But this community was unable to resist dipping into the Fund to pay for expansion of the community's works. This made it difficult to repay the capital owing to sisters who had decided to leave.[111] Ayckbowm had to remind herself of this constantly: she wrote to Sister Vera in 1897, saying

> The Community Fund [is] ... for the Sisters, before all. In many cases, it is given by parents and others that their daughters may be properly supplied with all that is necessary and desirable ... we have no right to use this money for the C.E.A. [the Church Extension Association; the charitable wing of the community] and leave the Foreign Sisters (especially) in an almost starving condition ... So the last two years – with the entire concurrence of the Assistants – they have a regular allowance and have clothing sent out besides.[112]

Even worse, the Community of Reparation did not differentiate at all between the two types of income, meaning that the community, as opposed to its projects, was permanently impoverished.[113]

Sisters' own incomes were the primary means of support for most communities. The money for the projects undertaken by the sisterhoods came from a combination of members' incomes and outside donations. Unlike the Sisters' Funds, which were always managed by the communities themselves, these were sometimes administered by a committee composed partly of sisters and partly of outsiders (usually clergy or prominent laymen). Sisters in communities where lay committees managed their project money disliked this situation, and often strove to get the group's finances into their own hands. The Community of All Hallows described its founder's struggle to take financial control of the sisterhood: in this account the managing of their own finances is clearly linked with the sisterhood's autonomy.

By 1870 she [Mother Lavinia] felt strong enough to dispense with the cumbrous 40 strong council of clergy and laymen who were trying to curb the Community's development and [she began] to administer the Community's finances herself. She made a profit! The Council did not.[114]

Fund-raising

A few sisterhoods, most importantly the Sisters of the Church, derived a substantial portion of their income from charitable donations. They needed such assistance, as child protection was expensive: one of their orphanages spent over £11,000 on operating expenses in 1894 alone. The community also borrowed largely to build three of their large schools.[115] Communities such as these relied on fund-raising drives and subscription lists headed by the great and the good. They emphasized the social utility of their work in order to draw in funding from the widest possible population.

Sisterhoods which established expensive projects but which did not have numbers of wealthy members could experience very real poverty. Dependent upon contributions from sympathetic laypersons, their finances could easily go wrong if contributions were not large and regular. Despite the success of their fund-raising efforts (the Sisters of the Church's income was £500 in 1871–2, £17,750 in 1887 and £38,000 in 1894), the founder of the community was plagued by money worries, especially by the constant need to attract donations: 'Miss Towers came for a little sympathy ... I am afraid I did not help her much; I was trying all the time not to think how very rich she was, and how easily she might help us in our difficulties.'[116]

In the 'Papal Aggression' hysteria of the 1850s, where ordinary British anti-Catholicism was exacerbated by the re-establishment of the Roman Catholic hierarchy in England, the fund-raising efforts of several communities were hurt by isolated secessions of community members to Rome. Such events, which were widely publicized by opponents of the sisterhoods, made people suspicious of the loyalty of remaining members and unwilling to donate money towards their work.[117] The sisters of Saint Saviour's Priory found it impossible to raise funds for several months after the notorious mass conversion to the Roman church of several of their leading members. During this time they often had no money in the house. They sold their old bottles to buy food, drank out of jam jars, and were overjoyed to discover a farthing in the pocket of an old coat.[118] When funds were in short supply, sisters could find that they could live like the poor as well as with the poor.

The Sisters of the Church suffered for a number of years from the attacks upon it published in Henry Labouchere's journal, *Truth*. Among other things, the sisters were accused of cruelty to orphans, confining children in 'spiked cages' and encouraging working-class children to attempt upward social mobility. While the third accusation was certainly true, the claims of cruelty were never substantiated. Although old friends of the community were not deterred by the hostile publicity (Ayckbowm noted that 'the attacks of our lunatic enemies don't seem to make much difference to our funds'), the attacks caused real financial problems in the short term. 'Our warm espousal of the cause of Religious Education, Foundlings, Starving men, and tortured animals all goes against the spirit of the age and brings us much ill-will and opposition.'[119] More generally, almost any kind of unfavourable publicity had a predictably negative effect on contributions. East Grinstead suffered an almost complete withdrawal of support for a period after the Lewes riots of 1857 (see p. 186). East Grinstead's financial state was complicated by its refusing, on principle, any endowment, saying that if the people whom they served were no longer willing to support the sisters, then they no longer deserved to exist. This may have created financial crises at more frequent intervals than other, more conventionally funded communities experienced: the founder of the Sisters of the Church, on a visit in 1885, felt that the East Grinstead sisters looked 'half-starved'.[120]

Sisterhoods were not businesses. However, those communities which ran penitentiaries for the rehabilitation of fallen women (the penitentiaries themselves are discussed in the following chapter) had a built-in form of revenue. This was the work done by the 'magdalens' themselves. Some penitentiaries were almost self-supporting, one sister-in-charge remarking appreciatively in the 1870s that laundry work was 'very remunerative'. Needlework, which penitents also did, was not, and their domestic services were confined to the penitentiary itself. An example of the disparity in earnings was the penitentiary run by Wantage, which by 1905 was earning £500 to £700 a year from laundry work and about £20 from needlework.[121] Generally, the money raised by penitents' employment did not cover the cost of running the penitentiary, as a significant number of the inmates were in weak health or unable to work at all, much less do the physically taxing laundry work. Additionally, penitents were expensive to keep, as they had to be provided with books and educational materials, treated for disease, and fed well in order to improve their general health. In 1855 the estimated difference between the cost of keeping a penitent for a year and the profits arising from their labour was £15, rising to £20 five years later. The actual income per penitent announced by the penitentiaries varied from less than £9 to £25, although most reported incomes which came close to, although not quite, meeting the costs of maintenance.[122] Building costs became a heavy burden as the penitentiaries expanded to meet the demand for their services, and this constant physical expansion ensured that the penitentiaries could never be truly self-supporting. A good example was Ascot Priory's House of Peace, which earned £488 from laundry work in 1871. This must be set against a shortfall for the year of £1089, due partly to the expense of enlarging the accommodation for penitents.[123]

Overall, the Clewer penitentiary was probably typical in its balance of profits and costs. It cost £1800 to £2000 a year to run, and the work of the inmates brought in roughly £600, with a Church Penitentiary Association grant providing an additional £150 to £250 extra each year. The balance was made up by private donations and contributions from the Sisters' Fund. (The size of Clewer's CPA grant is not representative, however. There were 31 CPA penitentiaries in 1873, who divided £1149 amongst themselves. With an average grant size of £37, and remembering that Clewer got around £200 a year, this must mean that many penitentiaries received no grant at all. By 1894 the Church Penitentiary Association was complaining that it was close to bankruptcy.[124])

Of outside sources of funds, probably the most reliable were the contributions of associates, women and men who sympathized with the aims of the community, followed a simple adaptation of the Rule and contributed both time and money to furthering the work. Most communities found that a newsletter, featuring updates on the order's activities and appeals for funds, was needed in order to maintain ties with their contributors. Some communities developed magazines which were of a very high quality and had wide appeal, while remaining essentially sophisticated vehicles for promotion and fund-raising. The Sisters of the Church's *Our Work* is a brilliant example of the efficacy of pathetic tales, heartrending appeals and attractive artwork. Attacked by the Charity Organization Society for their methods, they were undeniably effective, bringing in around £40,000 a year through their appeals in the 1890s.[125] In that time they reduced their £50,000 debt for school construction to £25,000. The community also ran fashionable and lucrative bazaars: they realized £700 from one three-day bazaar in 1887, and earlier made 300 guineas from a two-day doll show.[126]

An interesting form of fund-raising was door-to-door begging by community members. It is clear that this activity was popular among the participants, who thrived on the excitement and variety they encountered while soliciting for funds, and who competed among themselves to see who could raise the most money. However, begging was generally unremunerative. The average day's take for house-to-house begging in the north of England was £3 to £4 for the Sisters of St Mary at the Cross in the 1880s. During the summer of 1894, twenty-four of the Sisters of the Church went on begging tours throughout England, mostly working in pairs. They raised £268 plus their expenses, and their achievements and adventures were described in the community's in-house newsletter.[127] Given the Sisters of the Church's enormous annual income from donations and other sources, it seems likely that door-to-door solicitation was seen primarily as a morale-booster for the sisterhood rather than an important source of funding.

The most unusual form of funding was that provided by the rich benefactor. Only two communities had all, or nearly all, of their needs supplied in this way. The Community of St Peter, established in Kilburn as a nursing order, was funded for half a century by a wealthy couple who founded the sisterhood and considered themselves its patrons. These private donors could be astoundingly generous. By 1869, eleven years after the sisterhood's foundation, Mr and Mrs Lancaster had spent £40,000 on the community; they claimed that this sum comprised more than half of their private capital. When Mr Lancaster died in 1887 he left £30,000 to the sisterhood. However, until his will was read, no one had known whether the community would get anything at all.[128] Virtually all of the expenses of running a Brighton sisterhood, the Community of St Mary the Virgin, were provided by Arthur Wagner, a well-known local clergyman. In 1865 alone his contribution amounted to £2500, although the community, which ran a penitentiary and a school as well as an orphanage, must have received a small amount of income from the proceeds of the penitents' work and school fees.[129]

This kind of assistance was problematic for several reasons. The benefactor exerted a great deal of influence, and sometimes undue pressure, on the direction taken by the community. Perhaps in response to this, both sisterhoods experienced an appreciable change in focus shortly after their patrons' deaths. The Community of St Peter obviously tired of such uncertain munificence, especially when combined, as the Lancasters' donations were, with a very actively interventionist approach to the community. After his death, the sisterhood's statutes were revised to declare that 'no subscriber or donor' to the community's funds should have any right to 'interfere in any way in the management of this Society'.[130] Because the benefactors discouraged outside solicitation for funds, it was not until after the death of the patron that these communities were able to accumulate the large amounts of capital and property required for long-term prosperity. Even more seriously, when they were forced onto their own resources these sisterhoods lacked friends and contacts within the charitable classes, and found themselves competing for a limited amount of charitable money with communities who had been raising money effectively for several decades.

Convent building

Added to the expense of maintaining inmates and funding projects was the cost of buying land and erecting buildings. These could be very high. Wantage built a Victorian-Gothic home designed to house thirty penitents and eight sisters, with workroom, laundry and classrooms, for £2600 in the 1850s.[131] This building is unusual in that it was almost certainly built largely through donated funds, as the founding sisters of this single-order community were less socially elite and less well-off than their counterparts in most other orders. The Sisters of St Mary at Shoreditch constructed a hospital in Shoreditch which cost £15,600 by its completion in 1881, including a convent, and All Saints' hospital for incurables at Oxford cost approximately £33,000: the community's own members seem to have provided the greater share of the money.[132] Clewer, perhaps the most aristocratic of the sisterhoods, with a membership of only nine sisters in 1856, derived all of its support from their incomes. This money purchased the freehold of fifteen acres in Windsor for £2500, paid £6500 for the erection of the imposing buildings, and the community planned an extension costing another £3500.[133] One Ascot Priory sister donated £35,000 to her community's building fund.

Of course, not all communities followed the fashion for expensive neo-Gothic architecture when erecting convents, although Street and Butterworth were by far the most frequently used architects. Saint Saviour's Priory built a remarkably hideous convent in Hackney in the 1880s; utilitarian and low-cost, it resembled a massive brick barracks. Mother Kate designed it to emulate 'the early model tenements, with stone corridors and staircases and tiny windows'. The precariousness of the entire enterprise was emphasized by the convent's interior being divided into rooms and cubicles by wooden partitions, which could be removed if the community failed, and the building needed to be sold for flats. The mortgage on the building was finally paid off in 1912. The plain appearance of many of these buildings must have been made even plainer by the many injunctions similar to the following: 'money – which might be spent to better purpose – is not to be expended on keeping gardens in order'.[134]

Not all convents were purpose built, especially in the early years. All Saints' first convent was typical – 'a block of dark old London houses with narrow passages, made to communicate with one another. [It] was not an ideal conventual building: it was even suggestive of sordid poverty.' The Community of the Holy Comforter worked in Edmonton from a building whose floors had holes and which sported a leaking roof.[135] The Community of St Mary the Virgin, Brighton, lived in a series of connecting houses in Queen Square until the end of the century. This community was more than fifty years old when it erected its first purpose-built convent at Rottingdean in the early twentieth century. The Community of the Holy Cross had no convent, preferring to live wherever they were needed, until it became obvious that both elderly sisters and novices would benefit from having a permanent home.[136] As time passed, many communities found that the constant expansion of the work, with its corresponding demand for more land and more buildings, meant that the communities, although rich in property, were often short of cash.

Several communities built enormous complexes through donated funds. The gift of houses or land to communities was not uncommon: Bethany opened a hospital for incurables in a freehold house in Ramsgate which had been donated to the sisterhood.[137] The Community of St Peter benefited from a gift of houses and land in Woking, where their Kilburn motherhouse was eventually relocated. Most impressive of all, the Sisters of the Church collected money for the construction of St Mary's, Broadstairs, built during the 1890s as a tripartite institution: convalescent hospital, orphanage and convent. The community used innovative fund-raising devices such as encouraging donors to give money to named wards, for example the Holy Innocents ward in memory of deceased children. Women named Mary were encouraged to contribute to the Blessed Virgin Mary ward's costs. The hospital site cost £3000, with the central hospital costing £10,000. By the time the complex was complete in 1897, it housed 300 children, had two large warm-water swimming baths, special facilities for children with spinal disease, and a convent with novitiate, at a cost, including furnishings, of £60,000.[138] It is paradoxical that most of these organizations, often experiencing a period of poverty in their first few years of existence when numbers were few and the work was little known, had become owners of magnificent physical plants by the end of the century, paid for largely by their own members. It was estimated in 1897 that Anglican sisterhoods in Britain possessed about £2 million worth of property and annually distributed about £250,000 in charity.[139] This is certainly a serious undercalculation, as the calculator was clearly unaware of a number of communities; he also underestimated the size of those orders that he knew of. Ironically, while the individual sisters remained poor due to their vows of poverty, the inevitable tendency of the accumulation of capital resulted in most of the communities, as institutions, becoming moderately wealthy. What they did with their money and their time is the subject of the next chapter.

CHAPTER FOUR

'WE HAVE HEADS AND HANDS': SISTERHOOD WORK AMONG THE URBAN WORKING CLASS

In some ways it is paradoxical that sisterhoods emerged contemporaneously with a peaking of the anti-Catholic sentiment of the time. This crested in 1851 with the 'Papal Aggression' hysteria – a storm of protest in response to the restoration of the Catholic hierarchy in 1850, which some Protestant extremists blamed on the Puseyites. (Scotland's hierarchy was not restored until 1878.) The extremes of anti-Catholic feeling in Victorian Britain have been well chronicled elsewhere; suffice it to say that most Protestants in mid-century would have still expressed doubts about the loyalty, honesty and respectability of Catholics in general, while consorting happily with the Roman Catholics they happened to know personally.[1] The Protestant Alliance, probably the most extreme of the groups opposed to Roman Catholics, to the High Church and to sisterhoods, and which waged pamphlet war against all these groups until the 1890s, was founded in 1851. Brighton and Cambridge, which boasted perhaps the most active Protestant Alliance local associations in England, were centres of hostility to Anglican sisterhoods, if reports of insults in the streets are any indication. In Cambridge 'some horrid books about Nuns' were being lent about by zealous Protestants, and a sister reported to her Mother Superior that one 'lady [was] going round and giving shillings to make the people promise not to open their doors to us ...'[2]

The only possible defence for sisterhoods in the anti-Catholic atmosphere of the 1840s and 1850s was their social utility. It was claimed that only trained, dedicated and full-time women workers could mend the divisions gaping so alarmingly in Victorian society.[3] Sisterhoods were seen by their supporters as social work professionals in a system of voluntary welfare services that, more and more, seemed abysmally inadequate. Their initial justification for existing was simply that they were doing work that would otherwise remain undone: as Charles Booth described it, 'it is only an attempt ... to help the poor in their pinched lives and mitigate the hardships of their lot ...'[4]

Sisters were perceived as superior to part-time volunteer workers because of the continuity and coherence represented by their organized communities. Frances Power Cobbe, despite her hostility to the sisterhood movement, admitted as much in her description of the typical life-span of a lady's charity:

> the whole ... comes to a stand still while the ladies of the acting committee are gone to Switzerland and Italy, the principal subscribers have transferred their donations to a new charity, and the honorary secretary is going to be married ... Out of this discontent and impatience with the present machinery of philanthropy, comes the desire to ... substitute regular troops for volunteers who may be missing or married when most needed, and the good firm rule of a recognised Mother Superior for the vagaries of ladies' committees and the illicit omnipotence of an honorary secretary.[5]

Their efficiency was an important aspect of this acceptance: within communities, if one worker flagged or died, another stepped forward to take her place. This continuity was highly attractive to those dismayed by the amateurish quality of much voluntary endeavour: it was argued that individualism was positively detrimental to social work. When a devoted woman working alone died, her project died with her; 'some one may still walk in her steps and quote her sayings; *but the tradition of her life*, which, in a community, could have passed silently into the common life, and enriched it forever, *is lost*'.[6]

In short, sisterhoods were allowed space in public life as charitable professionals, what Cobbe called 'lady guerrillas of charity'. The possibility that women might be attracted to sisterhoods for contemplative and devotional reasons savoured strongly of Rome, and, as a result sisters in the few communities with a 'mixed' life rather disingenuously played up the active aspect of their vocations.[7] In most early communities sisters defined their vocations in terms not far removed from those of the social worker. The first Mother Superior of St Saviour's Priory summarized the pioneering years of Anglican communities thus: 'We were all young, all enthusiastic, all very keen on *doing*.'[8]

Victorian women philanthropists have been described as working to expand the domestic sphere into the public world. Victorian sisterhoods certainly took advantage of this thinking in order to broaden their field of action. In essence they argued that woman's mission was to Christianize and feminize the godless and masculine outside world, and that this work was a calling from God as valid as a man's calling to the priesthood. One wrote:

It is customary to urge men to the work of the ministry, missions, &c., and why should not kindred arguments be addressed to us, also, to stir us up to something ... more distinct and impressive than is now common to us? ... *We women have a little faith; we have warm affections and pure impulses; we have heads and hands ... too many of us are not living up to our vocations; not turning to good account the powers we are imbued with; ... at the best, allowing ourselves to be dwarfed and cramped into the niches of custom and worldly conformity ...*[9]

While some Anglican priests found the claim of women to have been called by God to any kind of ministry deeply disturbing, others took the then-radical position that women, by their very nature, were especially suited to it; claiming that 'for any Christian work, except that of the pulpit, the woman is at least the rival of the man'.[10] These clerical supporters of women's professional religious work were in a small minority, however: the more common clerical attitude will be examined in Chapter 6.

Most Anglican religious communities developed as a specific response to a perceived social need. They were deeply rooted in an immediate philanthropic impulse. Thus the majority of sisterhoods were founded in the London slums or in large towns, living and working among the poor. London's East End was the base for many of the communities, where by mid-century the gradual drift away of the upper classes and well-off tradesmen was almost complete, leaving a triple vacuum of generally lowered standards of living, the loss of a pool of parish workers, and few locals who could afford the luxury of charitable benevolence.[11] Sisterhoods took on a whole range of social welfare functions and seemed little concerned at duplication; they responded to immediate needs rather than engaging in long-term planning. In general they saw their mission being to break new ground and then move on to other groups whose needs were still unaddressed by the wider society.[12] The social functions performed by sisterhoods were 'nursing, healing, teaching, rescuing, and protecting', a cultural constellation that Jane Lewis has aptly termed 'social motherhood'.[13] Decades before the profession was defined, hundreds of Anglican sisters were working as full-time, unpaid social workers. Their work with the poor was primarily social rather than religious in orientation until well after the turn of the century.[14]

In the 1840s, at the time of the foundation of the first sisterhoods, it was imagined that communities would be a stabilizing and conservative force. Their loving charity, it was assumed, would enable the poor to 'forget the exasperating influence of the Poor Laws' and the contempt and neglect they suffered at the hands of the higher classes of society.[15] But when sisterhoods actually began, their work displayed a decided hostility toward the Poor Law, which the co-founder of East Grinstead called 'accursed of God, and intolerable to man'. Mother Emily of the Sisters of the Church described workhouses as 'whited sepulchres'; her profound hatred of them was the motivating force behind her work with workhouse children: 700 of the 1100 children in the Sisters of the Church orphanages in the late 1890s were pauper orphans.[16] Nor was the Sisters of the Church the only community to be concerned with the gross inadequacy of the Poor Law for a growing and mobile population. This resistance could take many forms: Wantage got a sister elected to the local Board of Guardians to express their point of view; the Community of the Holy Cross opened a hostel in direct response to the local Guardians' attempt to force the elderly poor into the workhouse; and a Clewer sister served as the President of the Workhouse Ladies Visiting Association.[17] Sisterhoods' traditional identification with the poor whom they served could run deep. Sister Rosamund of All Saints, in charge of Manchester Workhouse's infirmary from 1866 to 1877, lived in a workhouse cell identical to those inhabited by the paupers.[18] (Sister Rosamund lived an all-round adventurous life after joining All Saints: a wealthy woman and talented artist who was professed in her forties, she nursed in the Franco-Prussian war, spent over a decade in the workhouse, and died working in India in 1879.) Sisterhoods were not opposed to workhouses out of a theoretical distaste for legislated assistance, but from a conviction that workhouses abused, humiliated and demoralized the unfortunate. The role imagined for them by some social conservatives of the 1840s, as that of gentle feminine interpreters of laissez-faire economics to the poor, was not to be.

In searching for the significance of the active work of communities, it must be remembered that in the mid-nineteenth century, most public roles were male. There were few 'public' women accommodated in Victorian culture beyond the prostitute (and the Queen). Sisterhoods generated such outrage precisely because they expanded the boundaries of full-time work for women; sisters worked in public, without apology and without direct male supervision. It is clear that sisters treasured responsible work; reminiscences of Mothers Superior make it clear that one of their most valued qualities was their willingness to delegate serious responsibility to others and give them a free hand in their tasks. Mother Emily 'would give all out, she could hold nothing back to herself alone, trusting you entirely, especially when she gave you any charge to do'. Martha Vicinus is right when she states that sisterhoods offered women 'adventure linked with duty': a combination with enormous appeal for some Victorian women, whose options outside of marriage were so few.[19] Sisterhoods were an important innovator in that they gave their members the freedom to work in the non-domestic sphere, without waiting for outside permission, supervision or even approval.

Sisterhoods sometimes couched their arguments for their right to meaningful work in terms which suggested a conspiracy on the part of their society to deny them both personal fulfilment and the service of God. 'You may think such a life of "lowly charitable duties", unfit for educated, accomplished women – you may wish to confine their deep love – their mental powers – their passionate energies, to books, and cross-stitch, or a piano ...'[20] While being a respectable Victorian woman must have felt like imprisonment to many of these women, the sisterhoods' rescue and protection work in the cause of women and children provided outlets for both their 'deep love' and their 'passionate energies'. Their social vision was centred on the benevolent power and potential of women's communities.[21]

The range and scope of sisterhood initiatives was enormous: this discussion can only touch on some of the most important and most common of the projects undertaken. These activities are doubly important because of their place in the history of Victorian philanthropy: unlike most other groups, their focus was almost always primarily, if not exclusively, on assisting and strengthening women. By the 1890s sixteen sisterhoods had specially devoted themselves to the assisting of young working-class women.[22] A good example of this concern with the social as well as the spiritual well-being of women was the pioneer work of Ascot Priory in training working-class women for the printing trade. Almost a decade before Emily Faithfull set up what is usually considered to be the first press employing women only, Ascot Priory established a 'distinguished printing establishment' in Plymouth.[23] Here, for over fifty years, working-class women received a full training as formally apprenticed printers at the all-woman Devonport Society Press. This compares favourably to Faithfull's establishment in other ways as well; where the Victoria Press hired men to do the dirtier and heavier part of the job, the Devonport Society Press was genuinely all-woman in its workforce.

What would a woman seeking self-development and social responsibility find in a religious order? Nineteenth-century communities offered work freely to women. It was assumed that those who joined them would be both willing and able to be trained to undertake important and demanding responsibilities. This assumption that women were capable of, and indeed required, work was very different from the attitude toward the employment of women in mainstream Victorian Britain, where, if women could not demonstrate irrefutable economic necessity, work was seen as unnatural and even damaging. The significance of work to first-generation sisters cannot be overestimated. They painted the life in romantic colours, but described it in terms which were the very reverse of trivial: 'There is work for the best and noblest of our women. In our crowded cities, in our schools, our penitentiaries, our prisons, our workhouses, among the sin-stricken, the suffering, the sick, and the dying.'[24]

Communities took themselves, and their members, very seriously. They perceived their work as crucial to the well-being of the poor in this life and perhaps in the next: 'There was an earnestness about the life of each, as though she felt the deep importance and responsibility of her earthly mission as linked with eternity.'[25] In their world-view, nothing could be more important than carrying out the gospel imperative as defined by the apostle James: 'True religion and undefiled is this; to care for the widow and the orphan, and to keep unspotted from the world.' Work and purity of soul were to be all. They asked:

> Does any one object that this is not proper work for women? Are women then to be debarred from doing aught for Christ? Are women aliens from the Commonwealth of Christ? Are they denied all partnership in its self-sacrifices here, and its rewards hereafter?[26]

During the nineteenth century it began to be argued by advocates of an enlarged sphere for women that the female sex was specially suited to the management of public institutions. When hospitals or workhouses were run by men, it was claimed extravagance, irreligion and cruelty reigned; women, especially sisters, would use their special female attributes to make the operation of the Poor Law less brutal.[27] This claim reinforced the importance and value of domestic roles for the re-ordering of British society: in this view the public sphere was not truly separate. While not being particularly interested in justifying the ways of the Poor Law to man, sisterhoods accepted without question the advantageous assumption of women's superiority in 'female' fields. Indeed, some advocates of sisterhoods supported their establishment on explicitly 'separate sphere' grounds, saying that community life was the only way in which an unmarried woman could express her feminine temperament, which was seen as being naturally both caring and devout.

> It is natural to woman to render personal service to the sick, to children, and to others who need it. These employments stand to her in the place of the public

duties, or physical toils, which occupy men. It is also part of woman's temperament to be interested in the outward manifestations of religious life with more frequency, and with more devotion, than is commonly found among men ...[28]

Sisters thus appeared to be uniquely qualified to carry out social rescue work of every kind, and especially to undertake projects that were deemed unacceptable for other women. Foremost among such unacceptable projects was the reformation of prostitutes.[29]

Penitentiary work

Despite their name, penitentiaries were not prisons. They were places of penitence for women who had deviated from conventional sexual morality, or who had offended against Victorian decencies in other ways. The first penitentiary for the institutional reclamation of prostitutes was established in London in 1806. In the early 1840s there seem to have been fewer than a dozen penitentiaries within Great Britain, almost all of which had some link (nominal or otherwise) with the Established Church. Secular workers with prostitutes were normally male, and even those who acknowledged that ladies might be aware of the existence of prostitutes were by no means eager to involve women in the reclamation of women.[30] After the establishment of the first Anglican sisterhood in 1845, penitentiaries grew rapidly: by 1903 there were 238 Anglican penitentiaries and more than 200 of these were directed by sisterhoods.[31] The number of inmates in these institutions expanded rapidly; in 1840 there was room for 400 women in penitentiaries, by 1893 more than 7000 women and girls could be accommodated in institutions run by Anglican nuns.[32] (For purposes of comparison, in 1870 Roman Catholic sisterhoods were reclaiming 379 women; many Roman orders were not permitted to undertake such work.)

At first glance, it seems most incongruous that the growth in institutions for the rehabilitation of prostitutes should have accompanied the growth of conventual orders: the moral and social distance between the whore and the nun, in Victorian eyes, must have seemed immense. Two needs coincided in the 1840s: the growing demand for provision for prostitutes wishing to leave their profession and the newly established Anglican sisterhoods, seeking a means of justifying and defending their vulnerable new institutions, who saw in the provision of refuges for fallen women a clear justification for their own existence. Sisterhoods seized upon a variant of this argument in their struggle for acceptance in the 1840s and 1850s. Penitentiaries, it was argued, must be the special province of sisterhoods because ordinary women, those who were married or who were likely to marry, could not be permitted to work with the fallen. Such work would decrease their respect for men, 'creating feelings of disgust and indignation where there should be admiration and obedience'.[33] (It seems not to have mattered that sisters should learn to regard men with loathing.) It was a commonplace among the social theorists of the time that a religious orientation was necessary to successful reform work, again making sisterhoods an obvious source of workers.[34] Both Wantage and Clewer, two of the earliest and fastest-growing of the communities, were founded specifically in order to minister to this social need. Of the approximately eighty Anglican sisterhoods established by 1900, about fifty worked directly with prostitutes in penitentiaries.

For Anglican sisterhoods, the ultimate justification for reformatory work stemmed from the scriptural encounter between Jesus and Mary Magdalene. While society passed sentence of 'utter, final excommunication' on the fallen, the Church did not. Advocates of Anglican penitentiaries declared: 'It is time that the world's wretched prudery should be spurned ... we must no longer be too delicate to save souls.'[35] Sisterhoods seized eagerly on all of these justifications for shaking off the taboos forbidding the interaction of virtuous women and prostitutes.

The fact that sisters were mostly from the upper-middle and upper classes was important in their struggle to make penitentiary work their special province. First, it was commonly believed that only ladies could wield the moral influence necessary to reform 'fallen' women.[36] This created the interesting anomaly that the nuns were mainly upper class, while the inmates were working class – in a time when the two classes had minimal (and highly ritualized) social contact with one another. Also, it has seldom been noticed that the Church argued that the upper classes had an imperative moral duty to make restitution for preying sexually or economically upon the working classes; Frederick Temple, Bishop-elect of London in 1885, expressed this concern: 'Was it conceivable that any cruelty could be greater than that which the sensual passion of one class has inflicted on the other?'[37] While recent research has reminded us that the popular image of the upper-class man seducing the working-class innocent was largely a fiction, a more sophisticated version of this argument has focused on the economic responsibility of the upper classes for the condition of the lower, seen as the economic pre-condition for prostitution.[38]

And whose fault is it that the poor are so poor, that the severe toils of our women are so under-paid, that all the wretched shirt-makers and needlewomen are drudging away their lives, and often for very bread yield themselves to sin, after long resistance?[39]

These upper-class women may have seen their lives of self-sacrifice as a limited expiation of the sins of their order. At the same time, men who had resorted to prostitutes found an easier atonement. They were advised that 'large and constant alms offered to institutions formed for the reformation of female penitents make the nearest approach to restitution ... within [their] reach'.[40]

The purpose of the penitentiary was to rehabilitate prostitutes and 'fallen women'. Penitentiaries were developed with the intention of changing persons: Hughes calls them 'transformative institutions'. Penitentiaries sought to change prostitutes into 'honest' women. This incorporated both a spiritual change from sinner to penitent, and an equally important social change from dissolute outcast female to respectable woman.[41] Penitents of all types were to be reclaimed through hard physical labour, undertaken voluntarily, and directed by the sisters. Unlike the prisons also known by this name, female penitentiaries were always open institutions, in that women entered them voluntarily, and could leave at any time during the two-year 'course of penitence' typically undergone therein.

The first lesson learned by the communities was that penitentiary work demanded special skills and attitudes and that not all women were able to function effectively in it. In penitentiary-oriented sisterhoods, at most only one-fifth of the sisters worked directly with penitents.[42] Even those who were successful did not find it easy at first. The penitents seemed utterly foreign to them. They were almost invariably from a completely different social milieu, often entered as alcoholics, and fought with knives or fists on the slightest provocation. At worst, as one sister admitted, the penitents could be perceived as 'disagreeable, uninteresting, evil-tempered, low and repulsive'.[43]

Candidacy for a penitentiary was simple: to have fallen was to have had sexual intercourse with a man to whom one was not married. Some of the penitents were former street prostitutes, others had been kept mistresses, others had lived with a man to whom they were not married. More troublingly, the category of penitent encompassed the victims of sexual violence and incest as well.[44] Sisterhood reports mention the special problem of 'girls who have fallen owing to violence'. There are numerous suggestions in the records that many in this category had been victims of incest; this is implicit in the warning that their 'natural homes, if they have any, are generally the worst places for them'.[45] Valerie Bonham claims from her study of the Clewer penitentiary archives (largely closed to other researchers) that Clewer admitted female thieves, tramps, alcoholics and those who were described as 'feeble-minded' as often as it did outright streetwalkers.[46]

Penitentiary-oriented sisterhoods were unique in being the only type of sisterhood which normally settled outside urban areas. This was due to their need to isolate prostitutes from their former surroundings. Most penitents were sent to the communities by someone to whom they had appealed for help, while others simply turned up on the doorstep and asked to be taken in. Some communities actively recruited among prostitutes, with sisters visiting brothels from midnight to 3.00 a.m., in order to inform the women that a refuge was open to them if they wished to leave their work. Most sisterhoods had a policy of never refusing admission to anyone who requested it, although some believed that the younger the candidate, the better her chances of success. Success was defined as a return to respectability, not simply abstention from sexual connection for money.[47]

The penitents (or magdalens, as they were often called) tended to be young, usually in their late teens or very early twenties.[48] It was usual for penitents to come from disrupted family backgrounds. Most who entered were motherless and typically had left home upon the remarriage of the father, in response to conflict with the new stepmother. Some were as young as fourteen, most eighteen or nineteen. A very few were middle-aged and were working as prostitutes in order to support their children. The bulk of penitents seem to have been in prostitution for only a short time: for many, their 'fall' had occurred less than a year prior to their entrance into a penitentiary. Servants (and particularly maids-of-all-work) were by far the largest occupational group to seek refuge there throughout the century.[49] A letter to Mariquita Tennant, who founded the penitentiary work at Clewer, commented on the limited options available to unskilled servants in lower-middle-class households, and gives an indication why the situation was so common among servants of this type:

> none are, I think, more pitiable than the class of servants-of-all-work. I find that it is positively a common thing for them to be engaged without wages or clothes and only for food every other day. Who can wonder at girls so situated yielding to temptation and sin?[50]

Some penitents had been employed in local industries and turned to prostitution as the result of economic changes. (For example, most of the Cornish penitents had worked in the mines before going on the streets, probably in response to the increasing legal restrictions placed on women working in mining.[51]) The sisterhoods shared the general mid-Victorian recognition of the economic basis of prostitution: 'We talk of "fallen women"; but for the far greater number there is no *fall* ... They are starving, and they sell themselves for food.'[52]

Many communities attempted to classify their applicants, separating the professional or more hardened prostitutes from the 'unfortunates'. Several institutions set aside space for middle-class penitents, but most found that there was too little demand to justify continuing the experiment.[53] The Community of Saint John Baptist had six private rooms for 'lady penitents', but this area of the Magdalen wing was never full.[54] Presumably these women were able to re-integrate into respectable society without assistance, or were reluctant to associate themselves with working-class streetwalkers. Interestingly, those middle-class women who chose to enter penitentiaries were described as 'women of good condition, often ... clergymen's daughters'.[55] Could it be that clergymen's daughters, due to their religion-steeped upbringing, felt a more insistent sense of guilt after 'falling'? The middle-class penitents were separated physically as well as socially from the working-class 'fallen', sitting separate from their working-class sisters in latticed galleries in the penitentiary chapels. These higher-grade penitents had separate rooms, different occupation and were treated differently from working-class members.[56]

One community made provision for more permanent care for alcoholics, after discovering that these women's addiction made it difficult for them to retain respectable employment.[57] Some were admitted on the verge of delirium tremens, having been heavy drinkers for years. These penitents were allowed alcohol in moderation, and attempts were made to bring them off drink slowly.[58] Like middle-class penitents, inebriates were kept apart from the ordinary prostitutes. In the context of sexual violence and the treatment of alcoholic prostitutes, penitentiaries can be seen as therapeutic communities and the penitents as patients in treatment.[59]

It seems astonishing that women would request admission to an institution for a two-year course of penitence, when most prostitutes 'became respectable again' simply by moving away from the scene of their commercial activity. What could a woman of the streets gain by entering a penitentiary? As Taine rightly noted in his *Notes on England*; 'A penitentiary, ... [however]

well run, is never a place of pleasure.'[60] Neither do penitents seem to have been particularly impoverished or racked by remorse. As Sister Anna noted, 'The greater number of ... [those who enter] are not in what the world calls misery – nor are they in bodily want.'[61] Sisters who worked with magdalens wryly noted that most who entered were 'penitents' in name only.[62]

But the fact remains that the demand was there: sisterhood penitentiaries were developed in response to lack of accommodation in the existing institutions, and throughout the century women were routinely turned away for lack of room. This level of demand would seem to indicate that there were some advantages in penitentiary life. Most prostitutes left the trade by their mid-twenties, so these women were probably aware that they were not doomed to a lifetime of prostitution.[63] What brought them to the point of requesting admission to a penitentiary? On the most basic level, penitentiary life offered shelter, food, clothing and care for an extended period, as did the workhouse at an inferior level. It may be that the preference for the penitentiary over the workhouse is another testimony to the brutality of the 'less eligibility' policy enshrined in the Poor Law Amendment Act. Additionally, perhaps those who entered penitentiaries chose to leave the streets early as a result of feelings of guilt, or after finding it more distasteful than they had anticipated. Popular opinion supported the need for a period of 'penitence'; one Kent newspaper assured its readers that 'no respectable person will give them employment until they have been in some degree purged from the pollution in which they have lived'.[64] The penitentiary offered a public guarantee of restored respectability in the eyes of many.

If the prostitute had young children, they were separated for the duration of the reformation. Since the communities often ran one or more orphanages as well as penitentiaries, mothers were able to retain contact with their children while being relieved of the obligation to support them.[65] Families were reunited when the women went out as nurses, although those who went into service often left their children with the sisters, paying a small amount weekly for their maintenance, due to the difficulty of obtaining a domestic post which did not require living in.

Paradoxically, some young women of the very poorest of the poor may have seen a stint in a penitentiary as a way of bettering themselves. It was even claimed that there were several cases of young women pretending to have 'gone wrong' in order to gain access to the penitentiary run by the Community of the Holy Cross.[66] Sisterhood penitentiaries offered several practical advantages unavailable in the workhouse: the opportunity to train for the higher levels of domestic service or for nursing, the maintenance of contact with one's children, a complete outfit upon leaving, good references and assistance in finding positions.[67] In contrast, the ultimate goal of secular institutions for their penitents was emigration, while in sisterhood-run penitentiaries, only one penitent in fifty emigrated.[68] This may be one reason why sisterhood penitentiaries were so relatively popular; they did not pressure the women to leave the country.

While some women undoubtedly entered penitentiaries in a sincere attempt to make a fresh start, it soon became clear that others used them as a convenient rest-home before resuming their profession. Such 'penitents' would stay for as long as suited them, usually during the winter slow season or while recovering from illness or disease. They would then depart in the middle of the night, often stealing whatever objects of value they could carry. Thefts of clothes and money were not uncommon. At one sisterhood a penitent concealed 'money in her boots and went away laughing'. Some sisterhoods came to dread the first warm spring days, which could signal a general exodus, but consoled themselves by the hope that the women were the better for their care.[69]

It is difficult to discover what everyday life in a penitentiary was like for the penitents, since almost no written records have been left by the magdalens themselves.[70] The penitentiaries run by Anglican sisterhoods followed no uniform pattern, as rescue work was in its infancy. Initially, many penitentiaries were prison-like in atmosphere, with unattractive uniforms and strict regimentation. Some of the sisterhoods, believing that virtue had to be made attractive in order to keep the women from returning to their old life, provided pretty dresses and a slight degree of self-rule, and encouraged women to follow their own interests.

Sisterhoods emphasized that the indoctrination given the penitents should initially be domestic rather than religious:

> there should, at the first, be no religious teaching whatsoever ... I believe there are many who ... are repelled by the violent change from their free and easy life to the strict and severe system of a *so-called* Penitentiary; many who would gladly enter if they knew that they would find a quiet home, where they might rest and think, instead of a semi-prison, where they must commence at once, according to a fixed pattern, their reformation. Let them be admitted ... simply as inmates of a Home, requiring of them only quiet behaviour, obedience, and work, and leaving them perfectly free as regards religion, and entirely free to go away if they dislike the place.[71]

In almost all of the sisterhood penitentiaries, the inmates were disciplined by the loss or gain of 'marks'. Marks regulated the speed with which a penitent would be promoted through the ranks and the extent of her outfit upon leaving.[72] The ultimate discipline for a disruptive or disobedient inmate was dismissal, and the practices of the older penitentiaries, such as solitary confinement or bread and water diets, were not employed in the institutions run by Anglican sisters. In community penitentiaries no visible means of restraint were used. Sisters attempted to control behaviour by creating bonds of attachment to individual sisters, creating a sense of guilt over the past, and fostering feelings of obligation and gratitude to the community. Dependency and re-socialization were emphasized at every stage in the penitential process.[73]

Generally, the penitents were expected to remain for about two years, although cases were considered on an individual basis, and no woman was sent away if she felt unready to leave. Some women chose to stay for life.[74] Whilst in the penitentiary, the sisterhoods provided the penitents with housing, food, clothing, medical treatment, education and training for employment. Typically, laundry or domestic work occupied the daytime hours, and those who needed them were given school lessons in the evening, in an attempt to ensure that all left the penitentiary able to read, write and cipher competently. The Wantage penitentiary at Fulham included a lending library among its facilities.[75]

Most magdalens were equipped to take positions as domestic servants, usually specialist posts such as parlourmaid or cook, while those of more ability were trained as nurses. Needlework was taught to the less robust penitents, some of whom were permanently invalided by syphilis. Such instruction was necessary, as upon entrance most penitents were found to have only the most basic needlework skills or none at all.[76] However, for financial reasons these institutions employed most of their penitents as laundry workers in at least the first year of their penitential course, an occupation ideally suited to the location and design of the penitentiaries and gratifyingly lucrative. This occupation also provided a powerful symbolic image of the goal of the penitential process. The whitening of soiled garments was seen as an external sign of an inner transformation.

The strict regime for penitents was in many respects very similar to that observed by the sisters themselves, at least in externals. Like sisters, penitents wore a uniform dress, did not use their surnames, could be dismissed for cause, observed hours of silence, were not permitted to enter others' rooms without permission, were discouraged from talking about their families or their pasts, and were not permitted to find fault with one another. Penitents did gardening, joined in games and did fancy work during their recreation time. All of this is precisely what was expected of the sisters themselves, and in that sense penitents may have experienced the institution as fairly egalitarian. It is debatable whether the penitentiary regulations were much more repressive than the strict, authoritarian regime of a 'respectable' Victorian home.

That the experience of penitents could be relatively positive is also indicated by the fact that every Christmas sisterhoods received hundreds of letters from 'old girls'. Many former penitents took an interest in the work of the community and took pride in their ability to send contributions for favourite missions run by the sisters. It was common for former penitents to return to visit the sisters or to spend their holidays at the penitentiary. Sometimes close ties were formed, with the sisters and their former penitents keeping in touch for decades, to the extent of corresponding with the penitent's children.[77]

The sisters who worked with prostitutes gradually came to recognize that their perception of these women as being utterly different from themselves reflected differences of social class and upbringing more than it did the difference between purity and sexual experience. In 1881 the spokesman for one of the sisterhoods encapsulated their experience for Convocation, saying 'I have found that the great mass of the girls brought in are not at all worse in any manifest way than ordinary maid-servants ... with proper advantages they are not worse than many other girls.'[78] Sisterhoods, unlike secular investigators into prostitution, did not see prostitutes as irrevocably fallen or irretrievably damaged: their intellectual and moral faculties were not seen as permanently degenerate. Thus, Anglican penitentiary workers proclaimed the need to 'break down the artificial distinction between this and all other sins'.[79]

This realization must have led to a decreased sense of moral distance between the sisters and the penitents, although sisterhoods always insisted on silence about the penitent's prior experiences:

> The common feeling regarding the Penitents, among the Sisters, is, that their life is begun afresh. The object and bent of their work is to teach and train for the future, without realising the past, except that the poor girl has been the child of misery, and probably of neglect and misfortune.[80]

In the convent there was no meaningful distinction between staff and inmates because both were there to participate in the transformative process. Despite this, there was the problem of keeping separate two types of women who were regarded as qualitatively different, the prostitute and the nun. It was a highly charged opposition morally and religiously as well as actually and symbolically.

Remarkably, given the ambivalence of Victorian thought with regard to the fallen woman, sisterhoods made provision for the admission of former prostitutes as nuns. This provided an unparalleled bridge between the tainted and the pure, the gently born and the poor. The phenomenon of 'fallen women' becoming sisters not only implied that all taint of impurity had been removed by repentance, but placed these women in a higher spiritual and social class than they had been before their fall from virtue – a radical transformation, socially as well as morally. The slow but steady growth of these orders indicates that some women found the life congenial. Vicinus is mistaken when she claims that such magdalen sisters were never allowed to become full members of the community.[81] Magdalens were recognized as having a fully legitimate religious vocation. In the eyes both of the Church and of the sisters, magdalen sisters were following as valid a religious vocation as any other member of any sisterhood. They were described as 'an actual and substantive part of the community ... not merely raised penitents, or Magdalenes, in the common acceptation of the term, but an Order in a religious community ...'.[82] To the surprise of their mentors, penitent sisters sometimes developed what was called a 'genius for holiness'.[83] In most communities that had them, 'Magdalen sisters' usually assisted in the training and management of penitentiary inmates. In this sense they served as role models for newer generations of penitents.

The success of the penitentiaries is difficult to determine, although communities themselves generally considered that two-thirds of their penitents reformed. There is no evidence to indicate whether the more regimented or the more libertarian approaches succeeded better. What does seem to have been crucial was the attitude of the sisters to the penitents. Those who did not return to prostitution had graduated from penitentiaries which emphasized the idea that the community provided a new 'family' for the former prostitute. They left with the assurance not only that they could keep in touch with the sisters through letters and visits, but that they would be able to return to the community between jobs, thus avoiding the necessity of having to return to the street in order to obtain food and shelter.[84] This seems to have been the crucial factor in preventing recidivism.

Despite Martha Vicinus's sweeping assertion that sisterhood penitentiaries were prudishly repressive and uninterested in sexual justice, there is evidence that sisterhoods advocated the raising of moral standards for men long before the White Cross campaigns of the last two decades of the century. For example, many supported Florence Nightingale's demand for a Royal Commission of inquiry into venereal disease. Sisters who signed the 1898 venereal disease petition included Sister Constance of Clewer (who was President of the Workhouse Ladies' Visiting Association), Mother Alice of the East London Deaconess Community, Mother Emma of the Portsmouth Diocese Deaconess Community and Sisterhood, and Mother Cordelia, Superior of the Community of Sacred Compassion.[85] Compared to their secular counterparts, the workers in sisterhood penitentiaries were generally less obsessed with impurity and more open to seeing their penitents as women, rather than as stock figures of sin.[86] One sister summarized it thus: 'They are Christians; they have sinned; they are Penitents; they need the same teaching and help as other Christians ... their sin ... is not to be continually thrown in their faces.'[87] Some expressed their conviction that the social stigma attached to immorality should be extended to men as well, thus challenging the double standard. At the opening of All Hallow's penitentiary the following question was asked: 'Shall we welcome home the prodigal son, and drive the prodigal daughter from our doors?' Sisterhoods were convinced that men's standards must be raised to those of women, putting them firmly within that strand of female activism which saw the mission of women as one of purifying the outside world, tainted by men.[88]

The great unresolved contradiction in the philanthropic work done by the sisters with their penitents is the problem of the nature of women's work. Most of the penitents had 'fallen' while in domestic service, often as a direct consequence of the nature of that occupation. Yet after their rehabilitative course in the penitentiary, the sisters sent them out again to service. It was hoped that preparing the penitents for more specialist service jobs, such as parlourmaid or cook, would help, by increasing their earning power and status, to preserve them from temptation; certainly at least one community (All Saints) absolutely refused to place their penitents in maid-of-all-work posts.[89] But the sisters were able to gain no evidence that this training actually improved the penitents' job status. They recognized the problematic nature of their solution, and trained as many of the penitents as possible for other occupations, such as nurse, laundress or even teacher. Yet their penitents were more employable as servants than as anything else, and servants the great majority of them became, at least until rescued by marriage. The sisterhood penitentiaries were unable, given the limitations on women's occupations in the nineteenth century, to offer their penitents a sure means of escape from the cycle of service and 'sin'.

The penitentiaries are an important aspect of sisterhoods because they encapsulate in a uniquely dramatic form many of the Victorian debates over gender and class. The sisterhoods had to justify their work with fallen women to a society which saw such work as at best unnecessary, and at worst immoral. To do this they set up prison-like institutions that appropriated the metaphors of the family, where nun and whore lived together. Initiated by women who believed that the suffering of their social inferiors must be atoned for by the sacrifice of their own lives, penitentiaries brought devout upper-class women into unprecedentedly intimate contact with working-class women of the streets. Inextricably tangled within the working of the penitentiaries were ideas of paternalism, metaphysical motherhood, class and gender solidarity, and the double standard. And yet, ultimately, the sisters did not question the need to tame, control and lift the 'poor and pagan' working-class women with whom they lived.

Orphanages

Orphanages were a natural development for many communities. They grew alongside penitentiaries, hospitals for incurable children, crèches and ragged schools. Several were founded when it was discovered that so-called 'incurable' children, when well-fed and cared for, had a disconcerting habit of recovering from their apparently terminal illnesses and requiring more permanent provision.[90] However, in any discussion of orphanages in a Victorian context it must be remembered that an 'orphan' was not necessarily a child with both parents deceased, but was more typically the child of a single-parent family, with the surviving parent working hours which prohibited caring for children. While some sisterhood orphanages required a small weekly payment from the nearest relative, parentless orphans were often received for free. Several sisterhoods took virtually all of their orphans from workhouses, and at least one sisterhood orphanage was formed as a direct response to the cholera epidemic of 1866.[91]

The largest of the orphanage-oriented sisterhoods was the Sisters of the Church, founded in Kilburn in 1870: 'The ... idea of the orphanage was to take pauper orphans and foundlings; seeing they were excluded from every other institution on account of their supposed depravity.' Fifteen years later the Sisters of the Church were caring for 330 female and 50 young male orphans, mostly former workhouse inmates, in three homes, and by 1897 housed over 700 pauper children in eight orphanages; overall, over 2000 girls had grown up in the Sisters of the Church orphanages in those twenty-seven years. (This was in addition to the sisterhood's vast network of elementary schools.) Most other communities incorporated at least one small orphanage into their structure from very early on. Sisters who worked in orphanages were chosen for their ability to relate to children; the qualities stressed were a 'capacity for mothering' and 'shrewd commonsense'.[92] In general, women's 'innate' ability to care for children was assumed until experience proved otherwise. The training for this work was therefore slight, seldom extending beyond the touring of other orphanages in order to pick up techniques and study innovations.[93]

One problematic area was the acceptance of illegitimate children into orphanages. Most sisterhoods followed the example of secular institutions in demanding that children be proved legitimate by the production of marriage and birth certificates.[94] As the only national foundling hospital in existence was Thomas Coram's establishment in Guildford Street, London, this policy exacerbated the difficulty of providing for illegitimate children. Such policies created a fertile climate for infanticide and baby-farming. It was claimed that Londoners routinely avoided touching small bundles left lying in the street, 'lest the too familiar object – a dead baby – should be revealed, perchance with a pitch-plaster over its mouth, or a woman's garter round its throat'.[95] The Sisters of the Church endured years of vituperation and abuse from papers such as *Truth* for accepting illegitimate children and foundlings; the sisters believed that to refuse such children would be morally wrong and would encourage the evils of baby-farming. They were virtually alone in not restricting entry to the products of a 'first fall'; their 1892 prospectus stated 'The managers have no desire to inquire into the private affairs of those who desire to place children in the Home.'[96] The community, like St Saviour's Priory, campaigned vigorously against baby-farming. The Kilburn community took this crusade so far as to advertise their willingness to accept illegitimate children in cheap papers read by the working classes, such as *Reynolds' Miscellany*. As their founder, Mother Emily, explained, their aim was to save children rather than, as their opponents claimed, to encourage vice:

> Neither could the mothers know of the door of hope opened to them, except through the medium of an advertisement in a newspaper read by the working-classes ... We are, at present, the only Society which succours the children who are subjected to the cruel greed of the baby-farmer, and we should be unfaithful both to God and to our aim and object of our Order, if we allowed ourselves to be daunted.[97]

Mother Emily angrily characterized her opponents' position as forcing the unfortunate mother of an illegitimate child deeper into misery: 'if an erring sister fell she was to be sternly prevented from rising again. Righteous hands were to push her back into the mire, and keep her there.'[98]

Most sisterhood orphanages were for girls, although a few communities had facilities for young boys, and a very few specialized in male orphans. Ascot Priory operated an orphanage for the sons of deceased sailors, where the boys were trained for the sea, receiving instruction in navigation and French alongside more conventional studies. Most orphan boys were apprenticed to trades in their mid-teens. Female orphans were usually educated for domestic service, thus providing labour for the communities while at the same time teaching the girls domestic skills. However, not all were destined for a life of domestic service. Girls who showed intellectual ability were trained as pupil-teachers or nurses. The Sisters of the Church trained all but their least bookish orphans as elementary teachers for National Schools, convinced that school-teaching was the surest form of upward social mobility for working-class women.[99] The community prided itself on the large numbers of parentless and illiterate children it had received from workhouses, who as adults were respectable and prosperous as teachers, art masters and dressmakers, having been educated and apprenticed far beyond the normal reach of 'pauper brats'. Part of the attack on the Sisters of the Church's orphanages in the 1890s was based on the belief that they over-educated working-class children. The sisters not only encouraged the children to develop ambitions above their station, but assisted them in fulfilling them.[100]

Believing that the child's moral health was as important as its physical vigour, sisterhoods sought to counteract the institutionalization implicit in large-scale provision for children. While Sisters of the Church orphanages were very large, there was some awareness of the danger of institutionalizing orphans. One former orphan (who joined the sisterhood in adulthood) remembered that the community nursed a 'great ambition ... that each [orphan] should feel herself *somebody*'. In most other communities' orphanages, the children were subdivided into small 'family' groups under the care of a specific sister, who seems to have very often internalized the mother role to a profound extent. Pretty and colourful, albeit uniform, clothing also marked out sisterhood orphans from the beneficiaries of more traditional public benevolence; one Mother Foundress instructed her sisters to dress the orphans so that they looked 'like children who had mothers'. Because of the commonly held belief in the heritability of consumption, Mother Emily Ayckbowm laid great stress upon providing good food.

It must be borne in mind that most of our orphans inherit feeble constitutions, and that it is of extreme importance that good well-cooked food should not only be provided, but that the children should partake of it plentifully. Accordingly, they are never to be stinted in any way, or allowanced; but encouraged to eat as much as they can.[101]

Alone among the sisterhoods largely involved in the management of orphanages, the Sisters of the Church suffered from press accusations of cruelty to orphans. The community was accused of keeping the children in 'spiked cages' and of dismissing orphans without warning; it is instructive that the same sisterhood was simultaneously accused of over-indulging the orphans, refusing to use corporal punishment and encouraging them to aspire to upward social mobility.[102] The accusations of cruelty seem to have been without foundation but obtained wide circulation for a year or two in the 1890s. Discipline in the orphanages was not unduly harsh. The Community of the Sisters of the Church was probably not alone in their policy against corporal punishment, preferring to correct misbehaviour by the taking away of 'marks' and privileges. The ultimate sanction for misbehaviour was being sent away, as in what appears to have been a case of mutual masturbation in one orphanage. This was unusual: the same community reported that of the 1200 orphan girls they had reared, only thirteen had been returned to the workhouse as uncontrollable.[103]

The most convincing evidence in support of the orphanage's general good treatment of their charges comes in later life, when a significant minority returned to become sisters or to work for the community. It was not unusual for former orphanage girls to enter the community which had reared them, or another Anglican sisterhood, usually as lay sisters.[104] Some returned as waged employees: for example, the matron of the Sisters of the Church orphanages in the 1890s was a former orphan, as were some Bethany employees.[105]

We know more about the orphanage policy of the Sisters of the Church, thanks to the community's habit of preserving documents much more systematically than many other sisterhoods. They accepted girls up to the age of twelve, and undertook to care for them until they turned twenty-one. Female orphans entered the 'senior branch' at fourteen, and at eighteen they were no longer treated as children. At this stage they became paid employees of the Church Extension Association (the CEA was the charitable wing of the sisterhood) for three years, working as elementary school teachers, servants, assistant matrons, or assistants in the community's bookstore and printing establishment in Paternoster Row. At twenty-one the sisters found situations for all who did not wish to continue working for the CEA; many became matrons or assistant matrons in institutions, or gained appointments as National School teachers. Like penitents, orphans left sisterhood orphanages with the assurance that they could return when ill or between posts.[106]

Industrial schools, which were training schools for domestic service, were a common adjunct of orphanages. The symbiotic relationship between a community's desire to train girls for employment and its own need for labour is made clear in this diary entry, dating from the very early days of one sisterhood: 'The cook and housemaid gave notice to leave and it was decided that the training of 8 Industrial Girls should be undertaken.'[107] Older female orphans would often graduate to industrial schools and from there leave for service at the age of sixteen or seventeen. Other girls would enter sisterhood-run industrial schools in their early teens direct from the family home. They hoped to use the training they received in these eminently respectable establishments to acquire better posts as servants. Like the orphans, some 'industrials', as they were usually called, later entered Anglican communities.[108]

Nursing and hospitals

Anglican sisterhoods first came before the British public in a favourable light at the time of the Crimean War. More than half of the nurses who accompanied Florence Nightingale to Turkey were members of Anglican or Roman Catholic nursing orders.[109] Later, All Saints sisters nursed in the Franco-Prussian War; while in the military field camp, each sister nursed for twenty-four hours consecutively every fourth day. Despite this gruelling schedule, they were 'sorry' to return to England when their services were no longer needed.[110] Most of the early sisterhoods were established to nurse working-class patients: of the first ten communities formed, nine were partially or wholly devoted to the free nursing of the poor. The Nursing Sisters of Saint John the Divine (est. 1848) and the All Saints sisterhood (est. 1851) provided the nursing staff for several of London's large teaching hospitals, including King's College, Charing Cross and University College Hospitals, until close to the end of the century. In 1888 All Saints was forced to refuse the offer of a hospital in Hong Kong, explaining that they, like all other Anglican sisterhoods, were 'overstretched with work'. At this time they were nursing in two London hospitals (University College and the Metropolitan Hospital in Kingsland Road, Hackney), three in Bombay and one in South Africa.[111] East

Grinstead (est. 1855) specialized in nursing the rural poor, and advertised that their sisters would travel anywhere in the United Kingdom upon the receipt of a telegram requesting a nurse. Most communities demanded that their members avoid the temptation to proselytize over a sickbed, concentrating instead on ensuring the physical well-being of the patient.[112] One advantage Anglican nursing sisters enjoyed over their Catholic counterparts was that the latter were normally prohibited from nursing men or attending births: this limited their usefulness as hospital staff.[113]

The nursing sisterhoods generally operated on the principle that although their primary function was free nursing of working-class patients, they would also nurse the wealthy. At a time when the popular image of the nurse was still very close to Dickens' caricature of Sarah Gamp, the religious motivation and ladylike status of sisters seemed to guarantee nurses who would be clean, sober, reliable, honest and conscientiously devoted to the welfare of the patient. Rich patients paid large sums for this highly-regarded nursing, in this way providing funds which enabled the communities to nurse the poor without charge.[114] It was fashionable for a time to be nursed by Anglican sisters: lists of their paying patients are heavily sprinkled with prominent names, including that of Disraeli in his last illness.

The contribution made to the professionalization and improved status of nursing by the sisterhoods was a significant one: it was accepted by most authorities at the end of the nineteenth century that the Nursing Sisters of St John the Divine had been the first important agent of change in nursing reform, and that sisterhood nursing was still among the best available.[115] But just as sisterhoods experienced conflict with the hierarchy of the Church (see Chapter 6), they also came into conflict with hospital authorities over patient care and authority. Typically, the hospital would demand lower standards of patient care in an effort to reduce costs; such demands were ignored by sisters.[116] A former patient in the Holy Rood Accident Hospital witnessed one such confrontation, which illuminates the maternalist ethos underlying sisters' refusal to scrimp on patient care:

The final cause of the rupture was as follows: Sister Mary had got a sirloin of beef for the patients' dinner on the same day that The Committee were to meet (which they used to do in the dining room). Mr Isaac Sharp found fault about the patients having such choice joints when something less expensive would do ... [Sister Mary] asked The Committee if they had one of their own family suffering from accident what would they get for them: the best or the cheapest? They said that was different at their own houses. Sister Mary said 'These are my family'.[117]

Sisterhood nurses came to be viewed as troublemakers. Not only did they demand the best of everything for their patients, but they were convinced that their nurses had rights, authority and status as members of a religious community, in contradistinction to the medical profession's definition of a nurse in 'terms that referred ultimately to her obligations of service to the hospital in a permanently subordinate status'.[118]

> A St John's Nurse is not regarded by her superiors as a drudge, who is to be worked for the convenience of others until she can work no longer, and then cast aside as useless; but as a member of a community, entitled to sympathy and consideration ... Such relations are only possible between nurses and superiors of their own sex, and could neither be established or maintained between nurses and a committee of gentlemen.[119]

Sisters also refused to tolerate sexual harassment of female patients by doctors. They protested against the unnecessary aggravation of pain by doctors who they believed were more interested in research than in patient welfare. Their refusal to condone experimentation on patients made them enemies among doctors and administrators anxious to gain a reputation for research excellence.[120] In short, male hospital boards came to consider sisterhood nurses as interfering women who lacked deference, and who had not internalized the Nightingale ethic of unquestioning obedience to the doctors' orders.[121]

As Anne Summers has pointed out, class differences came into the conflict as well. Not only did the sisters insist that their working-class patients be treated with respect and given the best of food and medicine, but the doctors also resented having 'ladies' in the hospital, who worked without remuneration and who probably viewed the average physician as their social inferior.[122] The additional problems of class and gender are clear in a letter written to a newspaper in 1874 in which the Nursing Sisters of St John the Divine made public their dissatisfaction with the management of King's College Hospital. The indignant anonymous writer wrote:

> the Committee and the paid secretary can be satisfied with nothing less than immediate control over every woman working within the walls. The independent protest of educated witnesses against all wrong and abuses is no doubt often inconvenient.[123]

Although the 1874 dispute at King's was reconciled by reconstituting the council with the addition of the Mother Superior and other female members, the sisterhood ultimately stopped providing the nursing care for the hospital in 1883. The final breach was due to the hospital's refusal to discipline a doctor who harassed and humiliated female patients.[124]

Most of the early communities built several hospitals in the course of the century. This was in response to the urgent need for hospitals that were free or affordable for working class-people, joined to the sisterhoods' desire to have the medical staff under their own jurisdiction. Given their dissatisfaction with male doctors, it is unsurprising that nursing sisterhoods welcomed the advent of female physicians: when the Nursing Sisters of St John the Divine built St John's Hospital, Morden, in 1899, they appointed a 'resident lady surgeon' as doctor-in-charge.[125] Most sisterhood-built hospitals were institutions with a special emphasis upon caring for women and children. Sisterhood achievements included London's first baby hospital, and the pioneer provision of maternity hospitals for working-class women.[126] Because the sisterhoods did not expect their institutions to make a profit or even avoid running at a loss, they were able to establish hospitals for conditions requiring long-term or expensive care, including the care of incurables, convalescents and the tubercular. All Saints ran a convalescent hospital at Eastbourne which held over 300 patients, and the Community of the Holy Cross's home for convalescent children at Brighton was reported to be the best on the south coast. The Sisters of St Mary at the Cross, in their well-equipped children's hospitals, made no charge to patients, eschewing even the usual subscription and ticket systems, as did the Sisters of the Saving Name, in their free hospital for women and children in Hackney.[127] Accident hospitals were established by the northern sisterhoods; two of the best-known were the Middlesborough cottage hospital and the Rotherham Accident Hospital, both of which specialized in industrial accidents.[128]

The flexibility of having a built-in, mobile staff enabled sisterhoods to establish temporary hospitals quickly when exceptional circumstances arose, such as the outbreak of disease. The unique advantages that sisterhoods enjoyed is especially evident in the case of such short-term crisis care. They set up temporary hospitals during cholera, typhoid and smallpox epidemics throughout the century.[129] Ascot Priory sisters established a cholera hospital during the 1849 outbreak in Plymouth, and thirty-four years later their work was still remembered: an appreciative local priest then wrote, 'They were a band of heroines in the army of God: the thought of personal danger did not seem to enter their minds.'[130] Members of seven Anglican sisterhoods cooperated in nursing during the 1856 cholera outbreak in East London, and similar cooperation was evident in later cholera and typhoid epidemics.[131] As late as the 1880s sisters were seen as the natural source of assistance if the dreaded disease should return to England. In that year the Sisters of the Church received a letter from the Sick Metropolitan Asylums Board, asking the community to undertake the nursing if the expected outbreak of cholera were to manifest itself. The Mother Superior recorded in her diary, 'The Sisters all delighted with the request. Of course replied in the affirmative.'[132]

By the 1880s, however, most sisterhoods were placing less emphasis on nursing as it became a respectable secular profession and the quality and quantity of non-sisterhood nurses improved. The introduction of Jubilee Nurses into the East End in 1887 was the signal for at least one community to withdraw from local hospital work.[133] Although few communities gave it up entirely, the emphasis moved toward patient care in their own specialist hospitals, usually for convalescents or children, areas where they felt provision was still inadequate.

Schools

Most sisterhood schools in London and the large towns were free or cheap. They were intended for children who were too wretchedly dressed, and whose attendance was too sporadic, for the National Schools. These 'Ragged Schools' were co-educational, and lured children in with free buns and tea, plenty of singing, and short, enjoyable lessons. Typically lessons ran from 9.30 a.m. to noon, with afternoon lessons from 2.00 to 4.00 p.m.[134] Ragged school facilities were inadequate, as classes were typically held in rented rooms or buildings not designed for the instruction of large numbers of children. The sisters of Ascot Priory ran a 'shed school' in Plymouth, where street boys were educated for the navy in less than optimum conditions. Yet there is evidence that the sisters provided good education; one shed school alumnus was later knighted for his naval services.[135] Other ragged schools were run by sisterhoods in former public houses or over stables: always, however, in the heart of urban poverty. In an effort to educate girls hired to 'mind' infants, the babies could be brought to school, where they were fed and put to bed before lessons began. This must have added to the ragged schools' air of informality and improvisation. Discipline was sometimes rather crude in the early days; an adolescent novice, fresh from a Cheshire parsonage, experienced her first day of teaching in a Soho ragged school as something entirely outside her former experience.

School commenced at 9.30 and my first experience of London children was not pleasing. Rags and dirt I had rather a fancy for, even though the odour of tobacco and treacle impregnated their wearers, but as for managing the little imps! I was hopeless, until I saw the other Sisters whacking right and left, whereupon following their example I got on better.[136]

This rather drastic discipline did little to discourage scholars: within a few weeks of its opening the school had over 100 regular attendants.

Meals, including both breakfast and dinner, were an important feature of many sisterhood schools, as well as in the ragged schools: not only did they serve to attract children, but the sisters quickly realized that children could not be efficiently taught when hungry. The Sisters of the Church instituted daily meals more than a quarter of a century before the London County Council authorities would follow suit. Meals varied from simple 'feeds' of buns and milky tea, to substantial servings of soup, meat, vegetables and pudding. Shed and ragged schools were superseded by better equipped institutions as the communities grew in numbers and wealth.

In vivid contrast to the low-budget rented facilities of community-run ragged schools, the Sisters of the Church spared no expense on its schools, pouring money into the constant improvement of their facilities, even to the extent of borrowing from the Sisters' Fund, a problematic solution at best. Overall, the Sisters of the Church was the most important of the sisterhoods concerned with the care and education of young children, and it may be useful to briefly sketch the growth of the community's educational efforts. Beginning with a single Bun School in 1870 (a form of ragged school that rewarded attendance with food), the Sisters of the Church at first intended their schools, like so many sisterhood endeavours, to be for 'poor and ignorant girls' and infants only. They soon opened their doors to boys as well in response to local demand. In reaction to the School Act of 1870, the community quickly built and opened a number of cheap schools, charging pupils who could afford it a penny a day. Most of these schools were sited in north-west London, an area whose poverty was then ignored by charitable London.[137] Ayckbowm opened the Sisters of the Church's first infant school on 16 May 1870, with seven children present. By 25 May there were 100 pupils on the roll. Within a year, sisters of the community were studying for the government teaching certificates, and by 1883, there were over 900 girls and infants in the Sisters of the Church schools in London alone.[138] Sisters in charge of schools were instructed to stock the schoolrooms with good apparatus and cheerful pictures, and to ensure that teaching sisters were 'well supplied with all books, publications, and other ... appliances and advantages' that would enable them to carry out their 'most important work' efficiently. When the Free Education Act came into effect in September 1891, the Sisters of the Church decided that most of their cheap schools would become free.[139] By 1900 they operated eight government-inspected schools with over 6000 pupils in London, five schools in the provinces, twelve large schools overseas (where more than 1000 students were enrolled), and three penny schools. While some of the provincial schools were built by other groups, with the Sisters of the Church simply supplying the teaching and administrative staff, all the London and three of the provincial schools were built, maintained and staffed by the Sisters of the Church.[140] (In addition to their weekday labours, on Sundays sixty members of the Sisters of the Church taught 4695 children in Bun and Sunday Schools.[141])

This community believed not only in education, but in Anglican education. They travelled throughout Britain in the 1880s and 1890s, gathering hundreds of thousands of names on petitions for government assistance for Anglican schools, and routinely canvassed for votes for 'their' candidates at School Board elections.[142] This community also established a large Church Teacher's Union for elementary school teachers, which held regional conferences and annual retreats. So connected was this community in the public mind with the cause of Anglican education that some secular school campaigners saw in the Sisters of the Church's activities a serious threat to their campaign for non-sectarian education. In attempting to discredit the Sisters of the Church's work the community was depicted in a way that the most fervid anti-Ritualist propagandist would have found familiar.[143]

Outside London, sisterhood schools followed a similar pattern, generally beginning by establishing schools for the very poorest, and gradually expanding into the opening of institutions for the children of artisans and the lower middle class. The Society of the Sisters of Bethany's orphanage school received a glowing report from the HM Inspector in 1898, which commended the school's 'excellent' discipline, the 'bright and cheerful' children, and the 'very good' reading, writing, spelling and composition. The 'great attention' given to arithmetic was noted, and the report concluded that the primary grades 'deserve especial praise. They are extremely well taught and cared for.'[144] In light of this report, it seems very probable that the children in this Bournemouth orphanage were receiving a higher standard of education than many middle-class, fee-paying children in the unregulated private schools of the day.

Wantage was the other community which trained teachers on a large scale. The sisterhood opened a Middle School in 1864; this later evolved into a training school for National School teachers, run by Sister Bessie, who had come there at fifteen to train as a pupil-teacher.[145] Many other Wantage sisters were active in secondary and university school programmes: the Mother Superior of another community went so far as to lament that 'Wantage gets all the sisters with brains.' Excellence was not confined to this sisterhood, however: the Community of the Resurrection, a South African sisterhood founded by Englishwomen, sent 200 student teachers to the certification examinations every year; the students trained by the sisterhood received more first-class results than any other teacher training college in South Africa.[146] Both metropolitan and non-metropolitan sisterhoods established schools for poor gentlemen's daughters and good quality middle-class schools. These institutions, often boarding, were for girls only. (At least one community considered that middle- and upper-class education would violate their goal of being 'servants of the Poor' and refused to undertake them.[147])

Adult education was another area addressed by sisterhoods. That adult schools were intended to do more than educate is indicated by their being kept open until the public houses closed.[148] In addition, communities ran evening schools for employed children and adolescents, such as the large evening schools for women workers in the silk factories opened by All Hallows in Norwich.[149] These schools did much more than teach the 'factory discipline' suggested by E. P. Thompson, the Marxist cultural historian, in his *Customs in Common* (1991). The Sisters of the Holy Cross provided their adult working-class pupils with 'a good elementary English education; reading, writing, and arithmetic, with some instruction in history, geography, grammar and music.'[150] This thorough elementary education could not have been surpassed by many middle-class schools.

As with nurses' training within sisterhoods, teacher training varied substantially across communities. Some communities insisted on the best qualifications, and their community logs regularly list the scholarships and certificates won, and examinations passed, by their members.[151] This became even more important as sisters opened government-aided National Schools: a highly qualified teaching staff helped to ensure that sisterhood Schools would receive generous grants.[152] The Sisters of the Church's Mother Emily embraced educational excellence as a way of confuting secular critics of religiously based schooling.

It is the policy of infidels and secularists to stigmatise the Church as 'The Mother of Ignorance', and her teachers as narrow-minded bigots, desirous of keeping the working-classes in mental darkness. We *know* how false is this assertion, but we have to do our part towards *proving* it ... we must never rest until we can take the lead in Education, and show that we are ready to work harder, out of love to God, than do others for the sake of personal gain.[153]

After certification, teacher training did not cease: Sisters of the Church and Society of the Holy and Undivided Trinity teachers studied the work of continental educational theorists, including Pestalozzi and Froebel.[154] Froebel's radical ideas about the intrinsically good and creative nature of the child, which emphasized the relationship between affection and good teaching, especially influenced the Sisters of the Church's educational philosophy, as explained in the community's popular series of textbooks on elementary education.[155] Not all teacher education was theoretical, however. The sisters attended special lectures in botany, studied musical drill, and took courses in woodworking and cookery, in order to be able to offer these subjects in their schools. They observed educational methods in both religious and secular schools, travelling as far as Brighton and Edinburgh to do so, and they shared experiences and techniques with Roman Catholic teaching orders, crossing religious boundaries for the sake of educational effectiveness.[156] Teaching sisters were admonished that they should not 'shrink from [any] labour or study' which might 'increase their fitness for the great work of Education'.[157] Their work paid dividends, not least financial: most of the Sisters of the Church schools received the highest level of government grant after the positive reports of school examiners in 1891–92. One school inspector commented after seeing their Gordon Schools, 'No Board School could compete with such schools.'[158]

Sisters could complete their education after joining a community, although one teaching order qualified that by saying that it could 'accept no large proportion of Novices of narrow education and understanding'.[159] Emily Ayckbowm, the founder of the Sisters of the Church, was enthusiastic in the cause of higher education for women, and was amused by the panic-stricken reaction of some male church leaders to the opening of university degrees to both sexes. Candidates for the order were warmly seconded in their efforts to win scholarships before entering the novitiate. Members of the Sisters of the Church were encouraged to study for degrees at Bedford College and the University of London after profession. It was not at all unusual for the Sisters of the Church and Wantage sisters to have studied at Cambridge, attended classes at Oxford, or/and taken degrees at the University of London. Sisters of the Church, Wantage and Holy Name members sometimes found that they comprised a substantial proportion of the candidates when sitting the government examinations.[160] All teaching sisters in these communities had recognized qualifications long before the end of the century.

Other communities, generally the smaller sisterhoods, were more amateur in their educational provision. They relied largely upon the attainments their sisters had learned from their own governesses in their youth. As well, smaller communities were often unable to provide enough teaching sisters for all subjects, thus forcing them to pay salaries to secular assistants. The Society of the Holy and Undivided Trinity's school for young ladies had in 1890 a teaching staff composed of a sister as Regent, two sisters and two novices for academic subjects, and two sisters for music and drawing, with French, singing and the violin taught by seven secular teachers. (This distribution of teaching strength may also indicate something about the relative emphasis placed on accomplishments in genteel education.) Holy and Undivided Trinity did not have all of its teachers qualified until 1885.[161] Several of the small teaching communities seem to have sent all their best teachers to their free schools, probably feeling that ladies could educate young ladies without any training. As a result; the Society of the Holy and Undivided Trinity's orphan school, taught by several gifted lay sister-teachers, routinely got better reports from school inspectors than did the fee-paying schools the community ran for the daughters of clergy.[162]

There was always distinctively Anglican religious teaching in sisterhood schools, but at the same time there existed an awareness that too much could be counterproductive. Most sisterhoods quickly learned that excessive emphasis upon religion could have a regrettable effect upon children, and they generally expressed a decided distaste for 'pious practices' among the children. The religious teaching offered was geared to a child's comprehension. The Sisters of the Church limited religious education in its schools to forty minutes per day; this was probably typical.[163]

It was not uncommon for former school pupils to enter the communities that had educated them: indeed, for smaller teaching sisterhoods, this was a major avenue of recruitment. The available information suggests an impressive recruitment rate, and one which sisterhoods of all sizes could benefit from. Of 200 young women trained as pupil-teachers at St Michael's Training School (run by Wantage), twenty-one entered religious communities, one becoming Superior 'of a well-founded and increasing Sisterhood'.[164] Former pupils usually entered the choir novitiate, but a few students became lay sisters. One of the Society of the Holy and Undivided Trinity's working-class pupils became both a lay sister and a teacher in the community's schools.[165] Another of Holy and Undivided Trinity's former pupils, who had spent ten years at the community's school, returned twelve years later to enter the community, eventually becoming the third Mother Superior.[166] The opportunities offered by education for recruitment were recognized by both the sisterhoods and their enemies. Opponents of Anglican communities claimed that exposure to convent life through sisterhood schools made young women dissatisfied with home and family.

> from the CONVENTUAL standpoint it is well worth while to offer a fashionable education at a cheap rate; for the acknowledged effect produced upon a large proportion of girls ... is to make them dissatisfied with anything else than a so-called 'religious life'. The convent school-room is the recruiting ground for the nunnery; the pupil becomes the novice.[167]

The writer of this polemic seems not to have realized the flaw in his argument; implicit in it is the assumption that the convent is a genuinely attractive alternative to the home; if it were not, exposure to it would be without danger. But convent schools, Anglican and Roman Catholic alike, were commonly assumed to be mere ploys to lure young women into the religious life.

Not only former pupils, but former teachers and governesses regularly entered the teaching sisterhoods, often after initially working for the community as a secular instructor.[168] For a woman teacher or governess who did not wish to marry, community life offered the undeniable attractions of a permanent home, security in old age or illness, and a definite social status. This was much, compared with what a Victorian woman teacher would ordinarily acquire in the course of her career. Some communities actively recruited teachers. In 1885 the Sisters of the Church announced that they were beginning a new branch of the community, exclusively for elementary schoolteachers, remarking that it was 'a common error to suppose that practical work (such as teaching in a Government School ...) is incompatible with Sisterhood life ... Those who join this branch will have ample scope for the exercise of [their] talents.'[169] The Sisters of the Church also offered a quasi-religious life to qualified women teachers who wished to 'dedicate their lives to education without becoming sisters'. They shared a house with eight sisters in north London and followed a rule of life.[170]

The Sisters of the Church summarized their founder's achievements in the field of education in a passage which is worth quoting at length because it depicts so typically the intense pride communities took in the exploits and achievements of their founders.

> She built large schools, she raised funds for their maintenance, and secured excellent teaching, both secular and religious, for thousands of children; she encouraged the Sisters of her Community to qualify themselves as properly certificated teachers ... Neither ... would she ever be satisfied with a low standard of work; she would try and try again to perfect what she felt to be weak or inadequate, and in the schools made earnest efforts to stir up zeal and a spirit of wholesome emulation in the hearts of the teachers. 'We must not be content for our schools to be merely as good as Board Schools; they must be better,' she would say.[171]

District visiting

District visiting, unlike teaching, was an amateur activity usually organized by local clergy on a parochial basis. It involved visiting the poor in their own homes, and resembled in many respects prototypical social work.[172] At the time of the first establishment of sisterhoods, district visiting was the most generally acceptable public role for women of the middle and upper classes, involving as it did the bringing of middle-class virtues, as well as blankets and soup, to the labouring classes. This idea of woman's work had a long pedigree; it was described most concisely by Hannah More in her didactic novel *Coelebs in Search of a Wife*: 'I have often heard it regretted that ladies have no stated employment, no profession. It is a mistake. *Charity is the calling of a lady; the care of the poor is her profession.*'[173]

How did district visiting work? Ideally, the lady visitor would call regularly upon every family in her 'district' and report back to the clergy cases of distress, illness or unemployment.[174] Not all women were acceptable as district visitors: Charles Kingsley refused to allow young women to visit for fear that this would bring them into 'most undesirable contact with the coarser forms of evil'. Another clergyman allowed only mature married women, widows or spinsters who had 'arrived at a time of life when marriage is improbable' to work as district visitors; somehow, contact with the poor was so contaminating to young women that it would put them at risk of disqualification for marriage.[175] District visitors did not make decisions about the needs of the poor, or even distribute relief, without guidance from the parish clergy. Heeney describes the relationship of parish visitors to the parish priest as one of 'complete subordination'.[176] The mature married women who received clerical approval for district visiting did this work in their spare time, but with the average married woman experiencing ten pregnancies, spare time must have been something of a rarity, and volunteer work such as visiting suffered. Charles Booth gives an account of an East London parish where the district visitors did, on average, two hours a week each; this was probably not at all untypical, and abysmally inadequate.[177]

Sisterhoods seized on district visiting as a way of becoming intimately acquainted with the local population. They decried the casual attitude of other organizations, with even the formidable Charity Organization Society advising its visitors that 'you can keep up the acquaintance by irregular visits as you have opportunity, and if you go to see them after an absence from London for six months or more, they will appreciate the compliment involved in your not forgetting them'.[178] Such irregular and amateur visits seem to have been more for the benefit of the visitor than the visited. It is unlikely that the poor could conveniently postpone a crisis of illness or unemployment for the duration of their benevolent visitors' foreign tours. The religious community was always there, and this gave them an enormous advantage in their work with the poor.

As in many other aspects of active community work, the sisters used their status as ladies and as professional religious to give them a standing not unlike that of a parish priest.

> The people in the slums quickly recognise the authority of her state and vocation ... Her consecration gives her a special prerogative ... they know that it is not ... a passing phase of philanthropic sentiment, but ... a whole life given to Christ in their service. They can trust the Sister with secrets they would not trust to any other ... For them she represents religion in its most venerable aspect; she belongs to God permanently, therefore the poor have an unquestionable right to her.[179]

As a result of this semi-clerical status it was hard for sisters to convince the people with whom they worked that they were not qualified to celebrate the Eucharist, hear confessions or undertake other activities performed only by priests; they were, after all, active in baptizing infants.[180] The frequency of such requests demonstrates that for their poor neighbours, their status as professional religious workers overrode their gender disqualification for such ordinances.

Unlike lady visitors, who worked under strict clerical supervision, sisterhood visitors generally did not feel themselves confined to simply carrying out the clergyman's orders, although they were generally glad to cooperate with clergy who did not interfere with their actions. Neither did they feel obliged to confine themselves to parish boundaries. Sisterhoods generally came to an arrangement with the local rector which left them wholly responsible for the relief of bodily distress. Aid was distributed without regard to the religious beliefs of the needy, leaving the clergy to concentrate upon their pastoral functions.[181]

Sisters were willing to work in areas of extreme squalor where lady visitors were reluctant to venture. Indeed, the Sisters of the Church expressed both a powerful social conscience and a considerable amount of frustration at the wilful ignorance or hypocrisy of the better-off, who shunned such work.

All those well-dressed respectable people who fill our churches! Yet, probably not two percent of them ever enter a poor dwelling, or consider the working classes as other than a race created for, and ministering to, their comfort.[182]

One advantage the sisters had in their employment among the Victorian working class was their obvious poverty. In a time when the poor believed that clergymen were paid from the rates and made 'rather a good thing out of their jobs', the sisterhoods (unlike those who worked in settlements) tried to match their lifestyle to that of the poor instead of creating outposts of middle-class lifestyle among them.[183] Victorian sisters revelled in the contrast between their former affluent lifestyles and their chosen lives of poverty. A popular All Saints district visitor was Sister Margaret, an immensely rich heiress who had brought a fortune in diamonds into the community, but who also brought back vermin from her daily visits in a slum district.[184] Sisters did not make day-trips into the centres of urban poverty; they lived there themselves, and were accessible to those in need at all hours of the day and night. Local suspicion of sisters took some time to overcome, and sometimes this initial mistrust took unusual forms. For example the inhabitants of Southwark (who enjoyed a reputation for criminality) initially suspected the Society of Reparation sisters of being police spies in a new and particularly ingenious disguise, when the community settled there in 1869.[185]

Typical of the areas too rough for 'lady visitors' but where sisters worked was the parish of St George's-in-the-East, visited by the Community of the Holy Cross. Here four streets contained 733 houses, including 40 public houses and beer shops and 154 'houses of ill fame'. Charles Booth described

Southwark (home of the Reparation sisters) as a network of 'small streets which for vice, poverty, and crowding, are unrivalled in London'.[186] All communities working in such areas made their own provision for relief of the poor, usually in the form of money, food and material goods, schooling, or hospital admissions for the sick. When the sisterhoods no longer had money or food left to give, they contributed from their own scanty stores, always minimal because of the vow of poverty. The attitude which informed their district work is clear in Mother Kate's memories of work in the slummy streets around Soho:

> we lived *with* the people and *for* the people. Over and over again when some poor ragged body came round to the door, and we had nothing else to give her, we have shed our undergarments in the front hall, and walked about in our habits ... Sister Mary spared *nothing*, [saying] the poor *must* always come first.[187]

While it is difficult to imagine what local women could do with a nun's underwear except pawn it, such dramatic gestures must have had an impact and helped to create a sense of solidarity.

Some sisterhoods cooperated with charitable agencies such as the Charity Organization Society (COS), the Society for the Relief of Distress and the National Society for the Prevention of Cruelty to Children.[188] While few communities had ideological differences with the last two organizations, cooperation with the COS was always problematic, as it resented the sisterhoods interfering in any way with the ungentle administration of the Poor Law. The Sisters of the Church in particular were continually at loggerheads with the COS, who criticized the community for their food distribution practices: the sisterhood was selling food to unemployed workers at break-even prices, supplying 53,700 halfpenny dinners in 1892, with breakfasts for children on a corresponding scale.[189] Despite the severity of the recession, the COS considered this pauperizing and an interference with market forces. Another community which attracted COS complaints over the indiscriminate feeding of slum children was the Society of Reparation to Jesus in the Blessed Sacrament, who reminded 'rigid political economists' that their own children were well-housed and warm. The sisters advised such laissez-faire social theorists to 'dose' their own 'children with the principles of political economy as much as you like ... but do not apply this cold, unsympathetic reasoning to these poor children, whose lot in life is so hard'.[190]

Foreign mission work

Only two nineteenth-century Anglican sisterhoods were founded with an explicitly missionary purpose: the Missionary Community of St Denys originated in the 1870s as a training school for female missionaries and rapidly evolved into a missionary sisterhood; the Community of the Servants of Christ was founded by a former missionary as a missionary training school in 1897.[191] Additionally, three overseas communities, all in South Africa (St George's Sisterhood, the Community of St Michael and All Angels and the Community of the Resurrection), were founded by British women, and virtually all of their Victorian sisters were from the United Kingdom.

However, several of the larger English sisterhoods had a significant overseas presence by the end of the century. The first British-based community to undertake foreign mission work was Ascot Priory, which sent a number of sisters to Hawaii at the request of Queen Emma in 1864. There they opened schools for girls and founded a university preparation college for Hawaiian women. This initial overseas expansion, so typical in its emphasis upon women, is unusual in one respect: most sisterhood missionary foundations were centred on colonies and former colonies of the British Empire. All Saints and Wantage established branch houses in India, South Africa and the United States, and the Sisters of the Church sisters worked in Canada, Australia, New Zealand, South Africa and India. All Hallows educated indigenous children in northern Canada, and the Missionary Community of St Denys was active in many areas of India. Holy Rood began work in Canada in 1890, and soon expanded into work with black women in the American South.[192] The Sisters of Bethany worked with Kurdish girls and women in what is now northern Iraq during the 1890s, and the Community of St Peter stationed sisters in Korea from 1892 until the last sister died on the grim 'Death March' of 1950.[193]

Mission outposts established by sisterhoods performed the same range of functions as the communities at home. The usual gamut of hospitals, orphanages and schools were opened for both native and European residents. The sole important difference was that in many countries they concentrated even more exclusively upon working with women and girls than they did in Britain, largely because of cultural differences. Bethany sisters travelled from village to village in Iraq, teaching women and providing medical services for women and girls; Wantage did similar work in India.[194] Anglican sisters expressed concern with the position of women in 'heathen' cultures, and showed some sensitivity to cultural difference, especially in their concern to avoid over-Westernizing the girls they educated, and through housing and supporting Indian women studying medicine in the UK.[195] However, doubt was never expressed of the need for conversion to Christianity. It was unacceptable for 'native' women to enter English communities as professed members, with the exception of Wantage, which admitted Indian sisters among its ranks. Sisterhoods typically 'mothered' separate communities for women of colour who wished to enter the religious life, providing finance, structure and guidance during the initial period of establishment.[196]

Other services

Mainstream Victorian philanthropy focused its attention on the moral and physical condition of men.[197] But the sisterhoods generally saw their primary function as ministering to the needs of women and children. They did this with such success that the late-Victorian social purity activist, Jane Ellice Hopkins, wrote that when she began work it was only the High Church party (of which sisterhoods were the first practical demonstration) which did not shirk the issue of urban poverty.[198]

Several communities operated break-even or below-cost restaurants in areas where working-class men and women worked. They catered to commuting workers who were unable to return home for lunch. Such enterprises sold food at half its cost price in summer and one-quarter of cost in the winter. The Sisters of the Church were active in providing food for the strikers in the Dockers' Strike of 1889, and the sisterhood supported the industrial action wholeheartedly.[199] During periods of high unemployment free meals were provided. Once again, the Sisters of the Church's scale of operations (or at any rate their record-keeping) far outstripped that of other sisterhoods. By 1897 the community had provided 274,000 meals for adults, food and night lodging for 73,000 men, and 77,000 meals for poor children.[200] This was in addition to rearing 600 orphans in eight homes, operating three convalescent homes for children (one with 300 beds) and educating between five and six thousand children a year in their thirteen schools, as well as maintaining eleven other branches of educational work. It is not surprising that their bitterest opponents, the Charity Organization Society, described the community as 'one of the largest and best-known charities in London' in 1887, only seventeen years after the Sisters of the Church's foundation.[201]

Another sisterhood ran the Newport Market Refuge, which provided seven nights' free accommodation for newcomers to London, both male and female, in Soho. In addition to providing shelter, the sisters tried, usually successfully, to find these vulnerable strangers employment. They reported that most of the women who resorted to them were domestic servants out of place.[202] About twenty communities maintained night refuges for young women, believing (with good reason) that many women's first entrance into vice was the result of homelessness.[203] Most of these were on a small scale, providing lodging for no more than a dozen homeless women. A similar but more permanent provision was made for working-class women in industrial centres, where long-stay hostels were provided for female factory 'hands'. St Saviour's Priory established holiday homes at Brighton and Herne Bay to enable working-class adults to take vacations, and several other communities undertook 'rest homes' for male and female factory workers around the country, where workers could enjoy low-cost holidays seventy years before the Holidays with Pay Act. At the other end of the social scale, by the turn of the century several communities were preparing to undertake the running of hostels and residences for women university students.[204]

In most communities a number of miscellaneous services were aimed at easing, however slightly, the plight of the overburdened mother. Vitally important for the welfare of women was the establishment of some of the earliest day-care centres, which provided care for the children of working mothers. Among others, the Sisters of Charity at Bristol had a large free crèche from their foundation in 1868, and St Saviour's Priory provided childcare twelve hours a day in Haggerston from 1879 to 1930, for a maximum charge of threepence daily. (This price included milk, meals and unlimited cod-liver oil.[205]) Beside the many communities who established hospitals for ill children, St Saviour's Priory and other sisterhoods pioneered respite care: taking in sick children who needed a week or two of constant attention, and giving overburdened working-class parents a break from constant attention to the needs of a chronically ill child.[206] The special needs of the expectant mother were not neglected. The maternity societies run by the Sisters of the Church, the Nursing Sisters of St John the Divine and others lent baby-linen, supplied food and comforts for the mother, and would take young children off the mother's hands for a few days while she recovered from childbirth.[207] It was also usual for sisterhoods to open workrooms in times of distress. Here elderly or unemployed women worked at sewing, making such things as the sisters' habits and the clothes required by the orphans, in return for meals and a small daily wage.[208] The Sisters of the Church opened 'depots' (an early form of the charity shop), where donated used clothing was sold at very low prices to working-class customers, at about a dozen locations around England. St Saviour's Priory found that one of their most successful projects was a mutual loan and investment society.[209]

Clubs and guilds were important auxiliaries to work in most communities. These organizations gained friends for the sisterhoods, established a link between the local people and the community, and provided a sociable alternative to the public house. Different clubs were established for different types of clientele, from sailors in Plymouth to a club for costermonger women in the East End. Clubs such as these emphasized sociability and pleasure in a non-alcoholic atmosphere and, unlike most sisterhood initiatives, were available to adults of both sexes. A popular activity was singing classes for adults. Those who attended would give songs and recitations (the sisters did not perform, except by providing musical accompaniment), and there was no religious teaching.[210] Most clubs and guilds were aimed primarily at girls and women, although there were plenty formed for men. For the sisterhoods, the ultimate aim was to have a guild or club suitable for every member of the family.

A typical girls' guild was a club stressing personal purity, self-help and sociability for girls from the age of twelve to twenty-five. Guilds were organized similarly to those of Wesleyan class leaders: elected older girls called band-mistresses ruled their bands, which elected their own members; sisters had only a veto vote. Members paid a penny a week into a membership/savings scheme, which was used to supply support in illness, an outfit of clothing for those going out to work, and a sum of money upon making a respectable marriage. At the age of twenty-five a member's contributions were returned.[211] Typically, the guild would offer a clubroom open every night from 6 to 10 p.m., with cards, music, books, plants, needlework, cookery lessons, weekly clothing sales, plays and Bible classes.[212] This was not always as serene as one might imagine. What a Bible class in East London could be like is indicated by the rueful comment of a veteran of such ventures:

> by which name is not to be understood a nice orderly assembly of quiet, decent, [people], sitting all around with Bibles in their hands, and looking out their references – no; my Bible Class was a surging mob of noisy and blaspheming roughs, whom one had to quell by psychic force ... [213]

Several sisterhoods availed themselves of secular frameworks, establishing temperance societies, mothers' meetings, anti-vivisection lobbying groups and friendly societies for the people in their neighbourhoods.[214] One of the more spiritually centred activities was the sisters' habit of urging the poor to take communion regularly: in many areas it was believed throughout the nineteenth century that after confirmation, communion was only 'for the quality'.[215] Thus they contributed to the democratization of the Anglican Church, through their insistence that the Eucharist was for all believers, regardless of rank or social status.

The burial of the dead was one of the first four functions of the first Anglican sisterhood to be established. Most of the earliest sisterhoods provided mortuary services for working-class families who could not afford undertaking fees. These were greatly appreciated because such people had nowhere except their living space in which to keep their dead in the interval between death and burial. In this way, mortuary chapels were an important factor in gaining local support for sisterhoods. That this work could sometimes be repulsively hard is clear. Mother Kate recalled the experience of laying out the corpse of a child who had been dead of smallpox for five days before the mother could be persuaded to allow burial, and being obliged to carry the coffin through the streets after the refusal of the parish authorities to assist.[216]

The active work undertaken by the sisters was significant in several ways. Communities allowed women to work for a higher cause, and in the process of demanding their right to work for God, they saw something of how the urban working class lived, and did what they could to better their lot. Many of them wished, with Florence Nightingale, to 'regenerate the world with their institutions, with their moral philosophy, with their love'.[217] They did not accomplish this, but they did carry out worthwhile work in an atmosphere which celebrated their commitment to the poor around them as well as to their own community.

Crucially, sisterhoods originally conceived their work to be social as much as spiritual. Their orientation was maternalist: 'striving to compass every form of charity, to lessen every shape of ... suffering, to fill every gap in the social system as regards the needy'.[218] Perhaps this emotional extract from the Sisters of the Church's *Our Work* best expresses the motivations of the early Anglican sisters:

It is terrible, terrible ... this gulf between the classes, this awful disregard of the godly for the godless, of the respectable for the sinner. Oh! It puzzles me that hundreds do not press forwards to the help of these poor suffering ... creatures, taking their woes and burdens on themselves ... and forcibly rescuing them from the clutches of the devil. Could there be a happier, better work for any Christian woman?[219]

While sisterhoods and their activities could be criticized as examples of Tory benevolence or as 'ambulance workers' in a social system which denied its own ultimate responsibility for caring for its citizens, such a picture of social and religious conservatism would be incomplete. While Luddy's assessment of communities as providing wealthy single women with an opportunity to do social work, a career denied to their secular peers, is true, it is not the whole story.[220] Many of the early sisters would have agreed with Mother Kate's analysis of their motive; she saw it in part as a political purpose, fostered by the Christian Socialism with which many sisters were deeply imbued:

> In those late sixties and early seventies, there was a strong atmosphere of revolutionary socialism about, with which many of the very keen, ardent, earnest young people of that day were strongly impregnated . . . and I followed the lead.[221]

A late Victorian observer, looking back, saw sisterhoods as arising out a need for 'women of practical piety to battle with the ills ... poisoning the community'.[222] In a time when most people believed, like Mrs Sandford, that 'no woman can fulfil her social duties without being religious', these sisters would have unquestioningly accepted the link between social conscience and religious faith. In Anglican sisterhoods both tended to be radical.[223]

PART III POPULAR PERCEPTIONS OF SISTERHOODS

CHAPTER FIVE

'THEY WILL NOT OBEY': THE CLERICAL RESPONSE TO SISTERHOODS

The first Anglican sisterhood was established in the year of John Henry Newman's secession to Rome. Many assumed that the Tractarian Movement had lost its heart with the loss of Newman, and that it would be quickly embalmed as just another fad in the long line of Anglican vicissitudes. Initially this belief appeared to be confirmed by the small stream of Anglicans who followed Newman. The most important among these followers was probably Henry Edward Manning, who made his submission in 1851. But while some of the intellectual leaders of the Movement were leaving it, either for Catholicism or for scepticism (as with Mark Pattison), the practical consequences of Tractarian theology, with its two-fold emphasis upon the importance of symbolic ritual and on works as evidence of faith, found in sisterhoods one of its permanent expressions. As well as inheriting some of the beliefs and practices of Tractarianism, sisterhoods fell heir to much of the antagonism and suspicion with which the Anglican church hierarchy had regarded the Tractarian movement. Most communities, with the general exception of those in the province of York, tended to cluster at the Anglo-Catholic end of the Anglican spectrum, although not all of the women who joined them were in sympathy with the movement.

The relationship between Anglican sisterhoods and Church of England officialdom throughout the nineteenth century was ambivalent, complex and unhappy. Communities rejected the accepted roles for Anglican women, thus challenging belief systems dear to churchmen as well as to middle-class culture. A unified reaction to the sisterhood movement proved impossible, although the response was generally negative. At best, the bishops were always suspicious and cautious; normally they were simply and unrelievedly hostile. Given the structure of the Church of England in the nineteenth century perhaps nothing else could have been expected. However, little damage was done to the movement because the bishops themselves were reluctant to work together or to take any action which might bring on them adverse public comment.

This lack of a co-ordinated response from above was very different from the situation in the Victorian Roman Catholic Church, where communities of women were subjected to close supervision and enforced enclosure, despite often having originally had an apostolate which was as active as that of any Anglican sisterhood. The very fact of an established framework for women's orders in the Roman Church reduced freedom for potential founders of communities. Susan O'Brien points out that without official approval Roman Catholic women could not take vows and were not given the status of religious.[1] Maria Luddy reinforces this point, citing the experience of Catherine McAuley, who ended up founding a religious order against her will, but at the insistence of Archbishop Murray, who disapproved of lay women undertaking philanthropic work.[2] Having taken the vows, Roman Catholic sisters were subordinated to the needs of the Church as a whole, with scant regard for the community's own needs. They could be (and often were) tossed hither and thither at the whim of a priest, however incompetent, and they were dependent on 'their ecclesiastical superior' in even the crucial area of fund-raising.[3] By contrast, Anglican female founders were able to circumvent the problem by appropriating the status of 'ecclesiastical superior' for themselves, without reference to the authority of the Church as vested in the bishops. While Roman Catholic sisters were praised specifically because 'it is well known that the Lady Abbess is entirely subservient to her priest and Bishop, and never works in any department separately from them', Anglican sisters were seen as deplorably lacking in such tractability. One irritated priest explained to the Archbishop of Canterbury that the sisterhood at Malling Abbey had 'a freedom from external control which it probably would not enjoy in communion with Rome'. Sisterhoods were private enterprises within Anglicanism and as such were not answerable to any ecclesiastical authority.[4] One former Anglican sister, who later founded a Roman Catholic community, the control of which was swiftly wrested from her by her bishop, wrote that in the Church of England women 'could laugh at all restraints of ecclesiastical authority . . . a bishop was nothing to a lady.' This relative liberty within Anglican monasticism was closely tied to the differing self-definition and chosen structure of the two churches: while the structure of Roman Catholic orders closely resembled that of regiments in an army, Anglican sisterhoods were explicitly based on a family structure, which left them 'free to obey their spiritual parents as they choose – free to form new families or to alter their Rule of Life if and when they feel the need, and without previous reference to any higher authority'.[5]

Before the first sisterhood was established in 1845, there was no organization within the pale of the Church of England which provided full-time work for women. Florence Nightingale had bitter experience of the dilemma of the non-status of women within Anglicanism. It was women like her who founded sisterhoods, conscious of having talents and abilities which they longed to use within the English church. Nightingale expressed their frustration:

> The Church of England has for men bishoprics, archbishoprics, and a little work ... She has for women – what? ... They would give her their heads, their hearts, their hands. She will not have them. She does not know what to do with them.[6]

Because sisterhoods were set up within an Anglican religious culture which explicitly rejected the contributions (other than financial) of women, they found themselves in opposition to that religious culture. Those who entered the orders wished to remain Anglican, while continuing to live and work within communities, whereas the traditional solution had been for women to convert to Roman Catholicism in order to make themselves eligible for community life.

For the episcopate, the establishment of Anglican communities was not a development to be welcomed. Sisterhoods were first seen as a nuisance, and later as a threat, to be controlled from above if curtailment failed. Writing with reference to the Convocation of 1862, Frances Power Cobbe saw the irony of the situation clearly.

> High Churchmen and Low, Broad Churchmen and Hard, all seemed agreed that there was good work for women to do, and which women *were* doing all over England; and that it was extremely desirable that all these lady guerrillas of philanthropy should be enrolled in the regular disciplined army of the Church ... To use a more appropriate simile, Mother Church expressed herself as satisfied at her daughters 'coming out', but considered that her chaperonage was decidedly necessary to their decorum.[7]

Despite these constant attempts at official suppression, sisters seized and held space for themselves within their male-dominated church. 'Anglican sisterhoods were clearly in the vanguard of women's single-sex organizations, in both their organizational autonomy and their insistence upon women's right to a separate religious life.'[8]

Attitudes of the bishops

Initially, a few bishops attempted outright prohibition of sisterhood activity. Bishop Blomfield (London, 1828–56) warned in 1855, 'I will not suffer, if I can help it, Miss Sellon, or any of her Sisterhood, to intrude into this diocese.' This was the first of many such prohibitions of Ascot Priory's activities in London; the regularity with which they were repeated seems to indicate that Blomfield soon found that he could not control the community. He complained a few months later that 'it is not only without my consent, but in contravention of my direct prohibition' that the Ascot Priory sisters were labouring in East End cholera hospitals and among the Spitalfields slum dwellers.[9]

It rapidly became obvious that outright prohibition of the orders was impossible, because the Anglican Church, having never envisioned such groups, lacked any provision for disciplining them. Unlike most other church institutions, sisterhoods were not created by the Church, but within it. So the church hierarchy, opposed to sisterhoods, was forced to find new means of protecting male prerogative from the incursions of women. Such protection took the form of controlling communities for the ostensible good of everyone, as a York Convocation report made clear.

> these Communities are practically isolated and independent of external control. *Their present isolated position is full of danger alike to the communities and to the English Church* ... They need to be brought under Ecclesiastical control ...

Bishops were advised to 'confine' and 'protect' sisterhoods. As Anne Summers has pointed out, the concern of the male establishment was one of control; 'how best to *harness* the religious and charitable impulses' of women.[10]

In 1866 Archbishop Longley (Canterbury, 1862–68) consulted the bishops on the question of re-establishing religious orders; virtually all of them, he reported, were opposed to the idea. By the time that the bishops came to this conclusion, approximately thirty sisterhoods had been founded. The oldest of these had been functioning successfully within Longley's church for over twenty years. In light of this it is possible to see why Church of England sisters were regarded as virtual 'outlaws' in the eyes of the church hierarchy. Beginning as they did wholly outside the control or regulation of the Church, the move toward conformity with the demands of the episcopacy was slow, and for many sisterhoods was far from complete by the turn of the century. On their side, the bishops did not feel capable of issuing even the most cautious of *official* directives on the subject until 1908. Prebendary Sadler summarized the relations of sisterhoods to the episcopate admirably in a speech given at Convocation in 1878. (The comments from the floor are also instructive.)

> There are at this moment Bishops who would on no account have to do with anything coming under the name of Sisterhoods – ('Hear, hear') – and others who, if they could be induced to have anything to do with them, would impose such regulations as would entirely damp the ardour of the Sisters. ('Hear, hear.')[11]

Some of the episcopal opposition was based on the same essential distrust of women's psychological balance as that which was expressed by those who argued that any structure not headed by men was unnatural and intolerable. Such arguments were frequently couched in alarmingly mysterious and vaguely conspiratorial language.

> there is a particular danger incident to institutions of this kind where a number of ladies live together – a peculiar danger of excitement, which, if they are not under proper control, may tend to dangerous consequences both as regards the welfare of the institution itself and of the effects which it produces. I think it desirable that all those who have such institutions within their sphere should watch over them with great care.[12]

While it is not entirely evident from this warning whether Bishop Thirwall (St David's, 1840–72) feared outbreaks of lesbianism, mass hysteria or even wholesale conversions to Rome, it is clear from the reiterated use of the word 'danger' that he, at least, found the idea of communities of women threatening.

Danger of another type was perceived in the very success of the movement. The rapid growth of the communities meant that in the view of some bishops sisterhoods posed a threat to the popularity, and perhaps even the survival, of the male Church. In 1897 the Bishop of Ely declared that he feared there was 'a real danger' that sisterhoods would in time 'overshadow the Church'. His suggested remedy for over-prominent orders was that the archbishops should be given the power to dissolve any community which grew too powerful. Another, at an 1895 private meeting of the bishops convened to discuss communities, reverted to the idea that sisterhoods were potential sources for the undermining of the church establishment, saying that it was 'the growing independence and lawlessness' of the religious communities which made them a 'peril' to the bench of bishops.[13]

Most arguments used by the episcopate were less alarmist. A common one, used by the bishops as well as by laymen, was to depict women as intrinsically emotional and irresponsible, and therefore incapable of managing the large and complex projects undertaken by communities. To avoid the inevitable chaos that female control would produce, power over the communities should be vested in the bishop; 'the work must be under his personal control and rule; not under the irresponsible rule of any *woman*'.[14] A corollary of this argument was that women were capable of simple administration under male direction, but could not be entrusted with managerial or financial responsibility.

In a debate on sisterhoods in 1878, Prebendary Sellon told his hostile audience that most sisterhoods would have quickly disintegrated if the bishops had been able to interfere with them.[15] This was almost certainly true. Attempts to control communities tended to centre around the issue of vows, despite all Anglican priests also taking a lifetime vow at ordination. Most bishops, including those least hostile to sisterhoods, interdicted the taking of vows until the twentieth century, more than half a century after the first sisterhood had been formed. Most communities believed that they could not survive without the taking of vows, and it was over this issue that the most vigorous battles with the dignitaries of the Church were fought.

It is worth taking a closer look at the attitude toward vows of one bishop, Samuel Wilberforce of Oxford (1845–69). Wilberforce is largely remembered today as 'Soapy Sam', or as the clerical opponent of evolution who publicly debated Huxley. In his own time however, Wilberforce was best known as a bishop with Anglo-Catholic tendencies, and as the most sympathetic to women's communities. The evolution of his attitude towards religious orders is interesting: Wilberforce had originally insisted on episcopal approval before a sisterhood could be founded, but seems to have dropped this when presented with so many *faits accomplis*. He commented in an 1862 debate on sisterhoods that communities refused to become connected with the episcopacy either because of 'a love of independence' or because they knew that the bishop would not approve of all their activities. In this he expressed an opinion common to all bishops who had contact with communities in the nineteenth century. However, despite this, his diocese attracted a large number of communities; partly because of the attraction of Oxford for women influenced by Tractarianism, but primarily because he was the only important member of the episcopate who refrained from active harassment of sisterhoods.

However, Wilberforce's support was invariably conditional on the understanding that the women took no vows in any form. He consistently refused to approve women presented by their communities for profession, because they insisted on the right to take vows.[16] (They were professed anyway, but without his sanction.) Yet Wilberforce's attitude was seen as dangerously encouraging by his brother bishops, since instead of declaring that their gender rendered them incapable of making a religious vow, Wilberforce believed in the binding power of such promises when made by any adult. He apparently refused to allow women to make life commitments because he felt no bishop had the authority to dispense such vows.[17] It must have been intensely frustrating for sisters in Wilberforce's diocese to notice in 1866 that he permitted three *men* to take life vows after only a year's experience of community life. It is hard to see why he felt men were less likely to require dispensation than women, given the notorious instability of Anglican brotherhoods through much of the nineteenth century. (His more approving attitude toward male orders was echoed many years later by the Upper House of Convocation, who recommended that sisters not be allowed to take vows until the age of 30, but that brothers could take them at 25.[18])

Despite the restrictions he attempted to place on women's communities, Wilberforce could be personally supportive. After the first Mother Superior of Wantage joined the Roman Catholic Church during the flood of conversions at the time of the Gorham judgement on baptismal regeneration (which seemed to suggest that the official Establishment policy was anti-sacramental as well as Erastian), Wilberforce visited the community in order to offer support to those who remained; most bishops would have made frantic efforts to distance themselves at such a time. He was also unique in his insistence that the women in these communities should be left to govern themselves, aside from the issue of vows. In later life he seems to have become more interested in the communities' own vision of their mission, rather than in some theoretical idea of church order. Once (at a date unknown) Wilberforce invited the heads of several communities to visit him in order to discuss the general question of sisterhoods.[19] His ties with Wantage, the most male-dominated of the early communities, were relatively strong. He 'instituted' Mother Harriet as Superior in 1854, making her 'the first ecclesiastically appointed Superior in an English house of this kind since the Reformation.'[20]

In general communities seem to have quietly ignored the prohibitions against vows, and most took at least a modified vow at profession from very early on, irrespective of episcopal directives. The Archbishop of Canterbury complained of 'the secret, dishonest profession which they [the sisterhoods] have surreptitiously, though long before my time, introduced'. Some communities did not even preserve the fiction of obedience by taking the vows in secret. Ascot Priory took vows in open defiance of their bishop's expressed sentiments.[21] All Saints sisters took permanent vows from the beginning, and explained away the clause in their Constitution which stated that no life vows were taken (which had been added at the insistence of Tait, when Bishop of London) by saying that it was there for legal reasons only. Whether the vows were taken openly or in secret, the communities justified this on the grounds that what a group of women living together chose to do was their own business. Most communities at one time or another resorted to this 'family' defence to avoid episcopal protection or persecution. In this they argued that communities were essentially 'families of ladies', and therefore bishops had no more right to interfere with them than they would with any private family. When the Sisters of the Church began work in Australia the Bishop of Sydney protested that they had not sought his approval. Mother Emily wrote to the sisters:

> we cannot see that, in asserting our civil and religious liberty, to take up our abode wherever the voice of God seems to call us, we are guilty of the smallest disrespect to any Ecclesiastical authority ... what are we but an *enlarged Christian family*, and would any family of Church people, about to emigrate to one of our Colonies, dream of writing first to the clergy and bishops to ask if it would annoy them should they land on its shores?[22]

While usually the office of containment did centre around the issue of vows, it sometimes had a second, financial focus. This typically arose from bishops' attempts to remove financial control from the hands of community members. Bishops with sisterhoods in their dioceses were advised to prohibit communities from holding property in their own right. It was felt better to place all the property under the control of a group of male trustees; sisters, it was suggested, should view their convents as nothing more than 'places of retirement when disabled or in old age'.[23] This was manifestly unfair in that it ignored the fact that community property almost invariably came from the donations of the founding sisters. Obviously, no community ever came to regard their motherhouse as a nursing home for superannuated sisters, or as belonging to someone other than themselves. The financial argument was partly based upon resentment. After all, if these devout and well-heeled spinsters had not chosen to pour their money into the establishment and maintenance of religious communities, it was more than probable that not a little of their funds would have found its way into the coffers of church-run charities or enriched ecclesiastical fund-raising drives.

A good example of the problems which could be caused by financial interference was the experience of the Sisters of the Church with the Archbishop of Canterbury (E. W. Benson) in the 1890s. When Benson expressed a wish to examine the community's books, he also indicated that he would first exact a pledge that the community would agree to anything he suggested. The sisterhood's tactical manoeuvres, which essentially rendered him unable to act and which will be discussed below, were indicative of the ways in which sisterhoods responded to such requests. No bishop actually managed to wrest community holdings from community hands, largely because sisterhoods were not afraid of litigation and the accompanying negative publicity when their financial survival was in question.

Sometimes episcopal efforts at containment were seen as little more than a face-saving measure for the church hierarchy. Many were inclined to view episcopal sanction for sisterhoods as making the best of a bad job:

> We cannot stop the system. We might as well attempt to dam up the course of a river as to arrest the stream of female piety and charity which we see extending itself in so many, though often irregular, channels ... We cannot stop the stream; let us try to direct it aright ... into lawful channels under proper authority.[24]

Attempts at containment eventually came to centre on convincing communities to acknowledge that they were in some sort of special relationship to the episcopate. (It must be remembered that some clergy opposed even the idea of creating general rules for sisterhoods because they felt that even such indirect and confining sanction would 'touch upon dangerous ground'.) Sisterhoods did not always relish the idea of relationship: the 1870 inquiry into convents discovered that Anglican sisterhoods saw themselves as subject, not to the Archbishop of Canterbury, but to their Statutes. The private report of the Committee of Bishops into 'The Relation of Sisterhoods and Brotherhoods to the Diaconate' in 1885 concluded that 'nothing but good can arise from Communities of devout women' but that this depended on communities 'living and working in due subordination to the Church's Order and System, and under the authority of the appointed Rulers of the Church'.[25]

Bishop Creighton (London, 1897–1901) concluded that 'the bad point about sisterhoods' was that they wanted 'to be absolutely independent, obedient only to their own will'.[26] That there seems to have been some truth to this is indicated by the remarkable slowness with which the sisterhoods began to seek a formal association with the episcopate. In one very real sense, their Anglicanism was self-defined. Ascot Priory, founded in 1848, got its first visitor (Bishop Mackarness, Oxford, 1870–88) in 1880. East Grinstead, founded in 1855, 'entered into official relations with its diocesan for the first time' in 1895.[27] The Society of the Sisters of Bethany, founded in 1866, selected Bishop Temple (London, 1885–96) as their first visitor in 1889. The Community of Reparation to Jesus in the Blessed Sacrament, founded in 1869, had their first contact with a bishop (by letter) in 1897. The Sisters of the Church, founded in 1870, politely but firmly made it understood in 1903 that they were quite content without a visitor and that they did not wish the Bishop of London (Winnington-Ingram, 1901–39) to become officially associated with the community, although he would be welcome to visit as anyone else might.[28]

There were of course advantages to the communities in being outsiders; most importantly, there were no sanctions which could be imposed on those already outside the pale. Unlike Anglican clergy, who could be brought into line by the Consistory Courts as a last resort, sisters could not be punished by the church authorities. The sisters, outlaws already because of the attitudes of the bishops, had unprecedented liberty of action as a result.

Archbishop Benson (Canterbury, 1883–96) summarized the attitude of most of the Anglican hierarchy toward the sisterhoods in his own position: 'I have long considered that the attitude of certain Sisterhoods to their Diocesans is quite unwarrantable; they adopt a position of independence which is absolutely inconsistent with their profession.'[29] Benson was apparently unaware that a sister's vow of obedience was made to the Rule of her community, not to the local bishop, or even the archbishop. After an 1889 visit to the Sisters of the Church, Benson confided to his diary:

Here all was dignity, gravity, silence, beauty – most eager work for 600 orphans – two great chapels building – went to the embroidery room where many hundreds of ... complete sets of vestments ... are annually made and sent out to priests over the whole world. I told the Sister in Charge to communicate to the Mother Superior, who was at Broadstairs, my opinion that 'they are a very formidable body' – which amused her. The idea of 'putting down Ritualism' which a large number of these magnificent bodies are sedulously propagating with every advantage worldly and spiritual – their own saintly lives first and foremost. 'Agree with thine adversary quickly' is rather the course that now seems practicable.[30]

However, judging from his later clashes with the community, Benson soon seems to have regained his fighting spirit.

Bishop Phillpots of Exeter (1831–69), while originally welcoming the formation of Ascot Priory in his diocese, soon withdrew his approval, although he conceded that he could not find fault with the work Ascot Priory was doing in the Devonshire ports. According to Phillpots, the problem was one of authority: the Sisters ignored his instructions and disagreed with his claim to 'inquire into all the internal arrangements of a community of ladies'. Mother Lydia responded by issuing a pamphlet in which she retorted that the community was entirely independent of him: they did not consult the Bishop in cases of difficulty, that he had only once been conferred with on an internal matter, and that he had visited them on one occasion. She concluded by asserting that essentially the Bishop had no knowledge of the community beyond the published rules.[31] Phillpot's real reason for withdrawing his 'sanction' seems to have been his shocked response to the nation-wide outpouring of hostility toward the new venture.

The Bishop of Lincoln (Edward King, 1885–1910) tried in vain to 'get the Kilburn sisters [the Sisters of the Church] to obey authority but they would not'.[32] In the eyes of the bishops, this sisterhood was from its inception a particularly worrying community. Ayckbowm's disdain for the church hierarchy, as expressed on numerous occasions in her diaries, was apparently no secret to the clerical establishment. As a result, the community was singled out for special attack, especially in the 1890s, when (among other things) it was described as 'uniquely irregular, amorphous and abnormal with no spiritual head or visitor, Diocesan or provincial, under a Superior apparently as absolutely independent and autocratic as General Booth'. The community barely avoided censure by the Bishops in 1895 for its extreme independence. In a private meeting the Bishop of Peterborough (Mandell Creighton, 1891–97) bewailed the fact that within the Anglican Church no form of excommunication existed; if one could be found, he suggested, the members of the Sisters of the Church should be excommunicated.[33]

Church leaders began to doubt the Anglicanism of Church of England sisterhoods, Anglicanism being apparently defined (against all precedent!) as a general willingness to obey episcopal directions. Archbishop Benson described Ayckbowm's sisterhood as 'a dissenting community owning no Bishops or authority of any kind', concluding with yet another expression of the danger of such groups: 'there are no worse mines under the Church than such bodies'.[34] During his time at Lambeth, Frederick Temple went to the extreme of having an announcement inserted in *The Times* to the effect that 'the Archbishop of Canterbury ... does not recognise the Kilburn Sisters [the Sisters of the Church] in any way whatever'. The community retained its reputation for lawlessness after Ayckbowm's death; when a dispute over authority arose in 1903, the Archbishop of Canterbury wrote to the Bishop of London, warning him of, as he put it, 'the story of her triumphant progress trampling upon every authority in days gone by'.[35] The community's reluctance to subordinate itself to the church hierarchy is not surprising when one considers the Bishop of Worcester's advice on the treatment of women church workers: 'They are very willing horses to the collar; they desire the rein, and indeed may not be altogether unforgiving to the whip, when it is only just cracked over the ears.'[36] In the case of women's religious communities at least, the harness was not worn by the sisters.

Despite their reluctance to enter into official relations with the episcopate, sisterhoods did not hesitate to call the higher levels of the Church to their assistance when local clergy became troublesome. This strategy could also be used against the priests who were associated with communities. On one occasion the Archbishop of Canterbury was forced, after a number of letters of complaint from senior sisters, to write to the warden of All Saints (R. M. Benson), instructing him to stop interfering in the community's selection of a new Mother Superior. Although Benson seems to have ceased to promote 'his' (ultimately unsuccessful) candidate, he later put a great deal of pressure on the new Mother Superior to change the statutes of the community to give the chaplain more authority. When Mother Caroline Mary refused to sign any new regulations, insisting that the Statutes must reflect 'the generous freedom which characterizes the spirit of our foundation', Benson was prevailed upon by the Archbishop to desist.[37]

One area where the bishops were important was fund-raising. It was common practice for sisterhoods to attach the name of a bishop or bishops to their printed appeals, so as to raise the cachet of their efforts and convey that they enjoyed episcopal approval for their good works, even if not of their communal life. Some communities used bishops as bait for their fund-raising for only as long as the bishops remained quiescent; if they proved troublesome, they were removed. The Sisters of the Church calmly dropped the Archbishop of Canterbury from its list of patrons when he insisted on inquiring into the internal government of the community. When he protested against his summary removal, they assured him that he was much too busy to have time for such a minor group as themselves. When the Archbishop insisted that he had the right to interfere and demanded a promise from the community that they would obey his directives, the Sisters of the Church refused to make any promise of obedience, saying that 'twenty years experience and God's guidance could not be lightly gone against', thus effectively ending the dispute. Another sisterhood simply severed their connection with the Archbishop when he objected to their choice of a new chaplain.[38]

Oddly enough, women who were rejected by sisterhoods sometimes appealed to the relevant bishop or to the archbishop in the hope that church authority could convince or force the community to reconsider. Bishops were also appealed to by the other side; irate families often resorted to writing to the bishop in a last-ditch attempt to prevent a daughter or sister from entering a community.[39] Episcopal authority could, of course, do nothing in such cases. Sisterhoods made the final decision about whom they would admit into their communities.

Community responses to authority

Most sisterhoods throughout the nineteenth century remained essentially free from supervision by their diocesan or other bishop. Some successfully avoided coming into contact with any episcopal authority whatever. The small amount of contact which did take place was normally nominal, and extremely formal in its nature. Sisters also managed to circumvent direct prohibitions when they felt it was necessary; for example, the Park Village sisterhood, forbidden to pray for the dead, inserted a pause in their office at the place where the prayers were usually recited. In this pause the prayers were said silently. Similarly, Ascot Priory showed only an extremely abbreviated (one might say expurgated) version of their Rule to the bishop.[40] Hope Stone, in her excellent (and regrettably unpublished) research describes this sort of contact with the episcopate as the 'façade of compliance'.[41]

In the face of virtually unanimous disapproval from the leaders of the Church of England, the communities developed several effective strategies for coping with clerical authority. These included severing ties with the local bishop, opening houses in another diocese and thus confusing the issue of whose direction they were under, moving to another diocese, passive forms of equivocation, lobbying in protest, and simple defiance. When they felt their autonomy was threatened, sisterhoods launched organized letter-writing campaigns, singly or in cooperation with other communities. In 1862 Convocation was deluged with letters from sisterhoods deprecating episcopal imposition after the House of Laity recommended that the bishops form

Rules for sisterhoods. The idea was abandoned.[42] The Sisters of the Church used a similar strategy in the 1890s, mobilizing former orphans to write to Lambeth in the sisterhood's support, by defending their treatment while in the community's care.

Sisters found greater freedom from episcopal authority when working in more than one diocese. With some communities working in over half-a-dozen bishoprics, the problem of coordinating episcopal authority was used as the rationale for never seeking it. One writer compared them unfavourably with deaconesses in this respect: 'The sisterhoods are more independent in their character, not confining themselves to any particular diocese, nor always feeling it necessary to seek the Bishop's sanction before invading one.'[43] Perhaps the real root of episcopal hostility towards sisterhoods can be found in a comment made by the Bishop of Wakefield in 1897, a few months before his own death, in yet another of the interminable discussions of the 'problem' of sisterhoods: 'communities live and Bishops die'.[44] In the late nineteenth century, it would have been a rare bishop who did not feel that the sisterhoods were competing with the episcopate for the affection of the people, and generally winning.

Attitudes of priests

Sisterhoods experienced two types of relationship with the less exalted Anglican clergy: first, most communities had a priest co-founder, an important role which will be described below. Second, it was inevitable that any sisterhood working in a parish would come into contact with the local clergy. This local and unchosen relationship was necessarily a sensitive one. But let us first examine the most common causes for priestly disapproval of sisterhoods.

Sisters were often disliked by clergy because they could be perceived as somehow usurping their priestly role. This strand of opposition seems to have sprung from the idea that becoming a sister was in some way equivalent to becoming a priest, or might be seen to be so. Throughout the century, sisters were constantly being compared, directly or implicitly, to the clergy. One advocate wrote that their 'real character' was a calling equivalent to the priesthood. Opposition based on the clerical nature of sisters expressed 'fears and jealousies of a woman-power in the Church, which in fact would be a priestly power'. Some writers used this as another reason why sisterhoods should not be recognized by the Church. Stephenson concluded that episcopal recognition would be undesirable because it would give a 'semi-clerical character' to sisters.[45] One indignant anti-ritualist complained to his bishop that in his parish church 'the celebrating priest was accompanied by an assistant and eight veiled females', implying (almost certainly falsely) that the sisters were actively participating in the Celebration. Indeed, Sister Benedicta Ward concludes that the religious life was presented to women by the Tractarians as directly equivalent to the consecration through ordination to the priesthood.[46]

Not only was there a danger that women in communities might appear priestlike in the eyes of the theologically illiterate. Sisters, it was asserted, had already abrogated the authority and role of the clergy. It was seen as sinister by opponents of sisterhoods that the Mother Superior of one community carried a pastoral staff similar to that of a bishop. (In actuality, most Mothers Superior employed such symbolic objects in community rituals.) Another writer attacked All Hallows with the claim that the community had celebrated '*an ordination of the Lady Superior* ... very similar in character to that of the ordination of clergy'.[47] The wilder opponents of sisterhoods made this anxiety very explicit; take for example this accusation by an anti-convent lecturer against the Ascot Priory community.

> It is the first time ... in the whole history of the Church of Christ, that we read of such a thing as a female confessional; but perhaps ... our Tractarian friends are resolved that we shall have an order of Priestesses![48]

Hobart Seymour's statement above indicates that Ascot Priory's founder, Lydia Sellon, was believed to be hearing confessions, a shocking violation of both clerical prerogative and Protestant practice. In the distant past women religious had usurped the functions of male priests: they baptized infants in preference to a priest doing so, offered prayers in church, staffed the confessional, preached and celebrated the Eucharist. These abuses, claimed one Victorian clergyman sympathetic to sisterhoods, meant that such orders needed to be suppressed; and he cautions that women working in an unauthorized fashion in sisterhoods might eventually behave so again.[49] Sisterhoods indignantly denied any desire to move outside their non-priestly role. However, in actual parish work, sisters sometimes experienced pressure to take on priestly functions. The Community of Reparation, working in Southwark in the 1870s, found that the women in the Lambeth slums preferred to have the sisters baptize infants than to have this rite performed by a priest; some women also wanted sisters to perform other priestly functions, such as conducting the service called 'churching', normally celebrated after a woman had recovered from childbirth.[50] It is significant that these female religious professionals were seen as the appropriate persons to carry out rituals with a strongly female orientation, especially those that related to childbirth.

The vexed question of vows also became tangled with the argument that women were claiming a role analogous to that of a priest. The vows taken in community, argued those who favoured them, were equivalent to those taken by the clergy. The key assumption in this argument was that God could call women as he called men, and that both genders were capable of making a life-long commitment in response to that call. E. B. Pusey, who was associated with a number of the earlier sisterhoods, soon came to conclude that the vocations were equivalent:

> almost every objection which has been raised has arisen in *men's* ignoring or denying the possibility that God could call women to devote their lives to works of mercy ... But as we, the clergy, are expected to come to a conviction that [priests are called to their work by God] ..., so it must be possible for women to come to the same conviction ... *To deny the possibility that women can know that they are so called, is to deny the possibility that God could call them.*[51]

The church preferred deaconess orders as the channel for women's work, because of their reputation for obedience to episcopal authority. Sisterhoods were never under church control in the same way or to the same extent that deaconesses were. Archbishop Tait expressed his satisfaction with the three deaconess orders he was associated with, where 'anything I objected to as to dress, mode of life, or any other point, would be at once altered'. The Community of All Saints, on the other hand, permitted him no such say in such internal matters.[52] The work of the deaconess was typically described in extremely passive and subservient terms, as in this passage by Cecilia Robinson, founder of the most important of the deaconess institutions. 'The Deaconess is the servant of the Clergy; she does not plan out her own work, but receives it from her Vicar ... [she is a] handmaid of the Church.'[53]

Many contemporary writers on deaconesses expressed puzzlement over why they attracted so many fewer applicants than did sisterhoods. After all, they reasoned, deaconess institutions had the incalculable advantage of being closely and constantly supervised by the local clergy. The low recruitment figures for all deaconess associations throughout the nineteenth century suggest that this close contact may not have been as attractive to women as men liked to think. (It has been calculated that there were no more than 180

Anglican deaconesses by 1900.[54] This may in part have been because another Low Church option for women, the Church Army, was founded in 1887, and there may have been some competition for personnel.) My research suggests that the attrition rate for deaconesses was much higher than for sisters (close to 50 per cent), indicating a higher level of discontent with the life the deaconess orders offered. According to one contemporary observer, sisterhoods were preferred to deaconess orders for three reasons: communities were established by individuals, deaconess orders by committees; the ritualistic 'spirit of the age' attracted young and modern minds into sisterhoods, which reflected that spirit; and sisterhoods offered a permanent home, while deaconess orders did not.[55] However unpopular the deaconess orders were with potential members, they did receive their reward. The Archbishop of Canterbury and eighteen bishops gave formal recognition to their 'general principles' in 1871.[56] But women continued to avoid the deaconess option as envisioned by the hierarchy: the largest and most successful of them, the Deaconess Community of St Andrew, quickly became a sisterhood in all but name.[57]

Further evidence that this very freedom from clerical management might have been attractive to women can be found in articles written to promote sisterhoods among women who might be considering the life. These generally placed great stress on the autonomy of the community and on the pre-eminence of the elected Mother Superior; the clergy were rarely mentioned. One sister, responding to claims that women went into sisterhoods because they enjoyed being bullied by priests, protested, asserting the 'very little clerical guidance many Sisters receive: much less than falls to the lot of many women in the world'.[58] This statement could certainly be seen as implying that this lack of contact was perceived as one advantage of community life for devout women.

Priest co-founders

The doctrinal position taken by sisterhoods ensured that all priests associated with them would have been Tractarian or High Church, at a time when this allegiance was itself repugnant to the church hierarchy. The priests who were close to communities were, in a sense, maverick or rebel clergy, already in conflict with the episcopate. Because these men were in open and well-publicized rebellion against the accepted standards of their church, it is not surprising that women seeking a life wider than that found in the home were attracted to this subversive strand within Anglicanism. John Mason Neale was actually an inhibited priest when he co-founded the Community of St Margaret at East Grinstead; this meant he had been banned from the performance of normal clerical duties by the bishop of the diocese.[59] So even the clergy associated with sisterhoods shared their escape from the 'enervating influence of respectability' suffered by deaconesses.

The role of the priest co-founder has been misunderstood in the past. Virtually all writers on the subject have assumed, on very little evidence, that one man could, from the outside, create a way of life for a group of which he could never be a member.[60] This error stems from the first foundation of sisterhoods, and carries within it the assumption, so dear to the Victorians, that unassisted women could never achieve anything worth doing. It was concisely put by one of the earliest commentators on the growth of communities for women, and its open expression reveals its illogic: 'In our own time ... earnest *men* have been endeavouring to re-establish the true ideal of woman's work in the Church.' The eminent church historian E. R. Norman writes of the 'well-known band of slum priests whose work among the poor was one of the most noble achievements of the Victorian Church'.[61] Curiously, almost every priest listed worked in a parish which also had a sisterhood whose vocation was work among the poor: it seems probable that historians have sometimes given one hardworking priest credit for labours carried out by dozens of women, creating the myth of the superhuman priest and effectively erasing the women from history.

The habit of most historians of relying on biographies of priests for information about sisterhoods means that the role of the men has been magnified beyond all correspondence with reality. While it is natural for the biographer to place his subject centre-stage at all times, this may bear little relation to the reality of his role in some organizations. An examination of community records makes it very clear that the men involved in their foundation usually played a peripheral role, and generally dropped well into the background as the sisterhood's life developed.

For many communities, the role of the co-founder was useful and important, particularly in the early years; however, it was not absolutely necessary for the survival and well-being of a sisterhood; some large and successful sisterhoods had no co-founder at all. As one sister advised, 'No clergyman can begin such a society, ... he may ... foster and employ it after it has come into being, but he cannot create it.'[62] There is evidence that the sisterhoods themselves saw having a male co-founder as convenient rather than necessary; he served as midwife, not progenitor. The co-founder seems often to have been something of a figurehead, used to deflect criticism that the women involved in founding the group were lawless. Stone's concept of the 'façade of compliance' is again applicable here. Emily Ayckbowm, who did not seem to have a high opinion of men in general, deliberately formed her community in such a way that the Sisters of the Church's chaplain had 'no say whatsoever' within the community. She confided to her diary, 'It is very seldom that the suggestions of priests (however good and holy men they may be) would not do more harm than good to a Sisterhood.'[63] Most priests who actually had long and intimate contact with sisterhoods, like Charles Grafton and E. B. Pusey, came to believe that the idea of a man 'founding' a sisterhood was absurd. Grafton wrote:

> Clergymen think they would like a sisterhood in their parish, and, without any special knowledge, they form one of their own. Now a sisterhood is a school for the formation of a special character. This requires long and special training. But I have been asked to give the rules of a sisterhood, as if it could be made off-hand from a receipt.[64]

It should be noted that a male co-founder was not essential to the establishment of a community, although that tended to be the most common pattern. Not all communities had co-founders, and these communities tended to be more original in composition than the others. Ayckbowm's extraordinarily fast-growing Sisters of the Church had no clerical ties, and the first sisterhood to survive, Sellon's Ascot Priory, was entirely her own creation, absorbing the committee-created and priest-ridden Park Village sisterhood less than ten years after its foundation. As the founder of the Sisters of the Church tartly observed,

> In real truth the only Sisterhoods (in the English Church) that have done well, have been originated by women; and men have made such a mess of Religious Communities among themselves that it is absurd they should try to subject Sisterhoods now to their control.[65]

Like the Sisters of the Church, the Society of the Sisters of Bethany had no priest associated with their foundation at all. Their founder, Etheldreda Benett, is said to have remarked that she did not wish the religious to be known as 'Mr. ___'s Sisters'.[66] Bethany was the first community to explicitly reject the idea that the usefulness of sisterhood work was the only acceptable apologia for community life. From the outset of the Church's response to sisterhoods the Church had felt it necessary to discriminate between the active work and the lifestyle of communities; while the work was sometimes welcome, this was never the case with regard to the corporate life of the sisterhood. One of Bethany's major contributions was its insistence that women who wished to live a life of contemplation within the Anglican Church had the right to do so. It is even possible to see in the move to contemplation among a number of communities around the turn of the century a move away from external male control. The contemplative life made the sisterhoods which chose it more inner-directed and less susceptible to pressures based upon the mid-Victorian ideal of woman's ministering role as being expressed through the care of others.

Even in communities where the priest co-founder exerted real authority at first, he commonly lost influence over time, as the sisters gained confidence in their ability to run the community and as their numbers grew. One of the early sisterhoods, the Nursing Sisters of St John the Divine, soon refused to let the 'Master' have any voice in the internal workings of the group. When in 1869 the co-founder of the Community of the Holy Rood disagreed with the sisters' desire to take vows, the Mother Foundress, Teresa Newcomen, forced his hand by threatening to resign, knowing that there was no one who could replace her. Mother Teresa very definitely saw herself as the originator of the community, refusing the advice of priests who ventured to make suggestions.[67] Some co-founders expressed a respect for male authority in theory which they were unwilling or unable to carry out in practice. T. T. Carter, associated with Clewer, wrote to a friend, 'a *male* spiritual superior needs to have authority ... otherwise the female element has it all its own way ...'[68] Carter himself seems to have been often unable to exert this kind of authority over Clewer; evidently it was common knowledge that the Mother Superior, when she wished, could lead him by the nose.[69]

Only one large sisterhood had effectively strong clerical control throughout most of the nineteenth century. This was Wantage, founded by J. Butler and Elizabeth Crawford Lockhart in 1848. When Lockhart left the Anglican Church in response to the Gorham judgement, taking all the sisters except two with her, the authority gap thus created was to a certain extent filled by Butler himself. This may have been due in part to his upper-class status, as the Mother who replaced Lockhart was the daughter of a small farmer. Butler believed that, when there was a conflict between his authority and that of the Mother Superior of Wantage, his ought to take precedence. Despite this, he did not interfere in the most important area of all: the community's mission. The early sisters decided to change the sisterhood's work from education to penitentiaries, and Butler was powerless to stop them. In the light of the experience of other communities with strong ties to priests it is perhaps unsurprising that Wantage did not begin its period of rapid growth until after Butler's death.[70]

Not all clergy involved with the formation of sisterhoods believed that strong male guidance was necessary or desirable. John Mason Neale, the co-founder of East Grinstead, believed that sisterhoods would flourish despite the floundering of brotherhoods, because women were 'much better managers of these things than men'. Moreover, Neale did not feel that East Grinstead's autonomy ought to be an isolated instance. He advised a priest who was hoping to start a sisterhood in Liverpool that a community should be managed by its members.

> The governing body must be the Chapter and the Mother; ... the Priest should have no official authority. With ten years experience, I know that this is right. And were I a Sister, I would not for a second be under a Lay Treasurer.[71]

Another priest who co-founded a sisterhood found the idea that he controlled their activities amusing, despite his proprietorial pronoun. 'As for my *letting* them do it, not all the vicars in the Kingdom drawn up in a row, with all the police four deep behind them, could stop my Sisters.'[72]

It is clear that sisters themselves disapproved of overly-involved clergy interfering with community life. One sister described the problems of an unnamed embryonic sisterhood where a priest 'employed sisters' but refused to allow them to develop a unified community life. She clearly saw his over-involvement and the resulting lack of community support and structure as the root cause why the group could not retain members.

> Many women, of various characters, and belonging to various schools of religious opinion, ... have entered that House with thorough determination to devote themselves to the excellent work carried on within its walls, but no one permanently remains there ... one good woman after another leaves the work she heartily loves, either to return into the outer world, or to enter some regularly organised Sisterhood, of which she soon becomes a valuable and valued member.[73]

This portrait of one failing community was applicable to them all. It is strikingly obvious when one compares those communities which floundered with those that flourished, that a long period of strong clerical leadership was consistently detrimental to community survival. One example will suffice: with all his holiness, and despite the high esteem in which he was held by the Oxford Movement, E. B. Pusey had a consistently detrimental effect on any community with which he got involved. Given his insistence on a morbidly penitential spirituality, combined with his love of interfering (it is said that he once lifted the lid from a saucepan in a community kitchen and announced reprovingly 'These potatoes are too large for Holy Poverty'), it should not surprise us that any community he had much to do with remained small, chaotic and weak.

Another common feature of weaker or failed sisterhoods was the ejection of the Mother Superior. This key individual most commonly left as a result of the tensions arising from co-founder interference with the life of the community. The priest co-founder would chose a more tractable replacement, who then proved unable to attract women to the community. This occurred at both the Missionary Community of St Denys and the Wymering sisterhood of St Mary the Virgin. The Wymering sisterhood's experience was typical. When Wymering began to experience conflict with the co-founder, the sisters turned to the Superior of an older, well-established community for advice. The Mother of All Saints warned Wymering's Mother Superior against allowing the priest to 'assume the position he did' in the sisterhood. She also recommended that the community insist on having a proper Constitution. Wymering's Mother Superior eventually left as a result of the chaplain's insistence that he should be in control, and she established the Community of the Holy Comforter at Worthing in 1887.[74] This was not an isolated instance. The first Mother Superior of the Missionary Community of St Denys left the community after sixteen years of governing it, as the result of conflict with the priest co-founder over the nature of the Constitution.

When all else failed, sisterhoods would make a break from a co-founder who wished to rule the community from without. The Community of St Mary and St Scholastica broke away from their male co-founder (the notorious maverick, Brother Ignatius) after he refused to acknowledge Mother Hilda's authority. She was a more talented and more capable leader than he was, and found his interfering intolerable and many of his practices nonsensical.[75] All of the sisters of the Nursing Sisters of St John the Divine, except one, left to form a new community when the council running their affairs attempted to restrict their liberty. Some sisterhoods avoided an open breach by geographic relocation. The Community of the Holy Cross, like several other Victorian communities, simply moved out of their co-founder's parish, and thus out of his sphere of influence, after the community had developed to the point where it was capable of complete autonomy. The Community of Reparation marked their change of direction after the death of their domineering co-founder (he had advised them to study *his* mind in order to discover the true meaning of community!) by changing the community's name from the very particular Mission Sisters of St Alphage (a parish in Southwark where their co-founder had been vicar) to the far more universal Community of Reparation to Jesus in the Blessed Sacrament.

Many of the women who founded communities seem to have been sensitive to the hazards of priestly interference. The Society of the Holy and Undivided Trinity refused an otherwise attractive offer of amalgamation with the Community of St Thomas Martyr because the warden of St Thomas Martyr insisted on directing the community's affairs, both internal and external.[76] In fact St Thomas Martyr never managed to shake off their warden's yoke: an obituary remarked that with regard to the sisterhood, he 'exercised supervision over it to the hour of his death'; perhaps not coincidentally, the community remained small and chaotic and never achieved stability. During the nineteenth century, it lost 50 per cent of its members, either by their leaving, often to join other sisterhoods, or through expulsion. And the instability was not confined to the community's rank and file: one Mother Superior was ejected from the sisterhood by vote of Chapter for failing to observe the Rule.[77]

The chaplain

One other area of potential male dominance remained, even for communities which had successfully avoided becoming subordinate to their co-founder. This was interference from the priest whom the community chose as its chaplain. On one level, active male cooperation in sisterhoods was always essential; the sacrament was the focus of community worship, and the celebration of the Eucharist required an ordinand to perform it. (All communities eventually moved to daily celebration in their own chapels: however, initially, many simply attended the parish church on Sundays, and took the sacrament there.) This, at its most limited, was the role of the chaplain, but some priests who served as chaplains saw the community as coming under their control in larger ways. This may have been due to traditional male ideas about the natural subordination of women, but since the chaplains were actually employed by the sisters (they were normally paid a salary by the community), it seems likely that they believed that they should participate in the governance of the community as an aspect of clerical privilege.[78]

After the death of its founder, the extremely forceful and charismatic

Mother Harriet, the Community of All Saints experienced a classic struggle for control between the chaplain, R. M. Benson, and the community's senior sisters. Benson initially attempted to exploit the power vacuum by striving to influence the election of the new Mother. In a letter to the Archbishop of Canterbury Benson made his perspective clear, describing himself as the 'real Head of the Community, to whom obedience is due even more than to the Mother'. On another occasion he wrote that he viewed the 'Chaplain as the backbone of the Community. A meeting of the Sisters without the Chaplain, would not be a meeting of the *Community* and therefore not a real chapter.' Benson himself, however, was forced to admit that the 'autocracy' of the chaplain was a new doctrine which he was trying, with little success, to teach All Saints. In the lifetime of the Mother Foundress he had 'just advised and backed up the Mother and came forward in Chapter when she asked me to'. After receiving letters of protest from the All Saints sisters, the Archbishop compelled Benson to stop interfering in internal affairs. R. M. Benson clearly wanted to 'over-chaplain' the Society, as his later (unsuccessful) attempts to convince the new Mother to change the Rule, in a manner which would have given him more authority, show.[79]

When the Society of the Holy and Undivided Trinity was searching for a new chaplain in 1893 Mother Marion's notes on one candidate are illuminating: she began by saying that she has been advised that it is always

> better to be under than over Chaplained and in this case it proved quite true for when we came to enter into detail Mr. Hudson proposed some absurd points [involving the imposition of 'his will' on the community] ... I could in no way accept [this] so Mr. Hudson will not be the Chaplain ... such a Chaplain would be intolerable ...

The essential difference of opinion was made explicit in a later diary entry: 'the curious views he [the candidate for the chaplaincy] had upon the duty of a Chaplain which seems to me to interfere ... with the authority of the Mother Superior ...'[80] The Society of the Holy and Undivided Trinity was not alone in believing that a strong chaplain could damage a community's development. Ayckbowm advised her sisters, 'avoid being over-chaplained, over-committeed, over-managed, from without. I have seen much evil and much disappointment accrue from such a system. [Sisters] ... are the people best fitted to make their own rules and laws.'[81] Accordingly, most communities carefully crafted Rules ensuring that the election and deposition of chaplains remained the prerogative of Chapter. Some communities scrupulously made explicit the limitations of the warden's authority in their Constitutions: nominated and elected by the sisters, he had no financial or 'internal' authority, and could attend Chapter meetings only if summoned by the sisters. While there he had no vote.[82] Chaplains in such communities were clerical lapdogs, aside from their important sacramental role. This deliberate reduction of the chaplain's role in Chapter was probably necessary, as the men involved with sisterhoods sometimes found the consensus-seeking style of their councils difficult to tolerate. The Archbishop of Canterbury was told by one disgruntled warden that 'A woman has not the capacity, except very rarely, of grasping a subject constitutionally.' An Episcopalian bishop with considerable experience of communities gave the following advice to his Church of England peers in 1897:

> Then again there is government by a Chapter. Now women are not fitted for Parliamentary government. When things have to be settled and voted upon they do not agree but go on talking constantly.[83]

It is clear that this former community chaplain had been unable to dominate Chapter to his satisfaction.

Several communities, while tolerating chaplains because of their need for regular administration of the Eucharist, were quite ready to ignore the advice they proffered in other respects. Mother Emily of the Sisters of the Church, after a day spent discussing community rules with Sister Miriam of East Grinstead, recorded the following in her diary:

> Sister Miriam ... talked about the Cowley Fathers and the curious stress they lay upon bodily mortification. She thinks them utterly ignorant of the real temptations of women in Communities; and they therefore direct their teaching against evils which have no existence, and they even create these evils by the penances and remedies they suggest e.g. hair-shirts – chains etc. She says the Mother of East Grinstead is *certain* this is the case. What she said almost made me determine to have nothing ...[84]

When conflict between chaplain and Mother Superior arose, the chaplain, as a paid employee, tended to be worsted. There are many instances in the records of chaplains being given notice; some communities went through half a dozen chaplains in as many years, while they sought one who would not attempt to be 'masterful': an often-used word to summarize the attitude of an unsatisfactory chaplain-employee.

Parish priests

While not formally linked to sisterhoods in any fashion, parish priests posed a different set of problems. One of the most potentially destructive was when a local priest viewed a sisterhood located within his parish as 'his' sisterhood. Many initially enthusiastic clergymen experienced 'disappointment and disgust' when they discovered that sisterhoods saw themselves as more than just a parochial convenience and labour-saving device for local clergy. The founder of one early community claimed that her group was opposed by the clergy because she did not permit them to meddle with the sisterhood's projects or allow them to treat the sisters like district visitors.[85] Richard Littledale, who worked closely with East Grinstead's branch house in London, warned a correspondent that attempts at 'parish sisterhoods' were doomed to failure:

> a Parish Priest ought not to be director of a Sisterhood; ... I know not of one instance ... where the connexion, if kept up, has not proved harmful either to the Parish or the Sisterhood – often to both. A Parish Sisterhood must remain small and must become narrow; small, because there is not scope for many members; narrow, because of the limited field.[86]

E. B. Pusey argued on practical grounds against the idea that sisters should work under the parochial clergy. 'Those who in each society direct their works are, in these special works, far more experienced than our younger clergy, who are young enough to be their sons or much younger brothers; ... they ought not to need instruction in what has been the employment of their life.'[87] These clergy offered women a rare chance to be treated like professionals whose opinion and experiences were of value; not coincidentally, both Pusey and Littledale were connected with a number of religious orders for women.

The enduring struggle between the Evangelical and Anglo-Catholic wings of the church was sometimes fought out over the issue of sisterhoods. When this dispute confined itself to paper it was of little practical importance to the communities. It became a danger to community survival when a sisterhood, established in the parish of a sympathetic or indifferent priest, found itself, after a change of benefice, under an actively Evangelical incumbent. Strict Evangelicals placed great emphasis on the utter subordination of women to the private sphere. To men of this stamp, these undocile women were doubly dangerous, thanks to the Evangelical horror of anything reminiscent of the Church of Rome. Typical of this kind of frank hostility was the response of the fervently Evangelical vicar of East Grinstead, when informed that the town's new sisterhood, the Society of St Margaret, was a nursing order: 'The first case of infectious fever I have, I will ask them to undertake ... and then perhaps *we shall get rid of them.*'[88] Generally, while communities could protect themselves to a certain degree against unfriendly incumbents, such antagonism was certainly taken seriously. When a hostile rector was instituted in their North London parish, the Community of St Peter went to the extreme of considering moving its motherhouse. This would have meant the abandonment of their new purpose-built convent in the process.[89]

More realistically and more commonly, a hostile incumbent might seek to destroy a community through ruining its local reputation. Such open hostility, although it was an annoyance, was relatively easy to cope with; it simply divided the parish into camps, those who supported the sisters and those who were actively opposed to them. This opposition was more serious when it took the form of gossip or innuendo aimed at undermining a community's financial base. Mother Lucy of the Community of the Holy Comforter, Worthing, wrote to the archbishop to complain when the local clergy advised the local women who did their fund-raising to have nothing more to do with them. When the archbishop investigated, he discovered that the disapproval of the local clergy was based solely on the fact that Mother Lucy's sisterhood was 'a creation of her own mind and will', and it was readily admitted that their hospital for consumptives was a good one. In this case the archbishop seems to have agreed that working without a co-founder or other priest was provocation enough to justify the clergy's attempts to sabotage the community.[90] Archbishop Benson once received an indignant letter from the incumbent of a Bradford parish because a sisterhood was operating in his area 'quite irrespective of the Vicar of this or any other parish in which they may see fit to locate themselves'. Their offence? Opening 'unsectarian' clubs for working-class men and women in Bradford.[91]

Most sisterhoods responded to the problem of working with the local clergy by pointing out that since they ran projects in a large number of parishes, they held no special accountability to the parish priest of any one of them. They insisted that their position was entirely extra-parochial. In a number of instances, the mere threat that the community would withdraw its trained, organized and full-time staff was enough to quiet the parochial clergy's complaints. If declarations of independence did not produce the desired results, communities would in the last resort pull their workers out of the parishes of recalcitrant clergymen, often to the priest's dismay. The

Society of the Holy and Undivided Trinity withdrew its sisters from a Cambridge parish after the vicar insisted that he had the right to control which sisters should work there and in what manner. His plaintive letters asking for their restoration indicates how important the sisters had become to the work of the parish. Since, according to Charles Booth, the average district visitor spent two hours a week in parish work, there was a real danger that the entire administration of a parish would fall to the ground if a sisterhood left.[92]

The eventual subordination of the sisterhoods to church order took place in the years surrounding the First World War. The strategy which was ultimately to be successful had originally been proposed in 1873 in a letter of advice to the Archbishop of Canterbury. After acknowledging that the sisterhoods were succeeding because they had caught 'the spirit of the Age', the author gave this advice for containment, advice which from the onset of the next century was followed with some success:

> It is too late to enquire whether it is desirable to give this [community life] a place in our Reformed Communion ... you have seen how it is assuming really alarming proportions, how it defies all authority, is continually developing itself, [and] threatens our Church with disruption ... *Can we borrow a lesson from Rome, and as the Pope recognised the Franciscans when they became too strong for him, so might not our Bishops begin to countenance this movement* ... and gradually incorporate it into our Church's legitimate organisation?[93]

Finally, in 1908, the bishops bestowed upon sisterhoods some measure of official sanction and recognition by passing a list of regulations ('propositions') which emphasized the role of the bishops.[94] In this they followed earlier advice that the Church 'protect and confine' such groups, very much as middle-class Victorian women were protected and confined by the institutions of secular society. In light of their long tradition of resistance to church control, Allchin is wrong in his claim that 'the communities must be seen as a part of the Church's attempt to adapt herself to a rapidly changing society' if by Church he is referring to the bureaucratized, organized Church of England.[95] Sisterhood work was only reluctantly and tardily recognized by the Church of England as a legitimate part of its ministry to the people of the nation.

Until the absorption of sisterhoods into the structure of the Church was achieved, however, sisterhoods were perhaps the best known of the very few woman-originated, woman-peopled and woman-controlled institutions in

Victorian society. Despite the almost uniform discouragement of the formation of sisterhoods by the church hierarchy, sisterhoods were undoubtedly the most attractive channel of full-time work for women within the Church of England, although the least advocated by authority. This is certainly not coincidental.

CHAPTER SIX

'A BOMBSHELL TO PUBLIC OPINION': POPULAR PERCEPTIONS OF SISTERHOODS IN VICTORIAN BRITAIN

Defences of sisterhoods

Contemporary defences of sisterhoods were few. Some were based on the rather predictable ground that communities provided a source of cheap assistants for the clergy, or that they supplied a refuge for society's unwanted spinsters. However, a more interesting set of defences grew up around the claim that work was as important for women as it was for men, and that women had the right to choose work over marriage. The framework provided by sisterhoods, it was argued by some feminists, had potential as a transitional phase between decorative idleness within the family and completely independent work on an individual basis.

The idea of the convent as a community of women interested many who were concerned with the issue of women's place in Victorian Britain. Advocates of expanded roles for women, such as Frances Power Cobbe, saw the significance of sisterhoods in two aspects of their existence: first, they operated largely unaided by men; and second, they provided 'chosen life-tasks' to thousands of women who worked in cooperation, rather than as isolated individuals.[1] Both of these characterizations of the convent meant that some first-wave feminists saw the religious community not as an escape from life's stern realities, but as an opportunity for creative work in a permanent, woman-led, organization. Even the stridently conservative Mrs Sarah Stickney Ellis wrote of women's 'strange longing' for a community of women.[2]

It has often been pointed out that the discrepancy between what women were capable of doing and what they were permitted to do was perhaps greater in the mid-nineteenth century than at any other period in the modern era. In Victorian Britain there were very few jobs open to middle- and upper-class women, and those who attempted to undertake full-time work faced strong cultural opposition. Advocates for expanded roles for women routinely cited the mediaeval convent as an example of a lifestyle offering better opportunities for single women than did the nineteenth century. This extract from *Women and Work*, edited by Josephine Butler, later notorious as the leader of the anti-CDA movement, is typical in its dual emphasis on the work and status provided by the community to its members:

> The Convent opened its gates to rich and poor. In these communities, whoever could not marry, and whoever did not choose to marry, was sure of an honoured and secure asylum. There they were at least not idle. Besides the regular offices of religion, there was the management of property, the acts of charity, the learning and the teaching of the literature of the time ... To be unmarried was then to be the spouse of Christ, the revered 'mother', the member of a sisterhood surrounded with all the honour and sanctity of the Church – nowadays it is to live and die in the dreary lodgings, and under the half-contemptuous title of an old maid.[3]

And an eminent campaigner for women's legal equality, Barbara Leigh Bodichon, claimed that more than half of the women who converted to Catholicism and entered communities did so in a single-minded search for meaningful work. Furthermore, she judged that they did rightly in so doing: 'Happier far is a Sister of Charity or Mercy than a young lady at home without a work or a lover.'[4] Even the novelist George Gissing, no friend to organized religion in any form, has his hero encourage the agnostic heroine ('a lay sister of mercy') to join a religious order in order to have a greater scope for work than any independent individual could achieve.[5]

Florence Nightingale was fascinated by communities, seeing them as directly opposed to, and invariably challenging, the hegemony of the patriarchal family. In some ways her interpretation of the significance of sisterhood life is the most radical of any offered by outside observers of the movement. She frequently wrote of the advantages which the community offered women, especially the scope they offered for work outside the restrictions of home life. Indeed, Nightingale clearly envisioned sisterhoods as offering a degree of fulfilment that family life was not capable of providing.

> Monasteries ... were a much larger circle than the family, for there people did meet for a common object: those who had a vocation for work went into a house which supplied their kind of work – for contemplation, into a house of contemplation ... they were places where people who liked to work for the same object, met to do so; and the enormous rate at which they multiplied showed how they responded to a want in human nature. *Each was employed according to ... her vocation; there was work for all; but there is no such possibility in the family.*[6]

That there was a degree of truth in this Victorian analysis is certain. Some women used the experience of sisterhood work as the springboard to independent, sometimes radical, careers. The suffragette Emmeline Pethick-Lawrence, another (unnamed) early campaigner for votes for women, and the first secretary of the Labour Church movement (K. M. M. Scott) all started their public careers as Protestant sisters. It is extremely significant that the *Englishwoman's Journal*, the first periodical to campaign for the right of all women to work, regularly included sisterhoods (detailing the kind of work which each specialized in) among its listings of career opportunities open to women.

Why did Victorian women long for work? Anne Summers is right in seeing the 'argument from boredom', which claims that women worked among the poor as an antidote for their dull lives, as essentially a patronizing and belittling one. However, it cannot be overlooked, given the importance attributed to it at the time.[7] Frances Power Cobbe, who loathed sisterhoods, but was troubled by their undeniable vogue, finally explained away the popularity of Anglican communities by resorting to the familiar argument from boredom:

> They [women of the upper classes] are restrained from every effort at self-development or rational self-sacrifice, till, for the very want of a corrective bitter, they go and beat the hassocks in an Eaton Square church as a pious exercise, or perhaps finally lock themselves up in Clewer or East Grinstead. Small blame to them! *Ritualist Nunneries at present offer the most easily accessible back-door out of Belgravian drawing-rooms into anything like a field of usefulness.*[8]

The significance of Cobbe's outburst lies in its admission that what attracted mid-Victorian women to communities was the offer of meaningful work held out by them.

One of the motivations behind the foundation of the first community was a concern with providing employment for unmarried middle-class women. Sisterhoods were seen as providing a unique outlet for the energies and capacities of educated women. Certainly, women had few other choices. Even for the American-born Alice Horlock Bennett, with all the advantages of a liberal education and a wealthy background, the secular option was a dismaying one: 'It never occurred to me that there was anything to do except to stay on in the Community or return to the useless comfortable life I had experienced at home after I had "finished my education" ... '[9]

Not only could community life provide satisfying work, it was seen as improving the status of single women. The educationalist and supporter of female emancipation Maria Grey, although generally antagonistic toward communities, also hearkened back wistfully to the attitudes toward women she believed were fostered by communities.

> On the nun who voluntarily broke every human tie ... was bestowed none of the half contemptuous pity allotted to the old maid. In virtue of her voluntary sacrifice she was honoured above other women ... Here then we have quite a different view of the old maid and instead of being a social failure, a social superfluity, or a social laughing-stock, she is a social dignitary demanding respect and honour.[10]

In such circles, it was commonly asserted that communities valued women in a way that the wider Victorian culture did not. Some nineteenth-century feminists, like Lina Eckenstein in the 1890s, saw in women's communities evidence that a few women had always experienced autonomy by 'leaving' the male-dominated secular world. She argued that the convent had long offered the 'right to self-development and social responsibility' which contemporary women were seeking.[11] Emmeline Pethick-Lawrence's description of her years in a Methodist sisterhood emphasized the sense of liberation she experienced there. It was her 'first experience of that emancipation of mental and practical powers which is to be found by working as a free person in a community of equals ... '[12] The terms employed by Pethick-Lawrence in this passage are extremely significant: 'emancipation', 'free' and 'equals' all combine in a short sentence describing the effect of community life on an educated, intelligent, ambitious upper-class woman as late as the 1890s.

It is clear that for a great many Victorian women, life in a religious community was seen as a direct alternative to women's more conventional vocation of marriage. This created considerable conflict in the context of a society which believed that marriage offered the only respectable occupation for women. Alice Bennett, unhappy in her vocation, wrote 'I very nearly left the Sisterhood ... [but] I realised if I went back to the world ... I should give up everything ... '[13] This was a complete reversal of the common assumption that women gave up everything when entering a community; for members, the loss of work and friendship on leaving would be the real sacrifice.

Like marriage, profession offered life-long security and companionship, but with the advantages of a long 'engagement' (the novitiate) and the possibility of leaving the community when the life no longer satisfied: the equivalent secular choice offered no such escape.[14] Women who married made a lifetime commitment because of legal and social compulsion; sisterhoods offered a lifelong vocation with an opt-out clause, as well as some of the benefits of marriage. Even Anthony Trollope, who wholeheartedly believed that a happy marriage was the natural goal for all women, saw sisterhoods as offering a satisfying equivalent to the love of husband and children for some women.[15] Kate Warburton, who was a founding member of Saint Saviour's Priory in London's East End, wrote rather wistfully of the restricted opportunities in education or employment available to women when she was young, compared to their opportunities in the early twentieth century. Her account makes it clear that the desire for work could be a completely adequate motivation for seeking admission to a community.[16]

Superfluous women

Unlike the work orientation of feminist commentary on sisterhoods, the Victorian mainstream initially found only one condonation of this alternative for women. This was the claim that communities provided a sanctuary for women unable to find husbands. Marriage was considered woman's natural destiny, and an unmarried woman was popularly described as having 'failed in business'.[17] A female alone was seen as existing in an unnatural state: it was assumed that women, unlike men, were never single by choice. As an anonymous writer in the North British Review put it in 1862 – 'A single woman! Is there not something plaintive in the two words standing together? ... [Spinsterhood is an] estate alien to the whole constitution of woman's nature.'[18] Since Britain was home to a surplus of women over men, it was seen as a problem that not all of them could reasonably hope to fulfil their natural destiny. This panic over the excessive numbers of women assumed that women without husbands would be unable to find something to do.

Women had always outnumbered men in the population, but in the nineteenth century this disproportion was exacerbated by a number of factors, including male emigration. While it seems likely that most of the 'surplus women' were working-class, after the publication of the 1851 census, public attention took hold of and focused on the idea that the great bulk of the problem was in the middle classes.[19] Indeed, in the wake of the 'discovery' of the 'problem' of excess women, Dean Howson was surprised that one of the least important of his arguments for the institution of deaconess orders, that of employing some of the female surplus, was the one point seized on by reviewers. Howson and his ilk saw the working of God in the female surplus. Thus, accompanying the 'argument from boredom' was what might be called an 'argument from weakness', which claimed that sisterhoods would make useful women out of those who were too unattractive to marry and too weak, in mind and character, to work unassisted. The argument from weakness ignored the undoubted fact that sisterhood life was demanding. Advocates of communities protested against the idea that they offered a shelter for female incompetents who had failed to find husbands, arguing that the demands of community life strained the emotional and intellectual resources of even the most dedicated women.[20]

This curious defence of sisterhoods as shelters for undesired women was one which was always articulated by *non*-sisters. It depicted communities as safe retreats for women who had failed in their (presumed) life-goal of finding a man. These defenders saw sisterhoods as a sanctuary provided by Providence (no doubt spurred on by the 1851 census) in which to deposit 'superfluous women' – those who, without money or family, were precariously placed in a society which did not allow women to train for a career and did not make public provision for the unfortunate. They argued that these extra pairs of empty hands were divinely ordained in order to ease the suffering of the poor, and to make homelike the comforts of the affluent, rather than to seek independence for themselves. Not only would the sisterhoods care for these pathetic, dependent women; once enrolled, they would be a source of free labour as well. (Howson saw the great advantage of female work for the Church in market terms: women were cheaper, more numerous and more tractable than curates.[21])

Even those who held sisterhoods in despite liked to play with the idea that they were filled by women who had given up on the marriage market.

As to the dear little Sisters of St Margaret, one hardly knows what to say of them, poor things. Some, to be sure are old enough to know better. It's more years than she would like me to mention since I first saw one of them flirting and waltzing at an evening party. But then you know, Mr Editor, there is the sad statistical fact of half a million more females than males in the kingdom, and plentiful as curates seem, every pious little maiden cannot secure one to her own share. Excitement of some sort they must have.[22]

The conviction that many women in the middle classes were destined to remain unmarried was used as ammunition by supporters both of the sisterhoods and of other schemes for utilizing surplus females. Those who defined women's role as the opposite of men's held to the belief that, since women were born to dependency, the natural solution to the problem of surplus women was to transfer the surplus to where it was needed, either through female emigration or by putting women to work under the direct supervision of the parish priest. Those who thought that women could be trusted with autonomy were more likely to favour sisterhoods or opening the professions to women. Deacon and Hill classify Victorian solutions to the problem of surplus women in the following fashion: secular radicals advocated opening higher education and the professions to women, while secular conservatives supported wholesale female emigration. Religious conservatives were attracted to the idea of deaconesses, but religious radicals supported the establishment of sisterhoods.[23]

But the women who founded or entered early religious orders were not keen to provide a home and employment for all the 'female waifs and strays' of Victorian Britain. A former sister, Margaret Goodman, while expressing considerable reservations toward the institution she had left, pointed out the crucial flaw in the comfortable assumption that sisterhoods would function as nursing homes for incapables:

> [Some] think them [sisterhoods] desirable because calculated to prove a blessing to women who have nothing to do: a mode of existence for ladies, who after every effort on their part, from the supply not equalling the demand, are unable to find husbands; or a refuge for the woe-worn, weary, and disappointed. For neither of these three classes will a Sisterhood prove a proper home. The work is far too real to be performed by lagging hands ... [24]

Sisterhoods felt that women who entered solely out of a desire for a secure home were unlikely to contribute much to community life, or even to stay the course. Archival evidence suggests that this was probably true. One discontented sister was described, rather dismissively, as 'a good Christian of ordinary type before she came into the Community, which she seems to have sought as a place of quiet shelter'.[25] She was a rarity: women who came to communities as a solution for their own incapacity were seldom welcome, and very few persevered.

Opposition to sisterhoods

Anglican sisterhoods encountered enormous popular opposition. Many different aspects of their life came into question. Overall, eight arguments were used to discourage or discredit the work and very existence of these new organizations. These were: the 'family argument'; accusations of Romanism; attacks based on presumed female incapacity for self-government; the complaint that sisterhoods gave women a public face; accusations that ladies were doing the work of servants; disapproval of their financial affairs; anger at their refusal to subject themselves to church order; and a fear that sisterhoods were stripping social life of its best women. The three most important of these were the fear that communities were hostile to the family, an idea which remained important until the 1890s, but which peaked in the 1850s and 1860s; the accusations of Romanism, which predominated from 1845 to around 1870; and objections that sisterhoods worked independently of the hierarchy of the Church. This last argument became more important as the century drew to a close and it became clear that some communities within the now well-established movement were actively rejecting attempts to subordinate them to church order. Articulated most often by Anglican clergy, this last objection has been discussed in the previous chapter, while the remainder of this one deals with secular objections to sisterhoods.

Opposition to sisterhoods began almost immediately upon the foundation of the first community in 1845. Public protest reached a peak of intensity in 1848–52, but remained at a consistently high level until the mid- to late 1860s, when it began gradually to subside.[26] Expressions of hostility continued to re-emerge at intervals (usually in a weakened and transitory form) until World War One, so it can be said that a vocal thread of anti-sisterhood agitation did continue into this century.[27] As the anonymous author of *From the Curate to the Convent* wrote in 1877, more than thirty years after the first Anglican convent opened its doors, sisters were still commonly believed by many to be 'bound beneath a hideous nightmare of lies, impostures, tyranny, craft, vice; ... [sleeping] the sleep of spiritual, moral, social, domestic death'.[28]

'Domestic death': the family argument

Many of the Victorian arguments against sisterhoods were founded on a common set of assumptions about the God-mandated purpose of female life for women of the middle and upper classes. Often collectively referred to as the 'angel in the house' construct, no examination of the perceived threat of Anglican religious orders to Victorian cultural values would be comprehensible without reference to it.[29] The domesticity of the ideal is emphasized in the catch-phrase that has come to be her label: she was an angel *in the house*; this was a confinement which was almost cloistral in its intensity. While much recent scholarship calls the achievability of the ideal into question, it is generally conceded that the ideal as an ideal remained important to mid-Victorian women.

The concept of the angel in the house exalted middle-class women for their purity, affection and domesticity, while at the same time denying them self-determination and confining them to the domestic sphere. Its proponents regarded 'the domestic type of Christianity as the highest, if not its only, type'.[30] In light of the exaltation of domestic Christianity it is not surprising that the sisterhoods were perceived as threatening the very crux of mid-Victorian domestic ideology. These women wished to take their purity and their affection out of the domestic arena and into the public sphere of men, to 'pour into the corrupted stream the pure, healthy disinfectant of English womanhood'.[31]

The idealized, highly domestic feminine ideal seemed a necessity for ballast in the disequilibrium of the nineteenth century. As a result of the stabilizing role assigned to women, their experience in the nineteenth century was essentially one of increased role conflict. Angelically good yet in need of masculine guidance, they enjoyed high status in the private sphere but were powerless in the public sphere. Women were told that they had more influence on society than their sex had ever had before, yet they were increasingly expected to retreat into the home, and to concern themselves solely with the interiors of life. The sheer unnaturalness of the angel role for normal human behaviour meant that the wings must have been an uncomfortably tight fit for a great many women.

Nineteenth-century domestic ideology took the idea of the domestic and familial responsibilities of women to an extreme. In doing so, it attempted to ensure that the unmarried woman would never lack a home – or familial responsibility. If a woman remained single, she was expected to remain in the family home as long as it continued to exist. It was her duty to live with her parents until their deaths; she was then expected to transfer herself to the household of a sibling or other relative who might require her services. The unspoken half of this bargain was that in return she would be provided with a home for life. An advice manual written for unmarried women of middle age (interestingly, defined as being past the mid-twenties) refused to believe that any single woman could be without manifest home duties –

I do not see how they [single women] *can* employ their abilities better than among those of their own relations or friends who stand in need of help, or comfort, or companionship. Nor (with the exception of a few singularly unfortunate in their natural position) can I imagine any woman in the best-ordered sisterhood so advantageously placed as she who keeps to *home* duties; or who, in the possible default of these, devotes herself to those who have the strongest claim on her in private life.[32]

It must be emphasized that the presence of servants, nurses or other paid caregivers in no way obviated the duty of the unmarried daughter. If her family's wealth freed her from all domestic tasks, the daughter's role was to spread happiness, sweetness and piety within her family circle. Regardless of individual circumstances, the rule remained the same: an unmarried woman was called to single-heartedly devote her life to the peacefulness and comfort of her family much as her married counterpart did. The omnivorous Victorian family was capable of consuming all.

The family argument assumed that women should not act against their parents' lawful wishes, whatever the woman's own desires and ambitions. It carried within itself the conviction that unmarried women, in a very real sense, never came of age. Lydia Sellon, founder of Ascot Priory, was attacked for allowing a 26-year-old to try her vocation in the community; Sellon's surprised response was that she considered someone of that age a mature woman, capable of choosing for herself. Women could (and did) internalize the prevailing ideology: when Frances Pattison entered All Hallows at the age of forty-three, it was the first independent decision she had made in her life. She later became the community's second Mother Superior.[33] Time and again in the anti-sisterhood pamphlets, outraged fathers accuse the sisterhoods of seducing away women whom they portray as being essentially unable to make responsible decisions.[34] The most notorious of these attacks was that of the Rev. Scobell of Lewes, who claimed that the St Margaret's Sisterhood lured away his daughter Amy, whom he described as 'a mere child'. This 'child' was in her late twenties or early thirties when she left the paternal roof.

This attitude was not confined to the pages of polemical pamphlets. In 1874, an Anglican clergyman wrote to the Archbishop of Canterbury in the hope that his daughter's profession in a sisterhood could be prevented. Clementia Williams had supported herself for a decade as a governess, starting at the age of seventeen, before entering a community. Mr Williams did not want Clementia to return home (she had been away for twelve years by this date), as he still had two daughters there: he simply wished to exert his paternal authority in order to prevent his daughter from being professed.[35] This man felt that he still had absolute authority over his daughter's life choices, despite her dozen years of financial and domestic independence. And he was in no way unusual, except in appealing to a dignitary of the Church for assistance.

Indeed, these early Anglican sisters were called 'stolen daughters' by their opponents. This phrase encapsulated the attitude of the general public toward the communities. 'Stolen' summarized the belief that community life for women was so unnatural that well-brought-up women would not enter willingly; it was argued that they must have been '*seduced*' away from their families by '*promises of freedom of action*' (what could be more enticing?) or even hypnotized by the '*mesmeric abilities*' of the Mother Superior.[36] 'Stolen' is a word which is redolent of reassurance in this context – assuming as it does that women were so passive that they could be removed from the family without their active consent. If they were taken against their will (stolen), then the choice of a sisterhood over domestic life does not call the nature and structure of the Victorian family into question. 'Daughter', too, is significant. An unmarried woman in middle life was still seen first and foremost as a daughter, with a daughter's duties and a daughter's powerlessness. John Scobell, mentioned above as the best-known father of a 'stolen daughter', wrote several pamphlets on the issue. His argument, although clothed in a fulsome Evangelical cant reminiscent of Dickens's and Trollope's more repulsive clerical characters, contains within it a profound incomprehension of his daughter's desire to live a life separate from the family. He believed she should be content to have her path in life decreed by her father; the fact that Amy Scobell felt a sense of vocation which did not include father or husband as its central focus was unthinkable to Scobell. He wrote, and later published, a letter to Elizabeth Gream, Mother Superior of East Grinstead, which demonstrates to the full his sense of ownership of his adult daughter:

> I ask you to explain to me the character of the intercourse which I find, and am told by my daughter, has lately taken place between you and her ... I beg to ask by what right or authority – upon what principle of honour or religion – is my household broken into – my family peace invaded – my parental authority contemned. I shall be glad to have these touching questions replied to, and to be assured whether there is or not any segment of the Church of England whose system is to sap the unity of families; to creep into houses by person or by letter, unknown to the fathers and owners of them; and *that*, even when the offices of parent and parish priest are united in one person.[37]

And these 'touching questions' concerned many others as well: the most damning condemnation of the Ascot Priory sisterhood was that 'Miss Sellon has freed her household from the obligations of daughters'.

Figure 6.1 'Fashions for 1851; or, a page for the Puseyites', *Punch*, 27 December 1850. An example of the belief that Anglo-Catholicism threatened Victorian family life. (British Library Reproductions.)

Margaret Goodman's popular book attacking sisterhoods painted a lurid and sensational picture of popular fears. This former Park Village and Ascot Priory novice wrote, 'it is possible for a young girl to be kept secretly, in strict seclusion, in a convent professedly connected with the Church of England, not only against her own inclinations, but against the wishes of her parents and friends'. Goodman warned of communities whose inmates were taken from the 'protection and care of friends and relatives'. This sounds much more like abduction than the drawn-out battles to leave home that were the normal experience of women who wished to join sisterhoods. Anglican sisterhoods were often called 'prison-houses', and sisters were regularly described as 'captives' by Protestant extremists. The women who joined them were depicted as hapless victims of 'satanic plots against the peace of the domestic circle, the happiness of our free English firesides ... ' Another writer suggested that the members of All Saints were kept in a prison cleverly concealed behind an ordinary exterior.[38] Some people took these absurd claims seriously: when a group of ladies were taking their departure after touring an All Saints branch house, one grasped a sister by the arm and offered to help her 'escape' in their carriage. The sister, who so disliked being away from the community that she would not visit her own brother, was appalled by the suggestion.[39] While this last was certainly a sincere offer, most critics, and especially those with community experience such as Goodman (who herself had left not one, but two communities, without impediment), must have known that the claims of imprisonment were sensationalized and false. Community records contain long lists of postulants, novices and professed sisters who returned to the world. These bear witness to the ease with which the dissatisfied could leave. Many did not persevere, and left without opposition. But Goodman and her fellows needed the threat of forcible confinement to buttress the thesis that disobedience to the parental will could (and probably would) have truly nightmarish results.

That Goodman's dire warnings about sisterhoods must be taken in large part as special pleading is further indicated by her emphasis on the extreme youthfulness and malleability of the entrants. She warned of the danger inherent in 'the youthful mind and susceptible feelings of the postulant at the mercy of the matured and acute intellect and firm will of the Superior'. Not only was this a remarkable way of making an intelligent middle-aged woman sound somewhat sinister, but both Goodman's own experience and the records of the convents indicate that the typical choir postulant throughout the nineteenth century was much more likely to be in her late twenties or early thirties than in her teens.

The rights of parents over their middle-aged and often financially independent daughters are mentioned repeatedly and insistently throughout Goodman's book. She ascribes all the errors and inconsistencies of the orders, which were still experimenting with an unfamiliar form of living, as the evil results of such women being freed from their obligations as daughters. Goodman underscored her argument with some memorably bad verse, suggesting that those who rejected the paternal home were rejecting God:

> What echoes from the sacred dome
> The selfish spirit may o'ercome
> That will not hear of love or home?
> The heart that scorned a father's care,
> How can it rise in filial prayer?
> How an all-seeing Guardian bear?[40]

Goodman was not alone in her fear that sisters were tempting God's anger because of their willingness to leave their homes. Dean Howson was an influential advocate of deaconesses because they (unlike sisterhoods) worked under the supervision of the clergy. However, he objected to sisterhoods because they caused 'scandal' by their 'interference' with parental rights.[41] By contrast, deaconess institutions went to great lengths to ensure that they could not be accused of a similar fault. Every applicant to the Mildmay Deaconess Institute was closely questioned about her home duties before admission; in effect this meant that a male professional decided whether adult candidates were to be allowed to leave their families. Sisterhoods left such issues to the consciences of the women wishing to join.

Of all the groups which utilized the family argument against sisterhoods, during the 1840s and 1850s the most vigorous attacks came from the clergy: especially prominent were those with family in sisterhoods.[42] William Colles, writer of some of the most vitriolic pamphlets attacking Ascot Priory, was brother-in-law to a member of that community. Two of Bishop Whateley's sons were married to daughters of Lady Campbell, whose daughter Diana had been an Ascot Priory aspirant, and who instigated attacks by both Colles and Whateley.[43] Some anti-sisterhood clergy penned pamphlets little short of abusive. As well as theological differences, these pamphlets attest to the violent emotions evoked by affronted family loyalties. Interestingly, while the lesser clergy used accusations of family abandonment frequently, the bishops seem to have abandoned this means of reproach early. Indeed the only significant attempt was made in 1850 when Bishop Bloomfield complained that the Park Village sisterhood was admitting adult women against their parents' wishes. While he deplored this assertion of female independence, Bloomfield apparently was aware of his powerlessness to prevent such behaviour.[44]

Advocates of sisterhoods had an unrelenting response to the family argument: they insisted that women had the right (and indeed the duty) to obey the call of God, a call as unnegotiable as death.

> But where a daughter would think it right to leave her parents for the married state, she has a right to follow the call to a higher duty to be joined to Christ. It is most common, however, for parents ... to make objections. They do not want to give up their daughters or be separated from them ... *no parent has the right upon religious grounds to keep a child from [her vocation]* ... *God, who has a right to take their child away by death, has the right to take the child into religious life* ... [45]

It has long been suggested that daughters who wanted to escape from the pressure of family obligations often retreated into illness or intense religious devotion: Davidoff and Hall aptly term this 'passive resistance'.[46] Ill health could be a way of obtaining psychological and emotional power otherwise denied to women solely on the basis of their sex. Lorna Duffin suggested that upper-middle-class Victorian women sometimes escaped into illness as a response to the stifling dullness of their lives at home. In light of this, it is suggestive how very frequent in community archives are reports of the 'miraculous' improvement in the health of former invalids who join sisterhoods. There are a number of reasons why a woman's health may have improved after becoming a sister. The 'passive resistance' toward family domination would no longer be necessary. The work offered them was usually interesting and challenging; psychosomatic illnesses due to under-stimulation and boredom may well have been alleviated. The women who experienced this improvement in health perceived it as a reward from God for their obedience to their vocation; we may wonder if sometimes good health returned upon their assumption of an active, often exciting, always *chosen*, life.[47]

That the reality of devotion to one's family could be an unappealing or even horrific experience is shown very clearly in the life of Florence Nightingale. Treated as a 'shameful anomaly' at home because of her desire for meaningful work, for years she was the victim of her mother's and sister's neurotic and unreasonable demands: Nightingale later described this as being 'Devoured'. She endured fifteen years of intense conflict during which each of her plans for autonomy was vetoed by the other members of her family. In

1845 she hoped to establish a nursing/religious community of her own, but this ambition was overruled by vociferous parental objections.[48] In her diary Nightingale described feelings which must have been shared by other intelligent and ambitious women confined to the duties of young-ladyship: 'My present life is suicide; In my 31st year I see nothing desirable but death; What am I that their life is not good enough for me? ... why ... cannot I be satisfied with the life that satisfies so many people?'[49] With her own strong personality and drive for achievement thwarted at every turn, Nightingale saw nursing as offering a release from her domestic situation as well as a calling. As Nightingale sensed, the initial attraction of community life could be strengthened by the possibility it offered of escape from Victorian domesticity.

Of all the common attacks on the establishment of communities, the most consistently heard was the family argument, criticizing sisters for rejecting their place in the family and thus their biological role as women. Women who entered sisterhoods were depicted as rebels against parental rule and unamenable to family discipline: incredibly, some even claimed that the Victorian's cherished social order was seriously threatened by women who were free from the male dominion of husband, father or brother.

A sisterhood could seem an attractive option to women who were already in rebellion against the strictures of Victorian society. John Shelton Reed claims that the sisterhoods, and indeed Anglo-Catholicism in general, could be and was seen as a series of 'symbolic affronts' to Victorian cultural values. He points out that support for Anglo-Catholicism tended to come from groups whose members were threatened, oppressed or bored by the values of the mainstream culture. Part of the appeal of the movement was its

> challenge to Victorian family ideology and to received ideas about women's place
> and role ... its establishment of sisterhoods, often with women in positions of
> independent authority ... can be viewed, and was viewed at the time, as standing in
> at least symbolic opposition to the patriarchal Victorian family ... [50]

Greg puts this opposition most crudely in his famous definition of the feminine role: there are 'two essentials of woman's being; they are supported by, and they minister to, men'.[51] Sisters refused both roles. This may account in part for the peculiar viciousness and malice evident in many of the attacks on sisterhoods: they demonstrate a degree of almost hysterical enmity, often expressed over remarkably petty issues, which sits oddly with the high aims of the sisterhoods under attack.

It was a commonplace among opponents of religious orders for women to accuse those who entered sisterhoods as having abandoned family obligations in order to undertake the more attractive life of a sister.[52] There was a general consensus that there must be something very wrong with a woman who would deliberately seek to sever herself from the all-encompassing (and sometimes stifling) embrace of the family. It was never suggested that there might be something wrong with the family, although alternatives to it were regularly depicted as seductive and enticing. The inevitable tendency of community life to detach women from the family was invariably condemned: it was the most common accusation made against the communities, and the strength of this argument is shown by the number of times it is cited as the only necessary condemnation of the movement.

Anti-sisterhood literature is full of accusations of disloyalty to the family, and equally replete with dire predictions of what would happen to the women who left homes for communities. Death, or at the very least madness, were common forecasts. One of the more extreme of these is an entertaining novel by John Harwood. In it the daughter of a bishop, Miss Jane, defies parental authority to join an Anglican sisterhood (and no ordinary one: the sisters wear jewellery and go out to evening parties). She eventually has an illegitimate child, strangles it and pushes a clergyman who knows her guilty secret over a cliff.[53] In the eyes of some, a woman who became a sister was capable of any enormity.

The sisterhoods, in order to better defend themselves against the charge of subverting female domesticity, depicted themselves (and often saw themselves) as a transcendent family. Instead of denying the supremacy of the domestic obligation, in their defensive self-portrayal, women who became sisters sacrificed the comforts of home to serve as missionaries of Christian home life to the poor and pagan working classes: they were 'virgin mothers' to the poor, whom they depicted in terms of childlike dependence and ignorance. However, while they claimed that their work was simply an extension of the family into the public sphere, they neglected to mention that it also brought 'ladies' into contact with its underside: illegitimacy, incest, prostitution and the deepest and most squalid poverty. This was in part a purely defensive argument, but it is possible that the sisters deliberately subverted their critics' own language in order to protect their institutions. However, in the final analysis sisterhoods must be seen as hostile to the family because of their insistence that women had the right, and indeed the duty, to place the call of God to minister to the poor over any family claims. (One 1846 founder of a Roman Catholic order took this logic to an extreme; she became the Superior-General of the first native Roman Catholic order founded in England since the Reformation, while her husband took orders as a Roman Catholic priest, and their youngest child, aged six, was placed in the convent school.[54])

Sisters placed great emphasis on New Testament admonitions to obey the call of God before family demands. This religious justification for the denial of old ties, while impeccably orthodox, was extremely unpalatable to most Victorians, with their cult of idolatry toward the family – what Nightingale scathingly described as the *'fetish* of the family'. This divine sanction allowed sisterhoods to maintain that the intensity of their commitment necessarily involved some withdrawal from the intimacy of the biological family. This withdrawal was physical as well as psychological. The Rule of the Community of St Thomas Martyr in 1859 echoed biblical teaching in its declaration that 'Loving Him above Father, Mother, Brother, Sister, Husbands, all, they must *go forth* courageously ... '[55]

Anglican sisterhoods very explicitly set themselves up as surrogate families, and taught that a woman's duty to this second, *chosen* family transcended the demands of the biological one. The superior became their new mother, Christ became both father and husband, and the other sisters their sisters. All sisters were 'mothers' to the poor. It was a striking form of family reconstitution, and was done for the purpose of domesticating the godless outer world. The overriding mission of the communities was 'to supply mothers and sisters to the multitudes, who have none in any true sense of the words'.[56] Their opponents called their claim of spiritual motherhood blasphemous, but the sisters perceived themselves as having taken on metaphorical motherhood.[57]

Although these single women could not be mothers in the biological sense, it was argued that they were better 'mothers' than a biological mother could ever be, largely because they did not confine their maternal care and love to a restricted circle, but extended it to hundreds of needy children through orphanages, children's hospitals and convalescent homes, crèches, hostels for girls who worked in factories, schools, and reformatories. This is made explicit by the text chosen at the dedication festival for the Community of the Holy Cross: *'He shall make the barren woman to keep house, and to be a joyful mother of children.'*[58] The world became a home, and the sisters/mothers were free to move at will in it.

The entrance to sisterhood life, the novitiate, made the conflict between the biological family and the new 'family' of the community explicit. Not only was physical distance between woman and family created by communities, emotional distance was established as normative. Aspirants were instructed that letters home should be written with care; sisters should confide in their community, not their families. Novices were taught, in the interests of 'family' solidarity, to avoid disparaging the community or another sister to outsiders, including their families. Postulants were not allowed family visits during the six months of trial, although after clothing they could go home in case of urgent need. After profession sisters were allowed free intercourse with their near relations, who could visit them at the convent on specified days.[59] As discussed elsewhere, sisters could spend their holidays with their families if they wished. Few wished, or were able, to.

The entire community participated in decisions about a professed sister's biological family, especially when there was conflict between the demands of the two 'families'. For example, the All Saints sisterhood decided as a community whether Sister Mary Monica ought to return to her mother to support her after a change in family circumstances. Most Rules contained a provision that the community should vote when such circumstances arose.[60] This makes it clear that the chosen family of the sisterhood has superseded the biological one. Some communities articulated the new order of priority very directly, with only the most extreme situations allowing of a temporary return: 'A Sister's work is too important to admit of her interrupting it, to act as a sick-nurse to friends and relations, but she may always go to her parents, brothers and sisters if they are in danger of death.'[61] This caution was not always necessary. The decision to become a sister could strain family relations to such a degree that ties with home were severed, sometimes permanently.

Even the taking of a new name at clothing was a symbol of the substitution of new and higher ties for the old, as the family name was dropped and sometimes the Christian name was altered. Sisters were frequently criticized for changing their names, which was seen as being 'unEnglish' and as an act of disloyalty to parents, especially the father.[62] This criticism persisted despite the relative rarity of the abandonment of the Christian name; most sisters retained their baptismal name or a version of it. Certainly they abandoned the use of their surname, except for legal purposes. Being given a new name by a woman (the Mother Superior usually chose the sister's name in religion) upset the patriarchal applecart of the transmission of names through the father. But this kind of attack on the communities' practices relied less on what the sisterhoods were actually doing than on popular fears (or fantasies?) about what women untrammelled by family ties *might* do.

In the sisterhood new clothes replaced conventional garments. This symbolized the laying aside of the conventional role for women. In the distinctive habit of her order a woman could go anywhere and do virtually anything with impunity. One critic of the communities compared the sisters' habits to the Bloomer costume.[63] While outwardly very different, both garments signified a new and threatening freedom: the Bloomer costume gave a woman free use of her limbs and suggested that she would class herself among the 'New Women'. The habit, while similarly giving the body room and comfort in moving, also bestowed upon its wearers the freedom to transcend boundaries of class and conventional female behaviour.

The Mother Superior was seen as the 'superior Mother', both by those threatened by sisterhoods and by those who joined them. Just as the community gave sisters new names, it gave them the opportunity to choose a new mother. One Sisters of the Church member described the difference between the biological and chosen mother in terms which implied more than they stated about the strains which sometimes existed in the familial relationship:

> As a girl of eighteen, I had prayed that I might some day call a woman 'Mother', in whom I should see no flaw, and she [the Mother Superior] more than realized my desire.[64]

Whether flawless or not, Mothers Superior had advantages over mothers of families. Obedience was due to the Mother Superior; in the world of the Victorian family, mothers obeyed fathers, at least in theory. Mothers Superior possessed great authority and influence in a position of dignity and power. There were not many equivalent roles for ordinary women in Victorian society. Most importantly, the Mother Superior was an elected mother; any choir sister could aspire to eventually fill this role. All had a say in who their Mother would be.

This transformation, or perhaps reappropriation, of family ties was accompanied by an explicit celebration of celibacy, one of the three vows taken at profession. Borrowing from Catholic tradition, virginity was described as a higher state; this is a far cry from the common jeer that spinsters had 'failed in business'. In Victorian Britain the convent was almost the only place in which a celibate woman would be seen as superior to her married sisters. J. M. Neale, co-founder of East Grinstead, taught that marriage forced women into dependency; only the celibate woman could retain her autonomy and live a life of true freedom. The sisterhoods' celebration of celibacy was perceived by their culture as involving a rejection of the Victorian norms of biological reproduction and of men's sexual identity, by refusing to open themselves to the possibility of courtship, marriage and maternity. The sisterhoods, and the women who flocked to them, were a living witness to the belief that marriage and motherhood were not necessarily the highest and most desirable life for a woman. They thus flew in the face of the central tenets of Victorian ideas about womanliness.

The replacement of the biological family was illustrated again at another highly charged symbolic moment: the death of a community member. The account of the death of Sister Fridswida in 1857 makes the sister's usurpation of family prerogative explicit. The entire community is described as following her to her grave, 'going in the mourning carriage next the hearse, as being more nearly allied to her than her father and other friends who came in the carriage behind us'. Again, when one member sister of the Community of Reparation to Jesus in the Blessed Sacrament died of tuberculosis at her mother's house, sisters were dispatched to 'bring her body home' for burial at the convent.[65] These were not isolated incidents. A riot occurred at Lewes, Sussex, in 1857, at the funeral of Amy Scobell. Scobell had defied her father, rector of Southover in Lewes, by joining the Society of St Margaret at East Grinstead. When she died of scarlet fever caught while nursing, the sisters accompanied her body to the grave. As the funeral commenced, there was a dispute in the street over who should take the place of chief mourner, the sisters or Mr Scobell. At the church the nuns grouped themselves around the coffin in the place usually taken by family members. A riot broke out in the churchyard when the Warden of the East Grinstead community, J. M. Neale, insisted that he had the right to enter the mausoleum after the family had left.[66] The indignation of the rioters seems to have been sparked by the repeated usurpation of family prerogative they had witnessed; order in the town was not fully restored for another day. Such was the excitement that the *Sussex Advertiser* published an 'Extraordinary Edition' to chronicle the event on 1 December 1857.

The family argument proved to be both the most damaging and the most enduring of the cries raised against the establishment of sisterhoods. For decades sisterhoods were commonly depicted as attacking domestic life and flouting the most sacred ties. What the historian does not know is whether such protests were rooted in reality. If, as has been suggested, the very predominance of a Victorian value in print indicates that its power was beginning to fail, it may be that the outcry over the desertion of the family by these women demonstrated how much the authority of the family had already weakened by mid-century.[67]

Given the vigour of the family argument, it must have required considerable strength of will and firmness of purpose to overcome family opposition to entering a sisterhood. Anna Jameson explained that many women were deterred from joining Anglican communities out of a 'terror of the vulgar, stupid prejudices around them – chiefly ... masculine prejudices'.[68] Opposition was the most common response from one's family for at least the first two decades of the sisterhood movement. In 1884 Clewer was still acutely aware of 'the prejudices still existing in England' which made families go to almost any lengths to prevent their adult daughters or sisters from entering communities. Even in the 1890s, one woman from an elite background who entered a Protestant sisterhood described her decision to live in 'the comparative freedom of a community, in order to carry out rather subversive principles of social sharing' as being 'a bombshell' to her family and to public opinion.[69] Alice Bennett, a former Anglican sister who later converted to Roman Catholicism and who wrote a somewhat hostile but essentially fair-minded description of her experiences in All Saints, claimed that nearly every novice had to undergo 'much opposition and even petty persecution' before succeeding in entering a sisterhood. Another former sister, who went on to form a new order in the Roman Catholic Church, wrote of her Anglican companions that she did not believe that any had received the full and free consent of her parents for leaving home.[70] The very difficulty of breaking free of the family meant that a dread of the family welcome may have kept some women in communities who no longer wished to remain. Bennett's depiction of her personal dilemma makes it very clear that if a woman left the convent, she had no choice but to return to her family: there was no other alternative for a respectable woman of any age.[71]

For many women, the decision to become a member of a sisterhood involved the sacrifice of good relations with their families as well as a leap into an unknown and very demanding life. To my knowledge there is only one surviving contemporary example of the evaluation of sisterhood life by a woman who was later to become a member. The following passage is from the diary of Amy Scobell, written in 1853 and published after her death. In it the family looms large.

> Let me consider deeply about joining a sisterhood. First then as to what it is. I must give up marriage. And in giving up that I must give up love of any one human being before all others. There must be no love ... but the love of my heavenly Lord. And through him love for the poor ...

I must resign in my case entirely the love of all my relations, my father, my mother, in great measure my sisters and my eldest brother, aunt, and all my uncles ... and many of my cousins and friends ... I should be going with the fierce anger of my father, mother, and almost all my relatives, and many of my friends; thought at least foolish by all I know and going amongst strangers whom I may not like.

I will consider of this, and see if I can do it all ... [72]

Scobell's musings make it clear that the decision to enter a sisterhood must often have been a painful one, and made only after long thought about the reactions of others to the decision to leave home for a community.

The family argument was long-lived. One enthusiastic advocate of sisterhoods, and co-founder of the Community of St Denys, pleaded with parents who felt that only marriage should sever a daughter from the parental home. Written in 1885, his reasoning indicates that, for many, strictures and restrictions articulated forty years earlier still maintained their potency.

Hold not your daughters back from this work ... You are ready to spare those of them who may marry, to go out to India, or elsewhere. You place no difficulties in their paths. Give the same liberty to those who may choose another portion.[73]

Given the obsession with this issue, it is not surprising that sisterhoods came to see their separation from the family home as central to their self-image. The foundation of the Community of All Saints is considered to be the day Harriet Brownlow Byron left her family home, despite no other women joining her enterprise for a number of months. The community history describes how important this symbolic act was: 'On September 1 the house was taken, so that she might begin a life of separation *from her home* and from the world: so it came to pass that on St Luke's Day 1851 our Foundress *left her home*.'[74] Many women who wished to enter communities were torn between their desire to do so and their belief, realistic or not, that they were urgently required at home. Etheldreda Benett, founder of the Sisters of Bethany, delayed entering a sisterhood for twenty years after finding her vocation, because her father objected. The founder of All Saints was only free to establish a sisterhood after the death of one sister and the marriage of another released her from family ties. Due to family responsibilities, All Saints Sister Frances Emily waited eighteen years to enter the order, being finally professed at the age of fifty-four in 1886. For some, the conflict did not end with profession. After eight years as Superior of the Community of the Mission Sisters of the Holy Name, Mother Charlotte left the community in order to care for a family member. Her ambivalence about this step is indicated by her retaining the title of Mother Superior for another year.[75]

Some women, even after they had succeeded in their attempt to leave the family home for the convent, could not shake from themselves the fear that they had done wrong in taking to a life of their own choosing, rather than remaining passively at home. Parents sometimes played heartlessly on their torn loyalties. One sister received the news of her brother's sudden death in a letter from her mother, to which her affectionate parent added that his death grieved her less than the life her daughter had chosen. Given the enormous weight placed on the fifth commandment in Victorian culture, it is not surprising that another early sister came to believe that her fatal illness was the punishment of God for not doing as her father wished and returning home. Lest daughters should worry or tease reluctant parents into giving their consent to their choosing their own place in life, opponents of sisterhoods claimed that even reluctant consent did not free a woman from home ties.[76]

A good many sisters began their career as associates or outer sisters while they waited for parents or siblings to die. The idea of waiting for the death of a parent as the removal of an obstacle is abhorrent, but it seems to have been common; not a few women may have had to struggle against the temptation to wish to be freed from family ties by death. It must be said that parents did not hesitate to attempt to continue controlling their daughters after their deaths, usually by adding a clause to the will which revoked the daughter's inheritance should she enter a sisterhood. Sister Frances Emily was one woman who was unable to commence her religious career until both of her parents were dead. Although their only child, her parents tied up their money so that she was unable ever to touch the capital. Despite this, her income was so large that she was able to keep several community works in funds throughout her lifetime.[77]

Long after profession had taken place, families could exert enormous pressure on women to return to their 'natural' duties. Sister Florence of All Saints, the daughter of an alcoholic ex-soldier, with half a dozen comfortably married sisters, was professed as a lay sister in 1896. Sister Elspeth describes the ensuing drama with some relish:

> Then her troubles began. Her sisters were all married now but one: and they were all after Sister Florence to go home and take care of the mother, so that Katie, the youngest, could get married. The mother was very good and did not join in the chorus, though she was as good as (or worse than) a widow. Then the mother's health began to fail ... On a visit to her mother she found the whole family

assembled, sisters and husbands, and they said, 'Now Florrie, we are going to take you to town and get clothes for you.'

The pressure exerted by this formidable and somewhat threatening assemblage of family members must have been great. Sister Florence was only saved from being forcibly detained when one brother-in-law suddenly declared that she should not be kept at home against her will.

Another example of family pressure to abandon her vocation is similar, albeit occurring in a considerably higher social station. Sister Mary Rachael completed her novitiate and there was no doubt of her successful election to profession when suddenly one of her brothers died, leaving three small children. She was one of a large family of married brothers and sisters, but they all insisted that she, the only unmarried sibling, must look after the children. The most insistent of all was her brother, then a priest and later a bishop in America. She left the community with reluctance, and spent three years caring for the orphaned family, until the Mother Superior told her that she must make a final decision. She accordingly returned to the community, but for the rest of her life her family 'tormented' her with demands to leave in order to care for various members.[78] It is clear that her family was convinced that as a single woman, her God-ordained function was to act as a free nurse and babysitter for any relative who required such services, regardless of her own wishes. For Sister Mary Rachael, 'domestic death' was not the abandonment of the biological family, but her family's importunity that she sacrifice her own life to their convenience.

Romanists in disguise

An early and very persistent form of hostility to sisterhoods took the form of accusing them of Romish leanings, or even of being (in a popular phrase) 'disguised Roman Catholics'.[79] As one advocate of women's work commented in exasperation:

> Because a certain number of single women have agreed to live in one house, put on one dress, and join their earnings and efforts in one common stock for the relief of certain acknowledged social evils, the whole Apocalypse is ... ransacked for the millionth time, to prove that the mark of the beast is upon them![80]

This aspect of anti-sisterhood sentiment was in one sense a part of the larger anti-Catholicism which pervaded the Victorian age and which took on new life with every move toward equal rights for the Roman Catholic minority. But particular practices, and especially that of confession, were always tinder for the anti-Roman spark.

Great opposition was offered to the implementation of the confessional within the English Communion. The clamour of outrage raised around the practice of confession, which had never entirely died out in the Church of England but which was popularly revived with respect to communities in the 1840s and 1850s, shows how raw a nerve this practice touched. It awoke fears both of feminine betrayal of family solidarity and of Romish practice. It was commonly depicted as a threat to patriarchal authority by its subversion of the authority of husbands and fathers. It is absolutely central that, in almost every discussion of the perniciousness of the confessional, it is assumed that only women will avail themselves of it: women were perceived to be the potential weak spot in the fortress of family (and theological) unity. Anglican sisterhoods inevitably suffered from the most virulent strains of anti-Catholicism, the anti-confession and anti-convent agitations, whose propaganda sometimes descended to the level of something little different from pornography.[81] One relatively decorous example will suffice:

> under the cloak of religion, and where some truly religious persons are used as 'decoys' and 'masks,' Romish and Puseyite *Sisterhoods* and *Nunneries* are organised: 1. To ensnare beautiful and wealthy females: 2. To be coverts for evil-doers: 3. To be training-schools of vice and slavery: and 4. To serve as 'points of occupation'.

The author goes on to embroider the potential of communities for sexual vice, and even to suggest that convents served as arsenals and refuges for Fenians.[82]

While some of the opposition to sisterhoods must be seen as part of a larger response to 'Papal Aggression', in other ways this opposition was unique to the sisterhoods. In part the sisterhoods brought this criticism upon themselves, because they adopted a lifestyle which was so obviously derived, at least in externals, from continental religious communities. The simplest attacks were those claiming sisters were 'disguised Jesuits', working for the conversion of Britain to Catholicism from inside the Established Church. More sophisticated anti-Catholics (if that isn't a contradiction in terms) claimed that sisterhood life, due to its similarity to Roman Catholic models, was hostile not only to Christianity but also to the best interests of women themselves. Suspicion of all things Roman sometimes reached a pitch of absurdity. Mrs Tonna described the English spiritual classic, *The Garden of the*

Soul, written by Bishop Challoner in 1740, as an 'indecent book', 'put ... into the hands of young females'.[83]

Many saw the very idea of any community of women as irretrievably Romish, and thereby taboo. It is an interesting aspect of mid-century anti-Romish literature that although its purpose was ostensibly to expose the errors of Catholicism, it not infrequently discussed Anglican communities at greater length than Roman Catholic ones. Perhaps readers found it more thrilling to contemplate 'corruption' in their own church. Popular, too, was the allegation that sisters not only were corrupting the poor, but had successfully infiltrated the 'homes of the *very highest* in the land', including (it was claimed) the Queen and much of the Court.[84]

In general, communities made little effort to avoid being tarred with the 'Roman' brush. Sisterhoods often borrowed openly from Roman Catholic models with regard to dress, community administration and liturgy. For most, this was a supremely pragmatic decision: Roman orders had been functioning successfully for centuries, and imitating them might ensure the speedy regularization of the Anglican version; wholesale experimentation, although exciting, was also turbulent and destabilizing. In general, commun-ities' imitation of continental Catholic practice was not surprising: there were no other living examples of women's communities for them to emulate, with the exception of the Kaiserwerth deaconesses, who would not permit Anglican sisters to visit them. Family ties could also play a part: the founder of the Society of the Sisters of Bethany often turned for advice to two of her cousins who were Mothers Superior in the Société Marie Réparatrice. Both Mother Mary St John and Mother Mary St Joseph were converts.[85] Many Anglican sisterhoods also felt great sympathy for the Roman Catholic Church; a number of communities were deeply involved in movements which aimed at the reunion of the churches, most importantly the Sisters of Bethany, who were involved in this movement from their inception in 1866.[86] However, the mirror image which resulted from such uncritical imitation of Roman practice did allow their adversaries to describe them as having 'every peculiarity of a nunnery but the name'.[87] Early sisterhoods lost some of their already limited support as advocates were alienated by their 'non-Anglican' liturgy and practice. As an anonymous clerical writer put it, 'Establishments, scarcely different from the Roman Catholic convents and nunneries, are built and endowed; medieval ecclesiastical millinery is adopted in the costume of their inmates, and in every respect the Romish practice is carried out without any opposition or interference ... '[88] (It must be said that not all liturgical innovations were influenced by Roman Catholic precedents, however; in its formative years East Grinstead was always more interested in the Eastern Church's liturgy, and paid relatively little attention to that of the West.)

Because sisterhoods were seen by most English people as being intrinsically Roman in their nature, it was assumed by some that the good works they performed and the social utility which they professed were merely a smoke-screen for an intent essentially ascetic, and therefore pregnant with mediaeval evils. According to such commentators, sisterhood projects were simply a decoy for Romanism, and perhaps worse.[89] The anti-sisterhood literature, with its sexual edge, invariably assumed (against all the evidence) that women took the final vows while still in their teens, and that these vows somehow made them the prisoners of lecherous clerics and sadistic superiors for life. This extract from a committee of inquiry into convents unites ordinary anti-sisterhood arguments with a sanctimonious salaciousness:

> Thus, a girl who is just growing into womanhood and is at an age when her mind is most easily deceived, and she does not understand the cravings and instincts of woman's nature, or of a woman's heart, is called upon to take the last vows ... *and then the monks and priests possess her for life.* Her after life is a secret and mystery to the outer world. Every crime known to earth and hell may be perpetuated; there may be the cry of insulted innocence, there may be the shriek of outraged virtue; it may ring and ring again through the walls ... and never reach the outside world ... [90]

That this was not just the prurience and paranoia of one individual is indicated by the Protestant Alliance still agitating for state inspection of convents in 1898.[91]

It is possible, judging from the very frequency with which the assertion is made, that some of the wilder critics of sisterhoods genuinely believed that women were not permitted to leave after taking the vows. Certainly some of the authors of anti-sisterhood pamphlets claimed this. W. G. Cooksley claimed that a professed sister was 'irrevocably handed over, for the rest of her life, to the service of the Mother Superior; no power can redeem her from this bondage'.[92] However fervently his readers may have believed this, Cooksley was a clergyman with relatives in an Anglican community; it is hard to believe that he did not know that his claim was simply false.

Given the inflammatory nature of many anti-Roman attacks upon sisterhood, it is perhaps surprising that only one community suffered physical damage from anti-popery mobs, aside from the 1857 incident at Lewes. This was Mother Hilda's Benedictine community, which, when living at Norwich in the 1860s, found their school attacked by a mob which smashed the windows and rushed the doors. Sisters and pupils were forced to take refuge in a neighbouring house until order was restored. But violence aside, public interest in the early sisterhoods was immense. Objections to Ascot Priory's 'Romish' practices reached such a pitch in 1849 that the Bishop of Exeter was forced to hold a public inquiry into their behaviour. They were ultimately censured for having flowers on their altar.[93]

Closely allied to the accusation of Romanism was the claim that sisterhoods were essentially 'UnEnglish'. This can be traced not only to fear of clandestine Catholic infiltration of England, but also to sisterhoods' association with the High Church wing of Anglicanism, which was widely perceived as being somehow unpatriotic and effeminate. Communities were seen by some of their detractors as part of the feminization of the Anglican Church; the accusation of unmanliness is a constant theme in mid- and late-Victorian attacks on the High Church. Christianity, depicted as formerly being 'the most masculine of religions', had become, in its English manifestation, 'the most effeminate'.[94] Sisterhoods, it was declared, grew out of this undue female influence in the Church and were thus discordant with English attitudes and institutions. Evidence of this, such disputants claimed, was found in the fact that revolutions occurred in countries which were Roman Catholic, and hence had plenty of convents; this was seen as proof positive that the influence of communities was detrimental, in that it made people more dissatisfied with the social order.[95]

The 'female incapacity' argument

Part of the opposition to sisterhoods was based on a view of women as incapable: in this view, passive and helpless women were deprived of English liberty in convents, were denied womanly fulfilment as wives and mothers, were exploited by communities for their money and, worst of all, were led to Rome in a sort of spiritual abduction. A number of these attacks took the view that sisters were the deluded victims of 'crafty, insidious, Anglican Jesuits'.[96] Closely tied to the antagonism to sisterhoods on the ground of female incapacity, was the suspicion of communities as female-originated and woman-run organizations. Women, it was confidently asserted, harmed any cause they espoused, and any organization founded and staffed by women alone could lead only to disaster. Such critics worked from the premise that women were not capable of creating effective and dynamic organizations;

therefore, any sisterhood which appeared to succeed could not be genuinely women-run. It was not enough to argue that such communities worked; the response to this was to claim either that their female founders possessed mesmeric powers which they used to control the sisters and to keep them from leaving or that, again, 'a man was behind it somewhere'.[97] Those who took this line seem to have sincerely believed that the establishment of communities was a work of which women were incapable; hidden men, it followed, must be the secret mainspring of sisterhoods. It seemed all too probable to resisters of communities that these men were Anglican priests who preyed on the gullibility of devout women. Many of these early attacks combined anxiety about women-conducted organizations claiming to be part of the Established Church with distrust of women themselves, although this interesting condemnation of Ascot Priory was penned by a woman as late as 1907.

> Through the present permissive system in regard to the foundation by any woman whose love of power and desire of activity impels her to the assumptions [sic] of an office in which her humanity can garb itself in attributes that seem to be supernatural and in an authority which is imposed as divine, the Church of England is at the mercy of any adventuress ... [98]

In cases where it was patently demonstrable that no man was 'behind it', an alternative explanation was put forward. In it it was claimed that the use of authority by women desexed them, thus nicely easing the opponents out of a logical dilemma.[99]

Authority wielded by women was, almost by definition, 'irresponsible'. Even the progressive Frances Power Cobbe shared this view, writing that

> Enough has been revealed to us of the secrets of convents, to leave no doubt that the possession of unnatural authority by the superiors has continually proved too strong a temptation; and the woman who in her natural domestic sphere might have been the gentlest of guides, has become in a convent the cruellest of petty despots.[100]

Women and authority were seen to be essentially incompatible; to Victorian eyes the combination was against nature. After listing many dangers into which women without men may fall, one writer concluded that they were incapable of dispassionate administration. It then followed that a Mother Superior 'caged for life with her own sex' became a tyrant. Again, at the very end of the century, Walsh declared that 'it was her office which spoiled the woman in Miss Sellon'.[101] Just as many of the attacks on female education were based on a reluctance to bring girls into close and daily contact with other girls, this sort of deep-seated misogyny and suspicion of women was a constant accompaniment to many of the attacks on these new women's communities.

The threat of female sexuality also emerged in the sisterhood debate. Women would suffer, they were warned, if they rejected their natural roles as wives and mothers in favour of a life of celibacy lived only among other women. Negative stereotypes of spinsterhood were adduced as proof of the debilitating effects of long-term virginity. Women were caught in a cleft stick: they would become petty tyrants if they remained chaste, but even worse would befall if they did not. Part of the argument was based on the fear that women in this situation would not remain celibate, but would in fact indulge in 'the darker forms of moral depravity into which Satan tempts the rash defiers of that great law of . . . nature'.[102]

While it is perhaps understandable that the Victorians should have feared same-sex attraction in single-sex institutions (although few voices were raised against public schools and military barracks), sisters were sometimes seen as a threat which was overtly heterosexual in nature. The Bishop of Lincoln proposed that no woman should be allowed to take vows before the age of sixty unless she was willing to remain entirely cloistered within the convent. He explained this remarkable suggestion by making it clear that the very freedom of sisters could be considered provocative, calling them 'these youthful sisters, so free and so attractive' and warning of the 'danger' of putting such women 'under vows of perpetual celibacy'.[103]

Sisters' freedom from the toilsome and wearing business of childbearing and child-rearing did not go uncriticized either; it was perceived as providing another proof of their essential unwomanliness. The loss of a woman's mothering potential consequent upon the vow of chastity was seen as yet another rejection of the Victorians' family-centred ideal. As late as 1898, the Protestant Alliance could publish with a straight face a poem whose poignant title was 'On Hearing a Nun Say She Hated Children'.[104] This predictably provoked the poet's outrage, although one might think that a life of celibacy was certainly a sensible choice for nineteenth-century women who felt this way.

The single defence of old maids which the Victorians allowed was that spinsterhood was honourable as long as the spinster remained wistfully regretful that she never married. To such fanatic opposition, all was grist to their mill: to them it seemed deeply significant that one of the first sisters to join the first community broke her engagement in order to do so.[105] After such a dreadful precedent, anything seemed possible. Sisters' cheerful renunciation of the experiences of marriage, including sexual intercourse and childbirth, was seen as yet another evidence of the profound unnaturalness of religious orders and of the women attracted to them. The robust, cheerful, chosen singleness of women's communities could not be fitted into this pattern, and they were punished for it by being stigmatized as 'unfeminine' and unnatural.

Sometimes communities were seen not merely as rejecting Victorian domestic ideology but as actively assaulting it; they offered an alternative to marriage and the family by articulating a 'higher way' of celibacy and service to the community. F. D. Maurice, the Christian Socialist, joined ranks with more conservative thinkers on the issue. His objection to sisterhoods was based on a fear that such institutions withdrew women from their 'natural position' within society. In a critical essay on sisterhoods Maurice complained that communities believed that 'the prejudices of Englishmen [on the topic of women-inspired organizations] ... are to be resisted as low, grovelling, ungodly prejudices'. He also found it worrying that sisters believed that their communities were 'a chief instrument of combating the notion that it is not good for women to be alone'.[106] Maurice argued that such ideas were misguided, and that Englishmen had good reason to be suspicious of women's communities on the grounds of their ideological unsoundness and essential abnormality. Others feared that sisterhoods were holding out a temptation to renounce marriage (the avoidance of which was instructively described as a 'powerful' and 'dangerous' inducement to enter a community). Sisterhoods, perhaps worst of all, were single-sex institutions where the members were removed from the 'corrective influence of association with men'.[107]

The conclusion to all the arguments based on the premise that women living without family (and especially without men) were in an unnatural and undesirable position was that men should take a more active role in sisterhoods. Ludlow concludes his book *Women's Work* with a clarion call for female subordination to male control of women's communities.

The only thing that has been wanting to make the Devonport Sisterhood of Mercy a true normal school for all English female charity, from whence Christian women should issue forth to all quarters of our country to battle with all the evils of our social state, has been that the proud and noble spirit of its founder should have owed obedience to an earthly husband ... [108]

In other words, Mothers Superior, to be genuinely complete and acceptable women, needed to have experienced marriage, legal non-existence and the discipline of wifely subordination. Ludlow's was not an exceptional point of view; sisterhoods were under attack throughout the century for believing (so their critics claimed) in the superior sanctity of unmarried life. Sometimes the anti-woman opinions articulated were really grotesque. Take, for example, Ludlow's equation of women's 'harmlessness' with control by a non-celibate male. *'Every Sisterhood, to be really useful, to be really harmless, must, in my opinion, have at its head not only a man, but a married man.'*[109] In all seriousness, one critic of Anglican communities complained that nuns failed in their duty as women because they did not acknowledge men to be their superiors.[110] Perhaps these spinsters, who were bound by fewer emotional ties to their patriarchal society, were more likely to question its assumptions.

Another reason for opposing sisterhoods was inherent in the religious aspects of community life. Even those who welcomed the practical work done by sisters tended to share Ruskin's conviction that the one dangerous science for women was theology. The Community of the Sisters of the Church was attacked for writing and publishing catechisms and other religious works. These publications were seen as the unwise (because unauthorized) delving of women into the male sphere of religious teaching and authority. The founder of the secular Charity Organization Society resorted to a religious argument when unable to fault the work of Holy Cross and Clewer in London on practical grounds: Charles Bosanquet concluded that their efforts would do 'more harm than good in the long run' because they were 'not Scriptural'.[111]

As Vicinus points out, the idea of a successful woman's community was frightening, implying as it did female self-sufficiency and the dispensability (at least for some women) of men.[112] Collective female power was threatening; the women who joined Josephine Butler in her campaign against the Contagious Diseases Acts experienced similar and worse attacks from advocates of the woman's sphere. The entire ethos of sisterhood life, based as it was on cooperation, mutuality and corporate identity in a women's community, disturbed a whole series of comfortable Victorian assumptions about the nature of gender differences.

Living in public

While some critics of communities depicted them as prison houses, others saw danger in the non-domestic life they led. Sisters were criticized by the

Bishop of Lincoln, among others, for 'living in public'. This curious phrase confirms my claim that the convent, paradoxically, provided women with freedom from the Victorian ideal of claustration within the family home. There is irony in that the sisters (whose convents did sometimes contain cloisters) were charged with unwomanly freedom from confinement. While most philanthropic ladies avoided having any public face at all, sisters were accused of encroaching on the male monopoly of the public sphere.[113] This was another proof of their unladylike and unfeminine attitudes. But there was some truth in the accusation. The publicity attached to these new ventures did exact a psychological toll. The brother of an Anglican foundress described the drawback of 'living in public' as the constant, wearing scrutiny of the local community. Sisters in the pioneering communities soon became accustomed to locals attempting to press their faces against the convent windows, or trying to storm the doors to search for women believed to be being held against their will. Public interest in the new communities was extreme, and was sometimes expressed in unwelcome ways.

> Every action, almost every movement; where they went, whom they conversed with, their style of dress, their private as well as more public occupations, could not escape becoming most minutely criticized, and gradually gaining for ... the ... Sisters ... a notoriety as little to be envied by others, as desired by themselves ... [114]

Even this sympathetic observer felt that the sisters' violation of the 'sacred privacy' which should surround women was the most valid objection to their existence. He concluded that women who became sisters brought this unwelcome interest on themselves: 'those who engage in public actions become public property'. Sisters found that they could thus be condemned for doing, as well as for being.

Work and the role of 'ladies'

By the mid-nineteenth century the great indicator of social standing was the idleness of one's womenfolk; women worked, ladies did not. Unlike governesses, the standard example of the lady who was declassed as a result of her employment and as a result belonged neither in the kitchen nor in the drawing room, the nuns were often women of some wealth and belonged to families of influence. The Anglican sisterhoods created a paradoxical situation in that the sisters, mostly women of middle- or upper-class origin, worked hard and openly. It was inconceivable to argue that these women, who worked as the result of choice rather than in response to financial necessity, were not ladies. Much of the early anti-sisterhood pamphlet literature focuses on the fact that in communities upper-class women did work which would normally have been performed by servants. It is remarkable that even writers aiming at a neutral tone take on an hysteric intensity when this subject is broached.

Sisterhoods thus indirectly brought into question the very definition of female respectability, involving as it did complete abstention from open manual labour for all women above the working class. In fact, respectability was sometimes explicitly renounced. Lydia Sellon, the founder of Ascot Priory, condemned the 'idol of respectability, a word which bears NO Christian meaning whatsoever'. Sellon emphasized that the common definitions of 'female respectability' restricted women's activities to a point that was positively 'unChristian', as well as absurd.[115] Sisters argued that women who were debarred from public action would be debarred from obedience to the commands of Christ, who urged his followers to action, both spiritual and social, physical and moral.

The inappropriateness of physical labour for ladies was reiterated repeatedly in contemporary criticisms of community life. Typical of the degradation associated with manual work for women was the response of one man, who wrote to the Pall Mall Gazette, 'I call myself a gentleman and I am fond of my rank, – but I would sooner see a daughter or a sister of mine marry a shoemaker than become a sister ... '[116] Critics of the sisterhood movement were driven to disregard the fact that many women were desperately bored or unhappy in their comfortable homes and welcomed the opportunity to undertake hard, often unpleasant, work because it was meaningful and rewarding.

Most entrants into Anglican sisterhoods were women from upper-class backgrounds. The change from their leisured displays of conspicuous consumption to a life of cooperative poverty and manual labour must have been very great. Although the Country Gentleman depicted the change in a very romantic fashion, writing 'The lady who but last season might be seen at almost every fashionable ball, the admired of all, the life of the society she adorned, may now be seen doing the simplest work in the sisterhood, her only wish being a longing for her novitiate ... ', this portrayal did contain a grain of truth.[117] The change from lady of leisure to sister of mercy was an enormous one. To move from young lady on the Victorian marriage market to a woman under vows of chastity, obedience and poverty meant more than a change of dress and demeanour; it required a revolution in intent, in feeling and in values – in short, a new life.

Economic arguments

It was possible for those who found sisterhoods threatening to see sinister motives in almost anything. One example should suffice: most communities followed the practice of keeping secret the amount each member donated to their funds, in order to create the atmosphere of sisterly equality they believed necessary. Walsh, for one, believed that the 'profound secrecy' which surrounded sisters' contributions allowed dishonest Mothers Superior to embezzle community funds, saying that the vow of poverty 'is a grand scheme for relieving English ladies of their money'.[118] There was no instance of any claim, or even suggestion, of embezzlement in any Victorian community, yet this claim that sisterhoods were set up to dupe trusting and financially naive women was reiterated by otherwise disparate critics.

A more creditable attack with an economic basis was that launched by the Charity Organization Society against the Sisters of the Church in the 1890s. (The COS was convinced that pauperization of the poor was the almost automatic result of any assistance at all being given them. Beatrice Webb, a former member, described them as 'ideologues, convinced that a man who lacked work lacked character ... unpopular busybodies'.[119]) The COS was calling for a limitation of private charity in a period of high unemployment, and at the same time opposing state intervention. The Society attacked the sisterhood on two grounds: it disliked the nature of the assistance provided and was also opposed to the idea of women having responsibility for an organization's financial affairs. When the Sisters of the Church ignored the COS's demand that they cease providing meals for striking dockworkers, the unemployed and poor schoolchildren at below-cost price, the COS published a pamphlet accusing them of cruelty to children, demoralizing working-class people by giving them food and money, and suggesting that the community was misappropriating funds raised from the public. They were soon to retract the accusation of financial wrongdoing when Lord Nelson (one of the sisterhood's trustees) explained that the arithmetical error in the published audit had originated with him. The accusation of cruelty to children in the sisterhood's orphanages received widespread publicity for some time, but no proof of the charges made in the press was forthcoming, and no formal charge was ever made.[120] The most conventional of the many COS attacks on the Sisters of the Church in the 1890s based its argument on the hoary grounds that since 'everyone acknowledged' that ladies were no good at business, the all-woman sisterhoods were especially presumptuous in thinking they could manage their affairs without outside assistance. The COS report on this vigorous and prosperous community delivered this verdict:

> in our opinion, no body entirely composed of and governed by women, to the absolute exclusion of all members of the opposite sex, could be wholly successful in matters of policy, of finance, and business. Such a body we believe the Sisters to be.[121]

In other words, in the opinion of the COS, women were fit only to be the foot-soldiers of philanthropy, unquestioningly carrying out projects planned and managed by men. In light of this, the suggestion that the COS may have been 'over-anxious to grasp at pretexts to discredit an influential body which was working on different principles from their own' seems a reasonable one.[122]

Robbing society of moral women

One interesting objection to sisterhoods which emerged briefly in the 1860s portrayed them as a direct threat to the morality of society. The complaint was made that these organizations removed from social life 'qualities which might otherwise prove a bulwark against evil'. It was claimed that so many of the most intelligent and devout young women were entering Anglican communities that the moral tone of the upper classes was degenerating as the direct result of their withdrawal. Penelope Holland warned that convents 'sifted society', asserting that 'the noble and the strong, disgusted with the worrying littlenesses of society, turn to the convent in hopes of relief':

> convents ... have a tendency to absorb ... those who have any earnestness or solidity of character, leaving social life wholly to those who wish for nothing beyond amusement. It is worthy of observation, that the last ten years, during which it is said that such a marked change for the worse has been seen in English society, have coincided with the period at which the effects of the multiplying of Roman Catholic and Church of England convents began to be felt.[123]

Even *Punch* supported what seems an improbable claim. In an interesting illustration, Eliza Lynn Linton's 'Two girls of the period' (Figure 6.2), a frivolous creature, whose ostentatious cross is incongruously paired with her daring dress, is depicted in direct opposition to the image of serious and high-principled women, who were believed to be entering convents in droves.[124] What is interesting about this 'two girls of the period' objection is its insistence that community life was the *only* active alternative to 'the frivolity of the life which custom now enforces' on most women.[125] It, intentionally or not, forcibly underlines the lack of alternatives open to mid-Victorian women of ambition. After the 1860s, when recruitment to sisterhoods stabilized and publicity decreased, it must have become obvious that the appeal of communities was not going to strip the upper classes of their best women. This curious argument then disappeared.

Other pressures

Some communities faced dilemmas specific to themselves. The Community of Saint Mary the Virgin, Brighton, endured an extended period of obloquy when it was discovered that the celebrated (self-confessed) child murderer Constance Kent had lived with them for two years, working as a nurse and caring for orphans. The community was attacked both for harbouring a supposed killer and for encouraging her to turn herself in after she began to insist that she had committed the crime. Feeling rose so high that during Kent's trial in 1865, the convent was forced to have a police guard around it.[126]

The 'surplice riots' at St George's-in-the-East began eight days after the Bishop of London's *Charge*, in which he accused W. J. E. Bennett of encouraging women to work as sisters without their parents' consent.[127] The conjunction of the two events was almost certainly not coincidental. We have already looked at the Lewes riots which affected East Grinstead in the 1850s. The story of the unrest was still current in 1865, when the MP for Peterborough told a garbled version in the House of Commons, substituting the Brighton sisterhood for the East Grinstead group. He claimed that 'Miss Scovell' was sent to nurse fever cases in a deliberate attempt to kill her off, and enlarged the size of the legacy left to the community from £400 to £8000. Political hay could occasionally be made. In 1870 Gladstone was accused of being the 'head' of a convent: probably a confused recognition of his active involvement in the establishment of the first community, Park Village, in 1845 or of the fact that he was one of the Clewer trustees. This accusation against Gladstone remained current for much of the rest of his life.[128]

Given time, and increasing familiarity with the idea of women's life in community, the vigorous opposition of the 1840s and 1850s gradually faded: Priscilla Sellon marvelled in 1868 at the amount of change, writing that 'twenty-one years ago I was nearly killed for wearing the black dress and the black cross'.[129] The lack of national scandals involving communities, along with increasing tolerance of Anglo-Catholicism, resulted in the early nation-wide

PUNCH, OR THE LONDON CHARIVARI.—February 20, 1869.

TWO GIRLS OF THE PERIOD.

Ritualistic Priest. "THERE, MY CHILD, OBSERVE THAT EXAMPLE OF HUMILITY AND DEVOTION. HOW SWEET TO CHANGE THE VANITIES OF THE WORLD FOR A LOT SO HUMBLE!"

Fashionable Convert. "OH, BUT THAT IS NOT AT ALL WHAT I EXPECTED!—AND WEAR SUCH AWFUL SHOES? AND—— OH REALLY, ON SECOND THOUGHTS, I SHALL STICK TO BELGRAVIA."

Figure 6.2 'Two girls of the period', *Punch*, 20 February 1869. The fad for all things mediaeval (including monasticism) induced many upper-class women to consider sisterhood life, and some even argued that there was no *via media* between fashionable dissipation and the convent for intelligent women in the 1860s. (British Library Reproductions.)

fascination with the groups subsiding. Locally, three things worked in their favour. First, their anxious neighbours in the slum areas where sisterhoods settled gradually came to discover that no blood-curdling screams came from the convent and that the sisters were eager to be accepted as a normal and useful aspect of life in the local community. Ironically, the constant persecution which they had experienced in the early years probably assisted communities in their aim of solidarity with the poor; both were distrusted by the larger society, as well as being seen as incapable of managing their own affairs without the guidance of some 'other' (middle-class supervision for the poor, male supervision for the sisters).

Second, sisterhoods took advantage of every opportunity to disarm suspicion through contact, especially in times of local distress. Several communities commented on the difference in the degree of local acceptance before and after the cholera and smallpox epidemics which erupted intermittently from 1849 to 1870.[130] These events generally turned hostility and indifference into welcome and support, given that the sisters nursed indefatigably and at their own expense throughout such local calamities. One Bethnal Green native described the 1865 arrival of a community (probably Saint Saviour's Priory) in her neighbourhood as a source of prejudice and distrust, but demonstrates that this feeling was eventually overcome by the nursing of infectious disease and kindness to local children.[131] From the perspective of the sisterhoods, this could transform calamities into opportunities: as Mother Kate commented with some satisfaction, when discussing the outbreak of cholera in the East End of London in August–November 1866: 'Now doors were opened which had hitherto been closed to the Sisters; hands, which had pointed at them in scorn, now beckoned to them in anguish; voices, which had been raised at them in derision, now besought them to enter their houses.' Descending to a less exalted literary voice, Mother Kate concluded that the epidemic broke down barriers between the sisters and the local community.

> The people found them to be useful, ablebodied women, who would tuck up their sleeves, put on an apron, and either nurse them or clean the place, as the case required, and therefore ceased to look upon them as solemn-garbed recluses, as they had hitherto deemed them.

There does seem to have been some truth to this analysis: as we have already seen, the great waves of opposition and published abuse died out almost contemporaneously with the great epidemics at the end of the 1860s and reappeared only sporadically thereafter. Indeed communities were very aware of the publicity value of such exploits as nursing in local epidemics and attempted to ensure that their efforts received the widest possible attention. (The above extracts come from a brief publicity pamphlet of that nature.[132])

It must be mentioned that this tacit approval was limited to sisterhoods whose primary work was nursing; the sisterhoods who devoted themselves to the reformation of prostitutes found it necessary to keep their local profiles as low as possible. It is also possible to err on the side of optimism, as Cameron does when he claims that it was the communities' nursing work in the Crimean War in 1854–55 which ended the popular opposition to sisterhoods. The Crimean episode, while it alerted much of the British public for the first time to the existence of Anglican nursing sisterhoods, occurred in the decade during which community life for women was subjected to the most fierce, sustained and unrelenting opposition it was to encounter. Rowell makes a similar error when he links the cholera epidemic in Plymouth in 1849 with Sellon's sisterhood gaining local respect: in actual fact, 1849–50 showed the local anti-sisterhood movement at its fiercest.[133]

Third, communities worked through children. As Mother Kate pointed out, once the children had been won over to acceptance of the new element in their midst, the parents generally followed suit.[134] This meant that communities usually saw their first priority in a new location as the setting up of free or cheap schools, Sunday schools, guilds, clubs and clubrooms, and the sponsoring of social activities· designed to appeal to the young, as discussed in the chapter on community work.

In this lengthy discussion of how communities were viewed as threatening or undesirable by Victorian society, it is possible to lose sight of the basic question: why were sisterhoods perceived as such a problem? Sisters were in part so distressing to Victorian public opinion because of their willingness to discard the normal social and moral requirements for feminine respectability; they could not be identified with a man, they abandoned social markers such as material possessions, they directly reversed, and indirectly subverted, the Angel in the House image. The essential problem was this: sisters did not accept the Victorian ideas of what women should be, want and do. They chose to work when most of them could have lived in comfortable idleness; they chose to remain single in a culture which saw single women as failures; they chose to expose themselves to scenes and experiences commonly regarded as unfit for ladies; they chose to separate themselves from their families; and they chose to experiment with a woman-centred lifestyle which was, at this time, wholly foreign to the British way of thinking.

'A FIELD WIDER THAN PRIVATE LIFE': THE PLACE OF ANGLICAN SISTERHOODS IN VICTORIAN HISTORY

This book is a first attempt to sketch out the social history of Anglican and Episcopal sisterhoods in Victorian Britain. However, much remains to be learned about these communities, and even more material cries out for re-interpretation. Community finances, architecture and material culture and related subjects require much more research. The area of community spirituality, worship and ritual is still almost *terra incognita*. The interrelation-ships between the various sisterhoods require much more study. Even areas that seem absolutely central to a full comprehension of the communities, such as the influences upon, and development of, their Rules and Constitutions, have yet to be systematically examined.

The issues involved in any discussion of the sisterhood movement are extraordinarily complex: so many communities were formed, in a great variety of locations, and in response to a multitude of social needs and inner impulses. In light of the complexity of the establishment of these multifarious groups, their varied work and the strong response they evoked from the public, it may be useful to underline some of the findings of the research on which this book is based. My intention has been to show how several aspects of the sisterhood movement allowed women to extend the boundaries of the domestic sphere and thereby enlarge women's space into the public arena. By founding communities, by leaving home and family to enter them, by establishing a complex and self-governed corporate life, by creating and working in a wide variety of social welfare projects, and by insisting on their own control of their communities, despite social disapproval and the reservations of the established order of the church, the Anglican sisterhoods violated accepted Victorian expectations of female behaviour. Both as women and as religious professionals, these sisters were women who went beyond what their society believed women should be and do.

The first sisterhood was formed in the year of Newman's secession to Rome, and communities were one of the first and most durable practical outcomes of the Oxford Movement. They claimed as their own the

Movement's emphasis on the centrality of the sacraments and took to heart its teaching of the urgency of biblical commands to succour the poor. It is within the context of sisterhoods that we see one aspect of the significance of the High Church movement for women. Although in many ways their Anglicanism was self-defined, they found ways of expressing their religious and social convictions through the filter of Anglo-Catholic theology and practice. Religion was not an opiate for these women, except in that it may have assisted in easing their own personal pain. Religion provided the impetus and the structure that allowed them to violate social norms for their own behaviour, and to demand that their society change its way of dealing with the poor, the young and the deviant.

By 1900 more than ninety women's communities claiming allegiance to the Church of England had been formed; with only one or two exceptions, all of these were dedicated to active work. Anglican sisters rejected the necessity for female idleness as a demonstration of male success, and the class assumptions that accompanied the concept of conspicuous consumption. Instead, sisters displayed an unashamed willingness to undertake hard physical labour. In their communities sisters asserted their rights to work and regarded constant and regular employment as both a duty and a privilege, while their secular sisters still largely saw comfortable idleness as the appropriate feminine goal. In these ways, sisterhoods brought into question the very definition of female respectability, a concept they themselves unhesitatingly rejected.

Sisterhoods need to be understood in the context of the Victorian expansion of philanthropic activity, and especially of philanthropic work performed by women. The first communities were established at a time when both rural and urban poverty had assumed an unprecedented urgency and were causes for anxious public concern. They emerged in the aftermath of a long series of bad harvests and before the failure of the Chartists' third petition removed the fear of a working-class insurrection. For the first time, the divide between the 'two nations' had become a subject for anxious moral, as well as political, consideration, and it is certainly possible that such concerns may have been a factor in the expansion of the sisterhood movement. While their consciences may have been awakened by the growing awareness of the gulf between rich and poor, the sisters worked within the assumptions of their culture. They did not question the belief that private charity was a legitimate way of assisting the disadvantaged, as well as a divinely ordained duty. Except for those who were touched by Christian Socialism, sisters accepted without question the inequalities built into Victorian capitalism. They used the metaphor of 'metaphysical motherhood' to describe and justify their social work. Just as the Victorians exalted biological motherhood and its duties, the sisters demanded a privileged place for their mothering of the poor. While viewing the working class as needy and dependent, they nonetheless pioneered numberless initiatives aimed at helping ease the life of the urban slum dweller. As a late Victorian commentator pointed out, by the end of the nineteenth century sisterhoods were almost universally acknowledged as a significant advance for women and as important in the development of social work:

> A movement [sisterhoods] which has so permeated social life cannot be regarded as the mere ebullition of a sect. It is not only that the attitude of the Church towards women has altered, but the attitude of the Church as a body for social work has been affected. It brought the Church earlier than would otherwise have been the case to play a prominent part in that general altruistic movement which is the characteristic feature of the last half-century.[1]

If it were not for the work of sisters, the activity of the Anglican Church in late-Victorian social reform projects would have been negligible indeed.

The importance of the sisterhoods for Anglican women is demonstrated by the extremism of the reaction provoked from the public in general and from the clergy in particular. The church hierarchy was profoundly disapproving of the autonomy which sisters experienced in Anglican sisterhoods. The general public was suspicious of sisterhoods for several reasons, the most important being that communal living and the vow of celibacy seemed to involve a rejection of the family. In order to make this rejection comprehensible, the idea of the 'stolen daughter', suggesting somehow that women were seduced or tricked into rejecting their families for communities, gained wide acceptance. Their vexed relationship with both the family and the Church indicates that the autonomy which such communities bestowed was recognized and treasured by their members, and was not to be given up lightly in return for 'sanction' of dubious value.

What place, then, has the sisterhood movement within Victorian social history and within women's history? Communities must be seen in the context of that enormous proliferation of charitable and philanthropic organizations in Victorian Britain. Sisterhoods provided some of the most wide-ranging and long-lived charitable organizations originating in the nineteenth century, which by 1900 had been staffed by close to 10,000 full-time women workers. Sisterhoods are also of interest to historians of culture and ideas because of the attention they attracted. The vigour and longevity of the press attention devoted to them indicates that the idea of the 'nun' touched a sore place in Victorian anxieties about their society and women's place within it. The almost hysterical reaction which sisterhoods provoked from the British public centred around several core violations of the 'proper' role for women. Perhaps most consistently, they were attacked for rejecting their role in the family and their biological role as women.

For the women's historian, sisterhoods embody a powerful example of feminist practice. The sisters who formed them devoted their lives to the bettering of the lives of other women. This was demonstrated through the practical services which they provided for their client communities, themselves largely women and children. At the same time the convent provided careers for thousands of sisters. Sisterhood life called forth hitherto unsuspected administrative and managerial talents in individuals who, as women, would otherwise have been barred from pursuing such occupations. Unlike most roles for women, even the activism of the campaigners for women's rights, sisterhood work was a full-time activity, which constantly provided built-in affirmation of its own importance. The sisters created their own communities; ruled and served in them; and enjoyed great freedom from the normal controls on Victorian women. The history of these communities matters for many reasons: because of their size and importance, because of the amount of controversy they generated, because of the work they provided, and because they were a new departure within Anglicanism.

Victorian Anglican communities for women displayed an astonishing exaltation of female control, authority and spirituality. The sisters preached in their chapels, organized fund-raising campaigns, managed the finances of large and complex organizations, built convents, hospitals, orphanages and schools, took positions of authority and responsibility within the larger community, wrote books, lobbied MPs, presented petitions to Parliament and worked on every continent, all within a completely female authority structure. Naturally, all of this resulted in the pioneering members of Anglican orders taking tremendous pride in their *corporate* expansion, influence and achievements. They used, with great success, philanthropic and religious arguments to carve out for themselves satisfying careers outside of the normal sphere for Victorian women.

APPENDIX 1

ANGLICAN SISTERHOODS
ESTABLISHED 1845–1900[1]

1845	Sisterhood of the Holy Cross
1848	Community of St Mary the Virgin
1848	Society of the Most Holy Trinity
1848	Nursing Institute of St John's House
1850	Sisters of Charity (St Barnabas' Sisterhood)
1851	Society of the Holy and Undivided Trinity
1851	Community of St Thomas the Martyr
1851	Community of St John the Baptist
1851	Community of All Saints (Sisters of the Poor)
1851	Sisterhood of St Michael and All Angels
1854	Community of All Hallows
1855	Community of the Blessed Virgin Mary
1855	Society of St Margaret
1857	Community of the Holy Cross
1858	Sisterhood of St Peter
1858	Community of the Holy Rood
1858	Sisterhood of St Mary the Virgin
1860	Sisterhood of the Blessed Virgin
1861	Community of St Peter
1862	Deaconess Community of St Andrew
1863	Sisterhood of Mount Calvary, Norwich
1863	Community of the Good Samaritan, Coatham
1864	Sisterhood of the Compassion
1864	Sisters of St Joseph of Nazareth
1865	Community of the Holy Name (also known as the Community of the Mission Sisters of the Holy Name)
1865	Community of St Mary at the Cross (Sisters of the Poor)
1866	St Cyprian's Sisterhood
1866	Community of St Wilfred
1866	Society of the Sisters of Bethany
1867	Community of St Andrew of Scotland

1867	St Etheldreda's Sisterhood
1868	Sisterhood of SS Mary and John
1868	Sisters of Charity
1868	Benedictine Nuns
1869	Community of Reparation to Jesus in the Blessed Sacrament (Mission Sisters of St Alphege)
1870	Sisters of the Church
1870	Scottish Society of Reparation (Community of St Mary and St John)
1871	Community of SS Mary and Modwenna
1871	Community of the Paraclete
1872	Order of Holy Charity
1873	Sisters of St Mary and St John
1874	Community of St Laurence
1875	Sisterhood of the Compassion of Jesus
1877	Servants of the Cross
1879	Missionary Community of St Denys
1879	Community of St Katherine of Egypt
1881 (approx.)	Sisterhood of Faith, Hope and Charity
1881	Community of the Name of Jesus
1881	Sisterhood of the Holy Child
1883	Community of the Epiphany
1884	Sisterhood of St Agnes, Guild of St Alban
1884	Community of the Resurrection of Our Lord (branch)
1886	Sisterhood of St James
1887	Community of St Mary the Virgin
1890	Sisterhood of the Holy Ghost the Comforter
1891	Community of the Holy Comforter
1894	Community of the Ascension
1894	Sisterhood of the Holy Childhood
1894	Society of the Incarnation of the Eternal Son
1895	Community of St Michael and All Angels
1897	Servants of Christ
1898	Community of the Holy Family
1899	Community of the Compassion of Jesus
1899	Community of Our Lady of Nazareth

Other communities whose date of establishment or duration is unknown

(Dates given are those when the group is mentioned in other communities' records or in sisterhood literature.)

1846	Sisters of Charity, St Paul's, Knightsbridge
1858	Sisterhood of St Mary the Virgin, Ipswich, working in the parish of St Matthew's, Ipswich, for last 12 months[2]
1862	Sisterhood at Buckland Monachorum, nr Plymouth, which may be the Sisterhood of the Servants of the Church, Plymouth
1864	St Martin's Home, Blenheim St., Liverpool
1860s	St Mary's Community and Orphanage, Lambeth
1867	St James Sisterhood, Liverpool
1869	St Lucy's Home, Gloucester
1869, 1882	Community of St Cyprian, Park St., Dorset Sq.[3]
1870s–1892	Community of Hospitaller Nuns, Osnaburgh St.
1871	A community in Folkestone, parish of St Peters
1880s	'Mr Piscill's Sisters' active
1873	A community in the diocese of St Andrews, Perth
1873	Sisterhood of St Etheldreda
1878	St Michael's, Croydon
1880s	St Columba's (-by-the-Castle), Edinburgh (also worked in Carlisle and Ireland)
1880s	Sisters of the Saving Name, 279 Victoria Park Road, Hackney
1884, 1891	A community headed by Sister Beatrice (Parry) at Puffin View, Llangfrassfechum, North Wales
1884-98	St Gabriel's House of Rest, Folkestone,
1890s	A community in Clerkenwell, parish of Holy Comforter
1892	Order of the Holy Redeemer, Stamford Hill, London
1898	Community of Sacred Compassion, Hastings and Reading
?	House of Charity, 7 Johnson Terrace, Edinburgh
?	St Catherine's Convent, Folkestone
?	Benedictine Community of SS Mary and Scholastica
?	St Thomas' Home, Elson, near Gosport
?	Community of the Visitation

Notes

1. (Adapted from Anson and Campbell, *Call*.) This list despite my best efforts is still incomplete: Convocation calculated that there were 25 sisterhoods operating in 1862, and I have found tantalizing glimpses of several elusive groups besides those listed on pp. 211–13.

2. All Hallows Archives, 'The Sisters of Mercy in St Matthew's, Ipswich', clipping from *Suffolk Chronicle*, n.d.

3. Anson gives the date of foundation for this community as 1870; however, it is clear from CSC archives that the sisterhood was fully established before 1869 (CSC Archives, Account of the Beginnings of the Community, reference to 'Mr Gutch's Sisterhood').

PARENTAL OCCUPATIONS LISTED IN PROFESSION ROLLS

Aristocracy/Gentry

Various titles
Landowner
MP

Gentleman
JP

Professions

Admiral
Architect
Artist
Army officer
Barrister
Captain RN
Civil Servant
Clergy
Colonel
Commander RN
Consul

General
Lawyer
Lieutenant-Colonel
Major
Major-General
Naval officer
Physician
Professor
Solicitor
Surgeon
Vice-Admiral

Mercantile

Banker
Brewer
Manufacturer

Merchant
Newspaper proprietor/editor
Wine merchant

Trade and clerical

Chemist

Clerk

Manager

Music teacher

Ordinance survey (surveyor?)

Diocesan school inspector

Schoolmaster

Secretary

Tax collector

Teacher

Working-class trades

Artisan

Baker

Bootmaker

Builder

Cabinetmaker

Carpenter

Carver

Clockmaker

Coachman

Confectioner

Decorator

Draper's assistant

Farm labourer

Farmer

Fruiterer

Gardener

Gasfitter

Hatter

Jeweller

Leatherworker

Linen-draper

Mathematical instrument maker

Nurseryman

Organ-builder

Piano-maker

Printer

Prison warden

Private

Quarryman

Scripture reader

Sergeant

Servant

Soldier

Tailor

Tea grocer

Tinplate worker

Type founder

Wool sorter

THE CASE OF A SINGLE-ORDER COMMUNITY: THE COMMUNITY OF ST MARY THE VIRGIN, WANTAGE

Two hundred and twenty women joined CSMVW in the period to 1900. The average age of profession was 35.8 years. Thirty (13.6%) eventually left.

CSMVW was unique in recording the former professions of a substantial minority (29) of its members: occupations are given as described in the original source.

Teaching	
Private governess	9
Elementary schoolmistress	3
Held Oxbridge certificates	3
Teacher in private school	1
Founded school of embroidery	1

Service	
Servant	3
Matron	1

Nursing and related professions	
Children's nurse	3
Nurse	1
Deaconess	1

Trade and business	
Milliner	1
'In business'	1
Actress	1

Age at profession

20–24	1	40–44	28
25–29	37	45–49	11
30–34	58	50–54	11
35–39	44	55–60	2

CLOTHING AND PROFESSION RATES IN TWO COMMUNITIES

Clothing and profession rates 1855–1900: SSM

Clothed	247
Professed (73%)	181
Died as novices	4

Clothing and profession rates 1865–1900: Holy Name

Clothed	126
Professed (58%)	73

Lay sisters: 21 left; of these
5 were rejected
14 left at their own wish
2 health failed

Choir sisters: 32 left; of these
11 were rejected
12 left at their own wish
6 health failed
2 transfers
1 death

Overall, 42% of aspirants were never professed.

RATES OF GROWTH IN THE FIRST 25 YEARS AFTER FOUNDING: SELECTED COMMUNITIES

Date of foundation	Community	Number professed	Left (percentage)
1848	CSMVW	29	10.3
1851	CSJB	122	19.6
1855	SSM	86	37.2 [1]
1851	All Saints	80	21.2
1851	STM	29	44.8
1854	All Hallows	17	23.5
1858	Holy Rood	8	25.0
1865	Holy Name	28	21.4
1869	CRJBS	16	50.0
1870	CSC	110	34.5 [2]

Notes

1. This figure is misleadingly high: the majority of those who left SSM transferred to its 'daughter' communities, SSP and SSM Scotland.

2. Virtually all the CSC sisters who left went in 'the troubles' of the early 1890s; until then the community had been unusually retentive of members.

PROFESSIONS BY DECADE: 1840s–1890s

All professions[1]		Lay professions[2]	
1840s	10		
1850s	48	1850s	2
1860s	174	1860s	14
1870s	424	1870s	52
1880s	497	1880s	63
1890s	609	1890s	73

Note: There are 47 sisters with clothing but no profession dates, who seem to have been professed (i.e., they lived in the community for many subsequent years, and eventually died there). It is significant that 26 of these were lay sisters. Clearly, recording practices were laxer for lay candidates.

Notes

1. 174 who entered before 1900 were professed after that date.
2. 21 who entered before 1900 were professed after that date.

ATTRITION IN COMMUNITIES[1]

Conversion to Roman Catholicism	36.4
Transfer to other Anglican community	22.8
Dismissed by community	14.1
Requested release	6.7
Insanity	2.4
Left to found order	2.4
Illness	3.0
Left to marry	1.9
Wished to work independently	1.9
Parental demands	1.2
Left after discipline	1.2

Other (disliked new chaplain, life too rigorous, ran away, discontent with lay status, ambition to become Mother Superior, conflict with co-founder, isolation, nervous breakdown, deported, return to home country)

Lapse of time between profession and leaving[2]

No. of years	No. leaving
1–5	69 (average 2 years, 9 months)
6–10	60
11–15	45
16–20	30
21–25	22
26–30	9
31–35	13
36+	5

Notes

1. $N = 162$.
2. $N = 253$ whose date of leaving is known.

CRJBS: CONVENT ACCOUNT FOR 1906

	£	s	d
Rent	142	3	6
Rates and taxes	85	19	8
Fire insurance	3	0	0
Water rate	9	6	3
Gas rate	32	16	7
Repairs	60	6	1
Travelling expenses	31	17	11½
Postage, stationery, adverts	10	10	8
Chemist	2	15	10
Clothing and boots	23	6	10½
Convent housekeeping[1]	299	10	4½
Bank overdraft	1	16	10
Burial fee	3	3	0
Altar flowers, candles, oil	11	18	10
Office books	1	10	0
Chapel washing	1	3	4
Grants to charities[2]	28	10	1½
Total:	749	15	11

CRJBS: Convent Housekeeping (1906)[3]

	£	s	d
Butcher and fishmonger	58	8	7
Baker	23	3	3
Grocer	41	6	9½
Greengrocer	9	14	2
Milkman	32	2	9
Cheesemonger	30	17	2½
Coal	12	16	8
Oilman	5	9	2
Laundry	38	17	8
Wages	38	11	6

Crockery	1	18	10
House linen	15	13	$9\frac{1}{2}$
Total:	309	0	$4\frac{1}{2}$

Notes

1. CRJBS Archives, Annual Report for 1906. The housekeeping is broken down directly below. The inconsistency between the figure given here and the (correct) total below exists in the original set of accounts.

2. CRJBS Archives, Log of Community 1869–1936.

3. CRJBS Archives, Log of Community 1869–1936. This budget covered the living expenses of about fifteen sisters, several novices and postulants, and an unknown number of orphans.

THE SISTERS OF THE CHURCH: PRINCIPAL WORKS, AS REPORTED TO ARCHBISHOP BENSON IN 1894

1 Girls' orphanages
    Randolph Gardens, Kilburn
    St Mary's Home, Broadstairs
    Victoria Orphanage, Shirland Road, London
    Eastcombe, Somersetshire

2 Boys' orphanages
    Lady Adelaide Home, Brondesbury
    Hallam Hall, Clevedon
    Liddon Memorial Orphanage, Oxford

3 Day schools (London)

St Augustine's, Kilburn	1434	girls & infants
Gordon Memorial School, Kilburn	1286	mixed[1]
Princess Frederica, Kensal Green	1436	girls & infants
Keble Memorial, Harlesden	619	mixed
St Gabriels, Bromley	508	girls & infants
Waterloo College, Kilburn	225?	girls & infants
Wilberforce Schools, Kilburn	909	girls & infants
Upper School, Kilburn	?	girls
People's College, Harlesden	173	girls
National High School, Kilburn	530	girls
Upper School (Old Palace), Croydon	335	girls & infants
Liddon Memorial, Kentish Town	140	girls & infants

4 Other Schools

York	157	girls & infants
Salisbury	240	girls & infants
Nottingham	224	mixed
Liverpool High School	60	mixed[2]

5   Overseas schools[3]
     Hamilton, Canada
     Toronto, Canada
     Ottawa, Canada
     Adelaide, Australia
     Sydney, Australia
     Hobart, Australia
     Madras, India
     Rangoon, Burma
6   Higher Education
     Wordsworth College, Kilburn (women's teacher training college)
7   Other
     Lads' workshop, midnight shelter, night refuge, mission
     houses, restaurants, dispensary, rest home

Notes

1. Boys, girls and infants.
2. Newly opened in 1894.
3. Enrolment figures not given. There is a note saying that over 1000 children attended CSC schools abroad.

NOTES

Introduction

1. Mary Frances Cusack, 'Woman's place in the economy of creation', *Fraser's Magazine*, **9** (1874), p. 202.

2. Ursula King, 'Faith in females', *Times Higher Educational Supplement*, 1 May 1992, p. 19; Driver's 1976 review essay shows how new the field was at that date (Anne Barstow Driver, 'Religion', *Signs*, **2** (1976), pp. 434–42).

3. Gail Malmgreen, 'Introduction', in *Religion in the Lives of British Women* (London: Croom Helm, 1986), pp. 1, 3, 9.

4. This omission is beginning to be rectified by the publication of works such as Davidoff and Hall's *Family Fortunes* in 1985. However, even this book treats sisterhoods as unworthy of serious consideration; the few brief mentions are dismissive in tone (Leonore Davidoff and Catherine Hall, *Family Fortunes: Men and Women of the English Middle Class 1780–1850*, (London: Hutchinson, 1985), pp. 99, 432). Irish women's history is well served by Maria Luddy's excellent *Women and Philanthropy in Nineteenth-century Ireland* (Cambridge: Cambridge University Press, 1995).

5. Jane Rendall, *The Origins of Modern Feminism: Women in Britain, France, and the United States 1780–1860* (London: Macmillan, 1985), pp. 1–2.

6. Elaine Showalter, 'Florence Nightingale's feminist complaint: women, religion, and suggestions for thought', *Signs*, **6** (1981), p. 397.

7. John Shelton Reed, ' "A female movement": the feminization of nineteenth-century Anglo-Catholicism', *Anglican and Episcopal History*, **57** (1988), p. 238.

8. CRJBS Archives, Community Diary 1895–1936, entry for 1897. Because communities often had very long names, many of them have been shortened for the sake of brevity after first mention. A list of the communities whose names have been abbreviated can be found on pp. viii–ix.

9. Catherine M. Prelinger, 'The female diaconate in the Anglican Church: what kind of ministry for women?', in Malmgreen, p. 161.

10. It might seem odd that so little use has been made of the enumerators' reports in the nineteenth-century censuses. This decision was taken for several reasons. First, the student of sisterhoods initially faces the difficulty that there is often no clue to the street addresses of sisterhoods, especially of the branch houses. This problem is

exacerbated in the case of communities which no longer exist. Addresses of extinct communities are very hard to come by; post office directories are not always useful when one is searching for religious groups such as these, and local histories proved disappointing. Communities also tended to move frequently, especially the small, transitory ones, thus making their census records even more elusive.

Second, and separate from the difficulty of tracing such groups, the material available in the enumerators' reports is not entirely appropriate for the purposes of my study. There are several reasons why it was decided to exclude this material, after a brief test of its quality in one single-site, expired community. First, those in the motherhouse on the specific date of the census did not necessarily represent the community; for example, the listing inevitably omitted those working in branch houses, those who were temporarily away, and those who entered and left the community within the census decade. My tentative re-creation of the Community of Saint Mary the Virgin, Brighton, from census records produced a community about 60 per cent of its actual size, as ascertained from other sources. Also, the information provided by the census is not always useful for the purposes of my study, although the full name and place of birth is always supplied. There is usually no indication of whether the sisters were professed or merely novices, or whether they were choir or lay, thus obscuring any attempt to recreate the social climate of the convent. Most seriously of all, census data does not enable the researcher to discover the date of profession for individual members. Most of my calculations focus on date of profession, not because it is the most meaningful for my purposes (clothing is probably the best) but because the communities recorded it more regularly than any other date. From their perspective it was the most significant date: it marked the beginning of the individual's entrance into corporate life. For example, even at death, necrologies often failed to record the late sister's age in years, but such records normally gave the time elapsed since profession: '45th year of her profession'. Finally, I did not want to dilute my biographical data. Working with a variety of sources, I have managed to acquire some biographical information for slightly more than 2200 members of Anglican religious orders, with profession dates for about 1950 of these. The inclusion of large amounts of census data, all lacking the date of profession, could only have weakened the strength of this relationship.

1 'Those wicked nuns'

1. Lynne Strahan, *Out of the Silence: A Study of a Religious Community for Women: The Community of the Holy Name* (Melbourne: Oxford University Press, 1988), p. 44.

2. I have counted as a 'member' of a community anyone who stayed long enough to undergo the ceremony of clothing. Not only does this ceremony indicate a degree of commitment to the institution, but it means that the women involved had lived in the community for at least nine months.

3. [Penelope Holland], 'Two girls of the period: our offense and our petition, by a Belgravian young lady', *Macmillans Magazine*, **19** (1869), p. 324. See also Holland, 'A few more words on convents and on English girls', *Macmillans Magazine*, **19** (1869), pp. 535–8; 'Nature and the convent', *Macmillans Magazine*, **19** (1869), p. 519.

4. [Anne Mozley], 'Convent life', *Blackwood's Edinburgh Magazine*, **105** (1869), p. 607. Emphasis mine.

5. S. B. Wister, 'Charitable sisterhoods', *North American Review*, **117** (1873), p. 439. See also 'S.', 'Sisterhoods', *The Christian Observer*, NS **243** (1858), p. 156. In 1869 Holland dated the serious interest in sisterhoods from about 1859.

6. Martha Vicinus, *Independent Women: Work and Community for Single Women 1850–1920* (London: Virago Press, 1985), Table 3, p. 29.

7. There are innumerable histories of the Oxford Movement and the religious context in which it developed, including Owen Chadwick's magisterial *The Victorian Church*, parts 1 & 2 (London: A. & C. Black, 1971, 1972); Desmond Bowen, *The Idea of the Victorian Church: A Study of the Church of England 1833–1889* (Montreal: McGill University Press, 1968); W. J. Sparrow Simpson, *The History of the Anglo–Catholic Revival from 1845* (London: George Allen & Unwin, 1932); and the works of Geoffery Rowell and M.A. Crowther.

8. John Shelton Reed, ' "A female movement": the feminization of nineteenth-century Anglo-Catholicism', *Anglican and Episcopal History*, **57** (1988), p. 210; John Boyd-Kinnear, 'The social position of women in the present age', in Josephine Butler (ed.), *Woman's Work and Woman's Culture* (London: Macmillan, 1869), p. 357; M. G. Grey, 'Idols of society', *Fraser's Magazine*, NS **9** (1874), pp. 382–3.

9. Margaret Cusack, 'Woman's place in the economy of creation', *Fraser's Magazine*, **9** (1874), p. 202.

10. Arthur M. Allchin, *The Silent Rebellion: Anglican Religious Communities 1845–1900* (London: SCM Press, 1958), p. 116.

11. V. A. L., *The Ministry of Women and the London Poor* (London: S.W. Partridge, [1876], pp. 27–8. The same claim is made by Georgina Hill in *Women in English Life* (London: Richard Bentley & Son, 1896), vol. II, p. 243.

12. Margaret Anne Cusack, *Five Years in a Protestant Sisterhood and Ten Years in a Catholic Convent* (London: Longmans, Green & Co, 1869); Margaret Goodman, *Experiences of an English Sister of Mercy* (London: Smith, Elder, 1862).

13. John S. Sellon (ed.), *Memos Relating to the Society of the Holy Trinity, Devonport* (London: Terry & Co., 1907), p. i.

14. Wordsworth wrote a rather poor sonnet as a tribute to Sellon in 1849.

15. The information regarding Sellon's background is from P. F. Anson and A. W. Campbell's *Call of the Cloister* (new edn, London: SPCK, 1964), pp. 259–71. Sellon's career is examined in much greater detail, if rather uncritically, in Thomas J. Williams, *Priscilla Lydia Sellon: The Restorer after Three Centuries of the Religious Life in the English Church* (London: SPCK, 1950; rev. edn 1965). The most recent scholarship discussing Sellon is Sean Gill's 'Priscilla Lydia Sellon and the creation of Anglican sisterhoods', in

Stuart Mews (ed.), *Modern Religious Rebels* (London: Epworth Press, 1993), pp. 144–65.

16. G. Congreve, 'Sisters: their vocation and their special work', in *Pan-Anglican Papers: The Church and Its Ministry: The Ministry of Women* (London: SPCK, 1908), p. 4.

17. Peter Mayhew, *All Saints: Birth and Growth of a Community* (Oxford: Society of All Saints, 1987), pp. 24–5.

18. Other late foundations seem to have discovered that the competition for what was, after all, a limited number of potential members meant that they remained considerably smaller than the earlier communities.

19. Emily Janes, 'On the associated work of women in religion and philanthropy', in Angela G. Burdett-Coutts (ed.), *Women's Mission* (London: Sampson Low, Marston & Co., 1893), p. 135.

20. Charles Booth, *Life and Labour of the People in London*, Third Series, Religious Influences, vol. I (London: Macmillan & Co., 1902), p. 209.

21. See Appendix 1. This figure, while using Anson's lists as a base, also includes a few communities of which Anson seems to have been unaware. Casteras calculates that aside from 'unsanctioned or informal parish versions' there were 30 sisterhoods founded by 1900. This is a serious underestimate of the total number of sisterhoods, as well as assuming (against the evidence) that a significant number of communities were 'sanctioned'. (Susan P. Casteras, 'Virgin vows: the early Victorian artists' portrayal of nuns and novices', *Victorian Studies*, **24** (1981), pp. 157–84.)

22. David Hilliard, 'UnEnglish and unmanly: Anglo-Catholicism and homosexuality', *Victorian Studies*, **25** (1982), pp. 191–4 and note; see also Arthur Calder-Marshall, *The Enthusiast* (London: Faber & Faber, 1962).

23. Vicinus, p. 83.

2 'The eager life here just suits me'

1. Caroline Emilia Stephen, *The Service of the Poor: Being an Inquiry into the Reasons for and against the Establishment of Religious Sisterhoods for Charitable Purposes* (London: Macmillan & Co., 1871), p. 294.

2. All Saints Archives, Sister Elspeth, 'History of the Community', pp. 22, 27; Williams, *Sellon*, p. 195.

3. Frances Power Cobbe, *The Duties of Women* (London: Williams and Norgate, 1881), p. 3.

4. Malling Abbey Archives, 'Living Stones, the Obit Book of the Community of the Holy Comforter and the Benedictine Community of St Mary's Abbey, West Malling, Kent'. Bostock joined the Benedictine Community in 1918: although this post-dates 1900, the community was still in its first generation. See Charles Philip Stewart Clarke, *The Oxford Movement and After* (London: A. R. Mowbray, 1932), pp. 253–4.

5. Alice Horlock Bennett, *Through an Anglican Sisterhood to Rome* (London: Longmans, 1914), p. 16; All Saints Archives, Sister Etheldreda to Mother, 14 July 1895. Emphasis Etheldreda's.

6. Louisa Hubbard, 'The organization of women workers', in Angela Burdett-Coutts (ed.), *Woman's Mission* (London: Sampson Low, Marston & Co., 1893), p. 273.

7. Bennett, *Anglican Sisterhood*, p. 3; V.A.L., *Ministry of Women*, pp. 29–30; W. E. Sellon, *An Essay upon Sisterhoods in the English Church* (London: Joseph Masters, 1849), p. 11.

8. [Katherine Warburton], 'Mother Kate', in *Memories of a Sister of St Saviour's Priory* (Oxford: Mowbray, 1903), p. 3; Bennett, *Anglican Sisterhood*, pp. 10, 28, 30, 34, 36, 45.

9. Jennie Chappel, *Four Noble Women and Their Work* (London: S. W. Partridge, 1898), pp. 99–100; J. M. Povey [Sister Mary Agnes], *Nunnery Life in the Church of England: Or, Seventeen Years with Father Ignatius* (London: Hodder & Stoughton, 1890), p. 69; [Arthur John Butler (ed.)], *Life and Letters of William John Butler* (London: Macmillan, 1897), p. 139; [Augusta Dill], *Maude: Or, The Anglican Sister of Mercy*, ed. E. Jane Whately (London: Harrison, 1869), p. 4.

10. Louisa Twining, *Deaconesses for the Church of England* (London: Bell & Daldy, 1860), p. 17.

11. Thomas J. Williams and Allan Walter Campbell, *The Park Village Sisterhood* (London: SPCK, 1965), p. 28; PH, Ascot Priory Papers, Sister Clara's anecdotes of Dr Pusey.

12. CSMVW Archives, 'A Few Reminisces of Sister Eliza', p. 7.

13. Povey, p. 53; Bennett, *Anglican Sisterhood*, pp. 106, 109.

14. LPL, Temple Papers 1, ff. 1–3. R. S. Page to Temple, 5 June 1895; Bennett, *Anglican Sisterhood*, pp. 30, 45; see also 'Sisterhood life', in O. Shipley (ed.), *The Church and the World* (London: Longmans, Green, Reader & Dyer, 1867), pp. 166–95. All Saints Archives, Sister Elspeth, The American Congregation.

15. T. T. Carter, *Objections to Sisterhoods Considered, in a Letter to a Parent* (London: Francis & John Rivington, 1853), p. 18. Emphasis mine. This declaration may not be entirely disingenuous; it is probable that Carter also wished to defend CSJB against charges of imitation of the contemplative aspects of Rome.

16. LPL, Benson Papers 42, f. 320.

17. All Saints Archives, Sister Elspeth, 'History of the Community B'. Sister Mary Pauline was finally sent to be Mother of the Benedictines at West Malling, at their request.

18. SHUT Archives, Constitutions and Rule of the Sisters of Charity, Knowle (*c.* 1868), p. 38.

19. Mary H. Nicholl, *Augusta: Or, The Refuted Slanders of Thirty Years Ago on the Late Miss Sellon, Once More Refuted* (London: Remington, 1878), p. 16; All Saints Archives, All Saints Home and Sisterhood of Charity (London: J. Master & Co., privately printed, [1855], p. 6; CSC Archives, Mother Foundress' Diaries, 5 January 1880;

CSC Archives, The Sisters of the Church: Summary of Rule and Instructions for Novices (London: Sisters of the Church, 1891), pp. 52–3; Holy Rood Archives, Community of the Holy Rood: Extract of the Rule for Daily Use (1875); All Hallows Archives, Mother Lavinia: Extracts from letters, section D.

20. All Saints Archives, Chapter notes, 1895.

21. Allan B. Webb, *Sisterhood Life and Women's Work* (London: Skeffington & Son, 1883), p. 79; CSC Archives, Mother Foundress' Diary.

22. LPL, MS 3179, Rule of the Community of the Holy Family.

23. *The Kilburn Sisters and Their Accusers* (London: 'Church Bells' Office, [1896]), pp. 53–7. In the 1890s this sisterhood curtailed their devotions still further, feeling that the sisters were too busy and found them too much of a strain (LPL, Benson Papers 158, f. 353).

24. G. Congreve, 'Sisters: their vocation and their special work', *Pan-Anglican Papers* (1908), appendix SC iii b: p. 17.

25. SSP Archives, Sisters of SSP/SSM, vol. I; Soho Diary, 1860.

26. Henry Daniel Nihill, *The Sisters of St Mary at the Cross: Sisters of the Poor and Their Work* (London: Kegan Paul, Trench & Co., 1887), p. 298.

27. I have found only one still-preserved example of a letter of enquiry. This is in the archives of SHUT.

28. T. T. Carter, *Harriet Monsell: A Memoir* (London: J. Masters, 1884), pp. 95–6.

29. For example, see the list of associates who became sisters in various communities in the SHUT Archives, Register of the Associates of Mercy of the Oxford Society of the Holy and Undivided Trinity.

30. Brian Heeney, *The Women's Movement in the Church of England 1850–1930* (Oxford: Clarendon Press, 1988), pp. 55–6.

31. *The Founders of Clewer: A Short Account of the Rev. T. T. Carter and Harriet Monsell to Celebrate the Centenary of the Community of St John Baptist in 1952* (London: Mowbray, 1952), p. 65; see SSM's Community Log for examples.

32. CSC Archives, 'Sister Vera's paper on postulants', *Quarterly Chronicle* (January 1898), p. 11.

33. All Saints Archives, Sister Caroline Mary, 'Memories of Church Life'.

34. Bennett, *Anglican Sisterhood*, p. 31.

35. See Dinah Mulock Craik's description of a clothing ceremony, almost certainly at CSC ('About sisterhoods', *Longman's Magazine*, **1** (1883), pp. 303–6).

36. All Saints Archives, Notes on the Foundation of Our Community and Some Developments of Work, No. 11, p. 9.

37. CSC Archives, Sisters of the Church, 1888 Diary, 1 December 1888; CSC Archives, The Chronicle (July 1911), p. 52; All Saints Archives, Memories of Sister Caroline Mary, Second Mother.

38. John Duguid Milne, *The Industrial and Social Position of Women* (London: Chapman & Hall, 1857), pp. 136–7.

39. Bennett, *Anglican Sisterhood*, p. 16.

40. *A Hundred Years of Blessing Within an English Community* (London: SPCK, 1946), p. 57.

41. [Dill], p. 36.

42. All Saints Archives, Memories of Sister Caroline Mary, Second Mother; CSC Archives, Our Work (1884), p. 39.

43. CSC Archives, *General Rules for the Superintendence of an Orphanage or Community Kitchen, also the Regulations Binding on the Orphans, etc.* (London: Church Extension Association, n.d.); CSC Archives, *The Sisters of the Church: Summary of Rule and Instruction for Novices* (London: Sisters of the Church, 1891), p. 23.

44. All Hallows Archives, Revised and Consolidated Constitutions and Statutes, Jan. 1898, 18.7.

45. All Saints Archives, Sister Elspeth, History of the Community, p. 36.

46. CSP Archives, 'Primary Constitutions and Statutes of the Nursing Sisters of the Church of England, and the Convalescent Home', 1862; see CSC Archives, Quarterly Chronicle (July 1900) for a description of Sister Theresa's qualifications.

47. Emily Ayckbowm wrote as late as 1882 that it was still difficult to find 'ladies' who were willing to become nurses. CSC Archives, Ayckbowm to Canon Carr, 26 March 1882; J. Jones, *Memorials of Agnes Elizabeth Jones* (London: Strahan, 1871), p. 100.

48. NSSJD Archives, Report for 1910.

49. SSM Archives, Community Log, 27 April 1859; CSP Archives, Sister Rosamira, *The First Twenty-six Years of St Peter's Community* (Shrewsbury: Wilding & Son, 1917), p. 10; L. M. H., *Anglican Deaconesses: Or, Is There No Place for Women in Our Parochial System?* (London: Bell and Daldy, 1871), pp. 24–5.

50. Holy Rood Archives, Geoffery Stout, *History of the North Ormesby Hospital 1858–1948* (Redcar: privately printed, 1989), p. 116.

51. Williams, *Sellon*, p. 176; NSSJD Archives, Box 4 (labelled 'Nurse Wren's account'); Nightingale to Harriet Martineau, 24 September 1861, in Martha Vicinus and Bea Nergaard (eds), *Ever Yours, Florence Nightingale* (Cambridge, MA: Harvard University Press, 1989), pp. 226–8.

52. CSC Archives, Ayckbowm to Canon Carr, 26 March 1882.

53. Malling Abbey Archives, Living Stones, the Obit Book of the Community of the Holy Comforter and the Benedictine Community of St Mary's Abbey, West Malling, Kent.

54. Bennett, *Anglican Sisterhood*, p. 50; SHUT Archives, Statutes, XXII: Admission of New Sisters.

55. Bennett, *Anglican Sisterhood*, pp. 20–1. Chapters 3 ('The Mistress and the spirit of the novitiate') and 5 ('The other novices') contain a uniquely detailed description of the All Saints' novitiate in the 1860s.

56. The reason why the thirtieth candidate left is not recorded. All Saints Archives, All Saints Home: Novitiate 1900–1910; Maria Trench, 'English Sisterhoods', *The Nineteenth Century*, **40** (1884), p. 350.

57. Bennett, *Anglican Sisterhood*, p. 25.

58. Bennett, *Anglican Sisterhood*, p. 49.

59. 'Sisterhood Life', p. 187.

60. SHUT Archives, Mother Marion's Memories, vol. I, 1841–52, 14 January 1848; SHUT Archives, Mother Marion's Diary, vol. III, 1893–1902, 14 and 20 January 1893.

61. *A Hundred Years*, pp. 17–18.

62. All Saints Archives, Novices Received February 1891–1910; All Saints Archives, All Saints Home: Novitiate 1900–1910.

63. LPL, LC 38, f. 150; The Society of St Margaret added this fourth vow after the death of its priest co-founder, J. M. Neale.

64. SMHT sisters made their vows 'to' the Mother Superior: in this community, anything was possible. *Book of the Statutes of the Sisterhood of Mercy of the Holy and Undivided Trinity; With the Rules for Daily Life* (Oxford: By the Society, Convent of the Annunciation, 1882), p. 18; LPL, Temple Papers 1, f. 22. Profession Service of the Sisters of the Ascension. This is an unusually unequivocal life profession. After the usual Trinitarian formula, the sister to be professed says 'I promise and vow unto the Lord my God to devote myself spirit, soul and body in the holy estate of Poverty, Chastity and Obedience to the service of Christ and His poor forever.'

65. LPL, Winnington-Ingram Papers 3, ff. 132–3, 135. CSC Customs.

66. SHUT Archives, Mother Marion's Diary, vol. III, 1893–1902, 14 November 1893. Emphasis Hughes's.

67. [SHUT], *Book of the Statutes of the Sisterhood of the Mercy of the Holy and Undivided Trinity; With the Rules for Conduct* (Oxford: By the Society, Convent of the Annunciation, 1882), Appendix, p. 3.

68. SSP Archives, Sister Frances Clare, 'What I Know of the Sisters' Life'; LPL, Printed Book 8, p. 11; LPL, MS 3179, Rule of the Community of the Holy Family.

69. LPL [Mother Sarah Frances], *Vigilate et Orate: Spiritual Counsels on the Rule* (London: St Peter's Convent, 1903), p. 12. (Henceforth *Vigilate*.)

70. LPL, Temple Papers 12, ff. 313–14. Agnes Mason to Temple, c. 1898. Temple agreed that the woman could be professed but stressed that he should always be consulted in cases of this kind.

71. LPL, *Vigilate*, p. 21.

72. LPL, MS 3179, Rule of the Community of the Holy Family.

73. 'Sisterhood Life', p. 184.

74. Pusey House 6276, unidentified clipping, 'We are able to give Dr Pusey's paper verbatim.'

75. LPL, Temple Papers 1, ff. 7–8. Sister Margaret Emily returned to the world soon after profession.

76. *The Chronicles of Convocation*, Report No. 194, 'Report on Sisterhoods and Deaconesses' (July 1885), pp. 1–2.

77. W. J. Sparrow Simpson, *The History of the Anglo-Catholic Revival from 1845* (London: George Allen & Unwin, 1932), p. 237.

78. LPL, LC 38, ff. 141–2, Bishop of Wakefield.

79. All Saints Archives, Letters on vows, 1895. Emphasis in original. The Mother Foundress of this community described Archbishop Tait (the one referred to here in his earlier role as Bishop of London) as 'utterly ignorant of anything to do with the Religious Life'.

80. LPL, Creighton Papers 10, f. 274. Emphasis Sister Eanswythe's.

81. See, for example, the important correspondence on vows in the All Saints Archives; also Bennett, *Anglican Sisterhood*, pp. 52–3, 125.

82. Anne Frances Norton, 'The Consolidation and Expansion of the Community of St Mary the Virgin, Wantage, 1857–1907' (unpublished MPhil, King's College, London, 1979), p. 267. A copy of a very similar rule is also in the All Hallows Archives; it is unclear whether they borrowed heavily from CSMVW or whether both shared a common source. All Hallows Archives, *Rule of Life* (n.p., n.d.).

83. Henry Daniel Nihill, *The Sisters of the Poor at St Michaels, Shoreditch and Their Work* (London: printed for private circulation, 1870), pp. 4–5.

84. For a listing of parental occupations see Appendix 2; see also Appendix 3.

85. *Tractarian Sisters and Their Teaching* (London: William Hunt & Co., [1868]), p. 9; *The Great Want of the Church* (London: William Skeffington, 1868), p. 25.

86. S.D.N., *Chronicles of St Mary's* (London: Joseph Masters, 1868), p. 359. See also SHUT Archives, Sister Isabel Angela's Reminiscences 1872–1934, Feb. 1918.

87. S.D.N., *Chronicles*, pp. 357–9; *The Community of the Mission Sisters of the Holy Name of Jesus* (Worcester: Trinity Press, n.d.), pp. 22–3.

88. Charles Fuge Lowder, *Ten Years in St George's Mission* (London: G. J. Palmer, 1867), pp. 46–7.

89. Holy Name Profession Roll (photocopy); CSMVW Archives, Roll of the Sisters and Novices who have been admitted to the Community of St Thomas the Martyr, Oxford.

90. Holy Name Profession Roll (photocopy); CSMVW Archives, Roll of the Sisters and Novices who have been admitted to the Community of St Thomas the Martyr, Oxford. CSTM amalgamated the two orders in 1907; this was over a decade earlier than their amalgamation in most other communities, and seems to have been done largely in response to falling numbers. All Hallows Archives, Revised and Consolidated Constitution and Statutes, January 1898, part 3; LPL, MS 3179, Constitution of the Community of the Holy Family.

91. All Saints Archives, Sister Elspeth, Notes about Various Sisters, pp. 22, 36; All Saints Archives, Sister Elspeth's Recollections, p. 36. That this may have not been an entirely satisfactory solution is shown by the same community later rejecting a novice who was 'exemplary in her conduct' because she had a 'weak brain' (LPL, Benson Papers 42, ff. 377–8. Mother Caroline Mary to Benson, 5 March 1888).

92. The average age of all sisters listed in the database with both profession and birth dates was 34.22; of lay sisters 30.09 (range 21 to 51); of choir sisters 33.59 (range 20 to 74). N (all) = 709; N (lay) = 64; N (choir) = 254. See Patricia Branca, *Silent Sisterhood: Middle-class Women in the Victorian Home* (London: Croom Helm, 1975), pp. 4–5.

93. All Saints Archives, Memories: Sister Caroline Mary, Second Mother, p. 58.

94. Bennett, *Anglican Sisterhood*, p. 17; All Hallows Archives, Revised and Consolidated Constitution and Statutes, January 1898, part 2; LPL, Benson Papers 81, ff. 327–74.

95. SHUT Archives, Profession Roll. Ironically, this hot-tempered sister was styled Sister Rose Agnes of the Patience of God. SHUT Archives, Mother Marion's Diary, vol. 3, 1893–1902, 11 May 1899.

96. SHUT Archives, Sister Isabel Angela's Reminiscences 1872–1934, February 1918, and October 1920.

97. SSB Archives, Statutes and Constitutions of the Society of the Sisters of Bethany, p. 89.

98. S. D. N., *Chronicles*, pp. 30–1; All Saints Archives, Sister Elspeth, Notes about Various Sisters, pp. 22, 31.

99. All Saints Archives, Sister Elspeth's Recollections, p. 31.

100. All Saints Archives, Sister Elspeth, Notes about Various Sisters, p. 13.

101. All Saints Archives, Sister Elspeth's Recollections, p. 29.

102. CSC Archives, Sister Rosalie, Reminiscences of Mother Foundress; CSC Archives, Community Diary, 14 May 1881 and 7 October 1882; CSC Archives, *Quarterly Chronicle* (June 1892), p. 4; CSC Archives, *Quarterly Chronicle* (April 1903), p. 1.

103. All Saints Archives, Sister Elspeth, Notes about Various Sisters, pp. 22, 29, 32, 38–9.

104. Caitriona Clear, *Nuns in Nineteenth-Century Ireland* (Dublin: Gill & Macmillan, 1988), p. xx; All Saints Archives, Sister Catherine, Recollections of an Old Woman (November 1907), p. 8.

105. All Saints Archives, Sister Elspeth's Recollections, p. 22.

106. All Saints Archives, Notes on the Foundations of Our Community and Some Developments of Work, pp. 63–4.

107. For a discussion of this point in a Canadian context, see Marta Danylewycz, *Taking the Veil: An Alternative to Marriage, Motherhood and Spinsterhood in Quebec, 1840–1920* (Toronto: McClelland and Stewart, 1987), pp. 105–6.

108. SHUT Archives, Sister Isabel Angela's Reminiscences, 1872–1934; CSC Archives, Mother Foundress' Diary, 28 Dec. 1884; CSP Archives, Black notebook listing the outfit for a former lay sister.

109. Holy Rood Archives, CHR: The Rules of Associate Sisters or Sisters of the Second Order, rules 4 and 5; CRJBS Archives, The Manual for Outer Members of the Community of St Alphage, Southwark, p. 9; SSP Archives, *Constitutions and Rules of the Society of St Margaret* (Cambridge: J. Palmer, printer, n.d.), p. 48.

110. Vicinus, p. 60; SHUT Archives, Register of the Associate Sisters of Mercy of

the Oxford Society of the Holy and Undivided Trinity; CSMVW Archives, Associates of the Community of St Thomas the Martyr. No associates joined STM after 1886; of the eight who did join, three quit, one was expelled, and one entered the community.

111. All Saints Archives, Sister Catherine's Recollections, p. 4; All Saints Archives, Memories of Sister Caroline Mary, Second Mother, pp. 3, 27, 111. All Saints' *Rule* specified that for women over 21, parental consent was still required before they could enter the novitiate. Holy Rood placed the limit at age 23. (LPL, *The Statutes of the Sisters of Charity of the Holy Rood* (1894), p. 33.)

112. All Saints Archives, Memories of Sister Caroline Mary, p. 1. Emphasis in original.

113. All Saints Archives, Memories of Sister Caroline Mary, pp. 6, 28–9.

114. All Saints Archives, Sister Catherine, Recollections of An Old Woman (November 1907), p. 2; All Saints Archives, Records of the Early Days of the Community: Various Sisters, Sister Frances Emily's Recollections, p. 56.

115. All Saints Archives, Sister Elspeth, History of the Community, pp. 14, 27.

116. SSP Archives, *Constitutions of the Society of St Margaret* (Cambridge: J. Palmer, printer, n.d.), p. 48.

117. See Appendix 6 for rates of attrition in selected communities. Nineteenth-century North American Roman Catholic communities had attrition rates varying from 12 to 37 per cent (B. Misner, 'A comparative social study of the members and apostolates of the first eight permanent communities of women religious within the original boundaries of the US, 1790–1850' (PhD, Catholic University of America, 1981), pp. 92–3).

118. See Appendix 7 for reasons given for leaving after profession. It is important to remember that these are explanations proffered by the community involved after the event.

119. For more details of this community's unusual composition, see Appendix 3.

120. LPL, Benson Papers 110, ff. 383–4; 385–6.

121. Grafton, *Vocation*, p. 93.

122. CRJBS Archives, Community Log, 1869–1936, entry re: Sister Clare; CRJBS Archives, *The Elephant*, 'Memories of Mother Faith' (n.d.); Povey, *Nunnery Life*, p. 123.

123. CSC Archives, 'Private Account of "The Troubles"' (February 1895), pp. 7, 24; CSC Archives, Mother Foundress' Diary, 21 Dec. 1886.

124. All Saints Archives. See also the discussion of Sister Gertrude's motives in All Saints Archives, Sister Caroline Mary to Mother Mary Augustine (1895).

125. All Saints Archives, Sister Elspeth, History of the Community B; All Saints Archives, Letters on Vows, Sister Caroline Mary to Mother Superior (1895).

126. CSC Archives, *Our Work* (Sept.–Oct. 1955), pp. 88–9.

127. CSC Archives, *Our Work* (Nov.–Dec. 1964), p. 85.

128. CSC Archives, *Our Work* (Feb. 1922), pp. 19–20.

129. Susan O'Brien, ' "Terra incognita": the nun in nineteenth-century England', *Past and Present*, **121** (1988), p. 139.

130. Average age at death for all sisters, including novices, was 73.1; for lay sisters with profession dates, 72.1; for all lay sisters, 70.1; for choir sisters with profession dates, 73.8; for all choir sisters, 73.7. That disease of the young, consumption, carried off a number of younger novices and sisters in both orders. T. H. Hollingworth, 'A demographic study of British ducal families', in Michael Drake (ed.), *Population in Industrialization* (London: Methuen, 1969), p. 82. The precise life expectancy was 46.2 at the age of 20.

131. Some communities buried sisters with their novitiate crosses.

132. Most of the details of sisterhood funeral practices come from LPL, *Vigilate*, p. 41.

133. All Saints Archives, Memories of Sister Caroline Mary, pp. 77–8. Emphasis in original.

134. Holy Rood Archives, Sister Jean, *God Thorn* (Bognor Regis: New Horizon, 1981), p. 57.

135. LPL [Mother Sarah Francis], *Spiritual Counsels on the Rule* (London: Community of St Peter, Kilburn, 1903).

3 'A free person in a community of equals'

1. All Hallows Archives, Memoir of the Life of Lavinia Crosse, Mother Foundress of The Community of All Hallows, Ditchingham, Norfolk (1946), p. 1.

2. CSC Archives, 'Fragment of Mother Foundress' autobiography', *Quarterly Chronicle* (July 1901), p. 1; CSC Archives, *Our Work*, 'Sisters of Charity in the Church of England', *Our Work*, **7** (1884), p. 259. This serial is a thinly fictionalized account of the foundations of CSC, probably written by Ayckbowm or Frances Ashdown.

3. CSC Archives, 'Sisters of Charity', *Our Work*, **7** (1884), p. 261; CSC Archives, Account of the Beginnings of the Community.

4. SSB Archives, E. G. Benett to Ethel Benett, 24 November 1865. (Geoffrey Rowell, *The Vision Glorious: Themes and Personalities of the Catholic Revival in Anglicanism*, Oxford: Oxford University Press, 1983, p. 121.)

5. CSC Archives, Account of the Beginnings of the Community; Anson and Campbell, *Call*, pp. 290–1, 308–9, 407, 477; Charlotte F. Yonge, 'The beginnings of Sisterhoods', *The Treasury*, **23** (1914), p. 53; Denison, 'Sisterhood movement', pp. 1–2; Lough, *Influence*, p. 52.

6. CSC Archives, Ayckbowm to Sister Vera, 2 May 1900. Emphasis Ayckbowm's.

7. Carter, *Monsell*, p. 48.

8. T. Bowman Stephenson, *Concerning Sisterhoods* (London: for the author by C. H. Kelly, 1890), p. 41. For examples of their regulations, see *Book of the Statutes of the Sisterhood of Mercy of the Holy and Undivided Trinity; With the Rules for Daily Life* (Oxford:

By the Society, Convent of the Annunciation, 1882), pp. 4–8, 18. These Rules show Ignatian influence. Williams, *Sellon*, pp. 88 (note), 277.

9. Maria Trench, quoted in Arthur M. Allchin, *The Silent Rebellion: Anglican Religious Communities 1845–1900* (London: SCM Press, 1958), p. 134. Emphasis Trench's.

10. Nicholl, *Augusta*, p. 12.

11. See SHUT Archives, Diary III, 1893–1902, 14 and 20 January 1893, where Marion Hughes discusses the pressures on her to retire as Mother Superior.

12. Carter, *Monsell*, p. 188; *Founders of Clewer*, p. 76.

13. SHUT Archives, Diary, 1914, and Profession Roll; *Founders of Clewer*, p. 60.

14. SHUT Archives, Statutes, XX: Of the Superior; *A Kalendar of the Christian Church* (1863), p. 14; *The Sisters of Mercy at Devonport: Report of an Enquiry* (London: Joseph Masters, 1850), p. 15.

15. SHUT Archives, Sister Isabel Angela's Reminiscences 1872–1934, entry for 1914.

16. Valerie Bonham, *A Joyous Service: The Clewer Sisters and Their Work* (Windsor: Community of St John Baptist, 1989), pp. 78–9.

17. SSB Archives, Copy of Old Statutes [1871], pp. 9–10.

18. All Saints Archives, Mother Mary Augustine's Diary 1894–1921, entry for Oct. 1905–Oct. 1906; All Saints Archives, Sister Elspeth, History of the Community, B10.

19. CSC Archives, obituary of Sister Mabel, *Our Work* (July–August 1955), pp. 69–70.

20. Frances Power Cobbe, *Essays on the Pursuits of Women* (London: Emily Faithfull, 1863), pp. 134–5.

21. *Convent Tales, by a Religious of St Peter's Community, Kilburn* (London: SPCK, 1928), p. 97.

22. All Saints Archives, Sister Elspeth, The American Congregation.

23. CSMVW Archives, Constitutions and Rules of St Mary's Home for Penitents in the Parish of Wantage in Berkshire, in the Diocese of Oxford, 1854.

24. PH 6276, unidentified clipping headed 'We Are Able to Give Dr Pusey's Paper Verbatim'.

25. Grafton, *Vocation*, pp. 48–9. Emphasis mine. Anson and Campbell.

26. CSMVW Archives, Roll of the Sisters and Novices who have been admitted to the Community of St Thomas the Martyr, Oxford.

27. For a representative description of the nature and scope of government by Chapter, see SSB Archives, Rule of the Society of the Sisters of Bethany (amended) 1888, pp. 20–4.

28. LPL, Benson Papers 42, ff. 318–23; Williams, *Sellon*, p. 26; SSP Archives, *Constitutions and Rules of the Society of St Margaret* (Cambridge: J. Palmer, printer, n.d.), p. 7; LPL, *The Community of Reparation to Jesus in the Blessed Sacrament, Instituted 1869: The Constitution: The Rule: The Spirit of the Founder* (n.p., 1919), PB1, pp. 10–12; SSB Archives, Copy of Old Statutes [1871]; LPL, *Constitution of the Society of All Saints' Sisters of the Poor* (London: Harrison & Sons, [1886]), p. 12.

29. SSB Archives, Copy of Old Statutes [1871].

30. LPL, Benson Papers 158, f. 206. Emily Ayckbowm to Benson, 17 June 1895.

31. Carter, *Monsell*, p. 119. Emphasis mine.

32. SSB Archives, Rule [1888], pp. 12–14.

33. Nihill, *Sisters of the Poor*, p. 4; Nihill, *Sisters of St Mary at the Cross*, p. 22; *Statutes of the Society of the Holy and Undivided Trinity*, 1861, Part 2, Chapter 35, Statute 13, cited in Williams and Campbell, *Park Village Sisterhood*, p. 97.

34. CSC Archives, Sisters of the Church, Community Diary, June 1875; CSC Archives, *Quarterly Chronicle*, most issues; *Our Work*, **68** (obituaries of Sister Mabel and others), July–August 1955; LPL, *Sisters of Charity of the Holy Rood: Rule of Life* (1899), p. 55.

35. [Warburton], *Memories*, pp. 24–5.

36. [Dill], p. 127.

37. A.F.B., *Convent Experiences* (London: Thomas Scott, 1875), p. 16. Emphasis in original.

38. W. Gilbert, 'An Anglican sisterhood', *Good Words and Sunday Magazine*, **22** (1881), p. 836.

39. LPL, *Sisters of Charity of the Holy Rood: Rule of Life* (1899), p. 11; All Saints Archives, Sister Francis Emily's Memories of Mother Foundress, p. 3; All Saints Archives, Memories of Sister Caroline Mary, Second Mother, p. 94; SHUT Archives, Constitutions and Rule of the Sisters of Charity, Knowle (*c.* 1867), pp. 25–6.

40. Bennett, *Anglican Sisterhood*, p. 78.

41. Williams and Cameron, p. 31. An example of the more moderate approach is All Hallows Archives, *Rule of Life* (n.p., n.d.).

42. SHUT Archives, Constitutions and Rule of the Sisters of Charity, Knowle, p. 11; CSC Archives, The Rule in First Form; CSC Archives, 1888 Diary, 28 July 1888.

43. *I Am Not Worthy: A Voice from an English Sisterhood* (London: William Skeffington, 1870), p. 7; Owen Chadwick (ed.), *The Mind of the Oxford Movement* (London: Adam & Charles Black, 1960), p. 50.

44. All Saints Archives, Sister Francis Emily's Recollections, p. 20; Carter, *Monsell*, p. 106.

45. SSB Archives, Statutes and Constitutions of the Society of the Sisters of Bethany, pp. 59, 89.

46. SHUT Archives, Statutes of the Sisterhood of Mercy of the Holy and Undivided Trinity, XXXIII: Distribution of Time; SHUT Archives, Constitutions and Rule of the Sisters of Charity, Knowle, p. 48; LPL, Printed Book 8, p. 48.

47. SHUT Archives, Statutes, XXIII: On Recreation; All Saints Archives, Records of the Early Days of the Community: Various Sisters, Sister Frances Emily's Recollections, pp. 39–40.

48. Cited in Goodman, *Sisterhoods*, p. 7.

49. CSMVW Archives, Miss Butler's First Recollections of Wantage, p. 12.

50. 'A visit to Clewer sisterhood', *Penny Post* (1861), p. 35; Williams, *Sellon*, p. 72; All Hallows Archives, *Rule of Life*. This Rule may have been common to that community and to CSMVW.

51. Emily Sheriff, *Intellectual Education* (London: John W. Parker & Son, 1858), p. 409; Vicinus, *Independent Women*, p. 37; George Longridge, *Sister Bessie: A Memoir* (Oxford: James Parker & Co., 1903), p. 23.

52. Florence Nightingale, *Cassandra* (1852) (New York: The Feminist Press, 1979), p. 31. Emphasis Nightingale's.

53. SSB Archives, Statutes and Constitutions of the Society of the Sisters of Bethany, Part II: Constitutions, pp. 44–6; timetable in Rule of the Society of the Sisters of Bethany (amended), 1888. Lay sisters in this community had two 30-minute periods of private meditation to the choir sisters' 45.

54. PH, Ascot Priory Archives, D.C.H., *Thoughts on Religious Communities; Being the Letters of Two Friends* (London: Joseph Masters, 1860), p. 47; *Letters of Neale*, p. 271; [Katharine Warburton], *Old Soho Days and Other Memories* (London: Mowbray, 1906), p. 143.

55. William Rossetti, *The Family Letters of Christina Georgina Rossetti* (1908) (New York: Haskell House, 1968), p. 56; *Founders of Clewer*, pp. 46–7.

56. LPL, MS 3179, Rule of the Community of the Holy Family.

57. 'Sisterhood life', pp. 178–9; LPL, Rule of the Community of the Holy Cross, p. 7.

58. [Warburton], *Memories*, pp. 24–5; See CSC Archives, *Quarterly Chronicle*, esp. Jan. 1898, pp. 12–13; CSC Archives, 1888 Diary, 16 April & 12 May 1888.

59. CSC Archives, Ayckbowm to Sister Vera, 4 March 1892 and 4 May 1897; Williams, *Sellon*, p. 294; CSC Archives, *The Chronicle* (July 1911), p. 52. All Saints retains in its archives copies of the literary output of many of its sisters. See the *Victoria History of the Counties of England* series: *Bedfordshire*, I, pp. 309–404; *Buckinghamshire*, I, pp. 279–396; *Huntingdonshire*, I, pp. 357–98; *Leicestershire*, I, pp. 355–401; *Lincolnshire*, II, pp. 78–80, 96–104, 118–57, 161–79, 199–212, 230–44; *Rutland*, I, pp. 143–64 (London: Archibald Constable & Co., 1900–).

60. *A Hundred Years*, p. 59.

61. See, for example, *The Breviary of St Margaret's* (London: Ellis & Keene, 1st edn 1877, 2nd edn 1880, 3rd edn 1898); Deane Amelia's translation of *The Book of the Renowned Church of Salisbury [1556] Rendered into English According to the Use of the Society of the Holy Trinity, Devonport*, 2 parts (London: Gilbert & Rivington, 1889) was still in use in the 1960s.

62. *Church Times*, 12 January 1894; CSC Archives, Sister Vera Aletta's account of Ayckbowm; CSC Archives, Jane Ashdown obituary, clipping from *Church Standard*, 29 December 1921. See also advertisements in *Our Work*; CSC Archives, Mother Foundress' Diary, Feb. 1887; personal communication from the Archivist of CSC, Sister Margeurite Mae. For example, CSC Archives, *Quarterly Chronicle* (July 1904), pp. 4–5.

63. Shelton Reed, 'Feminization'.

64. *A Hundred Years*, pp. 30–4. The CSMVW archives preserve photographs of some of their embroidered art.

65. A.V.L., *Ministry of Women*, pp. 17–18.

66. CSC Archives, *Our Work* (obituary of Sister Caroline), **47** (1924), p. 169.

67. Christabel Coleridge (ed.), *Charlotte Mary Yonge: Her Life and Letters* (Macmillan and Co., 1903), p. 259. Letter from Yonge, 7 June, year not given.

68. Longridge, p. 64.

69. SHUT Archives, Statutes and Offices, p. 78.

70. *Founders of Clewer*, p. 69.

71. LPL, MS 3179, Rule of the Community of the Holy Family.

72. CSMVW Archives, A Few Reminiscences of Sister Eliza, p. 7.

73. Carroll Smith Rosenberg, 'The female world of love and ritual', *Signs*, **1** (1975), pp. 1–29, esp. p. 8. See also Jeffery Weeks, *Sex, Politics, and Society* (London: Longmans, 1989), p. 119; Hilliard, p. 187.

74. All Saints Archives, Sister Elspeth, History of the Community, pp. 3–4.

75. CSC Archives, Circular Letter (Easter 1887), p. 2; SSB Archives, Directions, interleaved in Rule, 1888.

76. CRJBS Archives, Memories of Mother Faith, p. 25.

77. CSC Archives, Account of the Beginnings of the Community.

78. [Craik], 'About sisterhoods', p. 304; John Scobell, *A Letter to the Rev. John M. Neale* (London: Nisbet, 1857), p. 11; 'Sisterhood life', p. 185.

79. A. A. [Anne Ayers], *Evangelical Sisterhoods: Two Letters to a Friend* (New York: T. Whittaker, 1864), p. 35.

80. *Letters of John Mason Neale, D.D., Selected and Edited by His Daughter* (London: Longmans, 1910), 6 March 1856, Neale to Benjamin Webb, p. 268; Stephen, *Service of the Poor*, p. 238.

81. T. Bowman Stephenson, *Concerning Sisterhoods* (London: For the author, by C. H. Kelly, 1890), pp. 70–1.

82. SSP Archives, Sister Kate to Mary (surname unknown), Easter Week, 1863.

83. Bowen, p. 298.

84. Suzanne Campbell-Jones, *In Habit: An Anthropological Study of Working Nuns* (London: Faber & Faber, 1979), p. 45; *The Foundations of the Sisters of Notre Dame in England and Scotland: From 1845 to 1895* (Liverpool: Philip, Son & Nephew, 1895), p. 2.

85. All Hallows Archives, Scrapbook of clippings, letter to the *Sussex Advertiser* (Nov. 1857); [Holland], 'Convents and English girls', p. 538; G. Congreve, 'Sisters: their vocation and their special work', in *Pan-Anglican Papers; The Church and Its Ministry: The Ministry of Women* (London: SPCK, 1908), p. 5.

86. Frances Power Cobbe, *Life of Frances Power Cobbe by Herself*, vol. I (Cambridge: Riverside Press, 1894), p. 155.

87. Vicinus, *Independent Women*, p. 42.

88. CSC Archives, Sister Leonora, More Memories of Mother.

89. Louisa Twining, *Deaconesses for the Church of England* (London: Bell & Daldy, 1860), p. 136; P. G. Hughes, 'Cleanliness and godliness: a sociological study of the Good Shepherd Convent refuges for the social reformation and Christian conversion of prostitutes and convicted women in nineteenth century Britain' (PhD, Brunel University, 1985), p. 80.

90. CRJBS Archives, Community Log, 1869–1936, entry for 1909.

91. Few, pp. 29, 30, 41–4; Malling Abbey Archives, The History of the Benedictine Community of St Mary's Abbey, West Malling, Kent, p. 81; See Appendix 8 for CRJBS's budget for 1906. There is an even less illuminating budget for the Community of the Holy Comforter in the Malling Abbey Archives, but it at least has the virtue of being nineteenth-century (Malling Abbey Archives, Genesis 1891–1916, interleaved '1898–99 Report: Community of the Holy Comforter'). Typically imprecise is CSC's 1895 report of orphanage expenditure in LPL, Temple Papers 4, ff. 237–52. See LPL, Benson Papers 55, f. 25, for the budget of All Saints' Hospital (for incurables) at Cowley, Oxford.

92. Charles C. Grafton to Mr Fay, 18 July 1865. *The Letters and Addresses*, vol. VII of *The Works of Bishop Grafton* (New York: Longmans, Green & Co., 1914), p. 54.

93. M. Hobart Seymour, *Convents or Nunneries* (Bath: R. E. Peach, 1852), pp. 29–30.

94. Bennett, *Anglican Sisterhood*, pp. 11–12.

95. LPL, Temple Papers 1, f. 7. 28 May 1896.

96. All Hallows Archives, Revised and Consolidated Constitution and Statutes, January 1898; SSB Archives, Statutes and Constitutions, pp. 87–8. Virtually all communities requested the annual £50 from choir sisters; SSB's lump sum option was more uncommon.

97. LPL, *Community of Reparation to Jesus in the Blessed Sacrament*, p. 16; All Hallows Archives, Revised and Consolidated Constitution and Statutes, Jan. 1898.

98. CSC Archives, Community Diary, 6 March 1885; CRJBS Archives, Community History, p. 3. Gifts of jewels became problematic if the giver later decided to leave, as a number of sisterhoods incorporated their founding members' jewellery into the community chalice.

99. SSB Archives, Old Statutes [1871], p. 4.

100. Pusey House, SHUT Archives, Sister Isabel Angela's Reminiscences 1872–1934; *The Law Times Reports*, **41** (1887), Allcard v. Skinner, p. 63, citing the unpublished Rule of the Community of St Mary at the Cross, *c.* 1871.

101. LPL, MS 3179, Constitution of the Community of the Holy Family.

102. Nihill, *Sisters of St Mary at the Cross*, p. vi.

103. *Law Times Reports* (1887), pp. 61–76; [Warburton], *Memories*, p. 104.

104. CSC Archives, Erroneous Statements Concerning the Church Extension Association (1897), p. 2; CSC Archives, *Circular Letter* (Oct. 1897); LPL, Benson Papers 148, f. 276; CSC Archives, The Rule in First Form; CSC Archives, Ayckbowm to Sister Vera [*c.* 1897]; CSC Archives, Mother May to Sisters, *Circular Letter* (14 May 1917).

105. LPL, Winnington-Ingram Papers 3, f. 138. CSC Customs.

106. Thomas Thellusson Carter, *First Ten Years of the House of Mercy, Clewer* (London: Joseph Masters, 1861), pp. 37–8; John S. Sellon (ed.), *Memos Relating to the Society of the Holy Trinity, Devonport* (London: Terry and Co., 1907), p. ii; R. Few, *An History of St John's House . . . With a Full Account of the Circumstances Which Led to the Withdrawal Therefrom of the Entire Sisterhood* (London: W. Skeffington, 1884), p. 44.

107. CSC Archives, Ayckbowm to Sister Vera (*c.* 1897).

108. *Statutes of the Clewer House of Mercy* (London: Spottiswoode & Shaw, [1853]), p. 3; Carter, *Ten Years*, pp. 37–8.

109. LPL, MS 3179, Rule of the Community of the Holy Family.

110. SSP Archives [Saint Saviour's Priory], *Memories of Mother Kate*, p. 37.

111. CSC Archives, Ayckbowm to Sister Vera, 13 February and 17 March 1900 and *c.* 1897, re: Sisters Katherine and Theodora.

112. CSC Archives, Ayckbowm to Sister Vera [*c.* 1897].

113. CRJBS Archives, Mother Eunice, Community History, p. 3.

114. Community of All Hallows Archives, 'Lavinia Cross'.

115. LPL, Benson Papers 158, ff. 102–10, 353; CSC Annual Report for 1894.

116. *Kilburn Sisters: Important Revelations*, 2nd edn (London: 'Church Bells' Office, 1896), pp. 10–13; CSC Archives, Mother Foundress' Diary, 2 Nov. 1884.

117. [Warburton], *Memories*, p. 104.

118. *The Story of St Saviour's Priory and Its Sixteen Years in Haggerston* (London: G. J. Palmer, 1882), pp. 26–7. This group had been planted by East Grinstead; all East Grinstead foundations were expected to find their own sisters and raise their own funds.

119. CSC Archives, Ayckbowm to Sister Vera, 1900; LPL, Benson Papers 158, ff. 218–21, Ayckbowm to Benson, 25 Jan. 1895; *Doing the Impossible: A Short Historical Sketch of St Margaret's Convent, East Grinstead, 1855–1980* (n.p., [1984]), p. 20.

120. CSC Archives, Mother Foundress' Diaries. 9 May 1885.

121. A. P. Ryder (comp.), 'A Paper . . . containing the replies of the various chaplains and Lady Superiors', in *Penitentiary Work in the Church of England* (London: Harrison and Sons, 1873), p. 12; CSMVW Archives, *Information Concerning the Works of the Community* (Wantage: Nichols, printer, 1905), p. 6.

122. Thomas Thellusson Carter, *The First Five Years of the House of Mercy, Clewer*, 2nd edn (London: Joseph Masters, 1855), pp. 30, 36; Carter, *First Ten Years*, pp. 35, 40; Lowder, *Ten Years*, p. 83; *A Kalendar of the English Church 1885* (London: Church Press Company, 1884), p. 47.

123. *Kalendar*, 1873, p. 175.

124. Carter, *First Ten Years*, p. 35; *Penitentiary Work*, p. 13; Edward J. Bristow, *Vice and Vigilance: Purity Movements in Britain Since 1700* (Dublin: Gill and Macmillan, 1977), p. 159.

125. *Kilburn Sisters*, p. x.

126. CSC Archives, Ayckbowm to Sister Vera, 10 February 1900; CSC Archives, *Our Work*, **7** (1884), p. 240; CSC Archives, Community Diary, 10 May 1887.

127. Nihill, *Sisters of St Mary at the Cross*, p. 81; CSC Archives, *Quarterly Chronicle*, **11** (1894), p. 3.

128. CSP Archives, Sister Rosamira, *First Twenty-six Years*, pp. 31–5, quoting Mrs Lancaster to Laura Oldfield, 3 September 1869, and Mrs Lancaster to the Archbishop of Canterbury, 20 February 1869, and p. 163.

129. Antony Wagner and Antony Dale, *The Wagners of Brighton* (London: Phillimore and Co., 1983), p. 134.

130. CSC Archives, Extracts from St Peter's Statutes.

131. CSMVW Archives, *Report for the Year 1855 of St Mary's Home for Penitents at Wantage* (Oxford: John Henry and James Parker, 1856), p. 8.

132. Williams and Cameron, p. 122; Nihill, *Sisters of St Mary at the Cross*, pp. 169–70; LPL, Benson Papers 55, ff. 18–21.

133. Thomas Thellusson Carter, *An Appeal for the House of Mercy, Clewer* (London: Joseph Masters, 1856), pp. 27–8.

134. LPL, Winnington-Ingram Papers, f. 137. CSC Customs.

135. Bennett, *Anglican Sisterhood*, p. 7; St Mary's Abbey Archives, The History of the Benedictine Community of St Mary's Abbey, West Malling, Kent, p. 35.

136. Community of the Holy Cross Archives, History of the Community Liturgy, p. 1. This part of their Rule may well have been based on that of the Sisters of St Vincent de Paul.

137. LPL, Temple Papers 33, ff. 270–2.

138. *Some Memories of Emily Harriet Elizabeth Ayckbowm, Mother Foundress of the Community of the Sisters of the Church* (London: Church Extension Association, 1914), pp. 197–8.

139. LPL, LC 38, ff. 149–50. Calculation by Charles Grafton, Bishop of Fond du Lac.

4 'We have heads and hands'

1. See, for example, E. R. Norman, *Anti-Catholicism in Victorian England* (London: George Allen & Unwin, 1968), and John Wolffe's *The Protestant Crusade in Great Britain 1829–1860* (Oxford: Clarendon, 1991).

2. Wagner and Dale, p. 102; letter to Mother Kate, August 1865, cited in [Warburton], *Old Soho Days*, p. 166. See also material relating to the Lewes riots. One sister, told by a woman in the street that she was 'denying Christ', admitted 'it is rather horrid to be so attacked', SHUT Archives, Sister Anne to Mother Superior (1877).

3. Carter, *Sisterhoods Considered*, p. 18.

4. Stephen, *The Service of the Poor*, p. 7; Charles Booth, *Religious Influences*, vol. II, p. 91.

5. Frances Power Cobbe, *Essays on the Pursuits of Women* (London: Emily Faithfull, 1863), pp. 109–10. The Home of Compassion, Hounslow, is a good example of this.

It was founded in May 1874, and by December of that year all three Lady Assistants had resigned, and only one new volunteer had come forward, leaving this refuge severely understaffed. (LPL, Fulham Papers, Bishop Jackson 491, Home of Compassion and Lambeth Refuge for ... Wayward Girls.)

6. Dora Greenwell, 'Our single women', *North British Review*, **36** (1862), p. 81. Emphasis Greenwell's. See also Webb, *Sisterhood Life and Work*, p. 74. Luddy makes a similar point with regard to Irish Catholic philanthropy, p. 36.

7. A.A. [Anne Ayers], *Evangelical Sisterhoods: Two Letters to a Friend* (New York: T. Whittaker, 1867), p. 29.

8. [Warburton], *Old Soho Days*, p. 6. Emphasis Warburton's.

9. [Ayers], *Evangelical Sisterhoods*, p. 16. Emphasis mine.

10. Stephenson, *Concerning Sisterhoods*, p. 17.

11. Twining, *Deaconesses*, p. 7.

12. Elizabeth, Mother Superior [Elizabeth Neale], *The Community of the Holy Cross: Short Account of Its Rise and History* (London: H. J. Wright, printer, [1884]), p. 6; O'Brien, 'Terra incognita', p. 115.

13. [Ayers], *Evangelical Sisterhoods*, p. 29; Jane Lewis, *Women in England, 1790–1950: Sexual Divisions and Social Change* (Brighton: Wheatsheaf Books, 1984), p. 95.

14. Charles Booth, *Religious Influences*, vol. 2, p. 90.

15. Samuel Fox, *Monks and Monasteries: Being an Account of English Monachism* (London: James Burns, 1845), pp. viii–xv.

16. John Mason Neale, *Ayton Priory* (Cambridge: Deightons, 1843), p. 113; CSC Archives, Sister Aletta's Memories of Mother Foundress; CSC Archives, Mother Foundress' Diaries, 20 April 1885; LPL, Benson Papers 148, f. 328.

17. L. E. Ellsworth, *Charles Lowder and the Ritualist Movement* (London: Darton, Longman & Todd, 1982), p. 125; LPL, Temple Papers 17, pp. 212–20, Signatories to the petition for a royal commission of enquiry into venereal disease.

18. All Saints Archives, Sister Catherine, 'Recollections of an old woman' (November 1907), p. 10.

19. All Saints Archives, Memories of Mother Foundress by Sister Mary Milicent; Vicinus, p. 48.

20. PH Archives, Ascot Priory papers, D. C. H., *Thoughts on Religious Communities*, p. 76.

21. Porterfield, p. 90.

22. E. Sellars, 'Women's work for the welfare of girls', in Burdett-Coutts, p. 43.

23. Neff, *Victorian Working Women*, p. 103; Florence Nightingale, *Cassandra* (1852), ed. Myra Stark (New York: The Feminist Press, 1979), p. 15; Goodman, *English Sister of Mercy*, p. 119; *The Times*, 'Protestant sisterhoods' (Sellon obituary), 25 November 1876, p. 9.

24. PH Archives, Ascot Priory papers, D. C. H., *Thoughts on Religious Communities*, p. 77.

25. V. A. L., *The Ministry of Women*, p. 6.

26. L. Coleman, 'Deaconesses, or sisterhoods', *American Quarterly Church Review*, **14** (1862), p. 631.

27. Twining, *Deaconesses*, pp. 2–3. There was also a class flavour to this argument, as in so many utilized by the sisterhoods. It was alleged that the present degrading system was due to the 'obtuse intellect and feeling of gross and boorish poor-law guardians' ('The social position of women', *The Churchman's Magazine*, **58** (1857), p. 205).

28. *Chronicle of Convocation*, Report No. 194, 'Sisterhoods and deaconesses' (1885), p. 1.

29. In recent years, studies of Victorian prostitution and the reformation of prostitutes have proliferated. A catalyst for much of this activity was Judith Walkowitz's study of areas affected by the Contagious Diseases Acts, *Prostitution and Victorian Society: Women, Class and the State* (Cambridge: Cambridge University Press, 1980). Other important pieces of research include local studies such as Finnegan's *Poverty and Prostitution* (Cambridge: Cambridge University Press, 1979), and Linda Mahood's *The Magdalens* (London: Routledge, 1990). There is an excellent chapter on Irish penitentiaries and refuges in Maria Luddy's book. Much of the following discussion of penitentiaries has appeared in revised form as 'Not worse than other girls: the convent-based rehabilitation of fallen women in Victorian Britain', *Journal of Social History*, **29** (1996), pp. 527–46.

30. Edward J. Bristow, *Vice and Vigilance: Purity Movements in Britain Since 1700* (Dublin: Gill & Macmillan, 1977), p. 62.

31. W. H. Hutchings, *The Life and Letters of Thomas Thellusson Carter* (London: Longmans, Green & Co., 1903), p. 92.

32. Mrs Boyd Carpenter, 'Women's work in connection with the Church of England', in Burdett-Coutts, p. 118. Great Britain, *Report from the Select Committee on Conventual and Monastic Institutions* (1870), question 903, p. 45.

33. Anna Jameson, *Sisters of Charity and the Communion of Labour* (London: Longman, Brown, Green, Longman & Roberts, 1859), p. 39.

34. S. B. Kanner, 'Victorian institutional patronage: Angela Burdett-Coutts, Charles Dickens and Urania Cottage Reformatory for Women, 1846–1856' (unpublished PhD, UCLA, 1972), p. 436.

35. John Armstrong, *An Appeal for the Formation of a Church Penitentiary* (London: John Henry Parker, 1849), p. 1; John Armstrong, *Essays on Church Penitentiaries* (London: John Henry Parker, 1858), p. 113.

36. T. T. Carter, *Is It Well to Institute Sisterhoods in the Church of England, for the Care of Female Penitents?* (London: John Henry Parker, 1851), p. 4.

37. Bristow, *Vice and Vigilance*, p. 102. No source given for Temple.

38. See Françoise Barret-Ducrocq, *Love in the Time of Victoria: Sexuality and Desire among Working-Class Men and Women in Nineteenth-Century London*, trans. John Howe (London: Verso, 1991).

39. John Armstrong, *A Further Appeal for the Formation of Church Penitentiaries* (London: John Henry Parker, 1851), pp. 5–6.

40. Armstrong, *Appeal*, p. 12; All Hallows Archives, clipping from *Penny Post*, **5** (1855), p. 237.

41. Hughes, 'Cleanliness and godliness', p. 2.

42. *Penitentiary Work*, pp. 28–9.

43. Lowder, *Ten Years*, p. 79; CSMVW Archives, Sister Kate Agnes, 'Reminiscences of Sister Anna'.

44. *Penitentiary Work*, p. 9. Given the judicial treatment of raped women, two years in a penitentiary may have been a more attractive option than attempting to take one's attacker to court. See Carolyn A. Conley, *The Unwritten Law: Criminal Justice in Victorian Kent* (Oxford: Oxford University Press, 1991), pp. 81–95. Luddy points out that many women in Irish Catholic penitentiaries had not actually worked as prostitutes, thus paralleling the English Anglican situation (p. 112).

45. T. T. Carter, *The First Five Years of the House of Mercy, Clewer* (London: Joseph Masters, 1855), p. 25.

46. Bonham, *Place*, pp. 19–21.

47. *Penitentiary Work*, pp. 24–5; *A Few Words to Servants about the Church Penitentiary Association* (London: J. H. Parker, n.d.), p. 7; H. N. [Harriet Nokes], *Twenty-three Years in a House of Mercy* (1866), 2nd edn (London: Swan Sonnchenstein, 1888), pp. 80–1.

48. Carter, *First Ten Years*, pp. 15-16.

49. Kanner, p. 191; Bonham, *Place*, p. 20. Luddy confirms that intact families were unusual in her study of the Irish penitentiaries (p. 133).

50. Unnamed correspondent to Mrs (Mariquita) Tennant, n.d., cited in *Founders of Clewer*, p. 22.

51. CSMVW Archives, Sister Kate Agnes, 'Reminiscences of Sister Anna'.

52. Jameson, *Sisters of Charity*, p. 39. Emphasis Jameson's.

53. All Hallows Archives, 'Shipmeadow Penitentiary', scrapbook clipping from *Penny Post*, **5** (1855), p. 259; Carter, *Five Years*, p. 22; Hughes, p. 126.

54. Bonham, *Place*, p. 25.

55. Sarah B. Wister, 'Sisterhoods in England', *North American Review*, **117** (1873), p. 567.

56. Carter, *Five Years*, p. 22.

57. CSMVW Archives, *St Mary the Virgin, Wantage: Information Concerning the Works of the Community* (1905), p. 8.

58. Hutchings, *Carter*, pp. 87–8.

59. Kanner, p. 513.

60. Hippolyte Taine, *Notes on England* (1872) (London: Thames and Hudson, 1957), p. 168.

61. CSMVW Archives, Sister Anna, undated letter.

62. [Noakes], *Twenty-Three Years*, p. 72.

63. Walkowitz, p. 196.

64. *Maidstone and Kentish Journal*, 25 January 1861, cited in Conley, p. 184.

65. 'Short homes: by a sister in charge of a refuge', pp. 52–6, and 'Small foundling homes', p. 142, both in *Penitentiary Work*.

66. Elizabeth Neale, *The Community of the Holy Cross*, p. 4; Russell, *Holy Cross 1857–1957*, p. 18; Maria Trench, 'English Sisterhoods', *The Nineteenth Century*, **40** (1884), p. 348.

67. *Penitentiary Work*, pp. 140–1.

68. Kanner, p. 5.

69. Carter, *My Dear Friend, You Ask for Some Result of Our First Five Years Work at the House of Mercy* (circular letter), Clewer, January 1856, pp. 1–3; Ann Frances Norton, 'The consolidation and expansion of the Community of St Mary the Virgin, Wantage, 1857–1907 (MPhil, King's College, London, 1979), p. 113; Armstrong, *Essays*, p. 14.

70. The only exception to this known to me is the MS notebook 'History of the Penitents' preserved in the CSJB archives; this document consists of the (dictated?) autobiographies of a few early penitents. The community also preserves a set of documents known as 'Letters of the Penitents'. Both of these are extensively used by Valerie Bonham in *A Place in Life: The Clewer House of Mercy, 1849–83* (Windsor: CSJB, 1992).

71. *Penitentiary Work*, p. 120. Emphasis in original.

72. CSMVW Archives, Report for the Year 1855 of St Mary's Home for Penitents at Wantage (1856), pp. 7–8; Sister Violet, *All Hallows, Ditchingham: The Story of an East Anglian Community* (Oxford: Becket Publications, 1986), p. 54; Norton, p. 119.

73. Hughes, p. 102.

74. Armstrong, *An Appeal*, p. 9; Norton, pp. 92–3.

75. LPL, Fulham Papers, Visitation Returns 1883, f. 313.

76. Carter, *First Ten Years*, p. 30; Hughes, pp. 94, 210.

77. Norton, p. 114–15, 120; All Saints Archives, Sister Elspeth, Notes about Various Sisters.

78. Quoted in Norton, p. 120.

79. Jane Ellice Hopkins, 'Work in Brighton', *Temple Bar* (1862), p. 40.

80. Carter, *Is It Well?*, pp. 2–3.

81. Vicinus, *Independent Women*, p. 79.

82. Vicinus, *Independent Women*, p. 78; *Penitentiary Life*, p. 23; 'The dedication of penitents as a religious order', *Seeking and Saving*, **3** (1886), p. 59.

83. Hutchings, *Carter*, p. 87.

84. LPL, Creighton Papers 15, ff. 165–8, report on St George's Rescue Home (All Saints).

85. Vicinus, p. 78; LPL, Temple Papers 17, ff. 212–20.

86. Vicinus, pp. 78–9.

87. *Penitentiary Work*, p. 121.

88. All Hallows Archives, 'Shipmeadow Penitentiary', scrapbook clipping from *Penny Post*, **5** (1855), p. 237; *Penitentiary Work*, p. 27.

89. LPL Creighton Papers 15, ff. 165–8.

90. CSC Archives, *Our Work* (December 1885), pp. 70–1; Nihill, *Sisters of St Mary*, pp. 56–9.

91. This was St Peter's, established by Catherine Tait (wife of the Archbishop) and run by the Community of St Peter. Davidson, *Life of Tait*, p. 471.

92. CSC Archives, 'The Sisters of the Church: Reply to Certain Statements Addressed by Two Ladies to the Bishops of the Lambeth Conference', p. 2 (henceforth 'Reply'); CSC Archives, *Orphanage for Workhouse Girls, in Connection with the Church Extension Association* (n.p., n.d.,); CSC Archives, *The Sisters of the Church and the Church Extension Association* (1897), p. 2; CSC Archives, 'Reply'; CSC Archives, *Our Work* (obituary of Sister Julia, born 1835, professed 1879), December 1924), p. 185.

93. CSC Archives, Community Diary, 25 December 1886 and 7 February 1887; CSC Archives, *Quarterly Chronicle* (April 1895), pp. 5–6.

94. See, for example, the legitimacy requirements listed in the *Guide to Schools, Homes and Refuges in England, for the Benefit of Girls and Women* (London: Longmans, Green & Co., 1888).

95. Henry Humble, 'Infanticide: its cause and cure', in Orby Shipley (ed.), *The Church and the World* (London: Longmans, Green, Reader & Dyer, 1866), pp. 55, 57.

96. LPL, Benson Papers 158, ff. 2, 10, 29–36, 328; CSC Archives, Sister Agnes' Reminiscences of Mother Foundress; CSC Archives, Sister Aletta's Account of Mother Foundress; CSC Archives, 'Reply', p. 4; *Kilburn Sisters: Important Revelations*, p. 27. The Sister Archivist of CSC informs me that this policy was changed a few years later.

97. CSC Archives, 'Reply', p. 4.

98. LPL, Benson Papers 158, f. 37, 1894.

99. CSC Archives, *Our Work* (Dec. 1885), p. 35. Holy Cross also trained its bright 'industrials' as teachers (Lowder, *Ten Years*, p. 67).

100. LPL, Benson Papers 158, ff. 253–6, 332–3; CSC Archives, Private Account of 'The Troubles', issued by the Community (February 1895), p. 37.

101. CSC Archives, *General Rules for the Superintendence of an Orphanage or Community Kitchen, also the Regulations Binding on the Orphans, etc.* (London: Church Extension Association, n.d.,), p. 16.

102. CSC Archives, Private Account of 'The Troubles', p. 37.

103. For evidence of this, see the many letters from former CSC orphans claiming that they and their companions were never ill-treated. LPL, Benson Papers 158; *Kilburn Sisters*, pp. 12, 16, 20, 72; CSC Archives, *General Rules*, p. 15; CSC Archives, *Quarterly Chronicle*, 7 (Oct. 1893), p. 1; CSC Archives, 'Reply', p. 3.

104. CSP Archives, Sister Rosamira, *First Twenty-six Years*, p. 11; CSC Archives, *Quarterly Chronicle* (June 1892), p. 4; 'Sisterhood life', p. 187.

105. CSC Archives, 'Sister Rosalie's Reminiscences of Mother Foundress'; SSB Archives, Packet of Letters from Mother Foundress to Sisters at H.O.B. Bournemouth, 1876–1906, Bennett to Sister Alice Flavia, [1892].

106. CSC Archives, *General Rules*, pp. 17–18; E. Janes, 'Associated work', in Burdett-Coutts, pp. 135–6; Holy Rood Archives, G. Stout, *History of the North Ormesby Hospital 1858–1948* (privately printed, 1989), p. 70.

107. CSC Archives, Community Diary, January 1873.

108. Lowder, *Ten Years*, p. 67; Lowder, *Twenty-one Years*, p. 121.

109. NSSJD Archives, 1855 Annual Report; Williams, *Sellon*, p. 137.

110. All Saints Archives, Letters from Mother Foundress to Various Sisters, pp. 91, 93.

111. NSSJD Archives, Annual Reports for 1856, 1867; LPL, Benson Papers 65, ff. 147–8, All Saints to Benson, 4 October 1888.

112. All Saints Archives, Letters from Mother Foundress to Various Sisters.

113. Luddy, p. 50.

114. CSP Archives, Sister Rosamira, *First Twenty-six Years*, p. 20.

115. Katherine Williams, 'From Sarah Gamp to Florence Nightingale: a critical study of hospital nursing systems from 1840 to 1897', in Celia Davies (ed.), *Rewriting Nursing History* (London: Croom Helm, 1980), p. 65; *Facta Non Verba* (London: W. Isbister, 1874), p. 329; Mrs Stuart Wortley, 'On nursing', in Burdett-Coutts, p. 217.

116. NSSJD Archives, *Statement of the Lady Superior*; Nihill, *Sisters of St Mary at the Cross*, p. 300.

117. Holy Rood Archives, marginal note by Isaac Haigh in hospital papers.

118. Williams, 'Sarah Gamp', p. 77.

119. NSSJD Archives, *Statement*, p. 5.

120. NSSJD Archives, F. F. Cartwright, 'The Story of St John's House', *King's College Hospital Nurses' League Journal*, **35** (1959), p. 29; NSSJD Archives, copy of 1886 memorandum; *The Times*, 14 February 1874; CSC Archives, Mother Emily Ayckbowm to Canon Carr, 26 March 1882; LPL, Benson Papers 4, f. 333.

121. LPL, Benson Papers 4, ff. 309–12, Sister Aimée to Benson; Williams, *Sellon*, p. 154.

122. Anne Summers, 'Ministering Angels: Victorian ladies and nursing reform', in Gordon Marsden (ed.), *Victorian Values: Personalities and Perspectives in Nineteenth Century Society* (London: Longmans, 1990), pp. 121–33.

123. NSSJD Archives, *The Echo*, 30 January 1874.

124. NSSJD Archives, 1874 Annual Report; Few, p. 22; LPL, Benson Papers 4, ff. 309–71.

125. NSSJD Archives, History of NSSJD.

126. Anson and Campbell, *Call*, pp. 282–3; NSSJD Archives, 1877 and 1883 Annual Reports; CSP Archives, Sister Rosamira, *First Twenty-six Years*, p. 17; All Saints Archives, History of the Community, p. 30; CSC Archives, 'What others are doing', *Our Work* (1884), p. 255.

127. LPL, Benson Papers 111, f. 415. Mother Caroline Mary to Benson, 19 August 1892; Russell, *Holy Cross*, p. 33; Nihill, *Sisters of St Mary at the Cross*, p. 83; CSC Archives, *Our Work* (1884), p. 228.

128. Holy Rood Archives, Sister Jean, *God Thom* (Bognor Regis: New Horizon, 1981), pp. 7–8; CSC Archives, *Our Work* (December 1883), p. 10.

129. NSSJD Archives, 1855 and 1856 Annual Reports; R. Brett, *Smallpox in Shoreditch, 1871* (London: printed for private circulation, 1871), pp. 3–6.

130. G. R. Prynne, *Thirty-five Years of Mission Work* (Plymouth: W. Brendon & Son, 1883), p. 11. All Saints archives list the names of sisters who died as a result of nursing the poor in various epidemics in Notes on the Foundation of Our Community and Some Developments of Work, No. 11, p. 36.

131. Charles Philip Stewart, *The Oxford Movement and After* (London: A. R. Mowbray, 1932), p. 255; *The Story of St Saviour's Priory and Its Sixteen Years in Haggerston* (London: G. J. Palmer, 1882), p. 40; Brett, pp. 3–6; Cecil Wray, *Sister Monica of St Martin's Sisterhood: A Funeral Sermon Preached at St Martin's Church, Liverpool* (Liverpool: Adam Holden, 1869), p. 11.

132. CSC Archives, Community Diary, July 1884.

133. CSP Archives, Sister Rosamira, *First Twenty-six Years*, p. 127; SSP Archives, Sister Frances, 'Priory Dates, 1866–1930'.

134. [Warburton], *Memories*, pp. 48–9.

135. Williams, *Sellon*, p. 100.

136. SSP Archives, Mother Kate's Crown Street diary, 16 December 1858.

137. CSC Archives, Sister Aletta's memories of Mother Foundress; CSC Archives, *Memories of Ayckbowm*, pp. 39, 59, 120, 204; CSC Archives, Mother Emily to Sister Vera, 13 Feb. 1900; Louise Creighton, *Life and Letters of Mandell Creighton* (London: Longmans, Green & Co., 1904), vol. II, p. 268.

138. CSC Archives, Community Diary, September 1883. See Appendix 9 for a listing of all community schools.

139. CSC Archives, *The Rules of the Sisters of the Church* (London: n.p., 1886), p. 93; LPL MS 3179, Rule of the Community of the Holy Family; CSC Archives, *Quarterly Chronicle*, **1** (March 1892), pp. 2, 5.

140. CSC Archives, *Memories of Ayckbowm*, p. 74.

141. CSC Archives, *Memories of Ayckbowm*, pp. 85, 74–5; CSC Archives, 'Circular letter, Michaelmas, 1887'. For a complete list of CSC's major projects in 1894, see Appendix 9.

142. CSC Archives, 1888 Diary, 21 January 1888 and 24 November 1888; *A Valiant Victorian: The Life and Times of Mother Emily Ayckbowm* (London: A. R. Mowbray, 1964), pp. 85–9.

143. Marjorie Cruikshank, *Church and State in English Education* (London: Macmillan and Co., 1963), p. 50.

144. LPL, *The Orphanage of the Sisters of Bethany, Springbourne, Bournemouth: Annual Report 1898–99* (n.p.: W. Mate and Sons, 1899), p. 3.

145. Allan T. Cameron, *Directory of Religious Communities of Men and Women in the Church of England* (London: Faith Press, 1920), p. 44; *A Hundred Years*, pp. 39, 41, 47; [Butler], *Life*, p. 156.

146. 'The training of teachers, professional and voluntary', in *Pan-Anglican Papers* (1908), vol. II, Section C, p. 180.

147. SHUT Archives, Constitutions and Rule of the Sisters of Charity, Knowle, (*c.* 1867), pp. 9–10.

148. Bennett, *Anglican Sisterhood*, p. 67.

149. Hugh W. Jermyn, *A Letter to the Right Hon. Sir John Coleridge, Visitor to the House of Mercy, Ditchingham* (Williton: S. Cox, printer, 1866), p. 8.

150. Lowder, *Ten Years*, p. 51.

151. CSC Archives, First Log of the Community of the Sisters of the Church, March, December, 1871; CSC Archives, *Memories of Ayckbowm*, pp. 70–2; CSMVW Archives, St Mary's Wantage (leatherbound index of sisters' qualifications); CSC Archives, Community Diary 1888, 24 February and 27 March 1888 and obituary notices in *Our Work*, **87** (Mar.–Apr. 1964), pp. 24–5; *Our Work* (Dec. 1943), p. 91; *Our Work* (July–Aug. 1955), pp. 69, iv.

152. CSC Archives, Mother Foundress' Diaries, 7 February 1887; *Quarterly Chronicle*, **1** (March 1892), pp. 5–6.

153. CSC Archives, Circular Letter (Lent 1892), pp. 2–3. Emphasis Ayckbowm's.

154. CSC Archives, Community Diary, 21 January 1888; [Kathleen White], *St Denys School Oxford: Originally Known as Holy Trinity School* (Oxford: privately printed, 1989), p. 26.

155. See, for example, *Elementary Education: The Kilburn Series* (London: The Education Union, n.d.); *The Kilburn Manual of Elementary Teaching* (London: The Education Union, n.d.); other titles in the series included *How to Maintain Discipline*; *Education in the Elementary School*, etc., as well as subject-specific manuals.

156. CSC Archives, Community Diary 1888, 8 February; 23 March; 26 March; 2 April; 19 May; 6 December, etc.; CSC Archives, Mother Foundress' Diary, 19 November 1884.

157. CSC Archives, *The Rules of the Sisters of the Church* (London: n.p., 1886), p. 93.

158. CSC Archives, *Quarterly Chronicle* (June 1892), pp. 5–6; CSC Archives, Community Diary 1888, 13 February 1888.

159. LPL, MS 3179, Rule of the Community of the Holy Family.

160. *Memories of Ayckbowm*, p. 171; CSC Archives. Mother Foundress' diary, 3 July 1884; CSC Archives, Community Diary 1888, 12 January 1888; 5 March 1888. See, for example, the obituaries of Sisters Susanna and Mabel in CSC Archives, *Our Work* (December 1943), p. 91; *Our Work* (July–August 1955), p. 69; *Our Work*, **87** (1964), pp. 24–5; *A Hundred Years*, p. 43; CSC Archives, Community Diary, 7 December 1875.

161. SHUT Archives, Logbook of orphanage school 1885–1913, entry for Sepember 1890; [White], p. 28.

162. SHUT Archives, Logbook of orphanage school 1885–1913 and School logbook (1885–1904). This was not unique to sisterhood schools; Asher Tropp states that middle-class schools often offered inferior education (*The School Teachers* (London: William Heinemann, 1957), pp. 23–4).

163. SHUT Archives, undated unidentified clipping, obituary of Sister Ursula; SHUT Archives, *St Denys School Oxford 1857–1957* (Oxford: Oxford University Press, 1957), n.p.; CSC Archives, *The Sisters of the Church: Their Life, Work, and Rule* (London: n.p., 1885), p. 35; CSC Archives, Circular Letter (Michaelmas 1887), p. 2.

164. CSMVW Archives, *A Diverted Hope*, p. 48.

165. [White], p. 40; All Saints Archives, Sister Caroline Mary, Memories by the Second Mother, pp. 107–8, CSMVW Archives, Roll of the Sisters and Novices who have been admitted to the community of St Thomas the Martyr, Oxford.

166. SHUT Archives, Mother Marion's appointment of her successor as Superior, 18 Oct. 1910; SHUT Archives, Sister Ursula, Obituary of Mother Ella Mary, undated clipping.

167. National Protestant Congress, 'The danger of conventual education', in *Romanism and Ritualism in Great Britain and Ireland* (Edinburgh: R. W. Hunter, 1895), p. 326. Emphasis in original.

168. CSC Archives, Community Diary 1888, 5 March 1888.

169. CSC Archives, 'For what purpose are thou here?' *Our Work* (December 1885), p. 69.

170. CSC Archives, Community Diary 1888. I can find no further reference to this neo-community at 29 Kilburn Park Road.

171. CSC Archives, *Memories of Ayckbowm*, pp. 83–4.

172. Bennett, *Anglican Sisterhood*, pp. 106–7.

173. Hannah More, *Coelebs in Search of a Wife* (1806), in *The Works of Hannah More*, Vol. 7 (London: Henry G. Bohn, 1853), p. 225. Emphasis More's.

174. J. H. Blunt, *Directorium Pastorale: Principles and Practice of Pastoral Work in the Church of England* (London: Rivingtons, 1864), pp. 322–3.

175. Charles Kingsley, 'Woman's work in a country parish', in *Sanitary and Social Lectures and Essays*, vol. 18 of *The Works of Charles Kingsley* (London: Macmillan & Co., 1880), p. 9; Blunt, pp. 331–2. Kingsley's strong disapproval of celibacy is ironic in that Emily Ayckbowm, founder of CSC, cited the reading of his novel *Yeast* as one of the determinants in her decision to form a sisterhood.

176. Heeney, *Women*, p. 28.

177. Jane Lewis, 'Reconstructing women's experience of home and family', in *Labour and Love* (Oxford: Basil Blackwell, 1986), p. 3; see also Davidoff and Hall, p. 334; Booth, *Religious Influences*, vol. 2, p. 13.

178. Charles B. P. Bosanquet, *London: Some Account of Its Growth, Charitable Agencies, and Wants* (London: Hatchard & Co., 1868), p. 155.

179. G. Congreve, 'Sisters: their vocation and their special work', in *Pan-Anglican Papers: The Church and Its Ministry: The Ministry of Women* (London: SPCK, 1908), p. 3.

180. CRJBS Archives, [Mother Faith], 'Community Memories', undated clippings from *The Elephant* (parish magazine).

181. Nihill, *Sisters of the Poor*, p. 6.

182. CSC Archives, 'Sisters of Charity', *Our Work*, 7 (1884), pp. 205–6.

183. Charles Booth, *Life and Labour of the People in London*, Third Series: *Religious Influences*, vol. 1 (London: Macmillan & Co., 1902), p. 27; Pusey House Archives 6276; E. R. Norman, *Church and Society in England, 1770–1970: A Historical Study* (Oxford: Clarendon Press, 1976), p. 165.

184. All Saints Archives, Sister Catherine, Recollections of an Old Woman (November 1907), p. 7.

185. CRJBS Archives, [Mother Faith], 'Reverend Mother's Memories', undated clippings from *The Elephant* (parish magazine).

186. Maria Trench, *Charles Lowder: A Biography*, 9th edn (London: Kegan Paul, Trench, 1883), p. 171; Charles Booth, *Life and Labour of the People in London*, Third Series: *Religious Influences*, vol. 4 (London: Macmillan & Co., 1902), p. 8.

187. [Warburton], *Old Soho Days*, p. 7. Emphasis Warburton's.

188. *Charity Organization Society Review* (Sister Constance's Report) (1895), pp. 518–21; SSP Archives, Sister Kate's Crown Street Diary, 1858–65 (Feb. 1861, etc.); Brian Heeney, *The Women's Movement in the Church of England 1850–1930* (Oxford: Clarendon Press, 1988), p. 65.

189. Mrs Molesworth, 'For the little ones', in Burdett-Coutts, p. 21.

190. CRJBS Archives, 'St Alphage, Southwark: 1894 Annual Report', pp. 39–40.

191. *C.S.D.: The Life and Work of St Denys', Warminster* (Warminster: MCSD, 1979); A. Perchenet, *The Revival of the Religious Life and Christian Unity*, trans. E. M. A. Graham (London: A. R. Mowbray & Co., 1969), p. 150.

192. Holy Rood Archives, Sister Jean, *God Thorn*, pp. 41–2.

193. SSB Archives, Sister Katherine Mildred, Scrapbook of drawings and photographs from the Assyrian Mission; Perchenet, p. 154; Mary S. Donovan, *A Different Call* (Wilton: Morehouse-Barlow, 1986), p. 133.

194. Benson, *Life*, vol. 2, pp. 191–2.

195. CSMVW Archives, *Monthly Letter*, January, March, August, 1887; see also Max Müller's mention of Pundita Ramabai's book on Indian women in *The Times*, 22 August 1887; Benson, *Life of Benson*, vol. 2, pp. 191–2.

196. Holy Rood Archives, Sister Jean, *God Thorn*, pp. 41–2; All Saints Archives, Memories of Mother Caroline Mary.

197. Rosemary Auchmuty, 'Victorian Spinsters' (unpublished PhD, Australian National University, 1975), p. 196.

198. J. Ellice Hopkins, *A Plea for the Wider Action of the Church of England in the Prevention of the Degradation of Women* (London: Hatchards, 1879), p. 12.

199. All Saints Archives, Sister Caroline Mary, Memories by the Second Mother, p. 73; Charity Organization Society, *Charity and Food: Report of the Special Committee* (London: Spottiswoode & Co., 1887), p. 7; 'The way the wind blows', *The Charity Organization Review*, 3 (1887), p. 81; CSC Archives, Circular Letter (Oct. 1889), p. 3.

200. CSC Archives, *The Sisters of the Church and the Church Extension Association* (1897), p. 2.

201. E. Janes, 'Associated work', in Burdett-Coutts, pp. 135–6; 'The way the wind blows', *The Charity Organization Review*, **3** (1887), p. 81.

202. Agnes Harrison, 'The under side', *Macmillans Magazine*, **19** (1869), pp. 331–9.

203. *A Hundred Years in Haggerston: The Story of St Saviour's Priory* (London: Saint Saviour's Priory, 1966), p. 23.

204. *A Hundred Years in Haggerston*, p. 37; All Saints Archives, Sister Elspeth's History of the Community, p. 25; All Saints Archives, Sister Caroline Mary, Memories by the Second Mother, pp. 61–2.

205. SHUT Archives, Constitutions and Rule of the Sisters of Charity, Knowle, Rule for the Sister in Charge of the Creche, [*c.* 1867], pp. 54–7; SSP Archives, *The Orient, or St Saviour's Priory Quarterly Papers*, **1** (1883), pp. 25–7; *The Story of St Saviour's Priory and Its Sixteen Years in Haggerston* (London: G. J. Palmer, 1882), pp. 60–1; *A Hundred Years in Haggerston*, p. 20.

206. *Story of St Saviour's Priory*, pp. 60–1.

207. CSC Archives, *The Rules of the Sisters of the Church* (London: n.p., 1886), p. 115; NSSJD Archives, 1885 Annual Report.

208. *The Story of St Saviour's Priory*, pp. 60–1; *Memories of Ayckbowm*, p. 120; Goodman, *English Sister of Mercy*, p. 120.

209. For an account of SSP projects in Hackney, see Charles Booth, *Religious Influences*, vol. 2, pp. 89–92.

210. *A Hundred Years in Haggerston*, p. 21; *The Story of St Saviour's Priory*, pp. 56–9.

211. *Guild of St Mary the Virgin, Parish of St Alban the Martyr* (London: W. Knott, 1870), pp. 7–8; Walter Walsh, *The Secret History of the Oxford Movement*, 4th edn (London: Sonnenschein, 1898), p. 258.

212. *Story of St Saviour's Priory*, pp. 44–50.

213. Charles Fuge Lowder, *Twenty-one Years in St George's Mission* (London: Rivingtons, 1877), p. 173.

214. NSSJD Archives, 1889 Annual Report.

215. Carpenter, *Church and People*, p. 255.

216. [Warburton], *Memories*, pp. 67–72.

217. Florence Nightingale, *Cassandra* (1852) (New York: The Feminist Press, 1979), p. 35.

218. Sarah B. Wister, 'Sisterhoods in England', *Lippincott Magazine*, **9** (1872), p. 568.

219. CSC Archives, 'Sisters of Charity', *Our Work*, **7** (1884), p. 73.

220. Luddy, p. 24.

221. [Warburton], *Memories*, p. 309.

222. Georgina Hill, *Women in English Life*, vol. II (London: Richard Bentley & Son, 1896), pp. 241–2.

223. Mrs Sandford, *Woman in Her Social and Domestic Character*, 5th edn (London: Longmans, Rees, Orme, Brown, Green & Longman, 1837), p. 194.

5 'They will not obey'

1. Susan O'Brien, 'Lay sisters and good mothers: working-class women in English convents, 1840–1910', in W. J. Sheils and Diana Wood (eds), *Women in the Church: Studies in Church History No. 27* (Oxford: Basil Blackwell, 1990), pp. 462–3; see also *Chronicle of Convocation*, 'Report of the Convocation of York on Sisterhoods', *York Journal of Convocation* (1885), Appendix III, pp. xxiv–xxv.

2. Luddy, pp. 24–9.

3. Hughes, 'Good Shepherd', pp. 90–5; Mary Ewens, *The Role of the Nun in Nineteenth Century America* (New York: Arno, 1978), pp. 256, 286–8.

4. V. A. L., *The Ministry of Women*, pp. 31–2; LPL, Temple Papers 25, f. 66, F. B. Smith to Temple, 2 August 1897. Smith obviously felt that the sisters should 'go over' to Rome without delay, where they would, he hoped, find their masters.

5. Cusack, 'Woman's place', p. 202. For a brief account of Cusack's subjection within the Roman Catholic Church see Clear, pp. 64–6. See also Daly, pp. 103–6, for a description of Mary Ward's similar experience. Peter Frederick Anson, *The Benedictines of Caldey* (London: Burns, Oates, 1940), pp. xxi–xxii.

6. Nightingale, *Suggestions for Thought*, vol. 2, p. 102.

7. Cobbe, *Pursuits of Women*, pp. 58–9. Emphasis Cobbe's.

8. Heeney, *Women's Movement in the Church of England*, p. 14.

9. LPL, Blomfield Papers 57, ff. 165–6, 2 March 1855, Blomfield to Pusey. Also vol. 57, ff. 195, 197, 228, 252.

10. *Report of the Convocation of York on Sisterhoods*, 1885, Appendix III, pp. xxiii–xxiv; *Chronicle of Convocation* (1862), p. 912; Anne Summers, 'Ministering angels', p. 126. Emphasis mine.

11. *Chronicle of Convocation* (1878), p. 253.

12. Stephen, *Service of the Poor*, p. 285; *Chronicle of Convocation* (1862), p. 967.

13. LPL, LC 38, ff. 163–4, 170.

14. Allen B. Webb, *Sisterhood Life and Women's Work* (London: Skeffington and Son, 1883), p. 57. Emphasis Webb's.

15. *Chronicle of Convocation* (1878), p. 253.

16. Thomas P. Dale (ed.), *Debate in Convocation on Deaconess Institutions and Protestant Sisterhoods* (London: Emily Faithfull, 1862), p. 37; Ashwell, *Life of Wilberforce*, vol. 3, p. 332; Davidson, *Life of Tait*, pp. 453–4.

17. Wilberforce was not alone in this belief. See LPL, Creighton Papers 10, ff. 282–7. This was not the view of most sisterhoods: All Saints' constitution stated that 'fidelity to these vows is not enforced by ecclesiastical authority, still less by physical compulsion or legal restraint' (LPL, *Constitution of the Society of All Saints' Sisters of the Poor* (London: Harrison & Sons [1886]), p. 18).

18. The formation of the Society of St John the Evangelist in 1866 is described in Allchin, *Silent Rebellion*, p. 196; *Chronicle of Convocation*, Resolutions of the Upper House, 4 February 1891, pp. iii–iv.

19. Bodleian Library, Dept. of Western MSS, Wilberforce Papers, Wilberforce to CSJB sisters, 19 May 1854, c 22, ff. 174–5; d 33, f. 43, 14 May 1854; Wilberforce to Carter, 18 May 1854, c 22, f. 172; Ashwell, *Wilberforce*, vol. III, pp. 324, 334.

20. [Butler], *Life*, p. 142.

21. Arthur C. Benson, *The Life of Edward White Benson, Sometime Archbishop of Canterbury* (London: Macmillan & Co., 1899), vol. 2, p. 397; Denison, pp. 223–5.

22. CSC Archives, *Quarterly Chronicle*, 7 (1893), p. 1. Emphasis Ayckbowm's. See also LPL, Benson Papers 116, ff. 331, G. North Ash to Benson, 2 October 1893.

23. W. A. Muhlenberg, introduction to A. A., *Evangelical Sisterhoods*, p. 9.

24. *Chronicle of Convocation* (1858), pp. 107–8, 110.

25. Great Britain, Parliamentary Papers, *Report from the Select Committee on Conventual and Monastic Institutions, &c., together With the Proceedings of the Committee, Minutes of Evidence, and Appendix*, vol. 7, [1870], question 3749, p. 172; LPL, Bishops' Meetings, BM 3, f. 51 (interleaved).

26. Louise Creighton, *Life and Letters of Mandell Creighton*, vol. II, p. 271.

27. Allchin, *Silent Rebellion*, p. 174.

28. *Society of the Sisters of Bethany*, p. 9; CRJBS Archives, Community Log 1869–1936, entry for 1897; LPL, Winnington-Ingram (Fulham) Papers 3, ff. 107–10.

29. Benson, *Life*, vol. 1, p. 594.

30. Benson, *Life*, vol. 2, p. 273. Diary, 6 August 1889.

31. Phillpotts, *A Letter to Miss Sellon*, pp. 6–8; [P. Lydia Sellon], *Reply to a Tract by the Reverend J. Spurrell* (London: Joseph Masters, 1852), p. 20.

32. SHUT Archives, Mother Marion's Diary, Vol. III, 1893–1902, 23 November 1895.

33. LPL, Benson Papers 159, f. 85; Heeney, *Ministry of Women*, p. 67; LPL, Bishops' Meetings, BM 1, f. 375.

34. Benson, *Life*, vol. 2, p. 643, citing diary entry 11 June 1895.

35. LPL, Winnington-Ingram (Fulham) Papers 3, f. 111.

36. 'The ministry of women', in *Pan-Anglican Papers* (1908), Vol. 4, Section C, p. 249.

37. LPL, Benson Papers 42, ff. 310–11. See also ff. 300–1, 306–7; Benson Papers 81, f. 424; Benson, *Life*, vol. 2, p. 286.

38. LPL, Benson Papers 158, ff. 218–21. Ayckbowm to Benson, 25 Jan. 1895; Davidson, *Life of Tait*, pp. 459–63.

39. Grafton, *Works*, vol. 4, *A Journey Godward*, p. 102; LPL, Tait Papers 428, ff. 327–8; Benson Papers 17, ff. 36–43; Davidson, *Life of Tait*, pp. 455–8.

40. Cusack, *Five Years*, pp. 27–8; *Book of the Statutes of the Sisterhood of Mercy of the Holy and Undivided Trinity; With the Rules for Daily Life* (Oxford: By the Society, Convent of the Annunciation, 1882).

41. Hope Campbell Barton Stone, 'Constraints on the Mother Foundresses: contrasts in Anglican and Roman Catholic religious headship in Victorian England' (PhD, Leeds, 1993).

42. *Chronicle of Convocation* (1862), p. 919.

43. Ludlow, *Women's Work*, pp. 118–19.

44. LPL, LC 38, f. 140.

45. Wray, *Sister's Love*, p. 9; Muhlenberg, introduction to A. A., *Evangelical Sisterhoods*, p. 9; Stephenson, *Concerning Sisterhoods*, p. 23.

46. Benedicta Ward, SLG, 'A Tractarian inheritance: the religious life in a patristic perspective', in Geoffrey Rowell (ed.), *Tradition Renewed* (Allison Park, PA: Pickwick Press, 1986), pp. 219–20.

47. All Hallows Archives, Scrapbook of clippings re: Church matters, 1850s. 'The Shipmeadow Penitentiary Again', clipping marked *Norfolk Chronicle*, Oct. 1856. Emphasis in original.

48. M. Hobart Seymour, *Nunneries* (London: Seeleys, 1852), p. x.

49. Bullough, *Subordinate Sex*, pp. 160–1; John Mason Neale, *Deaconesses, and Early Sisterhoods* (London: Joseph Masters, 1869), p. 8.

50. CRJBS Archives, Mother Faith's Memories.

51. PH 6276, unidentified clipping headed 'We Are Able to Give Dr. Pusey's Paper Verbatim'. Emphasis mine.

52. Davidson, *Life of Tait*, p. 458.

53. Robinson, *Deaconesses*, pp. 155, 105; see also J. R. Hayne, *Church Deaconesses* (London: John Henry & James Parker, 1859), pp. 10–12.

54. Vicinus, *Independent Women*, p. 58.

55. Sewell, 'Anglican deaconesses', *Macmillans Magazine* (1873), p. 465.

56. Prelinger, 'Female diaconate', in Malmgreen, p. 178.

57. Sister Joanna, 'The Deaconess Community of St Andrew', *Journal of Ecclesiastical History*, **12** (1961), pp. 215–30.

58. 'Sisterhood life', in Shipley, p. 171.

59. [Warburton], *Memories*, p. 15.

60. Typical is the assumption that men not only founded the sisterhoods, but ran them on a day-to-day basis. (James Bentley, *Ritualism and Politics in Victorian Britain: The Attempt to Legislate for Belief* (Oxford: Oxford University Press, 1978), p. 14; Charles Bigg, *Wayside Sketches in Ecclesiastical History* (London: Longmans Green, 1906), p. 439. It is dismaying to find this mistake repeated in more recent work: Davidoff and Hall, pp. 99, 432; and in Rowell's *Vision Glorious*, pp. 99, 110–11, 119.

61. Stephenson, *Concerning Sisterhoods*, p. 11. Emphasis mine; Norman, *Church and Society*, p. 134.

62. [Ayers], *Evangelical Sisterhoods*, p. 31.

63. LPL, Winnington-Ingram (Fulham) Papers 3, f. 116; CSC Archives, Mother Foundress's Diaries, 28 January 1885.

64. Grafton, *Journey Godward*, p. 104; Liddon, *Life of Pusey*, vol. 3, p. 32.

65. CSC Archives, Mother Foundress's Diaries, 7 June 1884.

66. *Society of the Sisters of Bethany*, p. 5.

67. Holy Rood Archives, Sister Jean, *God Rood*, pp. 21, 24, 31; Few, p. 9.

68. Hutchings, *Carter*, p. 149. Emphasis Carter's.

69. Bodleian Library, Wilberforce Papers, c 23, f. 160, Carter to Wilberforce, 7 April 1854; c 22, f. 172, Wilberforce to Carter 18 May 1854.

70. *Butler of Wantage*, pp. 45, 60.

71. LPL, MS 1604, f. 454. John Mason Neale to Cecil Wray, n.d.; *Letters of John Mason Neale*, p. 323 (May 1860).

72. Nihill, *Sisters of St Mary at the Cross*, p. 164. Emphasis Nihill's.

73. 'Sisterhood life', *Church and World*, pp. 168–9.

74. LPL, Benson Papers 87, ff. 90–6. Mother Lucy Jones to Bishop of Chichester, (copy) 16 July 1893. See MCSD Archives, notebook titled 'Sisters'; *C.S.D: The Life and Work of St Denys, Warminster, to 1979* (n.p.: MCSD, 1979), pp. 7–8.

75. Arthur Calder-Marshall, *The Enthusiast*, pp. 221–2.

76. SHUT Archives, Mother Marion's Diary, vol. 2, 1875–1882, interleaved note from E. B. Pusey [1880].

77. SHUT Archives, obituary of T. Chamberlain, album of newspaper clippings, undated, source unidentified; CSMVW Archives, Roll of the Sisters and Novices Who Have Been Admitted to the Community of St Thomas the Martyr, Oxford.

78. These salaries were generally low; for example, CSMVW paid the chaplain of their Fulham penitentiary £50 per annum (LPL, Fulham Papers, Visitation Returns 1883, f. 313).

79. LPL, Benson Papers 42, ff. 314–15, 318–23. R. W. Benson to E. W. Benson, Aug. 1887. Emphasis Benson's. See also LPL, Benson Papers 81, ff. 430–3.

80. SHUT Archives, Mother Marion's Diary, vol. 3, 21 February 1893; 13 June 1893.

81. CSC Archives, *Our Work*, 7 (1884), p. 169.

82. Scottish Record Office, CH12/58/4, Constitution of St Andrew's Sisterhood and House of Mercy, revised 1888, pp. 7–9; see also SSB Archives, Old Statutes [1871], pp. 7–8; LPL, Benson Papers 81, f. 387, and All Saints Archives, The Rule, Community of All Saints.

83. LPL, Benson Papers 42, f. 319; LC 38, f. 957. Grafton's misogynistic distrust of women's democracy is clear in his next remark: 'Have as few Chapter votes as you possibly can, (women are naturally tyrants when they have the power) . . . and in that way you will check them.'

84. CSC Archives, Mother Foundress's Diary, 7 Jan. 1880. Emphasis in original. Unfortunately, the diary is incomplete, and this entry ends with the word 'nothing'. One is tempted to surmise that the passage originally concluded 'to do with the Cowley Fathers'. (Cowley was the Community of St John the Evangelist.)

85. William Niven, *'Sisterhood' Nurses* (London: Hatchard, 1866), p. 24; [Dill], p. 123.

86. Richard Littledale to William Darling, 20 Jan. 1873, cited in *A Memoir of Hannah Grier Coombe, Mother-Foundress of the Sisterhood of St John the Divine* (London: Oxford University Press, 1933), p. 3.

87. PH 6276, unidentified clipping headed 'We Are Able to Give Dr Pusey's Paper Verbatim'.

88. Yonge, 'Beginnings of sisterhoods', p. 58. Emphasis Yonge's.

89. CSP Archives, Sister Rosamira, *First Twenty-six Years*, pp. 28–34.

90. LPL, Benson Papers 87, ff. 61–2, 64–5, 7 June 1890.

91. CRJBS Archives, Mother Eunice, Community History, p. 1; LPL, Benson Papers 42, ff. 381–2. Edward Brice to Benson, 15 Jan. 1887.

92. SHUT Archives, letters discussing work in Cambridge, November 1885, Marion Hughes and Mr Wood; Booth, *Religious Influences*, vol. 2, p. 13.

93. LPL, Tait Papers 92, ff. 7–10. Mr Blomfield to Tait, 19 January 1873. Emphasis mine.

94. LPL, LC 78, ff. 196–9.

95. Allchin, *Silent Rebellion*, p. 40. (This of course was true if seen in the context of the larger, invisible, Church Militant.)

6 'A bombshell to public opinion'

1. [Frances Power Cobbe], 'Female charity, lay and monastic', *Fraser's Magazine*, **66** (1862), p. 775; see Susan P. Casteras, 'Virgin vows: the early Victorian artists' portrayal of nuns and novices', in Gail Malmgreen (ed.), *Religion in the Lives of English Women, 1760–1930* (London: Croom Helm, 1986), p. 137.

2. Sarah Stickney Ellis, *The Daughters of England: Their Position in Society, Character, and Responsibilities* (London: Fisher, Son & Co., 1842), pp. 276–9.

3. John Boyd-Kinnear, 'The social position of women in the present age', in Josephine Butler (ed.), *Woman's Work and Woman's Culture* (London: Macmillan, 1869), pp. 351–2.

4. Barbara Leigh Smith [Bodichon], *Women and Work* (London: Bosworth & Harrison, 1857), p. 9.

5. George Gissing, *Workers in the Dawn* (1880) (Brighton: Harvester Press, 1975), pp. 219, 275.

6. Florence Nightingale, *Suggestions for Thought for Seekers after Religious Truth Among the Artisans of England* (London: Eyre & Spottiswoode, for private circulation, 1860), vol. 2, p. 225. Emphasis mine.

7. Anne Summers, 'A home from home – women's philanthropic work in the nineteenth century', in S. Burman (ed.), *Fit Work for Women* (London: Croom Helm, 1979), p. 38. Just a few of the multitude of references to the 'argument from boredom': William Rathbone Greg, *Why Are Women Redundant?* (London: R. Trubner & Co., 1869), p. 6; E. Monro, *Parochial Work* (London: John Henry Parker, 1850), pp. 168–9; Armstrong, *Further Appeal*, pp. 15–16; Jameson, *Sisters of Charity*, p. 56; *Morning Post*, 26 February 1849; [Holland], 'Our offence', p. 324; Stephenson, *Concerning Sisterhoods*, p. 22; Cobbe, *Duties of Women*, p. 92; Emily Shirreff, *Intellectual Education* (London: John W.

Parker & Son, 1858), pp. 419–20; Florence Nightingale, *The Institution of Kaiserwerth on the Rhine* (London: Colonial Ragged Training School, 1851), p. 7.

8. Cobbe, *Duties*, p. 93. Emphasis mine.

9. Bennett, *Anglican Sisterhood*, p. 46; see Cameron, *Directory of Religious Communities*, p. 28.

10. Maria G. Grey, *Old Maids: A Lecture* (London: Ridgeway, 1875), p. 5. Mary Daly sees in mediaeval sisterhoods a rare affirmation of 'the latent humanity of women', while their married sisters were valued primarily for their reproductive function (Mary Daly, *The Church and the Second Sex*, Boston: Beacon Press, 1985, p. 211).

11. Lina Eckenstein, *Women under Monasticism* (Cambridge: Cambridge University Press, 1896), p. ix.

12. Pethick-Lawrence, *My Part*, pp. 72–3.

13. Bennett, *Anglican Sisterhood*, pp. 61–2.

14. That marriage was seen to be a rather dubious risk by many is underlined by the *Daily Telegraph* receiving 27,000 letters in 1888 in response to the question 'Is marriage a failure?' See Harry Quilter (ed.), *Is Marriage a Failure?* (London: Swan Sonnenschein, 1888) for a selection of these letters.

15. [Anthony Trollope], 'The sisterhood question', *Pall Mall Gazette*, 14 Sept. 1865, p. 338.

16. [Katherine Warburton], 'Mother Kate', *Memories of a Sister of St Saviour's Priory* (Oxford: Mowbray, 1903), p. 6.

17. John Duguid Milne, *The Industrial and Social Position of Women* (London: Chapman & Hall, 1857), p. 136.

18. Dora Greenwell, 'Our single women', *North British Review* (1862), pp. 63–4.

19. Dinah Mulock Craik, *A Woman's Thoughts about Women* (London: Hurst & Blackett, 1858), p. 34; Alan Deacon and Michael Hill, 'The problem of "surplus women" in the nineteenth century: secular and religious alternatives', *A Sociological Yearbook of Religion in Britain*, **5** (1972), p. 91.

20. [Craik], 'About sisterhoods', p. 308; Stephen, *Service of the Poor*, p. 245; Maria Trench, 'English sisterhoods', *The Nineteenth Century*, **40** (1884), p. 350.

21. Howson, *Deaconesses*, pp. xviii, 61, 195–6. This was also seen as an advantage by subscribers to charities. See All Hallows Archives, Memoirs of the Life of Lavinia Crosse, Mother Foundress of the Community of All Hallows, Ditchingham, Norfolk, by a Sister of that Community (1946), pp. 3–4. The failure of this attitude was summarized by G. Congreve, 'Sisters: their vocation and their special work', in *Pan-Anglican Papers* (London: SPCK, 1908), p. 20.

22. Anonymous letter to *The Sussex Advertiser*, November 1857.

23. Deacon and Hill, p. 92.

24. Goodman, *Sisterhoods*, p. 268.

25. LPL, Temple Papers 1, ff, 1–4, 5 June 1895.

26. Sellon, *Memos*, p. i.

27. As late as 1898 Walter Walsh was warning his readers in the immensely popular

Secret History of the Oxford Movement (4th edn, London: Sonnenschein) that Protestant families were 'never safe' with 'Ritualistic nursing sisters' nursing in the family (p. 199). In the same year the Protestant Alliance was demanding state inspection of all convents. See also *Fourteenth Year of St Mary Wantage*, p. 4; Liddon, *Sister's Work*, p. 15.

28. A Churchman, *From the Curate to the Convent* (London: Houghton & Co., 1877), p. 405. This story claims, rather implausibly, to be based upon a true history (p. vi).

29. The phrase, of course, comes from Coventry Patmore's long poem of that name, published in 1854–6.

30. Anonymous woman writer in *North British Review*, n.d., cited by John Saul Howson, *Deaconesses: Or the Official Help of Women in Parochial Work and in Charitable Institutions* (London. Longman, Green, Longman & Roberts, 1862), p. 157. Taine, while admiring the English woman's devotion to home and family, displays some cynicism in his explanation of its existence. In his *Notes on England* he describes an English woman as 'a person who has always lived in a moral enclosure and never dreamed of leaving it'.

31. *National Review*, 1851, cited in Joan M. Burstyn, *Victorian Education and the Ideal of Womanhood* (London: Croom Helm, 1980), p. 31.

32. [Anne J. Penny], *The Afternoon of Unmarried Life* (London: Longman, Brown, Green, Longman & Roberts, 1858), p. 149. Emphasis Penny's.

33. Manton, *Sister Dora*, p. 153.

34. John M. Scobell, *A Letter to the Rev. John M. Neale* (London: Nisbet, 1857); John M. Scobell, *A Reply to the Postscript of the Rev. John M. Neale, Warden of Sackville College, East Grinstead* (London: Nisbet, 1858); John M. Scobell, *The Rev. J. M. Neale and the Institute of St Margaret's, East Grinstead* (London: Nisbet & Co., 1857); John Eddoes Gladstone, *Protestant Nunneries: Or, the Mystery of Iniquity Working in the Church of England; A Letter...Concerning Ann Maria Lane, Now a Sister of Mercy, Against Her Father's Wish, in Miss Sellon's Institution at Eldad, Plymouth* (London: Arthur Hall, Virtue, 1853).

35. LPL, Tait Papers 200, ff. 432–43, B. Compton to Tait, 1874. The Archbishop refused to act and presumably Clementia was professed.

36. These are actual arguments utilized in the above pamphlets and in Goodman, *English Sister of Mercy*.

37. J. Scobell to Miss Gream, 1855. Published in *John Mason Neale* (London: Nisbet & Co., 1857). Emphasis Scobell's.

38. Goodman, *Sisterhoods*, pp. vii, 76; Gladstone, *Protestant Nunneries*, p. 42; Daniel Allen, *The History of the Convent* (Sydney: Lee & Ross, 1878), pp. 112–24.

39. All Saints Archives, Sister Elspeth, Notes about Various Sisters, pp. 1–2.

40. Goodman, *Sisterhoods*, pp. viii, 9, 13–14.

41. Howson, *Deaconesses*, p. vii.

42. Sparrow Simpson, *History*, p. 232; W. G. Cooksley, *A Letter...On the Nature, Government, and Tendency of Miss Sellon's Establishment at Devonport, Called the 'Sisters of Mercy'* (London: James Ridgeway, 1853); W. M. Colles, *Sisters of Mercy, Sisters of*

Misery: Or, Miss Sellon in the Family (London: T. Hatchard, 1852); Gladstone, *Protestant Nunneries; Painful Account of the Perversion and Untimely Death of Miss Scobell, the Stolen Daughter of the Revd. J. Scobell, Inveigled from Her Home, Persuaded to Become a Puseyite Sister of Mercy* (Lewes, 1857); Goodman, *Sisterhoods in the Church of England*, p. 9.

43. Williams, *Sellon*, pp. 28, 200. Miss Campbell may have been an unreliable witness: *The Times* of 2 December 1852, p. 7, reported her arrest on a charge of theft. She admitted taking the jewellery concerned, but denied stealing it, as she claimed she intended to give it to the owner's daughters.

44. LPL, Blomfield Papers 50, f. 187. Blomfield to E. B. Pusey, 3 December 1850.

45. Grafton, *Journey Godward*, in *Works*, vol. IV, pp. 105–6. Emphasis added.

46. Davidoff and Hall, p. 334.

47. Lorna Duffin, 'Woman as invalid', in Sara Delamont and Lorna Duffin (eds), *The Nineteenth-Century Woman* (London: Croom Helm, 1978), pp. 30–1; Milne, *Industrial and Social Position*, p. 107; Douglas, *Feminization*, p. 92. More pragmatically, many vague aches and pains probably disappeared with the replacement of high-heeled boots and tight-laced stays by the habit. See Helene E. Roberts, 'The exquisite slave: the role of clothes in the making of the Victorian woman', *Signs*, **2** (1977), pp. 554–79. For an example of the improvement in health, see H. D. Nihill, *The Sisters of St Mary at the Cross: Sisters of the Poor and Their Work* (London: Kegan Paul, Trench & Co., 1887), p. 64.

48. Showalter, 'Florence Nightingale', p. 398.

49. Cecil Woodham-Smith, *Florence Nightingale 1820–1910* (New York: McGraw Hill, 1951), pp. 58–9.

50. Shelton Reed, 'Feminization', pp. 200–1.

51. William Rathbone Greg, *Why Are Women Redundant?* (London: N. Trubner, 1869), p. 26.

52. [Penny], *Afternoon of Unmarried Life*, p. 150.

53. John Harwood, *Miss Jane, the Bishop's Daughter* (London: Richard Bentley, 1867).

54. O'Brien, 'Terra Incognita', p. 120. Shunting off one's biological role could have its rewards: Cornelia Connelly is currently a candidate for beatification.

55. All Saints Archives, *The Holy Rule and Statutes of the Community of St Thomas-Ye-Martyr* (1859, revised 1892), preamble. Emphasis mine.

56. Howson, *Deaconesses*, p. 156.

57. Ludlow, *Women's Work*, p. 302; Henry (Phillpots), Bishop of Exeter, *A Letter to Miss Sellon* (London: John Murray, 1852), p. 8. I am indebted to Eileen Yeo of Sussex University for this phrase. F. Amanda Porterfield, in 'Maidens, missionaries and mothers: American women as subjects and objects of religiousness' (PhD, Stanford University, 1975) describes a similar concept as 'public maternity' (p. 93).

58. Charles F. Lowder, *Twenty-one Years in St George's Mission* (London: Rivingtons, 1877), p. 23.

59. All Saints Archives, *All Saints' Home and Sisterhood of Charity* (London: J. Masters

and Co., printers, 1855), pp. 8, 9; Holy Rood Archives, The Rules of Associate Sisters or Sisters of the Second Order.

60. All Saints Archives, Sister Caroline Mary to the Mother Superior, 1895; All Hallows Archives, Revised and Consolidated Constitution and Statutes, January 1898.

61. LPL, Winnington-Ingram Papers 3, f. 143. CSC Customs.

62. William A. Darby, *Monks and Nuns* (Manchester: John Heywood, 1864), p. 4.

63. All Hallows Archives, scrapbook of newspaper clippings.

64. CSC Archives, *Memories of Ayckbowm*, p. 165.

65. Goodman, *Sisterhoods*, p. 24; CRJBS Archives, Community Log 1869-1936, entry for 1883.

66. Highly coloured accounts of the funeral and subsequent riot can be found in 'Extraordinary Scene and Riot at a Funeral at Lewes', *Brighton Examiner* (24 November 1857); 'Extraordinary Scene after a Funeral at All Saints' Church, Lewes', *The Sussex Express, Surrey Standard, Herald of Kent Mail, Hants and County Advertiser*, (21 November 1857); 'Brighton Protestant Association', *Brighton Examiner* (24 November 1857).

67. Walvin, *Victorian Values*, p. 138.

68. Jameson, *Sisters of Charity*, p. 53.

69. Carter, *Monsell*, p. viii; Emmeline Pethick-Lawrence, *My Part in a Changing World* (London: Victor Gollancz, 1938), p. 72.

70. Cusack, *Five Years in a Protestant Sisterhood*, p. 158. This is corroborated in Goodman, *Sisterhoods*, p. 29.

71. Bennett, *Anglican Sisterhood*, p. 27.

72. Scobell, *Letter to Neale*, pp. 21–2. Amy Emily Scobell did enter SSM in 1857, but died before profession.

73. MCSD Archives, James Erasmus Phillips, *Call from the East* (Warminster: Coates, printer, 1885), p. 3.

74. All Saints Archives, Notes on the Foundation of Our Community and Some Developments of Work, p. 5. Emphasis mine. Much of the following discussion of the struggle to break free of the family is based on the archives of All Saints, which has kept unusually detailed records of the pre-profession histories of their early members.

75. All Saints Archives, Memories of Mother Foundress by Sister Frances Emily, Records of the Early Days of the Community by Various Sisters, & Memories of Mother Foundress by Sister Frances Emily; *The Community of the Mission Sisters of the Holy Name of Jesus* (Worcester: Trinity Press, n.d.), p. 19.

76. Goodman, *Sisterhoods*, pp. 14–16.

77. All Saints Archives, Sister Elspeth, Notes about Various Sisters, pp. 22, 33.

78. All Saints Archives, Sister Elspeth, Notes about Various Sisters, pp. 10–11, 36.

79. Cameron, *Religious Communities*, p. 39.

80. [J. M. Ludlow], 'Deaconesses; or Protestant sisterhoods', *Edinburgh Review*, **87** (1848), p. 446.

81. Much of this semi-pornographic literature was aimed explicitly at Anglican targets; a good example is *The Confessional in the Church of England* (London: Hatchard, Seeleys, & Houlston & Stoneman) (1852). Appropriately, it is this document which gives us perhaps the most limited as well as the most purely biological definition of women's role that I have encountered in mainstream Victorian discourse: 'Women are the moulds in which the bodies and minds of men are cast' (p. 35).

82. *Plea for the Inspection of Convents*, pp. 8–10. Emphasis in original.

83. H. Cooke, *Mildmay*, p. 55; [L. H. J. Tonna], *Nuns and Nunneries* (London: Seeleys, 1852), p. 305.

84. A good example is the anonymous *The Nunnery Question*, whose third edition was issued by the Protestant Alliance in 1853; See also *Tractarian Sisters and Their Teaching* (London: William Hunt & Co., 1868), pp. 3–4. Emphasis in original.

85. Hope Stone, Leeds University, unpublished paper, 'Anglican foundresses and the (re)founding of religious life in nineteenth-century England' (1992), p. 7.

86. SSB Archives, Statutes [1871], p. 2.

87. Bishop of London's charge, 2 November 1850, cited in Bennett, *Life*, p. 92.

88. *Facta Non Verba: A Comparison Between the Good Works Performed by the Ladies in the Roman Catholic Convents in England, and the Unfettered Efforts of Their Protestant Sisters* (London: Isbister, 1874), p. 6.

89. Cobbe, 'Female charity', *Frasers*, p. 783; *Facta Non Verba*, pp. 6–7; Whately, *Cautions for the Times*, p. 344; Conventual Inquiry Society, *Brief Abstract of Parliamentary Evidence on Monastic and Conventual Institutions* (London: John Kensit, 1889), p. 20.

90. Conventual Enquiry Society, *Brief Abstract*, p. 7. Emphasis in original. See also Churchman, *From the Curate to the Convent*, p. 414.

91. *Protestant Alliance Official Organ* (1898), p. 30.

92. Cooksley, *Letter*, p. 8.

93. *Report of the Inquiry Instituted by the Right Reverend the Lord Bishop of Exeter* (Plymouth: Roger Lidstone, 1849). The practices complained of included having flowers on the altar, bowing to the altar, using candles in worship and possessing pictures of the Madonna.

94. See Hilliard, 'UnEnglish and unmanly'; John Shelton Reed, '"Giddy young men": a counter-cultural aspect of Victorian Anglo-Catholicism', *Comparative Social Research*, **11** (1989); *Some Thoughts on Catholicism in the English Church, by a Country Gentleman* (London: Joseph Masters, 1874), p. 6; Scrutator, *Is the Christianity of England Real, or Is It Only a Sham?* (Manchester: Abel Heywood & Son, 1877), p. 11; *Malleus Ritualistarum: Or, the Ritual Reason Why Not* (London: Effingham Wilson, 1872), p. 57; Octavius J. Ellis, *Some Time among Ritualists*, 3rd edn (London: Hatchards, 1868), pp. 9–10. See also Shelton Reed, 'Feminization'.

95. *Women and Priests* (London: Haughton & Co., [1878]) p. 15; 'Deaconesses', *Penny Post*, **11** (1861), p. 161; Richard Seymour, *Women's Work* (London: Rivingtons, 1862), p. 6; 'The convents of the United Kingdom', *Frasers* (1874), pp. 17–20.

96. Review of *An Exposure of Popery*, in *The Sword and the Trowel*, **14** (1878), p. 415;

James Spurrell, *Miss Sellon and the 'Sisters of Mercy': An Exposure of the Constitution, Rules, Religious Views, and Practical Working of Their Society, Obtained Through a 'Sister' Who Has Recently Seceded.* 9th thousand (London: Thomas Hatchard, 1852), pp. 1–2.

97. *Some Thoughts on Catholicism*, p. 6; [Diana Campbell], *Further Statement*, p. 33; W. G. Cooksley, *A Letter to the Archbishop of Dublin*, pp. 9–10; CSC Archives, Memories of Mother Foundress; W. Martin Brown, *The Pathway to Rome! Or, Ritualism and Its Remedy!* (London: James Nisbet & Co., [1877]), p. 27.

98. Jerusha Richardson, *Women in the Church of England* (London: Chapman & Hall, 1907), p. 253.

99. Cobbe, *Pursuits of Women*, p. 135.

100. [Anne Mozley], 'Convent life', *Blackwood's Edinburgh Magazine*, **105** (1869), p. 617; Cobbe, *Pursuits of Women*, p. 136. Cobbe herself, a life-long spinster, professional writer and public advocate of theism, could hardly have been farther from her 'natural domestic sphere'.

101. *Malleus Ritualistarum*, p. 35; Walsh, *Secret History*, p. 188.

102. *Malleus Ritualistarum*, p. 34.

103. Christopher Wordsworth, *On Sisterhoods and Vows* (London: W. Rivingtons, 1879), p. 16.

104. S. W. P., 'On hearing a nun say she hated children', *Protestant Alliance Official Organ* (1898), p. 48.

105. Auerbach's *Community of Women* has a good discussion of this issue; Williams and Cameron, p. 10; Jameson, *Sisters of Charity*, p. 55.

106. F. D. Maurice, 'On Sisterhoods', *Victoria Magazine* (1863), pp. 290, 296.

107. Stephen, *Service of Poor*, pp. 289, 285.

108. Ludlow, *Women's Work*, pp. 301–2.

109. Ludlow, *Women's Work*, p. xiii. Emphasis mine.

110. [Mozley], 'Convent life', p. 613.

111. Charles B. P. Bosanquet, *London: Some Account of Its Growth, Charitable Agencies, and Wants* (London: Hatchard & Co., 1868), p. 109; Walsh, *Secret History*, p. 83.

112. Vicinus, *Independent Women*, p. 31.

113. Davidoff and Hall, pp. 422–3, 432.

114. Wordsworth, *On Sisterhoods*, p. 16; W. E. Sellon, *An Essay on Sisterhoods in the English Church* (London: Joseph Masters, 1849), pp. 15–16.

115. PH Archives, Ascot Priory papers, first Rule of SMHT.

116. See Cooksley and Whately's pamphlets, cited above; 'A gentleman', *Pall Mall Gazette*, 11 September 1865, p. 363.

117. *Some Thoughts on Catholicism*, p. 4.

118. Walsh, *Secret History*, pp. 170–4.

119. For example, see *Charity Organization Review*, **5** (1889), pp. 64–7, and **12** (1896), pp. 19, 406, 411–12, 520; Beatrice Webb, *The Diary of Beatrice Webb, Volume One 1873–1892: Glitter Around and Darkness Within*, ed. N. and J. MacKenzie (London: Virago, 1982), p. 70.

120. The Protestant Alliance was still accusing CSC of keeping their orphans in 'spiked cages' in 1901 (*Protestant Alliance Official Organ* (1901), p. 472).

121. *Kilburn Sisters*, p. 6.

122. Allchin, *Silent Rebellion*, p. 219.

123. [Holland], 'Convents and English girls', p. 537.

124. See Appendices 6 and 5 for profession rates by decade and in different communities.

125. [Holland], 'Our offence', pp. 323–31, esp. p. 324. Penelope Holland's essays on these and other woman-related subjects were reprinted posthumously in *Earnest Thoughts* (London: Macmillan and Co., 1874).

126. Antony Dale and Antony Wagner, *The Wagners of Brighton* (London: Phillimore & Co., 1983), pp. 106–18. After serving her prison term Kent returned to the community, who sheltered her until she emigrated to the colonies.

127. The actual instance cited was that of Miss Law, daughter of the Recorder of London. The bishop was misinformed: she had obtained her mother's full and father's reluctant consent to join the sisterhood (F. Bennett, *The Story of W. J. E. Bennett* (London: Longman's, Green, & Co., 1909), pp. 92–3).

128. Dale and Wagner, p. 111–12. The MP was George Hammond Whalley. *A Plea for the Inspection or Suppression of Convents* (London: Protestant Evangelical Mission & Electoral Union, [1870]), p. 12; Great Britain, *Report of the Special Committee on Conventual and Monastic Institutions* [1870], question 3921, p. 179. Gladstone's wife was a frequent vistor to St Saviour's Priory in Hackney.

129. Ascot Priory papers, No. 1, Sellon to unknown correspondent, 10 September 1868. Her memory may have been at fault: CMHT was founded in 1858.

130. Henry Phillpots, *A Letter to Miss Sellon* (London: John Murray, 1852), p. 18; Lowder, *Ten Years*, p. 131; *The Great Want of the Church* (London: William Skeffington, 1868), p. 24; Trench, *Charles Lowder*, p. 227.

131. Mrs Leyton, 'Memories of seventy years', in Margaret Llewelyn Davies (ed.), *Life As We Have Known It, by Co-operative Working Women* (London: Virago, 1977), pp. 10–12; *The Great Want of the Church* (London: William Skeffington, 1868), p. 24.

132. *Story of St Saviour's Priory*, pp. 6, 9.

133. Cameron, *Religious Communities*, p. 18. He may be following Cobbe in this; see her *Pursuits of Women*, pp. 104–6; Rowell, *Vision Glorious*, p. 127.

134. [Warburton], *Memories*, p. 84; Bennett, *Anglican Sisterhood*, p. 95; Williams, *Sellon*, p. 25.

Conclusion

1. Georgiana Hill, vol. II, p. 244.

BIBLIOGRAPHY

Contents

I. Archival sources

II. Printed works

Nineteenth-century sources

1. Government publications
2. Works on sisterhoods and related institutions
3. Other primary sources
4. Journal and newspaper articles on sisterhoods and related institutions
5. Other journal and newspaper articles

Twentieth-century sources

1. Secondary works on sisterhoods and related institutions
2. Journal and newspaper articles on sisterhoods and related institutions
3. Unpublished sources

I. Archival sources

Community archival sources

Community of All Hallows
Community of All Saints
Community of St Denys
Community of St John Baptist
Community of St Katharine of Egypt
Community of St Mary
Community of St Mary at the Cross
Community of St Mary the Virgin
Community of St Peter
Community of St Saviour's Priory
Community of St Wilfred

Community of the Holy Cross
Community of the Holy Name
Community of the Holy Rood
Community of the Resurrection
Community of the Servants of the Cross
Community of the Sisters of Charity
Community of the Sisters of the Church
Nursing Sisters of St John Divine
Saint Saviour's Priory
Society of St Margaret
Society of St Margaret of Scotland
Society of the Most Holy Trinity
Society of the Sisters of Bethany

Expired communities (with location of archives)

Bussage House of Mercy, Glos. (Gloucester Record Office)
Community of Reparation to Jesus in the Blessed Sacrament: Mission Sisters of St Alphage (PH)
Community of SS Mary and Scholastica (West Malling)
Community of St Andrew of Scotland (Scottish Record Office)
Community of St Thomas the Martyr (Wantage)
Community of the Holy Comforter (West Malling)
Society of the Holy and Undivided Trinity (PH)

Bodleian Library

Department of Western MSS, Wilberforce Papers

St Deiniol's Library, Hawarden

Gladstone Pamphlet Collection

Lambeth Palace Library and archives

Benson Papers
Bishops' Meetings
Blomfield Papers
Creighton Papers
Jackson Papers
Tait Papers

Temple Papers
Visitation Returns
Winnington–Ingram Papers

Scottish Record Office

Episcopal Church of St Columba's-by-the-Castle Papers
Sister Frances Langland Papers

II. Printed works

Nineteenth-century sources

1. Government publications

Great Britain. Parliamentary Papers. *Report from the Select Committee on Conventual and Monastic Institutions, &c., Together with the Proceedings of the Committee, Minutes of Evidence, and Appendix.* House of Commons, British Sessional Papers, vol. 7, [1870].

Great Britain, Parliamentary Papers. *Report from the Select Committee of the House of Lords Appointed to Inquire into the Deficiency of Means of Spiritual Instruction and Places of Worship in the Metropolis and Other Populous Places in England and Wales: Especially in the Mining and Manufacturing Districts.* House of Commons, British Sessional Papers, vol. 9, [1857–58].

2. Works on sisterhoods and related institutions

A. A. [Anne Ayres]. *Evangelical Sisterhoods: Two Letters to a Friend.* New York: T. Whittaker, 1867.

—. *Thoughts on Evangelical Sisterhoods, by a Member of One.* London: S. W. Partridge, 1872.

An Account for the Year 1852, of St Mary's Home for Penitents at Wantage, Berkshire, and an Appeal for Assistance Towards Its Support and Enlargement. Oxford: John Henry Parker, 1853.

Alison, L. *The Fast at the River Ahava: A Sermon Preached on the Occasion of the Opening of the New Chapel, East Grinstead.* Cambridge: J. Palmer, 1883.

Armstrong, John. *An Appeal for the Formation of a Church Penitentiary,* 2nd edn. London: John Henry Parker, 1849.

—. *A Further Appeal for the Formation of Church Penitentiaries.* London: John Henry Parker, 1851.

—. *Essays on Church Penitentiaries.* London: John Henry Parker, 1858.

Ascot Hospital for Convalescents and Incurables. n.p., 1879.

An Awful Exposure of the Awful Disclosures of Those Two Lying Females, Rebecca Reed and Maria Monk. Paisley: Caldwell & Sons, printers, 1836.

A. F. B. *Convent Experiences*. London: Thomas Scott, 1875.

Bagge, Henry T. J. *The Anglo-Catholics of Plymouth: A Few Remarks upon Miss Sellon's 'Reply' to the Rev. J. Spurrell's 'Exposure*. London: Seeleys, 1852.

Benson, Richard M. *The Religious Life Portrayed for the Use of Sisters of Mercy*. London: J. T. Hayes, n.d.

Bird, Charles. *Anglican Sisterhoods*. Protestant Alliance Tract No. 61. London: Protestant Alliance, 1864.

Book of the Statutes of the Sisterhood of Mercy of the Holy and Undivided Trinity. Oxford: privately printed, 1882.

Boyd-Kinnear, John. 'The social position of women in the present age', in Josephine Butler (ed.), *Woman's Work and Woman's Culture*, London: Macmillan, 1869, pp. 331–67.

Brett, R. *Smallpox in Shoreditch, 1871*. London: printed for private circulation, 1871.

The Breviary of the Renowned Church of Salisbury. London: Gilbert & Rivington, 1889.

Breviary Offices from Lauds to Compline. (1877) 2nd edn. London: J. T. Hayes, 1880.

[Broughton, Rhoda.] *Not Wisely But Too Well*. London: Tinsley Brothers, 1867.

Brown, W. Martin. *The Pathway to Rome! or, Ritualism and Its Remedy!* London: James Nisbet & Co., [1877].

Browne, W. A. F. *Sisterhoods in Asylums*. London: J. E. Adland, 1866.

Butler, Josephine (ed.). *Woman's Work and Woman's Culture*. London: Macmillan, 1869.

C., A. S. *The Two Ways of Christian Life*. London: Joseph Masters, 1862.

C., S. *The Sisters of the Church and Their Work*. London: Judd & Co., 1875.

Campbell, Diana. *An Elucidation of Facts, Connected with Miss Sellon's Society*. London: George Kingcombe, printer, 1852.

—. *Miss Sellon, and the Sisters of Mercy: A Further Statement of the Rules, Constitution and Working of the Society Called 'The Sisters of Mercy'*. London: T. Hatchard, 1852.

Carey, Rosa Nouchette. *Twelve Notable Good Women of the Nineteenth Century*. London: Hutchinson & Co., 1899.

Carpenter, Mrs Boyd. 'Women's work in connection with the Church of England', in Angela Burdett-Coutts (ed.), *Woman's Mission*. London: Sampson Low, Marston & Co., 1893, pp. 111–30.

Carter, Thomas Thellusson. *Is It Well to Institute Sisterhoods in the Church of England, for the Care of Female Penitents?* London: John Henry Parker, 1851.

—. *Objections to Sisterhoods Considered, in a Letter to a Parent*. London: Francis & John Rivington, 1853.

—. *The First Five Years of the House of Mercy, Clewer*. Second Edition, London: Joseph Masters, 1855.

—. *An Appeal for the House of Mercy, Clewer*. London: Joseph Masters, 1856.

—. *Mercy for the Fallen*. London: Joseph Masters, 1856.

—. *My Dear Friend, You Ask for Some Result of Our 'First Five Years' Work at the House of Mercy* (circular letter). Clewer, January 1856.

—. *The First Ten Years of the House of Mercy, Clewer.* London: Joseph Masters, 1861.

—. *Manual of Devotion for Sisters of Mercy,* 2 vols, 8 parts, 2nd edn. London: Joseph Masters, 1867.

—. *Are 'Vows of Celibacy in Early Life' Inconsistent with the Word of God?* London: Rivingtons, 1878.

—. *Vows and the Religious State. I. Vows, and Their Relation to Religious Communities. II. The Religious State and Age of Profession.* London: Joseph Masters, 1881.

—. *Harriet Monsell: A Memoir.* London: Joseph Masters, 1884.

—. *The House of Mercy, Clewer.* n.p., n.d.

Chappel, Jennie. *Four Noble Women and Their Work.* London: S. W. Partridge, 1898.

Charteris, A. H. *Christo in Pauperibus: The Organization of Women's Work in the Church of Scotland.* Edinburgh: William Blackwood & Sons, 1890.

Chronicle of Convocation. 1858, etc.

Church Congress Reports. 1862, etc.

A Churchman. *From the Curate to the Convent.* London: Houghton & Co., 1877.

Circumstances Connected with the Debate in the House of Commons on the Monastic and Conventual Institutions Inquiry Bill. London: George Slater, [1875].

Cobbe, Frances Power. *Essays on the Pursuits of Women.* London: Emily Faithfull, 1863.

—. *The Duties of Women.* London: Williams & Norgate, 1881.

Coleman, Leighton. *English Sisterhoods and Deaconesses.* Philadelphia: n.p., 1886.

Colles, W. M. *Sisters of Mercy, Sisters of Misery: Or, Miss Sellon in the Family.* 3rd edn. London: T. Hatchard, 1852.

Collier, Mrs. *The Autobiography of Mrs. Collier: A Biblewoman's Story,* rev. by Eliza Nightingale. n.p., c. 1880.

Community of St John Baptist, Clewer. (Rules for Associates). London: J. Masters & Sons, n.d.

Community of St Peter: Associate's Rule. Kilburn: St Peter's House and Sisterhood, 1900.

The Confessional in the Church of England. London: Hatchard, Seeleys, & Houlston & Stoneman, 1852.

Congreve, G. 'Sisters: their vocation and their special work', in *Pan-Anglican Papers; The Church and Its Ministry: The Ministry of Women.* London: SPCK, 1908.

The Conspirators' Schemes: Homes, Convents, Confession, and Education. London: Protestant Electoral Union, 1871.

Convents: A Review of Two Lectures. London: Thomas Richardson & Son, [1852].

Convents and Lunatic Asylums. Ideas, Opinions and Facts No. 2. London: Robert Hardwicke, 1865.

Conventual Inquiry Society. *Brief Abstract of Parliamentary Evidence on Monastic and Conventual Institutions.* London: John Kensit, 1889.

Cooke, Harriette J. *Mildmay: or The Story of the First Deaconess Institution.* London: Elliot Stock, 1892.

Cooksley, W. G. *A Letter to His Grace the Archbishop of Dublin, On the Nature,*

Government, and Tendency of Miss Sellon's Establishment at Devonport, Called the 'Sisters of Mercy', 3rd edn. London: James Ridgeway, 1853.

Cusack, Margaret Anne (Sister Mary Francis). *Five Years in a Protestant Sisterhood and Ten Years in a Catholic Convent*. London: Longmans, Green & Co., 1869.

—. *The Nun of Kenmare: An Autobiography*. London: Josiah Child, [1888].

—. *The Story of My Life*. London: Hodder & Stoughton, 1891.

Daily Offices of Prayer for the Use of the Church of England House of Mercy, Clewer; Also an Office for the Reception of a Penitent. London: John Henry Parker, 1851.

Dale, Thomas P. (ed.). *Debate in Convocation on Deaconess Institutions and Protestant Sisterhoods*. London: Emily Faithfull, 1862.

[Dallas, Alexander Robert Charles]. *Protestant Sisters of Charity: A Letter Addressed to the Lord Bishop of London*. London: Charles Knight, 1826.

Darby, William A. *Monks and Nuns*. Manchester: John Heywood, 1864.

[Dill, Augusta]. *Maude: Or, The Anglican Sister of Mercy*, ed. E. Jane Whately. London: Harrison, 1869. Cheap edition titled *The Anglican Sister of Mercy*, London: Elliot Stock, 1899.

Drummond, Henry. *A Plea for the Rights and Liberties of Women Imprisoned for Life*. London: T. Bosworth, 1851.

E., Catherine. *My Very Dear Friend* (circular letter). Devonport: n.p., 1852.

Eardley, C. E. *The Diocese of Exeter: Its State and Its Remedies*. London: James Ridgeway, 1852.

Education by Nuns: Its Failure and Injurious Tendencies. London: Protestant Alliance, 1890.

Extraordinary Trial of a Sister of Mercy: Saurin Versus Starr before the Lord Chief Justice and a Special Jury, February 3, 1869: Startling Revelations of Life in a Convent. London: E. Griffiths, [1869].

Facta Non Verba: A Comparison Between the Good Works Performed by the Ladies in Roman Catholic Convents in England, and the Unfettered Efforts of Their Protestant Sisters. London: W. Isbister, 1874.

Few, R. *An History of St John's House . . . With a Full Account of the Circumstances Which Led to the Withdrawal Therefrom of the Entire Sisterhood*. London: W. Skeffington, 1884.

Forbes, Alexander Penrose. *A Plea for Sisterhoods*. London: Joseph Masters, 1849.

The Foundations of the Sisters of Notre Dame in England and Scotland: From 1845 to 1895. Liverpool: Philip, Son & Nephew, 1895.

The Fourteenth Year of St Mary's Home for Penitents, at Wantage. Oxford: J. H. & J. Parker, 1864.

Fox, Samuel. *Monks and Monasteries: Being an Account of English Monachism*. London: James Burns, 1845.

Gilmore, Isabella. 'Deaconesses: their qualifications and status', in *Pan-Anglican Papers, The Church and Its Ministry: The Ministry of Women*. London: SPCK, 1908.

Gladstone, John Eddoes. *Protestant Nunneries: Or, The Mystery of Iniquity Working in the Church of England; A Letter. . .Concerning Ann Maria Lane, Now a Sister of Mercy,*

Against Her Father's Wish, in Miss Sellon's Institution at Eldad, Plymouth. London: Arthur Hall, Virtue, 1853.

Goodman, Margaret. *Experiences of an English Sister of Mercy.* London: Smith, Elder, 1862.

—. *Sisterhoods in the Church of England: With Notices of Some Charitable Sisterhoods in the Romish Church.* London: Smith, Elder, 1863.

Grafton, Charles C. *Vocation, or the Call of the Divine Master to a Sister's Life, and Other Writings on the Religious Life* (1886), in *The Works of Bishop Grafton*, vol. 5. New York: Longmans, Green, & Co., 1914.

The Great Want of the Church. London: William Skeffington, 1868.

Gresley, William. *Bernard Leslie*, part 2. London: Joseph Masters, 1859.

Guide to Schools, Homes and Refuges in England, for the Benefit of Girls and Women. London: Longmans, Green, & Co., 1888.

The Guild of St Mary the Virgin, Parish of St Alban-the-Martyr, Holborn: Office and Constitutions. London: W. Knott, 1870.

L. M. H. *Anglican Deaconesses: Or, Is There No Place for Women in Our Parochial System?* London: Bell & Daldy, 1871.

Hartley, John. *Monasticism: Its Origin, Influence and Results; With Some Observations on Sisterhoods, the Lay Diaconate, and the Pastoral Order.* London: John Hall, 1885.

Harwood, John. *Miss Jane, the Bishop's Daughter*, 3 vols. London: Richard Bentley, 1867.

Hayne, R. J. *Church Deaconesses: The Revival of the Office of Deaconess Considered.* London: John Henry & James Parker, 1859.

The High-Church Confessional: An Exposé. London: John Kensit, City Protestant Book Depot, 1887.

Hill, Georgina. *Women in English Life*, 2 vols. London: Richard Bentley & Son, 1896.

Hogan, William. *Auricular Confession and Nunneries.* London: Protestant Evangelical Mission and Electoral Union, [1880].

Holland, Penelope. *Earnest Thoughts.* London: Macmillan & Co., 1874.

Hopkins, J. Ellice. *A Plea for the Wider Action of the Church of England in the Prevention of the Degradation of Women.* London: Hatchards, 1879.

Howson, John Saul. *Deaconesses.* London: Longman, Green, Longman & Roberts, 1862.

—. *Diaconate of Women in the Anglican Church.* London: J. Nisbet, 1886.

Hubbard, Louisa M. *A Guide to All Institutions Existing for the Benefit of Women and Children*, part 5. London: Hatchards, 1883.

—. 'The organization of women workers', in Angela Burdett-Coutts (ed.), *Woman's Mission.* London: Sampson Low, Marston & Co., 1893, pp. 273–83.

—. 'Statistics of women's work', in Angela Burdett-Coutts (ed.), *Woman's Mission.* London: Sampson Low, Marston & Co., 1893, pp. 361–366.

I Am Not Worthy: A Voice from an English Sisterhood. London: William Skeffington, 1870.

Jameson, Anna. *Sisters of Charity, Catholic and Protestant, Abroad and at Home.* London:

Longmans, Brown, Green, & Longmans, 1855.

—. 'Sisters of Charity' and 'The Communion of Labour': Two Lectures on the Social Improvement of Women, new edn. London: Longman, Brown, Green, Longmans, & Roberts, 1859.

Janes, Emily. 'On the associated work of women in religion and philanthropy', in Angela Burdett-Coutts (ed.), Women's Mission. London: Sampson Low, Marston & Co., 1893, pp. 131–48.

Jennison, J. F. Deaconesses in the Primitive and Later Church. Baltimore: Isaac Friedenwald, 1891.

Jermyn, Hugh W. A Letter to the Right Hon. Sir John Coleridge, Visitor to the House of Mercy, Ditchingham. Williton: S. Cox, printer, 1866.

A Kalendar of the English Church. London: Church Press Company, 1863–4, 1867–9, 1870–4, 1882–6, 1889, 1900–1.

The Kilburn Sisters and Their Accusers. London: 'Church Bells' Office, [1896].

Larkin, Charles. A Refutation and Exposure of the Atrocious Forgery, Entitled 'Awful Disclosures of Maria Monk'. Newcastle-upon-Tyne: W. Fordyce, 1836.

A Letter to the Rev. James Spurrell: On the Subject of a Pamphlet Recently Published by Him Containing Certain Charges Against Miss Sellon and the Society of the 'Sisters of Mercy' at Plymouth. London: Joseph Masters, 1852.

Letters on the Plymouth Sisters, Suggested by the Recent Pamphlets and Letters of the Rev. J. Spurrell, Miss Sellon, and the Bishop of Exeter. London: T. Hatchard, 1852.

Letters to My Sisters: The Church – Church Influence – Confessions – Sisterhoods. London: T. Hatchard, 1858.

Liddon, H. P. A Sister's Work, 2nd edn. London: Rivingtons, 1869.

Lowder, Charles Fuge. Ten Years in St George's Mission. London: G. J. Palmer, 1867.

—. St George's Mission: Fourteenth Annual Report. n.p., 1870.

—. Twenty-one Years in St George's Mission. London: Rivingtons, 1877.

Ludlow, J. M. Woman's Work in the Church: Historical Notes on Deaconesses and Sisterhoods. London: Alexander Strahan, 1865.

Martin, John. Charity under Persecution: A Sermon on Behalf of the Sisters of Mercy and the Orphans' Home at Devonport. London: Joseph Masters, 1849.

The Marvelous Escape of 'Sister Lucy' and Her Awful Disclosures. Fifth edition. London: Protestant Evangelical Mission, [1867].

Massey, Edward. Love's Strife with the Convent, 3 vols. London: Ward & Lock, 1864.

McCrindell, R. The Convent; A Narrative, Founded on Fact. London: Aylott & Jones, 1848.

[Monk, Maria]. Awful Disclosures of Maria Monk, As Exhibited in Her Sufferings During a Residence of Five Years as a Novice, and Two Years as a Black Nun. London: Richard Groombridge, 1836.

Monsell, John S. B. English Sisterhoods. London: Joseph Masters, 1863.

Murphy, John N. Terra Incognita: Or, The Convents of the United Kingdom. London: Longmans Popular Edition, 1873.

H. N. [Nokes, Harriet]. *Twenty-three Years in a House of Mercy*. (1886), 2nd edn. London: Swan, Sonnenschein & Co., 1888.

—. *Thirty-two Years in a House of Mercy*. London: SPCK, 1895.

S. D. N. *Chronicles of St Mary's*. London: Joseph Masters, 1868.

—. *Holidays at St Mary's: Or, Tales in a Sisterhood*. London: Joseph Masters, 1871.

[Neale, Elizabeth]. *Elizabeth, Mother Superior. The Community of the Holy Cross: Short Account of Its Rise and History*. London: H. J. Wright, printer, (1884).

Neale, John Mason. *Ayton Priory: Or, The Restored Monastery*. Cambridge: Deightons, 1843.

—. *The Lewes Riot, Its Causes and Consequences: A Letter to the Lord Bishop of Chichester*, 4th edn. London: Joseph Masters, 1857.

—. *A Postscript in Reply to the Rev. J. Scobell's Statement*. London: Joseph Masters, 1857.

—. *Deaconesses, and Early Sisterhoods*. London: Joseph Masters, 1869.

Newdegate, Charles N. *Monastic and Conventual Institutions: A Speech Delivered in the House of Commons by C. N. Newdegate, M.P., on the 3rd of March, 1865: With the Correspondence*. Edinburgh: John Lindsay, 1866.

—. *Convent Inquiry*. London: Cornelius Buck, 1872.

—. *Speech of C. N. Newdegate, M.P., . . . in the House of Commons, on Tuesday, June 12, 1874*. London: George Slater, [1874].

Nicholl, Mary H. *Augusta: Or, The Refuted Slanders of Thirty Years Ago on the Late Miss Sellon, Once More Refuted*. London: Remington, 1878.

Nightingale, Florence. *The Institution of Kaiserwerth on the Rhine*. London: Printed by the inmates of the London Ragged Colonial Training School, 1851.

Nihill, Henry Daniel. *The Sisters of the Poor at St Michaels, Shoreditch and Their Work*. London: printed for private circulation, 1870.

—. *The Sisters of St Mary at the Cross: Sisters of the Poor and Their Work*. London: Kegan Paul, Trench & Co., 1887.

Niven, William. *'Sisterhood' Nurses*, 2nd edn, London: Hatchard, 1866.

The Nunnery. London: Macintosh, printer. n.d.

The Nunnery Bill: Its Absolute Necessity Proved. n.p., n.d.

The Nunnery: Or, Popery Exposed in Her Tyranny. London: Nisbet, 1851.

The Nunnery Question. London: Burns & Lambert, 1854.

The Nunnery Question, 3rd edn. London: Protestant Alliance, 1853.

Office of Installation of the Superior of a Religious House. Dundee: Chalmers & Winters, n.d.

The Orphans' Home, for the Orphan Daughters of British Seamen and Soldiers. London: William Odhams, 1849.

Orphanage for Workhouse Girls, in Connection with the Church Extension Association. n,p., n.d.

[Paget, Francis Edward]. *The Owlet of Owlstone Edge: His Travels, His Experience, and His Lucubrations*. London: Joseph Masters, 1856.

Painful Account of the Perversion and Untimely Death of Miss Scobell, the Stolen Daughter of the Revd. J. Scobell, Inveigled from Her Home, Persuaded to Become a Puseyite Sister of Mercy . . . (Lewes, 1857).

Penitentiary Work in the Church of England. London: Harrison & Sons, 1873.

Phillpots, Henry. *A Letter to Miss Sellon*. London: John Murray, 1852.

A Plea for the Inspection or Suppression of Convents. London: Protestant Evangelical Mission & Electoral Union, [1870].

Povey, J. M. [Sister Mary Agnes]. *Nunnery Life in the Church of England: Or, Seventeen Years with Father Ignatius*. London: Hodder & Stoughton, 1890.

Priest and Nun: A Story of Convent Life. London: Hodder & Stoughton, 1869.

A Proposal for the Establishment of a Female Penitentiary. Norwich: Charles Muskett, 1853.

Prynne, George Rundle. *An Address Delivered . . . in Consequence of Some Statements Contained in a Pamphlet with the Rev. James Spurrell*. London: Joseph Masters, 1852.

—. *Private Confession, Penance, and Absolution: A Reply to Some Remarks . . . on Nunneries*, 2nd edn. London: Joseph Masters, 1852.

—. *Thirty-five Years of Mission Work*. Plymouth: W. Brendon & Son, 1883.

L. N. R. *The True Institution of Sisterhood: Or, a Message and Its Messengers*. London: James Nisbet & Co., [1862].

Reed, Rebecca Theresa. 'The nun: or, six months' residence in a convent', in *The Mysteries of a Convent*. Philadelphia: T. B. Peterson, 1878, pp. 195–288.

'Religious and secular instruction', in *Penitentiary Work in the Church of England*. London: Harrison and Sons, 1873, pp. 117–21.

The Religious Houses of the United Kingdom. London: Burns & Oates, 1887.

Report for the Year 1853, of St Mary's Home for Penitents, Wantage. Oxford: John Henry Parker, 1854.

Report of the Inquiry Instituted by the Right Reverend the Lord Bishop of Exeter. Plymouth: Roger Lidstone, 1849.

Robinson, Cecilia. *The Ministry of Deaconesses*. London: Methuen & Co., 1898.

Rule of Life of the Society of the Holy and Undivided Trinity. London: privately printed, n.d.

St Margaret's Mission: Seventh Year, 1888. n.p., [1889].

St Mary's Home for Penitents, Wantage, Berkshire: The First Nine Years. Oxford: John Henry & James Parker, 1859.

Sandford, Daniel Fox. *A Pastoral Letter to the Clergy and Laity of His Diocese on the Resolution of Synod Regarding a Sisterhood*. Hobart: J. Walch & Sons, 1887.

Scobell, John M. *A Letter to the Rev. John M. Neale*, 2nd thousand. London: Nisbet, 1857.

—. *A Reply to the Postscript of the Rev. John M. Neale, Warden of Sackville College, East Grinstead*. London: Nisbet, 1858.

—. *The Rev. J. M. Neale and the Institute of St Margaret's, East Grinstead*. London: Nisbet & Co., 1857.

Sellon, John. S. (ed.). *Memos Relating to the Society of the Holy Trinity, Devonport*. London: Terry & Co., 1907.

[Sellon, P. Lydia]. *Reply to a Tract by the Rev. J. Spurrell*, 3rd. edn. London: Joseph Masters, 1852.

—. *Sisters of Charity, St Saviours, Osnaburgh St*. n.p., 1860.

—. *Two Letters to the Rev. Edward Coleridge, Eton College* (circular letter). n.d., n.p.

Sellon, W. E. *An Essay upon Sisterhoods in the English Church.* London: Joseph Masters, 1849.

Sellon, William R. B. *Miss Sellon and the Sisters of Mercy: A Contradiction of the Alleged Acts of Cruelty Exercised by Miss Sellon . . . With an Appendix Containing an Address from the Sisters of Mercy to the Mother Superior, and Her Reply,* 2nd edn. London: Joseph Masters, 1852.

Sermon and First Annual Report of the Church Penitentiary Association. London: Spottiswoode & Shaw, 1853.

Seventh Annual Report of the North London Deaconess Association. London: E. Varty, printer, 1868.

Seymour, Richard. *Women's Work.* London: Rivingtons, 1862.

—. *Sisterhoods, the Fruit of Christian Love.* London: Rivingtons, 1869.

Seymour, M. Hobart. *Convents or Nunneries.* Bath: R. E. Peach, 1852.

—. *Nunneries.* London: Seeleys, 1852.

'Short homes: by a sister in charge of a refuge', in *Penitentiary Work in the Church of England.* London: Harrison & Sons, 1873, pp. 52–6.

'Sisterhood life', in O. Shipley (ed.), *The Church and the World.* London: Longmans, Green, Reader, & Dyer, [1867], pp. 166–95.

Sisterhoods Considered: With Remarks upon the Bishop of Brechin's 'A Plea for Sisterhoods'. London: Francis & John Rivington, 1850.

Sisters of Charity, and Some Visits with Them. London: Joseph Masters, 1855.

The Sisters of Mercy: A Tale for the Times We Live In. London: Houlston & Stoneman, 1854.

The Sisters of Mercy at Devonport: Report of an Enquiry. London: Houlston & Stoneman, 1849.

Sisters of Mercy in the Church of England. London: Joseph Masters, 1850.

The 'Sister of Mercy', the Priest, and the Devil: An Allegory. London: E. W. Allen, [1881].

'Small foundling homes; by a sister in charge of a refuge', in *Penitentiary Work in the Church of England.* London: Harrison & Sons, 1873, pp. 136–42.

Some Account of St Mary's Home for Penitents, at Wantage. Oxford: John Henry Parker, 1851.

Some Account of the Deaconess Work in the Christian Church. n.p., [1852].

Southey, Robert. *Sir Thomas More: Or, Colloquies on the Progress and Prospects of Society* (1829). London: John Murray, 1831.

A Special Appeal on Behalf of the Sisters of the Holy Cross. n.p., [1884].

Spurrell, James. *A Rejoinder to the Reply of the Superior of the Society of the Sisters of Mercy.* London: Thomas Hatchard, 1852.

—. *Miss Sellon and the 'Sisters of Mercy': An Exposure of the Constitution, Rules, Religious Views, and Practical Working of Their Society, Obtained Through a 'Sister' Who Has Recently Seceded,* 9th thousand. London: Thomas Hatchard, 1852.

Stanley, Mary. *Hospitals and Sisterhoods*. London: John Murray, 1854.

Statutes of the Clewer House of Mercy. London: Spottiswoode & Shaw, [1853].

Stephen, Caroline Emilia. *The Service of the Poor: Being an Inquiry into the Reasons for and against the Establishment of Religious Sisterhoods for Charitable Purposes*. London: Macmillan & Co., 1871.

Stephenson, T. Bowman. *Concerning Sisterhoods*. London: For the author, by C. H. Kelly, 1890.

The Story of St Saviour's Priory and Its Sixteen Years in Haggerston. London: G. J. Palmer, 1882.

[Tonna, L. H. J.]. *Nuns and Nunneries*. London: Seeleys, 1852.

Tractarian Sisters and Their Teaching. London: William Hunt & Co., [1868].

Tracts on the Doctrine and Discipline of the Church, No. 2, *Monks and Nuns*. London: G. J. Palmer, 1860.

[Trench, Maria]. *The History of Ascot Priory and Memorials of Dr. Pusey*. London: 'The Churchwoman' office, 1897.

[Trollope, Anthony]. 'The sisterhood question', *Pall Mall Gazette*, 14 Sept. 1866.

[Turnbull, Elizabeth]. *Appeal of the Sisters of Charity for Spitalsfields and Bethnal-green*. n.p., 1859.

Twining, Louisa. *Deaconesses for the Church of England*. London: Bell & Daldy, 1860.

—. *Recollections of Life and Work*. London: Edward Arnold, 1893.

Ullathorne, William B. *A Plea for the Rights and Liberties of Religious Women*. London: Thomas Richardson & Son, 1851.

—. *A Letter . . . on the Proposed Committee of Enquiry into Religious Communities*. London: Thomas Richardson & Son, 1854.

A Visit to East Grinstead. London: Joseph Masters, 1865.

Walker, Charles. *Three Months in an English Monastery: A Personal Narrative*. London: Murray & Co, 1864.

[Warburton, Katherine]. 'Mother Kate', in *Memories of a Sister of St Saviour's Priory*. Oxford: Mowbray, 1903.

—. *Old Soho Days and Other Memories*. London: Mowbray, 1906.

Webb, Allen B. *Sisterhood Life and Women's Work*. London: Skeffington & Son, 1883.

A Woman's Way: Or, The Chelsea Sisterhood, 3 vols. London: Tinsley Brothers, 1865.

Women and Priests. London: Haughton & Co., [1878].

Wordsworth, Christopher. *On Sisterhoods and Vows*, 2nd edn. London: W. Rivingtons, 1879.

Wortley, Mrs Stuart. 'On nursing', in Angela Burdett-Coutts (ed.), *Woman's Mission*. London: Sampson Low, Marston & Co., 1893, pp. 216–23.

Wray, Cecil. *Sisterhoods on Their Trial*. London: G. J. Palmer, 1864.

—. *A 'Sister's' Love* London: Rivingtons, 1866.

—. *Sister Monica (of St Martin's Sisterhood): A Funeral Sermon Preached at St Martin's Church, Liverpool*. Liverpool: Adam Holden, 1869.

3. Other primary sources

The Adventures of a Gentleman in Search of the Church of England. London: John Chapman, 1853.

Armstrong, John. *The Confessional: Its Wickedness*. Brighton: Edward Verrall, printer, 1856.

Auricular Confession Proved to Be Contrary to Scripture; Not Countenanced by the Church of England . . . By a Voice from the Grave of a Living Curate. London: For the author, by William Macintosh, [1875].

Bayly, Mrs [Mary]. *Ragged Homes and How to Mend Them*, 6th thousand. London: James Nisbet & Co., 1860.

Benson, Arthur C. *The Life of Edward White Benson, Sometime Archbishop of Canterbury*, 2 vols. London: Macmillan & Co., 1899.

Bird, M. Mostyn. *Woman at Work: A Study of the Different Ways of Earning a Living Open to Women*. London: Chapman & Hall, 1911.

Blunt, J. H. *Directorium Pastorale: Principles and Practice of Pastoral Work in the Church of England*. London: Rivingtons, 1864.

[Bodichon], Barbara Leigh Smith. *Women and Work*. London: Bosworth & Harrison, 1857.

Bosanquet, Charles B. P. *A Handy Book for Visitors of the Poor*. London: Longmans & Co., 1874.

—. *London: Some Account of Its Growth, Charitable Agencies, and Wants*. London: Hatchard & Co., 1868.

—. *The Organization of Charity: The History and Mode of Operation of the Charity Organization Society*. London: Longmans, Green & Co., 1874.

Bosanquet, Helen Dendy. *Social Work in London, 1869–1912* (1914). Brighton: Harvester Press, 1973.

Brockman, H. J. *The Confessional Unmasked*. London: Protestant Evangelical Mission and Electoral Union, [1871].

Broome, Mary Anne. *Colonial Memories*. London: Smith, Elder, & Co., 1904.

Browne, Edward George Kirwan. *Annals of the Tractarian Movement from 1842 to 1860*, 3rd edn. London: The Author, 1861.

Burdett-Coutts, Angela (ed.). *Woman's Mission*. London: Sampson Low, Marston & Co., 1893.

Burgon, John William. *Woman's Place*. Oxford: James Parker & Co., 1871.

[Butler, Arthur John (ed.)]. *Life and Letters of William John Butler*. London: Macmillan, 1897.

Butler, Josephine E. (ed.). *Woman's Work and Woman's Culture: A Series of Lectures*. London: Macmillan, 1869.

[Chambers, J. C.]. *The Priest in Absolution*, Part 1, London: Joseph Masters, 1866; Part 2, privately printed for the use of the clergy, [c. 1873].

Charity Organisation Society. *Charity and Food: Report of the Special Committee*. London: Spottiswoode & Co., 1887.

Cobbe, Frances Power. *Life of Frances Power Cobbe, by Herself*, 2 vols. Cambridge: Riverside Press, 1894.

The Community of the Mission Sisters of the Holy Name of Jesus. Worcester: Trinity Press, n.d.

Confession and Absolution, Considered under Their Religious, Moral, and Social Aspects. Essays on Modern Religious Thought No. 2. London: Longmans, Green, & Co., 1868.

Craik, Dinah Mulock. *A Woman's Thoughts about Women*. London: Hurst & Blackett, 1858.

Creighton, Louise. *A Purpose in Life: A Paper Read at the Brighton Conference of the National Union of Women Workers*. London: Wells, Darton & Co., 1901.

Eckenstein, Lina. *Women under Monasticism*. Cambridge: The University Press, 1896.

Ellis, Octavius J. *Some Time among Ritualists*, 3rd edn. London: Hatchards, 1868.

Ellis, Sarah Stickney. *The Daughters of England: Their Position in Society, Character, and Responsibilities*. London: Fisher, Son & Co., 1842.

—. *The Wives of England: Their Relative Duties, Domestic Influence, and Social Obligations*. London: Fisher, Son, & Co., 1843.

Faithfull, Emily. *On Some of the Drawbacks Connected with the Present Employment of Women*. London: Victoria Press, 1862.

Feasey, Henry John. *Monasticism: What Is It? A Forgotten Chapter in the History of Labour*. London: Sands & Co., 1898.

A Few Words to Servants about the Church Penitentiary Association. London: J. H. Parker, n.d.

Gavazzi, Alessandro. *The Priest in Absolution: An Exposure*. London: Simpkin, Marshall, & Co., 1877.

Gissing, George. *Workers in the Dawn* (1880). Brighton: Harvester Press, 1975.

Grafton, Charles Chapman. *The Works of Bishop Grafton*, 7 vols. New York: Longmans, 1914.

Greg, William Rathbone. *Why Are Women Redundant?* London: N. Trübner & Co., 1869.

Grey, Maria G. *Old Maids: A Lecture*. London: Ridgeway, 1875.

Grey, Maria G., and Emily Shirreff. *Thoughts on Self-Culture, Addressed to Women*, 2 vols. London: Edward Moxon, 1850.

Hamilton, Cecily. *Marriage as a Trade* (1909). London: The Women's Press, 1981.

Hints on District Visiting. London: SPCK, 1877.

Hopkins, J. Ellice. *Work in Brighton: Or, Woman's Mission to Women*. London: Hatchards, 1877.

Humble, Henry. 'Infanticide: its cause and cure', in O. Shipley (ed.), *The Church and the World*. London: Longmans, Green, Reader & Dyer, 1866, pp. 51–69.

Jones, J. *Memorials of Agnes Elizabeth Jones*. London: Strahan, 1871.

Kingsley, Charles. 'Women's work in a country parish', in *Sanitary and Social Lectures and Essays*, vol. 18 of *The Works of Charles Kingsley*. London: Macmillan & Co.,

1880, pp. 1–18.

A. V. L. *The Ministry of Woman and the London Poor*, ed. Mrs Bayley. London: S.W. Partridge, 1870.

Landels, William. *Woman's Sphere and Work Considered in the Light of Scripture*. London: James Nisbet & Co., 1859.

'The last thirty years in the Church of England: an autobiography', in O. Shipley (ed.), *The Church and the World*. London: Longmans, Green, Reader & Dyer, 1866, pp. 215–47.

[Lewis, Sarah]. *Woman's Mission*. (1839) 10th edn. London: John W. Parker, 1842.

Littledale, R. F., and J. E. Vaux (eds). *The Priest's Prayer Book*, 7th edn. London: Masters & Co., 1890.

Longridge, George. *Sister Bessie: A Memoir*. Oxford: James Parker & Co., 1903.

Malleus Ritualistarum: Or, The Ritual Reason Why Not. London: Effingham Wilson, 1872.

Meadows, Alfred. 'Hospital and workhouse nursing', in O. Shipley (ed.), *The Church and the World*. London: Longmans, Green, Reader & Dyer, 1866, pp. 113–40.

Milne, John Duguid. *The Industrial and Social Position of Women*. London: Chapman & Hall, 1857.

Molesworth, Mrs. 'For the little ones', in Angela Burdett-Coutts (ed.), *Woman's Mission*. London: Sampson Low, Marston & Co., 1893, pp. 13–34.

Monro, E. *Parochial Work*. London: John Henry Parker, 1850.

More, Hannah. *Coelebs in Search of a Wife* (1808), in *The Works of Hannah More*, vol 7. London: Henry G. Bohn, 1853.

Muhlenberg, William Augustus. *The Woman and Her Accusers*. New York: Pliny F. Smith, 1870.

National Protestant Congress. *Romanism and Ritualism in Great Britain and Ireland*. Edinburgh: R. W. Hunter, 1895.

Neale, Miss. *An Offering to St Margaret's Convent*. London: Joseph Masters, 1873.

[Neale, John Mason]. *Annals of Virgin Saints, by a Priest of the Church of England*. London: Joseph Masters, 1846.

—. *Letters of John Mason Neale, D.D., Selected and Edited by his Daughter*. London: Longmans, 1910.

Nightingale, Florence. *Cassandra* (1852). New York: The Feminist Press, 1979.

—. *Suggestions for Thought for Seekers after Religious Truth among the Artizans of England*, 3 vols. London: Eyre & Spottiswoode, for private circulation, 1860.

Official Yearbook of the Church of England. 1883, etc.

Parker, Theodore. *The Public Function of Women*. Woman's Rights Tracts No. 2. London: n.p., 1853.

Parkes, Bessie Rayner. *Essays on Women's Work*. London: Alexander Strahan, 1865.

Pearson, Charles H. 'On some historical aspects of family life,' in Josephine Butler (ed.), *Woman's Work and Woman's Culture*. London: Macmillan, 1869.

[Penny, Anne Judith]. *The Afternoon of Life*. London: Longman, Green, Longman, &

Roberts, 1858.

Percy, Josceline. *Reply to the Rev. W. Niven's Letter on Sisterhood Nurses*. London: Rivingtons, 1866.

Prynne, G. R. *Thirty-five Years of Mission Work*. Plymouth: W. Brendon & Son, 1883.

Quilter, Harry (ed.). *Is Marriage a Failure?* London: Swan Sonnenschein & Co., 1888.

Rigg, James H. *Oxford High Anglicanism and Its Chief Leaders*. London: Charles H. Kelly, 1895.

Rome's Recruits: A List of Protestants Who Have Become Roman Catholics Since the Tractarian Movement, 3rd edn. London: Whitehall Review Office, 1879.

Rossetti, Christina. *Maude: Prose and Verse* (1850), ed. R. W. Crump. Hamden: Archon Books, 1976.

Rossetti, William. *The Family Letters of Christina Georgina Rossetti* (1908). New York: Haskell House, 1968.

Ruskin, John. 'Of Queen's Gardens', in *Sesame and Lilies* (1865). London: Collins, 1900.

Sandford, Mrs. *Woman in Her Social and Domestic Character*, 5th edn. London: Longmans, Rees, Orme, Brown, Green & Longman, 1837.

Scrutator. *Is the Christianity of England Real, or Is It Only a Sham?* Manchester: Abel Heywood & Son, 1877.

Sellars, E. 'Women's work for the welfare of girls', in Angela Burdett-Coutts (ed.), *Woman's Mission*. London: Sampson Low, Marston & Co., 1893, pp. 35–48.

Sellon, Lydia. *A Few Words to Some of the Women of the Church of God in England*, 3rd edn. London: Joseph Masters, 1850.

Shirreff, Emily. *Intellectual Education*. London: John W. Parker & Son, 1858.

Shipley, Orby (ed.). *The Church and the World: Essays on Questions of the Day*. First Series, 1866; Second Series, 1867; Third Series, 1868. London: Longmans, Green, Reader, & Dyer.

Soltau, G. W. *A Letter to the Working Classes on Ritualism*, 12th edn. Plymouth: I. Latimer, 1873.

Some Thoughts on Catholicism in the English Church, by a Country Gentleman. London: Joseph Masters, 1874.

Stretton, Hebsa. 'Women's work for children', in Angela Burdett-Coutts (ed.), *Woman's Mission*. London: Sampson Low, Marston & Co., 1893, pp. 4–12.

Taine, Hippolyte. *Notes on England* (1872), trans. Edward Hyams. London: Thames & Hudson, 1957.

Walker, Henry. *East London: Sketches of Christian Work and Workers*. London: Religious Tract Society, 1896.

Walsh, Walter. *The Secret History of the Oxford Movement*, 4th edn. London: Sonnenschein, 1898.

Webb, Beatrice. *The Diary of Beatrice Webb*, vol. 1, 1873–92, *Glitter Around and Darkness Within*, ed. N. and J. MacKenzie. London: Virago, 1982.

Whately, Richard (ed.). *Cautions for the Times*. London: John W. Parker & Son, 1853.

Wise, Daniel. *The Young Lady's Counsellor: Or, Outlines and Illustrations of the Spheres, the Duties, and the Dangers of Young Women.* Otley: Yorkshire J. S. Publishing Co., (1851).

Woman's Influence. Philadelphia: J. W. Bradley, 1854.

A Woman's Reply to a Sermon Preached by the Rev. J. W. Burgon . . . on 'Woman's Place', with a General Review of the Woman's Question. Oxford: George Shrimpton, 1871.

Wright, Joseph Hornsby. *Investigation in Some of Its Features.* London: Charity Organization Society, for circulation among officers of the Society, 1872.

Yonge, Charlotte M. *On Womankind.* London: Walter Smith, 1881.

4. Journal and newspaper articles on sisterhoods and related institutions

[Armstrong, John]. 'The Church and her female penitents', *Christian Remembrancer*, (NS) **17** (1849), pp. 1–17.

Beale, Lionel S. 'Nursing the sick in hospitals, private families, and among the poor', *Medical Times and Gazette*, 6 Dec. 1873, pp. 630–2.

'Brighton Protestant Association', *Brighton Examiner*, 24 Nov. 1857.

C., F. P. (Frances Power Cobbe). 'Women's work in the Church', *Theological Review*, **2** (1865), pp. 505–21.

[Capes, J. M.]. 'Hospitals and sisterhoods', *The Rambler*, (NS) **2** (1854), pp. 209–29.

—. 'Protestant accounts of French convents', *The Rambler*, (NS) **4** (1855), pp. 37–50.

[Cobbe, Frances Power]. 'Female charity, lay and monastic', *Fraser's Magazine*, **66** (1862), pp. 774–88.

Coleman, L. 'Deaconesses, or sisterhoods', *American Quarterly Church Review*, **14** (1862), pp. 617–34.

'Convent of the Belgravians', *Punch*, **19** (1850), p. 163.

'The convents of the United Kingdom', *Fraser's Magazine*, (NS) **9** (1874), pp. 14–24.

[Craik, D. M.]. 'About sisterhoods', *Longman's Magazine*, **1** (1883), pp. 303–13.

Cusack, M. F. 'Woman's place in the economy of creation', *Fraser's Magazine*, **9** (1874), pp. 200–9.

'Deaconesses', *Penny Post*, **11** (1861), pp. 161–2.

'Deaconesses and Protestant sisterhoods', *Christian Guardian*, **40** (1848), pp. 444–9.

'The dedication of penitents as a religious order', *Seeking and Saving*, (1886), pp. 58–63.

'Disgraceful scene at funeral: Puseyite demonstration, and violence of the mob', *Sussex Advertiser and Surrey Gazette, &c.*, 24 November 1857.

'Extraordinary scene and riot at a funeral at Lewes', *Brighton Examiner*, 24 Nov. 1857.

'Extraordinary scene after a funeral at All Saints' Church, Lewes', *Sussex Express, Surrey Standard, Herald of Kent Mail, Hants and County Advertiser*, 21 Nov. 1857.

[Fearson, D. R]. 'The ladies' cry, "Nothing to do!"' *Macmillans Magazine*, **19** (1869), pp. 451–4.

Gilbert, W. 'An Anglican sisterhood', *Good Words and Sunday Magazine*, **22** (1881), pp. 833–7.

Gooch, Robert. 'Protestant Sisters of Charity', *Blackwood's Edinburgh Magazine*, **18** (1825), pp. 732–5.

[Harltey, May Laffen]. 'Convent boarding schools for young ladies', *Fraser's Magazine*, NS **9** (1874), pp. 778–86.

Harrison, Agnes T. 'The under side', *Macmillans Magazine*, **19** (1869), pp. 331–9.

[Holland, Penelope]. 'Our offence, and our petition, by a Belgravian young lady', *Macmillans Magazine*, **19** (1869), pp. 323–31.

—. 'A few more words on convents and on English girls', *Macmillans Magazine*, **19** (1869), pp. 534–9.

Hopkins, J. Ellice. 'Work in Brighton', *Temple Bar* (1862), pp. 39–43.

'A house in Westminster', *Cornhill Magazine* (1862), pp. 258–68.

[Howson, John Saul]. 'Deaconesses: or the official help of women in parochial work', *Quarterly Review*, **58** (1860), pp. 342–87.

'The kidnapper: a case for the police', *Punch*, **20** (1851), p. 129.

'Letters from Dr Pusey', *Convent Magazine*, **2** (1888), pp. 265–7.

[Ludlow, J. M.] 'Deaconesses, or Protestant sisterhoods', *Edinburgh Review*, **87** (1848), pp. 430–51.

—. 'Ruth (review)', *North British Review*, **19** (1853), pp. 151–74.

—. 'Sisterhoods', *Good Words*, **4** (1863), pp. 493–502.

Maurice, F. D. 'On sisterhoods', *Victoria Magazine*, **1** (1863), pp. 289–301.

'Miss K. M. M. Scott', *Labour Prophet*, **1** (1891), inside cover.

[Mozley, Anne]. 'Convent life', *Blackwood's Edinburgh Magazine*, **105** (1869), pp. 607–21.

'Nature and the convent', *Macmillans Magazine*, **19** (1869), pp. 539–43.

'No business of ours', *Punch*, **20** (1851), pp. 125–6.

'A nursery tale for novices', *Punch*, **20** (1851), pp. 138–9.

'A page for Puseyites', *Punch*, **19** (1850), pp. 227–8.

'Protestant deaconesses as nurses in hospitals', *Monthly Journal of Medical Science*, **7** (1847), pp. 684–9.

'Prudentia'. 'Sisterhoods', *Christian Observer*, **244** (1858), pp. 330–4.

'Puseyite doings and consequent riot at Lewes', *Brighton Herald*, 21 Nov. 1857.

S. 'Sisterhoods', *Christian Observer*, NS **243** (1858), pp. 156–61.

Sewell, Elizabeth M. 'Kaiserwerth and the Protestant deaconesses', *Macmillans Magazine*, **21** (1870), pp. 229–37.

—. 'Anglican deaconesses', *Macmillans Magazine*, **28** (1873), pp. 463–7.

'Sisterhoods', *London Review* (superseded by *Westminster Review*), **4** (1862), pp. 178–9.

Trench, Maria. 'English sisterhoods', *Nineteenth Century*, **40** (1884), pp. 339–52.

'Two girls of the period', *Punch* cartoon (1869), p. 71.

'A visit to Clewer sisterhood', *Penny Post*, **11** (1861), p. 35.

'We are able to give Dr Pusey's paper verbatim', 16-in. col., from unknown periodical, Pusey House 6276.

Wister, Sarah B. 'Sisterhoods in England', *Lippincott Magazine*, **9** (1872), pp. 564–71.

—.'Charitable sisterhoods', *North American Review*, **117** (1873), pp. 439–60.

'Y'. 'Sisters of Charity', *Educational Magazine*, NS **2** (1840), pp. 351–6.

5. Other journal and newspaper articles

Cobbe, Frances Power. 'What shall we do with our old maids?', *Fraser's Magazine*, **66** (1862), pp. 594–610.

'The female agency in the Church', *London Quarterly Review*, **25** (1865), pp. 163–88.

Greenwell, Dora. 'Our single women', *North British Review*, **36** (1862), pp. 62–87.

[Greg, William Rathbone]. 'Why are women redundant?', *National Review*, **14** (1862), pp. 434–60.

Grey, M. G. 'Idols of society', *Fraser's Magazine*, NS **9** (1874), pp. 377–88.

Hill, Octavia. 'A few words to fresh workers', *Nineteenth Century*, **26** (1889), pp. 452–61.

'Hospital nurses as they are and ought to be', *Fraser's Magazine*, **37** (1848), pp. 539–42.

[Kaye, J. W.]. 'The non-existence of women', *North British Review*, **23** (1855), pp. 536–62.

Low, Frances H. 'How poor ladies live', *Nineteenth Century*, **41** (1897), pp. 405–17.

—. 'How poor ladies live: a rejoinder and a Jubilee suggestion', *Nineteenth Century*, **41** (1897), pp. 161–68.

'Old maids', *Blackwood's Edinburgh Magazine*, **112** (1872), pp. 94–108.

Pollard, Alfred W. 'The salaries of lady teachers', *Murray's Magazine*, **4** (1888), pp. 780–89.

'The social position of women', *Churchman's Magazine*, **58** (1857), pp. 201–6.

Twentieth-century sources

1. Secondary works on sisterhoods and related institutions

Adderly, James Granville. *In Slums and Society: Reminiscences of Old Friends*. London: T. Fisher Unwin, 1916.

Allchin, Arthur M. *The Silent Rebellion: Anglican Religious Communities 1845–1900*. London: SCM Press, 1958.

Anson, Peter Frederick. *The Benedictines of Caldey*. London: Burns, Oates, 1940.

—. *Building up the Waste Places*. Leighton Buzzard: Faith Press, 1973.

Anson, Peter Frederick and A. W. Campbell. *Call of the Cloister*, new edn. London: SPCK, 1964.

Arnstein, Walter L. *Protestant Versus Catholic in Mid-Victorian England: Mr Newdegate and the Nuns*. Columbia: University of Missouri Press, 1982.

As Possessing All Things: All Saints Sisters of the Poor. n.p., [c. 1972].

Ashwell, Arthur Rawson, and Reginald G. Wilberforce. *Life of the Right Reverend Samuel Wilberforce ... with His Diaries and Correspondence*. 3 vols. London: John Murray, 1880–2.

Atkinson, Clarissa W. " 'Your servant, my mother": the figure of Saint Monica in the ideology of Christian motherhood', in Clarissa W. Atkinson et al. (eds), *Immaculate and Powerful: The Female in Sacred Image and Social Reality*. Boston: Beacon, 1987, pp. 139–72.

Atkinson, Clarissa W., et al. (eds). *Immaculate and Powerful: The Female in Sacred Image and Social Reality*. Boston: Beacon, 1987.

Attwater, Donald. *Father Ignatius of Llanthony: A Victorian*. London: Cassell & Co., 1931.

Auerbach, Nina. *Communities of Women: An Idea in Fiction*. Cambridge, MA: Harvard University Press, 1978.

Austin, Anne L. *History of Nursing Source Book*. New York: G. P. Putnam's Sons, 1957.

Bacon, F. D. *Women in the Church*. London: Lutterworth Press, 1946.

Baldwin, Monica. *I Leap Over the Wall: A Return to the World after Twenty-eight Years in a Convent*. London: Hamish Hamilton, 1949.

Banks, Olive. *Faces of Feminism: A Study of Feminism as a Social Movement*. Oxford: Martin Robertson, 1981.

Bellamy, V. Nelle. 'Participation of women in the public life of the Anglican Communion', in R. L. Greaves (ed.), *Triumph over Silence: Women in Protestant History*. Westport, CT: Greenwood Press, 1985, pp. 229–60.

Bennett, Alice Horlock. *Through an Anglican Sisterhood to Rome*. London: Longmans, 1914.

—. *English Medical Women: Glimpses of Their Work in Peace and War*. London: Sir I. Pitman & Sons, 1915.

Bennett, Frederick. *The Story of W. J. E. Bennett*. London: Longmans, Green, & Co., 1909.

Bentley, James. *Ritualism and Politics in Victorian Britain: The Attempt to Legislate for Belief*. Oxford: Oxford University Press, 1978.

Bernstein, Marcelle. *Nuns*. London: Collins, 1976.

Best, G. F. A. 'Popular Protestantism in Victorian Britain', in Robert Robson (ed.), *Ideas and Institutions of Victorian Britain: Essays in Honour of George Kitzan Clark*. London: G. Bell & Sons, 1967, pp. 115–42.

Birkett, Dea. 'Mary Kingsley and West Africa', in Gordon Marsden (ed.), *Victorian Values: Personalities and Perspectives in Nineteenth Century Society*. London: Longman, 1990, pp. 171–86.

Bolster, Evelyn. *The Sisters of Mercy in the Crimean War*. Cork: Mercier Press, 1964.

Bonham, Valerie. *A Joyous Service: The Clewer Sisters and Their Work*. Windsor: Community of St John Baptist, 1989.

—. *A Place in Life: The Clewer House of Mercy, 1849–1883*. Windsor: Community of St John Baptist, 1992.

Booth, Charles. *Life and Labour of the People in London*, Third Series, *Religious Influences*. 7 vols. London: Macmillan & Co, 1902.

Bowen, Desmond. *The Idea of the Victorian Church: A Study of the Church of England, 1833–1889*. Montreal: McGill University Press, 1968.

Bradley, Ian. *The Call to Seriousness: The Evangelical Impact on the Victorians.* London: Cape, 1976.

Branca, Patricia. *Silent Sisterhood: Middle-class Women in the Victorian Home.* London: Croom Helm, 1975.

Brandreth, Henry Reynard Turner. *Dr Lee of Lambeth: A Chapter in Parenthesis in the History of the Oxford Movement.* London: SPCK, 1951.

Bridenthal, Renate, and Claudia Koonz (eds). *Becoming Visible: Women in European History.* Boston: Houghton Mifflin, 1987.

Bridges, Yseult. *Saint with Red Hands?* London: Jarrolds, 1954.

Bristow, Edward J. *Vice and Vigilance: Social Purity Movements in Britain Since 1700.* Dublin: Gill & Macmillan, 1977.

Brooke, Audrey. *Robert Gray: First Bishop of Cape Town.* Cape Town: Oxford University Press, 1947.

Brown, C. K. Francis. *The Church's Part in Education, 1833–1941.* London: National Society, 1942.

Bull, Paul B. *The Revival of the Religious Life.* London: Edward Arnold, 1914.

Bullough, Vern L. *The Subordinate Sex.* Baltimore: Penguin Books, 1974.

Burman, S. (ed.). *Fit Work for Women.* London: Croom Helm, 1979.

Burme, Kathleen E. *Love's Fulfilment.* London: A. R. Mowbray, 1957.

Burn, W. L. *The Age of Equipoise.* London: George Allen & Unwin, 1964.

Burstyn, Joan N. *Victorian Education and the Ideal of Womanhood.* London: Croom Helm, 1980.

Butler of Wantage: His Inheritance and His Legacy. Westminster: Dacre Press, [1948].

C.S.D: The Life and Work of St Denys', Warminster to 1979. Tempsford: The Community of St Denys, 1979.

Calder-Marshall, Arthur. *The Enthusiast: An Enquiry into the Life, Beliefs, and Character of The Rev. Joseph Leycester Lyne, alias Fr Ignatius, O.S.B., Abbot of Elm Hill, Norwich and Llanthony, Wales.* London: Faber & Faber, 1962.

Cameron, Allan T. *The Religious Communities of the Church of England.* London: Faith Press, 1918.

—. *Directory of Religious Communities of Men and Women in the Church of England* (1920), 2nd edn. London: Faith Press, 1924.

Camm, Bede. *The Call of Caldey: The Story of the Conversion of Two Communities.* London: Burns, Oates, & Washbourne, [1940].

Campbell-Jones, Suzanne. *In Habit: An Anthropological Study of Working Nuns.* London: Faber & Faber, 1979.

Carpenter, Spencer Cecil. *Church and People, 1789–1889.* London: SPCK, 1933.

The Centenary of the Community of St Wilfrid, Exeter, 1866–1966. Exeter: J. Banks & Son, printers, [c. 1966].

Chadwick, Owen. *The Mind of the Oxford Movement.* London: A. & C. Black, 1960.

—. *The Victorian Church,* 3rd edn. London: Adam & Charles Black, 1971.

Charles Borromeo, Sister M. [Maryellen Muckenhirn] (ed.). *The New Nuns*. London: Sheed & Ward, 1968.

Clarke, Charles Philip Stewart. *The Oxford Movement and After*. London: A. R. Mowbray, 1932.

Clear, Caitriona. *Nuns in Nineteenth-Century Ireland*. Dublin: Gill & Macmillan, 1988.

Cockshut, A. O. J. *Anglican Attitudes: A Study of Victorian Religious Controversies*. London: Collins, 1959.

Coleman, B. I. *The Church of England in the Mid-nineteenth Century: A Social Geography*. London: Historical Association, 1980.

Coleridge, Christabel Rose. *Charlotte Mary Yonge: Her Life and Letters*. London: Macmillan, 1903.

Collet, Clara E. *Educated Working Women: Essays on the Economic Position of Women Workers in the Middle Classes*. London: P. S. King, 1902.

The Community of the Mission Sisters of the Holy Name of Jesus. Worcester: Community of the Holy Name, 1950.

The Community of the Nursing Sisters of St John the Divine: 1848–1948. n.p., [c.1948].

[Compton, Mrs, et al.]. *From Theatre to Convent: Memories of Mother Isabel May, C.S.M.V.* London: SPCK, 1936.

Conley, Carolyn A. *The Unwritten Law: Criminal Justice in Victorian Kent*. Oxford: Oxford University Press, 1991.

Convent Tales, by a Religious of St Peter's Community, Kilburn. London: SPCK, 1928.

Cooke, Edward T. *The Life of Florence Nightingale*, 2 vols. London: Macmillan, 1913.

Creighton, Louise. *Life and Letters of Mandell Creighton*. 2 vols. London: Longmans, Green, and Co., 1904.

Crowther, M. A. *Church Embattled: Religious Controversy in Mid-Victorian England*. Newton Abbot: David & Charles, 1970.

Cruickshank, Marjorie. *Church and State in English Education*. London: Macmillan & Co., 1963.

Cruikshank, Anna. *Startling Facts under the Convent Veil*. London: Protestant Alliance, 1913.

Daly, Mary. *The Church and the Second Sex*. Boston: Beacon Press, 1985.

Danylewycz, Marta. *Taking the Veil: An Alternative to Marriage, Motherhood, and Spinsterhood in Quebec, 1840–1920*. Toronto: McClelland & Stewart, 1987.

Davidoff, Leonore. *The Best Circles: Women and Society in Victorian England*. Towata, NJ: Rowman & Littlefield, 1973.

—. 'The separation of home and work? Landladies and lodgers in nineteenth-century England', in S. Burman (ed.), *Fit Work for Women*. London: Croom Helm, 1979, pp. 64–97.

—. and Catherine Hall. *Family Fortunes: Men and Women of the English Middle Class, 1780–1950*. London: Hutchinson, 1985.

Davidson, Randall Thomas, and William Benham. *Life of Archibald Campbell Tait,*

Archbishop of Canterbury, 2 vols., 3rd edn. London: Macmillan & Co., 1891.

Davies, Celia (ed.). *Rewriting Nursing History*. London: Croom Helm, 1980.

Davies, Horton. *Worship and Theology in England: From Watts and Wesley to Maurice 1690–1850*. Princeton: Princeton University Press, 1961.

Davies, Margaret Llewelyn (ed.). *Life as We Have Known It, by Co-operative Working Women* (1931). London: Virago, 1977.

Deacon, Alan, and Michael Hill. 'The problem of "surplus women" in the nineteenth century: secular and religious alternatives', in Michael Hill (ed.), *A Sociological Yearbook of Religion in Britain*. London: SCM Press, 1972, pp. 87–102.

Delamont, Sara, and Lorna Duffin (eds.). *The Nineteenth-Century Woman*. London: Croom Helm, 1978.

Doing the Impossible: A Historical Sketch of St Margaret's Convent, East Grinstead, 1855–1980. n.p., [1984].

Donovan, Marcus Fitzgerald Grain. *After the Tractarians*. London: Philip Allan, 1933.

Donovan, Mary S. *A Different Call*. Wilton, CT: Morehouse-Barlow, 1986.

Douglas, Ann. *The Feminization of American Culture*. New York: Alfred A. Knopf, 1978.

Drain, Susan. *The Anglican Church in Nineteenth-Century Britain*: Hymns Ancient and Modern. Toronto: Edward Mellon, 1989.

Drake, Michael (ed.). *Population in Industrialization*. London: Methuen & Co., 1969.

Ducrocq, Françoise. 'The London Biblewomen and Nurses Mission, 1859–1880: class relations/women's relations', in Barbara Harris and John K. McNamara (eds), *Women and the Structure of Society*. Durham, NC: Duke Press Policy Studies, 1984, pp. 98–107.

Dyhouse, Carol. 'Mothers and daughters in the middle-class home, *c.* 1870–1914', in Jane Lewis (ed.), *Labour and Love: Women's Experience of Home and Family 1850–1940*. Oxford: Basil Blackwell, 1986, pp. 27–47.

Edwards, David L. *Leaders of the Church of England, 1828–1944*. London: Oxford University Press, 1971.

Elliott-Binns, L. E. *Religion in the Victorian Era*. London: Lutterworth Press, 1964.

Ellis, S. M. *Wilkie Collins, Le Fanu, and Others*. London: Constable, 1931.

Ellsworth, L. E. *Charles Lowder and the Ritualist Movement*. London: Darton, Longman & Todd, 1982.

Essex, Rosamund. *Woman in a Man's World*. London: Sheldon Press, 1977.

Ewens, Mary. *The Role of the Nun in Nineteenth Century America*. New York: Arno, 1978.

Finnegan, E. *Poverty and Prostitution*. Cambridge: Cambridge University Press, 1979.

The Founders of Clewer: A Short Account of the Rev. T. T. Carter and Harriet Monsell to Celebrate the Centenary of the Community of St John Baptist in 1952. London: Mowbray, 1952.

Frere, Walter Howard. *English Church Ways*. London: John Murray, 1914.

Gage, Matilda. *Woman, Church, and State: A Historical Account of Woman Through the Christian Ages*. Chicago: C. H. Kerr, 1893.

Gay, John D. *The Geography of Religion in England*. London: Duckworth, 1971.

Gilbert, A. D. *Religion and Society in Industrial England: Church, Chapel, and Social Change, 1740–1914*. London: Longman, 1976.

—. *The Making of Post-Christian Britain: A History of the Secularization of Modern Society*. London: Longman, 1980.

Gill, Sean. 'The power of Christian ladyhood: Priscilla Lydia Sellon and the creation of Anglican sisterhoods', in Stuart Mews (ed.), *Modern Religious Rebels*. London: Epworth Press, 1993, pp. 144–65.

[Gilmore, Isabella]. *Deaconess Gilmore: Memories*, ed. Elizabeth Robinson. London: SPCK, 1924.

Gordon, Linda. 'What's new in women's history', in Teresa de Lauretis (ed.), *Feminist Studies/Critical Studies*. London: Macmillan Press, 1986, pp. 23–35.

Gorham, Deborah. *The Victorian Girl and the Feminine Ideal*. London: Croom Helm, 1982.

Grafton, Charles C. *A Journey Godward* (1910), in *The Works of Bishop Grafton*, vol. 4. New York: Longmans, Green & Co., 1914.

Grierson, Janet. *Isabella Gilmore: Sister to William Morris*. London: SPCK, 1962.

—. *The Deaconess*. London: Church Information Office, 1981.

Hackett, Jo Ann. 'In the days of Jael: reclaiming the history of women in ancient Israel', in Clarissa W. Atkinson (ed.), *Immaculate and Powerful: The Female in Sacred Image and Social Reality*. Boston: Beacon, 1987, pp. 15–38.

Hall, Catherine. 'The early formation of Victorian domestic ideology', in S. Burman (ed.), *Fit Work for Women*. London: Croom Helm, 1979, pp. 15–32.

Hall, M. Penelope, and Ismane V. Howes. *The Church in Social Work: A Study of Moral Welfare Work Undertaken by the Church of England*. London: Routledge, International Library of Sociology and Social Reconstruction, 1965.

Hammond, Peter C. *The Parson and the Victorian Parish*. London: Hodder & Stoughton, 1977.

Harrison, Alan. *Bound for Life*. London: Mowbray, 1983.

Harrison, Brian. *Separate Spheres: The Opposition to Women's Suffrage in Britain*. London: Croom Helm, 1978.

Heeney, Brian. *The Women's Movement in the Church of England 1850–1930*. Oxford: Clarendon Press, 1988.

Hennock, E. P. 'The Anglo-Catholics and Church extension in Victorian Brighton', in M. J. Kitch (ed.), *Studies in Sussex Church History*. Brighton: Harvester Press, 1983, pp. 173–88.

Hill, Michael. *The Religious Order: A Study of Virtuoso Religion and Its Legitimation in the Nineteenth-Century Church of England*. London: Heinemann, 1973.

Hill, Michael (ed.). *A Sociological Yearbook of Religion*. London: SCM Press, 1972.

Hollingworth, T. H. 'A demographic study of the British ducal families', in Michael Drake (ed.), *Population in Industrialization*. London: Methuen & Co., 1969, pp. 73–102.

[Hughes, Dorothea Price]. *The Life of Hugh Price Hughes*. 4th edn. London: Hodder & Stoughton, 1905.

A Hundred Years in Haggerston: The Story of St Saviour's Priory. London: St Saviour's Priory, 1966.

A Hundred Years of Blessing within an English Community. London: SPCK, 1946.

Hutchings, W. H. *The Life and Letters of Thomas Thellusson Carter*. London: Longmans, Green & Co., 1903.

Inglis, K. S. *Churches and the Working Class in Victorian England: Studies in Social History*. London: Routledge & Kegan Paul, 1963.

James, Janet Wilson (ed.). *Women in American Religion*. Philadelphia: University of Pennsylvania Press, 1980.

Johnson, Dale A. (ed.). *Women in English Religion 1700–1925*, in *Studies in Women and Religion*, vol. X. Toronto: Edward Mellen Press, 1983.

Kate, Sister. *Mother Cecile: Venturer for God*. London: SPG, 1922.

Kitson-Clark, George. *The English Inheritance: A Historical Essay*. London: SCM Press, 1950.

—. *The Making of Victorian England: Ford Lectures, 1962*. London: Methuen, 1962.

Knowles, Josephine Pitcairn. *The Upholstered Cage*. London: Hodder & Stoughton, [1912].

Lewis, Jane. *Women in England, 1870–1950: Sexual Divisions and Social Change*. Brighton: Wheatsheaf Books, 1984.

—. 'Introduction: reconstructing women's experience of home and family', in Jane Lewis (ed.), *Labour and Love: Women's Experience of Home and Family 1850–1940*. Oxford: Basil Blackwell, 1986, pp. 1–24.

— (ed.). *Labour and Love: Women's Experience of Home and Family 1850–1940*. Oxford: Basil Blackwell, 1986.

Leyton, Mrs. 'Memories of seventy years', in Margaret Llewelyn Davies (ed.), *Life as We Have Known It, by Co-operative Working Women* (1931). London: Virago, 1977, pp. 1–55.

Liddon, Henry Parry. *Life of Edward Bouverie Pusey*. 4 vols. London: Longmans & Co., 1893.

Lochhead, Marion. *Episcopal Scotland in the Nineteenth Century*. London: John Murray, 1966.

Lonsdale, Margaret. *Sister Dora*. London: C. Kegan Paul, 1880.

Lough, Arthur Geoffrey. *The Influence of John Mason Neale*. London: SPCK, 1962.

—. *John Mason Neale – Priest Extraordinary*. Newton Abbott: privately printed, 1976.

Luckock, Herbert Mortimer. *The Beautiful Life of an Ideal Priest*. London: Simpkin, Marshall, Hamilton, Kent & Co., 1902.

Luddy, Maria. *Women and Philanthropy in Nineteenth-Century Ireland*. Cambridge: Cambridge University Press, 1995.

Mahood, L. *The Magdalens*. London: Routledge, 1990.

Maitland, Sara. *A Map of the New Country: Women and Christianity*. London: Routledge & Kegan Paul, 1983.

Malmgreen, Gail (ed.). *Religion in the Lives of English Women, 1760–1930*. London:

Croom Helm, 1986.

Manton, Jo. *Sister Dora: The Life of Dorothy Pattison* (1971). London: Quartet Books, 1977.

Margaret Teresa, CSMV, Sister. *The History of St Dunstan's Abbey School 1848–1928*. Plymouth: Underhill, printer, 1928.

Margaret, Sister. *The Deaconess*. London: Faith Press, 1919.

Matthews, H. C. G. 'Gladstonian finance', in Gordon Marsden (ed.), *Victorian Values: Personalities and Perspectives in Nineteenth Century Society*. London: Longman, 1990, pp. 110–20.

Mayhew, Peter. *All Saints: Birth and Growth of a Community*. Oxford: Society of All Saints, 1987.

McCarthy, Kathleen D. (ed.). *Lady Bountiful Revisited: Women, Philanthropy and Power*. London: Rutgers University Press, 1990.

McGuire, Meredith. *Religion: The Social Context*, 2nd edn. Belmont, CA: Wadsworth, 1987.

McLeod, Hugh. *Class and Religion in the Late Victorian City*. London: Croom Helm, 1974.

—. *Religion and the Working Class in Nineteenth-Century Britain: Studies in Economic and Social History*. London: Macmillan, 1984.

Meehan-Waters, Brenda. 'From contemplative practice to charitable activity: Russian women's religious communities and the development of charitable work, 1861–1917', in Kathleen D. McCarthy (ed.), *Lady Bountiful: Women, Philanthropy and Power*. London: Rutgers University Press, 1990, pp. 142–56.

A Memoir of the Life and Work of Hannah Grier Coombe, Mother-Foundress of the Sisterhood of St John the Divine. London: Oxford University Press, 1933.

Miles, Margaret R. 'Introduction', in Clarissa W. Atkinson *et al.* (eds), *Immaculate and Powerful: The Female in Sacred Image and Social Reality*. Boston: Beacon, 1987, pp. 1–14.

Mother Cecile in South Africa 1883–1906: Compiled by a Sister of the Community. London: SPCK, 1930.

A Mother Superior. *The Life of an Enclosed Nun*. London: A. C. Fifield, 1910.

Mudie-Smith, Richard (ed.). *The Religious Life of London*. London: Hodder & Stoughton, 1904.

Neff, Wanda Fraiken. *Victorian Working Women: An Historical and Literary Study of Women in British Industries and Professions, 1832–1850*. London: Allen & Unwin, 1929.

Newton, Judith L. *Sex and Class in Women's History*. London: Routledge & Kegan Paul, 1983.

Nicholls, David. 'Two tendencies in Anglo-Catholic political theology', in Geoffrey Rowell (ed.), *Tradition Renewed*. London: Darton, Longman & Todd, 1986, pp. 140–52.

Norman, E. R. *Anti-Catholicism in Victorian England*. London: George Allen & Unwin, 1968.

—. *Church and Society in England, 1770–1970: A Historical Study*. Oxford: Clarendon Press, 1976.

Nutting, M. *Adelaide, and Lavinia L. Dock: A History of Nursing*, 2 vols. New York: G. P. Putnam's Sons, 1907.

O'Brien, Susan. 'Lay sisters and good mothers: working-class women in English convents, 1840–1910', in W. J. Sheils and Diana Wood (eds), *Women in the Church*. Studies in Church History No. 27. Oxford: Basil Blackwell, 1990, pp. 453–65.

O'Dea, Thomas, and Janet O'Dea Aviad. *The Sociology of Religion*, 2nd edn. Englewood Cliffs, NJ: Prentice-Hall, 1983.

Ollard, S. L. *A Short History of the Oxford Movement* (1915), 3rd edn. London: Faith Press, 1963.

Owen, Alex. *The Darkened Room: Women, Power and Spiritualism in Late Nineteenth-Century England*. London: Virago, 1989.

Parsons, Gerald (ed.). *Religion in Victorian Britain*, vols 1–2, 4, *Tradition; Controversies; Interpretations*. Manchester: Manchester University Press, 1988.

Peck, W. G. *The Social Implications of the Oxford Movement*. New York: Scribner, 1933.

Perchenet, A. *The Revival of the Religious Life and Christian Unity*, trans. E. M. A. Graham. London: A. R. Mowbray, 1969.

Pethick-Lawrence, Emmeline. *My Part in a Changing World*. London: Victor Gollancz, 1938.

Pickering, W. S. F. 'The development and function of religious institutes in the Anglican Communion', in *Vie ecclésiale: communauté et communautés*. Paris: Diffusé par Didier-érudition, 1989, pp. 193–212.

Pope, Barbara Corrado. ' "Angels in the Devil's workshop": leisured and charitable women in nineteenth-century England and France', in Renate Bridenthal and Claudia Koonz (eds), *Becoming Visible: Women in European History*. Boston: Houghton Mifflin, 1977, pp. 296–324.

Pope, Barbara Corrado. 'Immaculate and powerful: the Marian revival in the nineteenth century', in Clarissa W. Atkinson *et al.* (eds), *Immaculate and Powerful: The Female in Sacred Image and Social Reality*. Boston: Beacon, 1987, pp. 173–200.

Power, Eileen. *Medieval English Nunneries, 1275–1535*. Cambridge: Cambridge University Press, 1922.

Poynter, F. N. L. *The Evolution of Hospitals in Britain*. London: Pitman Medical Publishing, 1964.

Prelinger, Catherine M. 'The female diaconate in the Anglican Church: what kind of ministry for women?', in G. Malmgreen (ed.), *Religion in the Lives of English Women, 1760–1930*. London: Croom Helm, 1986.

Pringle, J. C. *The Social Work of the London Churches*. Oxford: Oxford University Press, 1937.

Prochaska, Frank K. *Women and Philanthropy in Nineteenth Century England*. Oxford: Clarendon Press, 1980.

—. *The Voluntary Impulse: Philanthropy in Modern England*. London: Faber, 1988.

Radford Ruether, Rosemary (ed.). *Religion and Sexism*. New York: Simon and Schuster, 1974.

Reffold, A. E. *A Noble Army of Women: The Story of Marie Carlile and the Church Army Sisters*. Church Book Room Press, 1947.

Rendall, Jane. *The Origins of Modern Feminism: Women in Britain, France and the United States 1780–1860*. London: Macmillan, 1985.

Report of the Women's Meetings Held in Connection with the Pan-Anglican Congress of 1908. London: Christian Knowledge Society, 1908.

Richardson, Jerusha. *Women of the Church of England*. London: Chapman & Hall, 1907.

Robins, Margaret W. *Mother Cecile* (1910). London: Wells, Gardner, Darton & Co., 1949.

Rowell, Geoffrey. *The Vision Glorious: Themes and Personalities of the Catholic Revival in Anglicanism*. Oxford: Oxford University Press, 1983.

Rowell, Geoffrey (ed.). *Tradition Renewed*. Allison Park, PA: Pickwick Press, 1986.

Russell, Alan. *The Community of the Holy Cross 1857–1957*. Haywards Heath: Holy Cross Convent, 1957.

Russell, George W. E. *Dr Pusey*. Oxford: A. R. Mowbray, 1907.

—. *St Alban the Martyr, Holborn: A History of Fifty Years*. London: George Allen & Co., 1913.

Sheils, W. J., and Diana Wood. *Women in the Church*. Studies in Church History No. 27. Oxford: Basil Blackwell, 1990.

Simey, M. *Charitable Efforts in Liverpool in the Nineteenth Century*. Liverpool: University Press, 1951.

Simpson, W. J. Sparrow. *The History of the Anglo-Catholic Revival from 1845*. London: George Allen & Unwin, 1932.

The Society of the Sisters of Bethany, 1866–1966. Oxford: Church Army Press, 1966.

Sockman, Ralph Washington. *The Revival of the Conventual Life in the Church of England in the Nineteenth Century*. New York: W. D. Gray, 1917.

Some Memories of Emily Harriet Elizabeth Ayckbowm, Mother Foundress of the Community of the Sisters of the Church. London: Church Extension Association, 1914.

Strachey, Ray. *The Cause*. New York: Kennikat, 1969.

The Story of A Vocation: A Brief Memoir of Mother Florence, Second Superior of the Community of the Resurrection of Our Lord. Grahamstown: The Church Book Shop, n.d.

Summers, Anne. 'A home from home: women's philanthropic work in the nineteenth century', in S. Burman (ed.), *Fit Work for Women*. London: Croom Helm, 1979, pp. 33–63.

Summers, Anne. 'Ministering angels: Victorian ladies and nursing reform', in Gordon Marsden (ed.), *Victorian Values: Personalities and Perspectives in Nineteenth Century Society*. London: Longmans, 1990, pp. 121–33.

Taylor, Barbara. *Eve and the New Jerusalem: Socialism and Feminism in the Nineteenth Century*. London: Virago, 1983.

Toon, Peter. *Evangelical Theology 1833–1856: A Response to Tractarianism*. London: Marshall, Morgan & Scott, 1979.

[Trench, Maria]. *Charles Lowder: A Biography*, 9th edn. London: Kegan Paul, Trench, 1883.

Tropp, Asher. *The School Teachers*. London: William Heinemann, 1957.

A Valiant Victorian: The Life and Times of Mother Emily Ayckbowm. London: A. R. Mowbray & Co., 1964.

Vicinus, Martha. *Independent Women: Work and Community for Single Women 1850–1920*. London: Virago Press, 1985.

Vicinus, Martha, and Bea Nergaard (eds). *Ever Yours, Florence Nightingale*. Cambridge, MA: Harvard University Press, 1989.

Violet, Sister. *All Hallows, Ditchingham: The Story of an East Anglian Community*. Oxford: Becket Publications, 1986.

Voll, Dieter. *Catholic Evangelicalism: The Acceptance of Evangelical Tradition by the Oxford Movement During the Second Half of the Nineteenth Century*, trans. Veronica Ruffer. London: Faith Press, 1963.

Wagner, Antony and Antony Dale. *The Wagners of Brighton*. London: Phillimore & Co., 1983.

Walkowitz, Judith. *Prostitution and Victorian Society: Women, Class, and the State*. Cambridge: Cambridge University Press, 1980.

Walton, Ronald G. *Women in Social Work*. London: Routledge & Kegan Paul, 1975.

Ward, Benedicta, SLG. 'A Tractarian inheritance: the religious life in a patristic perspective', in Geoffrey Rowell (ed.), *Tradition Renewed*. Allison Park, PA: Pickwick Press, 1986, pp. 214–25.

Weeks, Jeffrey. *Sex, Politics, and Society: The Regulation of Sexuality since 1800*. London: Longman, 1989.

Welter, Barbara. 'The cult of true womanhood', in B. Welter (ed.), *Dimity Convictions*. Athens: Ohio University Press, 1977, pp. 21–41.

[White, Kathleen E.]. *St Denys School Oxford: Originally Known as Holy Trinity School*. Oxford: privately printed, [1989].

Widdowson, Frances. *Going up into the Next Class: Women and Elementary School Teacher Training, 1840–1914*. London: Women's Research & Resources Centre Publications, 1980.

Williams, Katherine. 'From Sarah Gamp to Florence Nightingale: a critical study of hospital nursing systems from 1840 to 1897', in Celia Davies (ed.), *Rewriting Nursing History*. London: Croom Helm, 1980, pp. 41–75.

Williams, Thomas J. *Priscilla Lydia Sellon: The Restorer after Three Centuries of the Religious Life in the English Church* (1950), rev. edn. London: SPCK, 1965.

Williams, Thomas J., and Allan Walter Campbell. *The Park Village Sisterhood*. London: SPCK, 1965.

Wolffe, John. *The Protestant Crusade in Great Britain 1829–1860*. Oxford: Clarendon, 1991.

Yates, Nigel. *The Oxford Movement and Anglican Ritualism*. London: Historical Association, 1983.

2. Journal and newspaper articles on sisterhoods and related
institutions

Aldridge, A. 'In the absence of the Minister: structures of subordination in the role of deaconess in the Church of England', *Sociology*, **21** (1987), pp. 377–92.

Anderson, Olive. 'Women preachers in mid-Victorian Britain: some reflexions on feminism, popular religion, and social change', *Historical Journal*, **12** (1969), pp. 467–84.

Arnstein, Walter, *et al.* 'Recent studies in Victorian religion', *Victorian Studies*, **33** (1989), pp. 149–75.

Bellamy, V. Nelle. 'Participation of women in the public life of the Church from Lambeth Conference 1867–1978', *Historical Magazine of the Protestant Episcopal Church*, **51** (1982), pp. 81–98.

Brent, A. 'Newman's conversion, the Via Media, and the myth of Romeward movement', *Downside Review*, **101** (1983), pp. 261–80.

Casteras, Susan P. 'Virgin vows: the early Victorian artists' portrayal of nuns and novices', *Victorian Studies*, **24** (1981), pp. 157–84.

Clegg, Herbert. 'Evangelicals and Tractarians', *Historical Magazine of the Protestant Episcopal Church*, **35** (1966), pp. 111–53, 237–94.

Cominos, Peter. 'Late Victorian sexual responsibility and the social system', *International Review of Social History*, **8** (1963) pp. 18–48, 216–50.

Davidoff, Lenore. 'Mastered for life: servant and wife in Victorian and Edwardian Britain', *Journal of Social History*, **7** (1974), pp. 406–28.

Davin, Anna. 'Imperialism and motherhood', *History Workshop*, **5** (1978), pp. 9–65.

Driver, Anne Barstow. 'Religion: review essay', *Signs*, **2** (1976), pp. 434–42.

Freedman, Estelle. 'Separatism as strategy: female institution building and American feminism, 1870–1930', *Feminist Studies*, **5** (1979), pp. 512–29.

Frere, W. H. 'The religious life', *Church Times*, 20 September 1901.

Gillis, John R. 'Servants, sexual relations and the risks of illegitimacy in London 1801–1900', *Feminist Studies*, **5** (1979), pp. 142–73.

Heeney, Brian. 'The beginnings of Church feminism: women and the councils of the Church of England 1897–1919', *Journal of Ecclesiastical History*, **33** (1982), pp. 89–109.

—. 'Women's struggle for professional work and status in the Church of England, 1900–1930', *History Journal*, **26** (1983), pp. 329–47.

Hill, Bridget. 'A refuge from men: the idea of a Protestant nunnery', *Past and Present*, **117** (1987), pp. 107–30.

Hilliard, David. 'UnEnglish and unmanly: Anglo-Catholicism and homosexuality', *Victorian Studies*, **25** (1982), pp. 181–210.

Inglis, K. S. 'Patterns of religious worship in 1851', *Journal of Ecclesiastical History*, **11** (1960), pp. 74–86.

Joanna, Sister. 'The deaconess community of St Andrew', *Journal of Ecclesiastical History*, **12** (1961), pp. 215–30.

Kollar, R. 'Lord Halifax and monasticism in the Church of England', *Church History*, **53** (1984), pp. 218–30.

Krenis, L. 'Authority and rebellion in Victorian autobiography', *Journal of British Studies*, **18** (1978), pp. 107–30.

Mcleod, Hugh. 'Recent studies in Victorian religious history', *Victorian Studies*, **21** (1978), pp. 245–55.

O'Brien, Susan. '"Terra incognita": the nun in nineteenth-century England', *Past and Present*, **121** (1988), pp. 110–40.

—. '10,000 nuns: working in Catholic archives', *Journal of Catholic Archives*, **9** (1989), pp. 6–33.

Peck, Winifred Frances. 'The ladies of the Oxford Movement', *Cornhill Magazine*, NS **75** (1933), pp. 3–14.

Peterson, Jeanne. 'No angel in the house', *American Historical Review*, **89** (1984), pp. 677–708.

Reed, John Shelton. '"A female movement": the feminization of nineteenth-century Anglo-Catholicism', *Anglican and Episcopal History*, **57** (1988), pp. 199–238.

—. '"Ritualism rampant in East London": Anglo-Catholicism and the urban poor', *Victorian Studies*, **31** (1988), pp. 375–403.

—. '"Giddy young men": a counter-cultural aspect of Victorian Anglo-Catholicism', *Comparative Social Research*, **11** (1989), pp. 209–26.

Roberts, Helene E. 'The exquisite slave: the role of clothes in the making of the Victorian woman', *Signs*, **2** (1977), pp. 554–79.

Showalter, Elaine. 'Florence Nightingale's feminist complaint: women, religion, and *Suggestions for Thought*', *Signs*, **6** (1981), pp. 395–412.

Smith-Rosenberg, Carroll. 'The hysterical woman: sex roles and role conflict in nineteenth-century America', *Social Research*, **39** (1972), pp. 652–78.

Soloway, Richard Allen.'Church and society: recent trends in nineteenth century religious history', *Journal of British Studies*, **11** (1972), pp. 142–59.

Summers, Anne.'Pride and prejudice: ladies and nurses in the Crimean War', *History Workshop*, **16** (1983), pp. 33–56.

Thompson, D. M. 'The making of the English religious classes', *Historical Journal*, **22** (1979), pp. 477–91.

Yonge, Charlotte F. 'The beginnings of sisterhoods', *The Treasury*, **23** (1914), pp. 51–9.

3. Unpublished sources

Auchmuty, Rosemary. 'Victorian spinsters', PhD, Australian National University, 1975.

Denison, Keith M. 'The sisterhood movement: a study in the conflicts of ideals and spiritual disciplines in nineteenth century Anglicanism', PhD, Cambridge University, 1970.

Hammersmith, S. K. 'Being a nun: social order and change in a radical community', PhD, Indiana University, 1976.

Hill, Michael. 'The religious order in a sociological context: a study of virtuoso religion and its legitimation in the nineteenth-century Church of England', PhD, University of London, 1971.

Hughes, P. G. 'Cleanliness and godliness: a sociological study of the Good Shepherd Convent refuges for the social reformation and Christian conversion of prostitutes and convicted women in nineteenth century Britain', PhD, Brunel University, 1985.

Kanner, S. B. 'Victorian institutional patronage: Angela Burdett-Coutts, Charles Dickens and Urania Cottage Reformatory for Women, 1846–1856', PhD, UCLA, 1972.

Misner, B. 'A comparative social study of the members and apostolates of the first eight permanent communities of women religious within the original boundaries of the US, 1790–1850', PhD, Catholic University of America, 1981.

Norton, Ann Francis. 'The consolidation and expansion of the community of St Mary the Virgin, Wantage, 1857–1907', MPhil, King's College, London, 1979.

Porterfield, F. Amanda. 'Maidens, missionaries and mothers: American women as subjects and objects of religiousness', PhD, Stanford University, 1975.

Smulders, S. G. M. 'Christina Rossetti: response and responsibility', DPhil, Sussex University, 1988.

Stone, Hope B. 'Anglican foundresses and the (re)founding of religious life in nineteenth-century England', Leeds University, unpublished paper, 1992.

Stone, Hope B. 'Constraints on the Mother Foundresses: contrasts in Anglican and Roman Catholic religious headship in Victorian England'. PhD, University of Leeds, 1993.

INDEX

food
  convents 31, 68–9
  orphanages 112–13
  schools 119
foreign mission work 76–7, 129–30
founders, *see* Mother Foundresses
friendships 75–6
fund-raising 86–90, 148
funerals 55

Gissing, George 167
Gladstone, W.E. 6, 203
Goodman, Margaret 172, 178, 179
Grafton, Charles 64, 155
Grey, Maria 169
guilds 132

habit, the 76–9, 184–5
Harwood, John 182
Heeney, Brian 21
holidays 69
Holland, Penelope 4, 202
Holy Cross, Community of the 104,
  117, 121, 158, 183
Holy Family, Community of the 33, 40,
  75–6
finance 83, 84
Holy Name, Community of the 41, 218,
  219
Holy Rood, Community of the 18, 32,
  49, 67, 115, 129, 156, 219
Holy and Undivided Trinity, Society
  of 28, 30–1, 75
  chaplain 160
  and the clergy 159, 164
  and education 122, 123, 124
  habit 76
  Mother Superior 61–2
  status of sisters 38, 42–2
homeless women, refuges for 131
Hopkins, Jane Ellice 130
hospitals 46, 49, 90, 114–18
household work 67–8
  lay sisters 44, 45
  novitiate 24–5
Howson, Dean 170–1, 179
Hughes, Marion 28, 101

illegitimacy
  children in orphanages 111
  eligibility for sisterhood 32
industrial girls 56, 114
invalid sisters 31, 45

Jameson, Anna 187

Kent, Constance 203

King, Edward, Bishop of Lincoln 147
Kingsley, Charles 125

Labouchere, Henry 87
'ladies', role of 173, 199–200
Lancaster, Mr and Mrs 89
lay sisters
  age of death 54
  age of entering communities 42
  and Chapter 65
  domestic work 44–5, 68
  former school pupils as 124
  habits 43, 77, 78
  leaving the community 47, 50,
    51
  money 82, 83
  new members 21
  novitiate 23
  professed novices 28–9
  status and social background 35–8,
    39–47
leaving communities 47, 50–3, 221
leisure 69–71
Lewes riots (1857) 87, 186, 203
Lewis, Jane 95
Littledale, Richard 162
Luddy, Maria 138
Ludlow, J.M. 197–8

McAuley, Catherine 138
Manning, Henry Edward 40, 137
marriage 52, 169–70
maternity services 131
Maurice, F.D. 197
men
  clubs for 132
  sexual morality 108–9
men's communities 9, 143
Monsell, Harriet 8, 79
moral women, robbing society of 173,
  202–3
More, Hannah 125
Mother Foundresses 32, 57–61, 66, 156,
  160, 188
Mothers Superior 61–2
  attacks on 195–6, 197–8
  authority of 63–4, 65, 185
  and episcopal authority 148, 151
  and families 185, 188–9
  and Mother Foundresses 57, 61
  and priests 153, 158, 159, 161
  selection of new members 20
  sisters aspiring to role of 52–3
  social background 40, 41
  vow of obedience 32
motives for joining sisterhoods xv, 13–19,
  51